D1087631

Winter Quarters

The 1846–1848 Life Writings
of
Mary Haskin Parker Richards

Volume 1
Life Writings of Frontier Women

A Series Edited by
Maureen Ursenbach Beecher

Mary Haskin Parker Richards. Photo by Fox & Symons, Salt
Lake City, Utah; Dorothy Streeper collection.

Winter Quarters

The 1846–1848 Life Writings
of
Mary Haskin Parker Richards

Edited by

Maurine Carr Ward

UTAH STATE UNIVERSITY PRESS
LOGAN, UTAH
1996

Utah State University Press
Logan, Utah 84322-7800

Publication of this book was supported by a subvention from Brigham
Young University

Typography by WolfPack
  Dust jacket design by Michelle Sellers

Cover illustrations: Mary Haskin Parker Richards from a painting in the
possession of Maurine Carr Ward. Winter Quarters from a painting by
C. C. A. Christensen. The Church of Jesus Christ of Latter-day Saints. Used
by permission.

Library of Congress Cataloging-in-Publication Data

Richards, Mary Haskin Parker, 1823–1860.
    Winter quarters : the 1846–1848 life writings of Mary Haskin
  Parker Richards / edited by Maurine Carr Ward.
      p. cm. – (Life writings of frontier women ; v. 1)
    Includes bibliographical references (p.).
    ISBN 0-87421-207-3
      1. Richards, Mary Haskin Parker, 1823-1860. 2. Women pioneers–
  Missouri River Valley–Biography. 3. Mormon women–Missouri River
  Valley–Biography. 4. Pioneers–Missouri River Valley–Biography.
  5. Mormons–Missouri River Valley–Biography. 6. Missouri River
  Valley–Biography. I. Ward, Maurine Carr, 1939- . II. Title. III. Series.
  F627.M66R53 1996
  978'.02'092–dc20
  [B]   96-4509
                                                               CIP

To my mother, Ivy Streeper Carr,
who taught me to believe in myself

CONTENTS

ILLUSTRATIONS

FOREWORD
Maureen Ursenbach Beecher

The life experiences of frontier women inform a new history that over the past two decades has begun to appear. The search for documents to tell that story has led to the discovery of many splendid diaries, autobiographies, and letters, which, until recently, had remained stashed away in attics and closets, little valued and less consulted. Even now, those documents that are in archives and repositories, available to researchers if not to general readers, are usually handwritten, difficult to read, time consuming, and, as one researcher termed them, low grade ore for his historical mill.

Until recently, the documents of men have formed the basis of our history of the western movement, men's activities having been credited with the making of the modern West. Many multivolume diaries, including from Mormondom, for example, those of John D. Lee, Hosea Stout, Charlie Walker, Charles Ora Card, and Wilford Woodruff, have appeared in the last two decades, supporting the view that the stuff of western history, as of history generally, is the public, political, commercial world, the sole province of men.

But life consists of cabbages as well as kings; what was happening in the kitchen, the parlor, the bedroom, and the birthing room affected civilization as much as–I venture to say more than–what was happening to the field and forest or being decided in the council chamber and the exchange house. Heartening indeed is the breadth afforded to the writing of the past by the introduction of social history and the related inquiries of ethnic, demographic, and women's studies. Supporting that enlightened broadening has been the appearance in the recent past of some few volumes of women's life writings. These, to be sure, are not the hefty tomes of the John D. Lee journals, nor the nine volumes of the Wilford Woodruff diaries, but are as valuable for their contribution: Annie Clark Tanner, Mary Jane Mount Tanner, Martha Spence Haywood, the two Ellens–McGary and Clawson–and most recently Ida Hunt Udall and Catherine Cottam Romney are among the life writers. As a notable continuation of this enrichment process, Utah State University Press offers this volume, the first of a new series, Life Writings of Frontier Women.

This larger expanse of historical concern is mirrored in related disciplines: literature, anthropology, sociology, and political science, all are asking more pointedly female questions of their material and finding female-related source materials that answer some questions and raise many more new ones. And all are realizing how their findings inform knowledge of human endeavour. In order that scholars in all the disciplines might use these texts with confidence, the transcriber–editors of each manuscript have observed the most rigid standards of documentary editing. Beginning with the accepted authority in the field, Mary-Jo Kline's *Guide to Documentary Editing* (Baltimore and London: Johns Hopkins University Press, 1987) and with Dr. Kline's personal assistance, the editors evolved a series of guidelines to guarantee that in transcribing handwritten texts, we not sacrifice fidelity to the writers' originals. As much as possible, each typescript reflects both the process of its creation and the author's product as it exists.

In addition, each volume editor has provided commentary, documentation, maps, and photographs to help the reader or researcher to understand the circumstances surrounding the writer's narrative. People named or alluded to in the text are, wherever possible, identified in notes or appendices. The author's omissions and deletions are explained where possible, and supplementary documents are provided where they may enhance the reading.

For all the editors' diligence, however, there will remain in each text puzzling spaces, silences, which even the most diligent researcher cannot fill. The questions raised may be troubling to some readers, intriguing to others; the reality is they exist, and scholarly integrity forbids reader or editor overstepping the available evidence.

As useful as women's texts are as sources of data for other disciplines, it is their significance as literary works in their own right that motivates this present series. Whether we consider them a genre of their own or a subgenre of autobiography or a stepchild not quite accepted in the literary family, the unrefined and artless life writings of ordinary women are compelling reading for their own sakes. They have an appeal as honest as the smell of baking bread, as cleansing and nurturing as a rainstorm, as full of beauty and surprise as the aurora borealis. Never quite compete, always concealing something, they are as gripping as a mystery story, as engaging as a play unfolding on an intimate stage. So powerful is the format that novelists have mimicked the personal forms in order to add credibility to their fabrications.

But these are no conscious fabrications; their truth is as profound as the souls of their authors. Even the distortions of demonstrable factuality that call the texts into question are subjective truths that rise from the complexity of their writers' lives. Like mirrors, the written pages of a woman's life cannot reflect that life in its fullness. As a mirror cannot reflect the third dimension of reality, so these texts cannot display the writers' lives from all points of view. But the images they do present are true, genuine, and born of the writer's need to express herself, to create herself, to perpetuate herself.

The diaries, letters, and autobiographies of frontier women in this series are as interconnected as the struts in a geodesic dome. Each is its own entity, but each takes on its full meaning only in connection with the others of its like. One piece at a time, and then a triangle at a time, this series begins to put in place the parts of the whole. The present volume, for example, sees the Winter Quarters portion of the Mormon migration west through the words of Mary Haskin Parker Richards. Despite the austere living conditions of the Latter-day Saints there, and their tenuous hold on life, Mary is optimistic, outgoing, cheerful, and helpful. Her closest companion through that 1846-48 period is her sister-in-law Jane Snyder Richards. Jane did not keep a diary but in later years wrote an autobiography recounting, from a much altered perspective, the times the sisters-in-law shared. Written for readers at large with intent to invoke pity toward the Saints and tolerance of their religious practices, her sketch is bleak and sparse, recreating only the pitiable moments.

At the time that Jane wrote her reminiscences, she was part of the inner circle of Mormon women leaders, the hub of which was Eliza Roxcy Snow, whose name enters Jane's writing. And into Eliza Snow's life writing come the names of their contemporaries from the Ohio roots of Mormonism and on, until the zenith of Mormon women's organizational effectiveness, the 1870s and 1880s. Through Emmeline B. Wells, whose diaries are laced with references to both Eliza Snow and Jane Richards, we become aware of the national web of women—Susan B. Anthony and her eastern associates—linked in the struggle for suffrage and divided by the battle for and against the Mormon practice of polygyny. As their eastern contemporaries misunderstood the Mormons' aberrant marriage patterns, so also have later historians misrepresented them, presuming the few later statements of women leaders to exemplify the whole of women's lives on the Mormon frontier. Not so. Only in sensitive study of complete and contemporary records such as this one of Mary Haskin Parker Richards can we gain insight, one by one, into women's intimate experiences and emotions.

Such intertextuality as exists in the documents in preparation for this series compounds the value of each text and provides the impetus for the series. Because of the Mormons' long tradition of life writing, and the richness of the manuscripts available, we begin with their women's stories. But as documents become available, we hope to include texts by the Jennie Froiseths, the Corinne Allens, and the Elizabeth Cohens whose lives on the western frontier were more closely tied to those of their east coast sisters than to those of their Utah neighbors. For all their differences of belief and practice, their similarities of place and time, role and background bound these women in one female world.

For one woman's story is everywoman's story, and every woman's story is each woman's story. The life experiences common to women, the universals of menarche, marrying, birthing, nurturing, working, building and maintaining domestic units, menopause, and maturing, form the warp on which each woman weaves her own pattern. Not all women's fabrics have all the strands, nor are the threads exclusive to women; nevertheless there is enough commonality in women's lives to make useful a comparison of their variations. Begin with one woman, this woman, Mary Haskin Parker Richards, and continue on. Only when all the stories are gathered, and their interweavings made apparent, will we begin to know what it meant to be a woman on America's western frontier. Or anywhere.

ACKNOWLEDGMENTS

This book has been a labor of love, not only for me, but for the many people who helped bring it to fruition. First, and foremost, I wish to thank my husband, Gary A. Ward, and my sons, Lyle and Adam, who lived with this project for the past four years as it gradually engulfed the entire house. Next, I am deeply grateful for my daughter, Betsy, who helped me with some transcribing, did early editing, encouraged me, and believed in me. My sister, Leslie Carr Jorgensen, traveled Illinois, Iowa, Missouri, and Nebraska with me as we searched areas mentioned in Mary's journals and has always given me emotional support. I appreciate relatives Rosabelle Streeper Gwynn, Rose Adele Gwynn, and Dorothy Streeper for the use of their family histories, genealogy records, and photographs and for financial support from Dorothy that allowed me the opportunity for research. Other genealogical records and photographs were made possible through the generosity of Joseph Grant Stevenson, genealogist for the Richards Family Organization.

A special thank you to the staff of the Historical Department of the Church of Jesus Christ of Latter-day Saints: William W. Slaughter, who first suggested to me that I should write a book about Mary, who worked with me on the photographs, and who became my sounding board; W. Randall Dixon, who, with his knowledge of Salt Lake City, helped me understand the land records and maps for that part of Mary's story; Ronald O. Barney, who researched restricted files for me; Ronald G. Watt, who answered questions and gave encouragement; James L. Kimball Jr. for his knowledge and help on the Nauvoo period; April Williamsen and Linda Haslam for their friendly assistance in obtaining films and manuscripts; and many others who helped look up records or decipher Mary's writings.

I am thankful to Julie Hartley-Moore, who not only edited my manuscript but helped me analyze the vast amount of material gathered; Richard Neitzel Holzapfel for his editorial and historical input, as well as his last-minute support; Allison Feinhauer for reading the manuscript and offering literary suggestions; Ann Buttars, Utah State University Special Collections, for suggesting research material and locating sources; Noel Carmack for rendering the maps; and James Allen and Kenneth W. Godfrey for reading an early draft and offering constructive comments. I thank William G.

Hartley, who has been my mentor for many years. He researched the trail used by Mary as she crossed Iowa, planned my research trip to the areas covered in her journal, and answered innumerable questions. Gail George Holmes also patiently answered questions on Winter Quarters and the surrounding areas as he drove me to locations, answered letters, and conversed on the telephone. I am indebted to Frederick S. Buchanan and his wife Rama Richards Buchanan, a great-granddaughter of Mary Haskin Parker Richards. They were able to add unknown information on the Scottish Mission of Samuel Whitney Richards, to give me access to some letters between Samuel and Mary, and to allow me to include a photo of the valentine Samuel sent Mary from Scotland.

Finally, I would like to thank Maureen Ursenbach Beecher, the general editor of this series of women's writings, for her love and knowledge of Mary and for having confidence that I could write Mary's story. Maureen's efforts to write the history of women in the Latter-day Saints church are an inspiration to me. I also appreciate John Alley and the staff at Utah State University Press for preparing the book for publication. The publication received generous financial support from Brigham Young University.

CHAPTER ONE

The Fabric of Life: An Introduction

Nevver shall I forget the feeling that shriled through my Bosem this day. while parting with all my dear Brothers & Sisters. and all my kindred who were near & dear to me by the ties of nature. and expecialy my Dear Sick Sister and her companion. who needed my assistance. to travil to a distant Port. from there to venture upon the wide Expanded Ocean. behind wich to wander in a strange Land in wich I should be a stranger. hope at intervales would glimer in my bosem. there dwells my Dear Parents. but what if God should please to take them to himself. E'er I be permited to see them. I must bid an everlasting adue to my native Land and to that dear spot that gave me birth. wich had been the dwelling Place of my dear Parents for more than 40 years also of my forefathers for many years before them. 'tis true I was going with a family who had promised to befriend me. but what if they should forget their covanant and leave me a Stranger. in a Strange Land. the trial of parting with my Friends. together with these reflections. caused me to give vent to my tears. wich until this time I had endeaverd to conseal.[1]

The "native land" which diarist Mary Haskin Parker Richards laments in the above passage is the verdant Ribble River Valley in northern England's County Lancashire. Divided into counterpane squares of farms by ancient stone borders, the valley and its villages had been the ancestral home of Mary's family for generations. Mary grew up in Chaigley, in what she later proclaimed

> one of the most Beautyfull valeys. that my Eyes Ever Beheld. . . . The mountain Stream Ran Singing by the Door. joind by the Warbleing notes of unnumbered Birds Whose melody in the Spring & Samer together with other ajoining Beautys. made my Home apear Delightfull.

Lancashire, England's land of cotton since the Industrial Revolution, shipped material from its large weaving mills to ports throughout the world. The industrious, thrifty, and innovative people of Lancashire saved their money to invest in the mills or to purchase their own looms for work in their cottages. Others continued to farm the fields and live off the land.

Mary's "Dear Parents," John Parker and Ellen Heskin, married in the Mitton Parish in neighboring Yorkshire County on January 14, 1799, and settled three miles away in Chaigley, Lancashire. Their small farm home lay at the foot of Mount Longridge, between two mountains and near the River Hodder, which flowed through the valley and joined the River Ribble. The main road skirting the Parker farm connected the two nearest towns of Preston and Clitheroe.

During the twenty-four years following their marriage, John and Ellen had ten children: Isabella, Robert, Richard, Roger, Ann (Nancy), John, William, Ellen, Alice, and Mary. Mary was born on September 8, 1823.[2] She was christened, as were all of her older brothers and sisters, in the Mitton Parish where her parents had married.

Mary eventually added her mother's maiden name to her own and became known as Mary Haskin Parker.[3] She acquired other, intangible attributes during her childhood: an appreciation and love of beauty, the ability to withstand hard work and do her share, close knit ties to her family and friends, and trust in her Lord. These qualities, woven together, created the fabric of Mary's life, a life which would comfort others much as the woven fabric from her native country comforted and clothed people worldwide.

The Parker family was poor and rented its farm land from wealthier landlords. Some of the older children collected small willows called besoms, wove them into brooms which could sweep stables and yards, and sold the brooms for pennies. John also invested in a large fly-shuttle loom that he set up in the home. Here, the whole family helped in the weaving process. Even four-year-old Mary did her part by learning to wind the bobbins.

John and Ellen believed in the importance of education for their children. They sent Mary and perhaps others of her closest brothers and sisters to school, one mile away at the chapel in the village of Walkerfold. A young woman named Jennetta Richards taught the basics of reading, writing, and arithmetic. Mary was a quick student and attended Miss Richards's school until she was ten.

At the age of eleven, Mary left home to work, probably as a maid, in the home of a Mrs. Willson. This was an unsatisfactory situation, so young Mary returned home to help her parents weave. Again, at the age of fourteen, Mary was persuaded by Mrs. Willson to move into her home to work. As before, this proved to be an unhappy arrangement. After two months, Mary went to work in the home of a Mr. Seeds as a nursemaid for his "Sweet little babe."

The Parker family attended church in the Walkerfold Chapel, where Jennetta Richards's father, the Reverend John Richards, was the Congregationalist minister.

However, in 1837, missionaries from the American-based Church of Jesus Christ of Latter-day Saints arrived in the Lancashire area, bringing news that forever changed the lives of John and Ellen Parker's family. The Church of Jesus Christ of Latter-day Saints had its beginning in Palmyra, New York, when fourteen-year-old Joseph Smith knelt in prayer to God, asking which church to join. Joseph recounted that God the Father and Jesus Christ the Son appeared to inform him that he should join none of the existing churches and that he would be guided to perform an important work. In 1829-30 he translated the Book of Mormon, from which came the popular nickname Mormonites, or Mormons.

On April 6, 1830, Smith organized the restored Church of Christ. As the young church grew, conflict with neighbors, mobbing, and harassment of its members increased. Smith moved his followers first to Kirtland, Ohio, and then to Missouri. Criticism from within the church became almost as intense as from outside, and some of the original leaders left the fold. To strengthen the fledgling church, Smith sent seven missionaries to the British Isles.

The missionaries arrived in Preston during the excitement of election day, July 22, 1837. There they saw a political banner unfurled overhead, reading "Truth Will Prevail." Within ten days, the missionaries had baptized nine converts in the River Ribble at Preston, as thousands of people strolled through the river park and lined its banks to witness the event.

Social, political, religious, and economic change in Great Britain had created an environment in which the people were eager to hear the message of the American missionaries. Chief among these changes was the industrialization of the British nation. This undermined traditional livelihoods, forced people into crowded cities, broke up families, and intensified class conflict. Class distinctions were apparent in the State church and in nonconformist religions, such as those of the Congregationalists, Baptists, and Methodists. As upper classes reasserted their religion, the working class searched for something new.

Most religious leaders of this period were careful not to criticize the economic or political conditions affecting their members. The Mormon missionaries, however, were bold in describing the whole of society as "Babylon." The appeal of rejecting the British Babylon, of possibly fleeing to a new Zion in America, greatly enhanced the success of the first missionaries. Not all of the 57,000 Mormon converts in the British Isles between 1837 and 1852 actually left their homeland, but the attraction of a growing transoceanic Zion drew many to the church.

After their initial success in Preston, the missionaries branched out, with Heber C. Kimball, Orson Hyde, and Joseph Fielding moving up the Ribble through Lancashire and into Yorkshire. In March 1838, some of the Parker family heard their gospel message and believed. Three days later, John and Ellen were baptized by Heber C. Kimball, as were their son John Jr.; his wife, Alice Woodacre or Whitaker; another son, Roger; and their daughter Alice. Another daughter, Ellen, would be baptized the following year.

Five months after her parents' baptism, Mary followed their example and was baptized on August 6, 1838, by William Kay. Kay had been one of the first persons baptized in the Chaigley-Walkerfold area. Willard Richards and Joseph Fielding confirmed Mary five days later. When Mary affiliated with the strange, new American church, her employer, Mr. Seeds, turned her out. Once again, she moved back home with her parents.

From that time forward, the home of Old John Parker[4] became a center for the church. Mary recalled that missionaries frequently visited the family members, instructing and strengthening them. In the spring of 1840, Mormon leader Heber C. Kimball became ill on a return visit to England and stayed in the Parker home. He also stayed there regularly when he was visiting in the Chaigley area to do missionary work or hold meetings.

Mary recalled that on one such visit, Kimball laid his hands upon her head, pronouncing that "it Shall be said of you after many years. that you washed the feet of the searvants of the Lord and administered to their wants" and promising her blessings and rewards.[5]

A spirit of gathering to Zion, the church headquarters now established at Nauvoo, Illinois, intensified. At first church leaders were reluctant to give their approval. But at a conference in Preston on April 15, 1840, they decided that any Latter-day Saints wishing to migrate could do so, after first receiving recommends from the leaders in England. John and Ellen listened to those advocating a gathering and began to make preparations to join the Saints in the new city of Nauvoo. John was sixty-five and Ellen sixty when, on September 5, 1840, they left their home and family for the Mormon haven in America. They boarded the *North America*, the first ship chartered by the church especially to bring immigrants from Europe. Under the direction of Elder Theodore Turley, they became part of the 300 British Latter-day Saints who reached the United States in 1840.[6]

Mary's parents were perhaps apprehensive about leaving their seventeen-year-old daughter behind; however, Mary's brothers and sisters were all nearby. Some neighbors of the Parker family who were members of the church also planned to sail to America as soon as arrangements could be made. They may have agreed with John Parker to bring Mary with them.

When twenty-six-year-old George Rhodes informed Mary of his impending departure with other friends, William and Margaret Bleasdale, and offered to pay her way, Mary decided to accompany him. She made one final visit to each of her brothers and sisters, who tearfully bade her farewell. When she left her brother Robert, he accompanied her about a mile, and Mary later noted that he not being a saint I gave him my testmony in regard to my faith in the work wich I had imbraced and desird him to join the Church. & to gather with the Saints that I might hope. that one day ere long I might see his face again. I then bade him good bye & left him in tears. with but little hope that [I] should ever See his face more.

At her brother John's home, a number of Mary's brothers and sisters had gathered to say goodbye. She sang a few verses which she had composed as a farewell song for them.

When Mary, Rhodes, and the Bleasdales arrived in Liverpool, they discovered that the man who had arranged their ship's passage intended to charge them each ten shillings more than what they had earlier agreed upon. At this, William Bleasdale scheduled passage for them himself on the ship *Alliance*. Unlike the vessel John and Ellen Parker had sailed on, this was not a Mormon church-sponsored emigration ship.

Mary's little group awaited their voyage for eleven days in a rented room. On the evening before their departure, George Rhodes was robbed of all his money. Unfortunately, Rhodes had been the only one in the group with any money at all and had been financing not only Mary but William and Margaret Bleasdale. As the discouraged group contemplated their options, Mary suggested,

> our Passage is paid. our provisions are on Board. let us go to NY the Lord is just as able to sustain us there' as he is' if we should remain here. and so long as we walk uprightly before him' we shall have no cause to fear. for he has promised that he will never forsake those who put their trust in him.

The rest of the group agreed, boarded the ship, and left England for Zion.

The *Alliance* docked at New York on January 26, 1841. Because they had no money, Mary and her co-travelers were forced to remain in the East and work before they could continue their journey to Nauvoo.[7] Nothing is known of Mary's life during this period. The Bleasdales were not yet in Nauvoo later in 1841 when their youngest daughter, Jeannette, arrived from England to meet them. Nor had Mary arrived by June 1842, when a British convert, Ellen Briggs Douglass, wrote to her family in Lancashire that "Old John and Ellen Parker are both in good health and spirits and are expecting their daughter Mary every day."[8]

However, Mary was in Illinois by the fall of 1843. On October 1, Mary's former teacher, Jennetta Richards, who had married missionary Willard Richards and was living in Nauvoo, wrote to her parents that "Old John and Ellin Parker are well, and I never saw them look as fleshy as they now do. Mary is living with them, and going to stay."[9] Mary had first lived for awhile with the Bleasdales at Camp Creek, a branch of the Latter-day Saints church

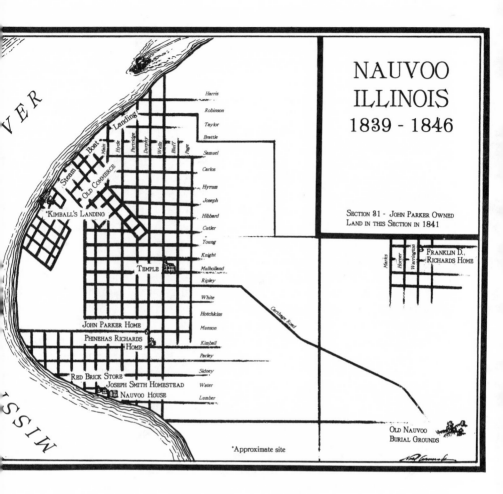

NAUVOO
ILLINOIS
1839 - 1846

SECTION 31 - JOHN PARKER OWNED
LAND IN THIS SECTION IN 1841

FRANKLIN D.
RICHARDS HOME

Marks Horner Warrington

*Approximate site

OLD NAUVOO
BURIAL GROUNDS

RIVER

MISSI

Steam Boat Main Old Commerce Hyde Partridge Durphy Wells Bluff Page

Landing

*KIMBALL'S LANDING

TEMPLE

JOHN PARKER HOME

PHINEHAS RICHARDS HOME

RED BRICK STORE
JOSEPH SMITH HOMESTEAD
NAUVOO HOUSE

Harris
Robinson
Taylor
Brattle
Samuel
Carlos
Hyrum
Joseph
Hibbard
Cutler
Young
Knight
Mulholland
Ripley
White
Hotchkiss
Munson
Kimball
Parley
Sidney
Water
Lumber

Carthage Road

twelve miles east of Nauvoo. It was while living there that she became friends with the family of Samuel and Hannah Burton. This close friendship would continue throughout Mary's life.

Mary's brother, John Parker Jr., who had remained in Chaigley when she left, eventually decided that the time had come for him to emigrate to Zion too. His wife, Alice, had died in childbirth, leaving him with three small children ages three to seven. So in January 1845, John Jr. set sail alone with his children. The voyage was extremely difficult on John, compelling him to remain in bed most of the trip and to leave the little ones to take care of themselves. When they finally arrived in Nauvoo in April, John and his family were warmly embraced by Ellen, John Sr., and Mary.

Two months later, John Jr. came down with malaria. Commonly known by the Nauvoo inhabitants as the shakes, the ague, or chills and fever, malaria attacked most families.[10] At times in the mosquito-infested city there were not enough well persons to care for the afflicted. John Jr. also suffered slightly from inherited muscular dystrophy,[11] which further weakened him, and it was many months before he recovered from his illness. Before her son could recover, Ellen Parker contracted the disease herself and died with her second chill on September 22, 1845. Father John was feeble from his own muscle infirmity, so the responsibility of caring for the family rested solely on Mary. During this time a strong bond developed between Mary and her young nieces and nephew. The separation would be very difficult for her a year later when she left for the Missouri River and John Jr. moved his small family to St. Louis. Mary's letters then would indicate that she thought a great deal about the children and wished to see them. She would specifically wonder about little Mary Ann and worry that her niece might have forgotten her. "I expect she do'nt care any thing about Aunt Mary any more," she wrote, asking John to give each of the children a kiss for her.[12]

In the meantime, life in Nauvoo was exciting for Mary. The city was a refuge for the persecuted and driven American Latter-day Saints and the new British converts. Here they had begun building their "City Beautiful" from the swamps of old Commerce, Illinois, in 1839. The Saints drained the land, planted crops, and built homes and businesses. By August 1840, the inhabitants of Nauvoo numbered nearly three thousand, half the population of Chicago. At its peak, Nauvoo would consist of twelve hundred hand-hewn log cabins (most of them whitewashed inside), two to three hundred substantial brick houses, and three to five hundred frame houses. Most of these homes were quite primitive as compared to former homes of the Saints. Poverty and illness abounded. Nevertheless, craftsmen of all kinds plied their trade, school children attended classes, and newspapers and a library allowed adults to further their own learning. Debates, singing school, dancing school, and productions of the Nauvoo Dramatic Company, the Nauvoo Brass Band, the Nauvoo Quadrille Band, and the

Lyceum of Music provided diversions and enlightenment for all the citizens of Nauvoo.

Besides granting Mary her parents' company again, Nauvoo allowed her to renew friendships with many British Saints, as well as British missionaries Willard Richards, Heber C. Kimball, and Orson Hyde. During the six years that Nauvoo was the center of church activity, more than 4,600 Latter-day Saints from Great Britain immigrated to the city and its vicinity.[13] Mary likened her "City of Joseph" to a garden in an 1845 letter to family members remaining in Lancashire. She noted that the walls of a Mormon temple were growing higher and higher and that the Saints worked and prayed for the day they would be able to use it for sacred ordinances.

It was also in Nauvoo that Mary met Samuel Whitney Richards, the handsome son of Phinehas and Wealthy Dewey Richards, who lived one block from the Parker home.[14] With his dark hair bobbed below his ears and his strong jaw showing a hint of a cleft in his chin, Samuel apparently stole Mary's heart.

Samuel had been born August 9, 1824, in Richmond, Massachusetts, and was one year younger than Mary. He was baptized at the age of fourteen and moved with his family to Nauvoo in November 1842. Before that, at age fifteen, he had been ordained to the Mormon priesthood and had gone on a mission to New York, Connecticut, and Vermont.

In later life, Samuel recounted a remarkable spiritual experience he had at nineteen. He was one of twenty-five men who met with the Prophet Joseph Smith to discuss finding a place in the West for the Saints to settle. Joseph had remarked that he "wanted young men for the mission who could go upon the mountains and talk with God face to face, as Moses did upon Mount Sinai, and learn from Him where His people should make a home." According to Samuel,

> My first thought was to resign at once. The idea of going into the mountains and talking with God face to face, was more than I, as a boy, could think of encountering. But after a few moments' reflection I thought I would ask my heavenly Father before I decided the matter.[15]

Samuel said he then went home and prayed for a manifestation of some kind to let him know what he should do. He retired to bed and had a vision or dream where he was transported to the Salt Lake Valley, then on to Southern California, into Northern Mexico, and back to Jackson County, Missouri, where he helped build a temple. He said that his spirit left his body and he traversed the continent from end to end, seeing many wonderful things. When he awoke, Samuel was prepared to go on the journey and do anything that Joseph Smith might ask of him, even though this particular assignment never materialized.

In Nauvoo, Mary may have been drawn to Samuel through her affection for his uncle Willard Richards, one of the British missionaries who introduced her to the Mormon church. Uncle Willard seemed to have a special place in his heart for Mary too, and he encouraged Samuel to propose to her. Continued criticism within the church and a renewal of anti-Mormon sentiment from without soon disrupted life in Nauvoo though. The tension culminated in the martyrdom of the Prophet Joseph Smith and his brother Hyrum at the hands of a mob, who ignored Illinois Governor Thomas Ford's promise to protect the Mormon leaders. After the murders, a number of people claimed to have the authority to lead the prophetless church. Brigham Young, as the senior member of the Council of the Twelve Apostles,[16] persuaded a majority of the distraught Saints that he and others of the Twelve held the keys of the priesthood. Those who could not accept Young's leadership gradually left the main fold of the church, some individually and others in small groups.

As conflict from outside the church escalated, Brigham Young and the Council of the Twelve initiated plans to leave their city. Then, in September 1845, mobs systematically started burning outlying Mormon homes, forcing the families to move into Nauvoo. Young promised Governor Ford that the Mormon leaders and a thousand families would leave Nauvoo by the following spring. The Saints prepared to leave the city. At the same time they intensified their efforts in building the Nauvoo Temple, believing that ordinances essential to their salvation must be performed there. Finally, on December 10, they completed and dedicated the upper rooms of the temple and there administered the first "endowments."[17]

Throughout this time, Samuel assisted his father in carpentry work and painting on the Nauvoo Temple. He received his own endowments on January 7, 1846, after which he was called to work in the temple and assist others with their ordinances. In the meantime, Mary and Samuel continued courting. On Friday, January 23, 1846, Samuel recorded in his journal the words,

> By my interposition, Father John Parker's family received their endowments, his daughter Mary being my intended wife. Afterwhich I obtained permission of Pres. Joseph [Young][18] for her to have the privilege of spending her time in the temple, also, where she commenced her labors on the morn of the 27th, and in the evening of the 29th we were sealed upon the altar, husband and wife for all eternity, by Amasa Lyman, at 25 minutes to nine. Witnessed by Phinehas Richards, and C. W. Wandall and recorded by F. D. Richards.

Samuel was twenty-one and Mary was twenty-two when they married. The young couple divided their time between the homes of both their parents.

Although Brigham Young had planned to move his people out of Nauvoo in April, rumors of increasing conflicts caused him to change his plans. Those Saints who were ready to leave crossed the frozen Mississippi River on February 2 instead. President Young later admitted that at the time he led the Saints across the Mississippi, he was unsure where he was going. However, he soon chose to build a camp to the west on the Missouri River; there they could sojourn until their final destination in the West could be decided.

Samuel's parents, Phinehas and Wealthy Richards, were among those preparing to leave Nauvoo later, that spring. Samuel and his brother Franklin Dewey Richards, however, had been called to serve church missions in Great Britain. Knowing that he would have to leave Mary, Samuel arranged for her to travel with his parents. Any time he did not spend at or in the temple he devoted to getting Mary ready for the long move west.

Samuel's journal furnishes some information on the newly married couple's activities during these furtive short months together:

> In the eve of the 31st I left the Temple with my wife, and went to her fathers house where I spent the night with her for the first time. Feb 23, 24, 25. At the temple as usual in the eve of the 25th went to Joseph Youngs, where my wife was visiting and on our return home called at the Masonic Hall, and saw the Paintings, representing the Carthage murder of Joseph & Hyrum . . . in the eve was at Bro. Burton's in company with Rebecca & Malissa . . . Mar 27. In the P.M. went to father Parkers to get my wive's things she being with me at my father's.

They spent other evenings visiting Mary's good friend Elizabeth Fory at the home of Father Fory, and they found time to attend singing school together. On March 29, Samuel and Mary went about one mile north of the city to attend the wedding of Mary's brother John Parker Jr. and Ellen Briggs Douglass, performed by Samuel. Ellen's husband George had died shortly after arriving in Nauvoo from England, leaving her with seven children.

Despite her happiness at being in Nauvoo, Mary was not a strong woman. Like her brother John, she had inherited muscular dystrophy from her father. She had also contracted typhoid fever before leaving England, further weakening her body. In addition, she suffered frequently from attacks of malaria and was often ill with the "ague and fever."

Samuel's journals at this time show that he worried about Mary's health. He consulted with his uncles, Willard and Levi, and his father, Phinehas, who had all studied to become Thomsonian practitioners.[19] This method trained doctors in the use of herbs and natural means of healing the body. Samuel's father and uncles helped him prepare the necessary medicines for Mary, teaching him how best to administer them to her and how to use steam and other cures.

On Saturday, April 4, after she had been very ill for a few days, Samuel wrote, "Mary quite sick with a death like feeling, fainting and reviving and expressing herself as if she could no longer stay. With faith and prayers, warm drink and hot stones, she commenced to sweat and was much relieved of her abdominal pain." Five weeks later he wrote, "In the P.M. staid with my wife, being quite sick, not having recovered from her illness, quite a distressed day with her."

As Mary recovered, she and Samuel carried on many discussions with his parents Phinehas and Wealthy, his Uncle Levi, and other family members relative to the forthcoming journey. Willard, Phinehas's brother, had been with the first company to leave Nauvoo, and he sent instructions back to his extended families to help them get ready. Although younger than his siblings, Willard was the undisputed leader of the Richards family as well as a leader in the church. His family usually listened carefully and followed his words and advice.

Samuel and Franklin postponed their church mission until they had provided for the departure of their wives and families from Nauvoo. However, on April 28, the brothers learned in a letter from the leaders now encamped in Iowa that they and others who had not yet left for their missions were to leave immediately.

The next day, after painting in the temple until ten o'clock, Samuel, Franklin, and other Mormon brethren, with their wives, met in the attic story of the temple. There they held a prayer circle, preached the gospel, administered to the sick, feasted on pies, cakes, and wine,[20] and rejoiced with music and dancing until near midnight. The next day, Thursday, April 30, a private dedication of the temple occurred. On Friday, this was followed by a temple dedication for strangers, who were charged $1.00 admission. Mary was there with Samuel, who was appointed one of three men responsible for seating the congregation.

On Sunday, May 3, Samuel and Mary met in the temple again. Here Orson Hyde addressed them, after which he gave instructions to the missionaries going to England. Monday, Tuesday and Wednesday, Mary continued to be much distressed and ill. Samuel spent most of the time with her, preparing her medicines and trying to comfort her. On Saturday, after a visit to Mary's father, they went to a party comprised mostly of priesthood quorum members and their wives, where they learned the rudiments of dancing. Mary managed to attend a meeting in the temple with Samuel one last time before she left, there partaking of the sacrament. She also went to dancing school with him two more times.

During these few months Mary and Samuel spent together in Nauvoo, they discussed the prospect of having children, weighing the blessing a child would be for Mary against the negative effects of compounding her already poor health with pregnancy complications. They apparently decided parenthood was worth the risk. The first few letters from Samuel to Mary asked about her condition. Mary's reply to the first letter was still one of uncertainty. A later answer, however, informed Samuel that Mary was not pregnant, much to her disappointment.

On May 15, Samuel began to pack the wagons for his mother, father, and Mary.[21] He also put on the wagon covers. Four days later he took one wagon to the Mississippi River ferry, then returned to the house after the other. At one o'clock, the group boarded the ferry and bade farewell to Nauvoo. Family members leaving at the time included Phinehas Richards and his wife Wealthy Dewey; their sons Joseph and Henry and daughter Maria; her husband, Walter Wilcox; Phinehas's plural wife, Mary Vail Morse (whom he had married on February 8, 1846); and their daughter-in-law Mary Haskin Parker Richards.[22]

Throughout the following two years, Mary would live with Phinehas and Wealthy, whom she called "father" and "mother" in her journals. Phinehas was described as a man of "strong character, firm in his religious convictions and consistent," by Mary's sister-in-law Jane Snyder Richards. In contrast, Jane described Wealthy as a "noble-hearted woman who gave me a daughter's place in her home and in her love."

Phinehas wrote in his journal that "having no team of my own, Br. John Van Cott, of a noble soul and high minded liberality, profered me a team of 4 yoke of oxen and 2 waggons to convey my family and goods to the City of Winter Quarters, for which I shall ever feel myself in duty bound to honour & respect." Phinehas drove one team and his son Joseph drove the other.

Samuel continued westward with his family for a few days, as if he wanted assurance that they would be all right. Up the slight incline from Montrose to Charleston Mary clung to him. In her journal she lamented, using imagery that many of her peers would have found compelling:

> [T]his indeed was one of the most trying Scenes that I ever witnessed. To part with him to whome alonee I look for protection & comfort. & who alone is the most dear to my heart. to wander for hundereds of miles in a dreary wildernss wile he is traviling for thousands of miles in another direction is a trial beyond decription.

In fact, her journal and letters would prove her quite capable of describing the trials of her wandering.

A few days after Samuel left camp, John Van Cott also left, going back to meet Levi's group and bring it in to camp. Like Phinehas, Levi was able to leave Nauvoo because of Van Cott's generosity. Levi's family group included his wife, Sarah Griffith Richards, and their one-year-old son, Levi Willard; some of Willard Richards's plural wives; Eliza Ann Peirson, a niece of Phinehas and a close friend to Mary; and Levi's sister, Rhoda. Also

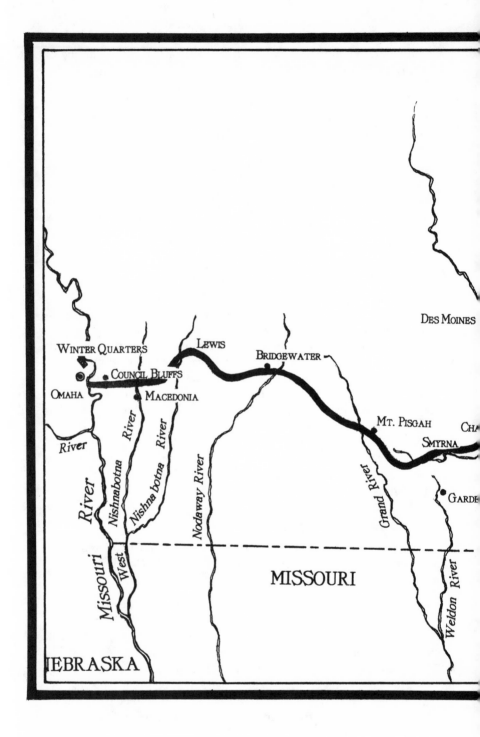

DES MOINES

WINTER QUARTERS   LEWIS
        COUNCIL BLUFFS   BRIDGEWATER
OMAHA   MACEDONIA   MT. PISGAH   CH
                                                          SMYRNA
River
                                                                            GARD
River
Nishnabotna
River
Nishna botna River
Nodaway River
Grand River
MISSOURI
Missouri
West
Weldon River
NEBRASKA

MARY'S TRAIL
ACROSS IOWA
1846

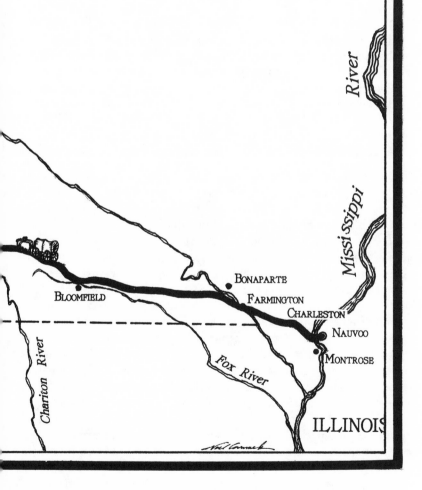

River

Missi ssippi

BONAPARTE

BLOOMFIELD

FARMINGTON

CHARLESTON

NAUVOO

MONTROSE

Chariton River

Fox River

ILLINOIS

traveling with John Van Cott was another friend, Abigail Abbott, who helped Mary through the separation from Samuel.

Mary's group under Van Cott followed the trail of the first pioneers, leaving Nauvoo by way of Montrose, to Sugar Creek, then to Farmington, where they crossed the Des Moines River, stopping at Richardson's Point, and continuing along Fox River to the present city of Drake. However, it appears that they then took a variant emigrant route, as neither Phinehas nor Mary mentions stopping at Garden Grove. The original Mormon Trail stayed close to Missouri settlements, allowing the Mormons to purchase feed for their teams. By May, though, there was ample grass available for the later companies like those of the Richards families, allowing them to take a more direct route. Willard had written to Levi from Garden Grove on May 1, 1846, instructing his brothers on the route they were to follow:

> Come up on the divide from Richardson's Point between Demoines and Fox rivers to a location we are about to make some 30 or 50 miles north of this instead of coming to this place, and bring 1 & a half years bread stuff if you can, or purchase it before you leave the settlements. One half pound of meal or flour per day for every man woman and child. The Missourians have risen on their oxen from 25 to 60 and 80 dollars, and corn from 10 to 25 and 37 &. a half cents and we recommend to the brethren to have little to do with them as possible. If you go up the divide you will not go near them.

The Mormon experience between the Mississippi and the Missouri Rivers, across present day Iowa, was the worst part of the entire journey from Nauvoo to the Salt Lake Valley. The rolling prairie was a monotonous expanse of blue-stem prairie grass and hickory forests. Numerous rivers, streams, swamps, and bogs made the travel dangerous. Where roads did exist, they were usually very primitive. Those Saints who left Nauvoo in the first companies through mid-April had to cut the trails themselves, many times in mud three feet deep, mud that dried in deep wagon wheel ruts still visible today. By the time Phinehas and his family crossed in May, the routes were pretty well established, but it was still a difficult journey.

Mary's Iowa journal indicates that her daily chores were much the same as those of other women on the overland trail. John Mack Faragher has argued that these women usually arose about one hour earlier than the men to stoke the fire and get the kettles of water boiling before breakfast.[23] Also before eating, they baked the bread, which they usually mixed the night before, and milked the family cow. Following breakfast, the women washed up the tinware and packed the cooking equipment and food while the men were getting the wagons ready. There was a brief stop at noon for a cold lunch and a few minutes of rest, then the wagons pushed on until evening, most of the party walking alongside throughout the day. The women were also responsible for collecting firewood or fuel of some sort, which often resulted in them walking extra miles through the area surrounding the wagons.

In the evening, the women still had four or five hours of work ahead of them as they hauled water, cooked the evening meal, milked the cow again, prepared jellies or preserves from wild berries, mixed bread, and prepared the following day's lunch. After dinner, the women made up the bed, cleaned the wagons, and aired the provisions to prevent spoilage. Then they relaxed by mending clothes or knitting socks. Mary also occupied her spare time in the evening writing to Samuel or in her journal.

Many of Mary's daily entries during this stretch of her journey portray the rain falling in torrents, the muddy sloughs, creeks so high they could not be crossed, or the uncomfortable weather. She does not, however, describe the spectacle of struggling through bogs while her many layers of modest skirts and underskirts soaked up mud and weighed her down or her efforts to dry her saturated clothing over a campfire at night. Mary's trek was relatively easy, though, since she was not pregnant or responsible for young children.

It took Franklin Richards longer than his brother Samuel to get his family moved out of Nauvoo. His family at that time included his wife, Jane Snyder Richards, who was expecting her second child at any time and who was very ill; their three-year old daughter, Wealthy Lovisa; and his plural wife, Elizabeth McFate.[24] He had arranged for a friend, Philo Farnsworth, to be the teamster of his wagon. On June 11, Franklin, Samuel, who was still in Nauvoo, and one of Mary's friends, Ellen Wilding, were able to get the wagon and family across the river and safely away from mobs, although they were still not equipped to travel.

On the fifteenth, Samuel received a letter from Mary, dated June 9. Upon receiving it, he wrote a love poem to Mary and sent it with a return letter.[25] Three days later, he went to Brother Foster and "had his likeness done," then sent the photograph to Mary. He and Franklin continued to cross the river back and forth many times getting Jane ready to leave. At her departure, Samuel gave her a small box of items to give to Mary.

On June 12, Phinehas arrived at Mt. Pisgah, located on the middle fork of the Grand River on Potawatomi Indian land. The first Mormon company in Mt. Pisgah had immediately upon stopping planted thousands of acres in potatoes, corn, beans, peas, cucumbers, buckwheat, pumpkins, and squash. Ezra Benson, a fellow Latter-day Saint, wrote of Mt. Pisgah, "This was the first place where I felt willing in my heart to stay at, since I left Nauvoo." Mormons maintained a camp there until 1852. Many of the Saints who lived at Mt. Pisgah did not move on to the Missouri River camps but waited until the final move directly to the Salt Lake Valley. At its height the camp had two thousand inhabitants.

Samuel Whitney Richards. He wrote in his journal on June 18,
1846, from Nauvoo, "went to Bro. Foster's office and got my
likeness taken." On July 15, 1846, in St. Louis, Missouri, Samuel
wrote, "got bro McKenzie to take off my beard at his shop."
Photo courtesy of International Daughters of Utah Pioneers.

Phinehas did not have time to exchange his goods for additional provisions if he was to continue on to Council Bluffs, the main stopping point of the "Camp of Israel," where Young's lead party had camped. So Phinehas set up camp in the townsite and planned to stay awhile. Levi and the rest of his group, including Walter and Maria Wilcox, decided to continue straight on to the bluffs, so they camped across the Grand River, where they could get forage for their animals. Early the next morning, Phinehas's family forded the river to bid farewell to Levi's camp, then returned to Mt. Pisgah.

Mary's sadness at losing her friends Abigail and Eliza Ann changed to joy when she discovered she had other friends from Nauvoo and Camp Creek at Mt. Pisgah: the families of John Haven and Samuel Burton. Mary's close association with the Haven and Burton children is evidenced by the frequent appearances in her journal and later letters of Maria Haven, who was married to Robert Taylor Burton; Rebecca Burton, married to Nathaniel V. Jones; Melissa Burton; and Mary Burton, who was married to Samuel White.

After lingering one month in Mt. Pisgah, Phinehas received a letter from Willard telling him to come on and join with the rest of the Richards family. Because John Van Cott had left him with only one wagon, Phinehas decided to leave Mary Vail Morse temporarily at Mt. Pisgah with whatever things he could not crowd into his wagon. Then, obeying Willard's call, the little group headed west, crossing a "roveing Praira with intervening slews," once having to unload all of their loose things to lighten the burden. They forded several creeks, experienced a tremendous thunderstorm, and passed through the Potawatomi Indian village near present-day Lewis, Iowa. Nine days after leaving Mt. Pisgah, the family arrived at the Missouri River.

The Grand Encampment near Council Bluffs extended nine miles to the east of the present-day Iowa School for the Deaf on Highway 92, ever stretching its boundaries as new Saints arrived. Similar to other Mormon settlements, it was neatly divided into squares with split and rail fences. Mary's excitement grew as her party reached the camp, and she cheerfully called out greetings to friends as she passed. Soon the group came to Walter and Maria Wilcox's tent, then farther on to the Samuel Burton camp. Then, on Saturday, July 11, 1846, they left the Grand Encampment, crossed Mosquito Creek, and stopped near John Van Cott and members of the extended Richards family, at what Phinehas called "Liberty Pole." Situated on a nearby hill were the tents of church leaders John Taylor and Parley P. Pratt. After eating breakfast with Pratt's company, Phinehas prepared his tent, then immediately set out to help build a leafy bowery at the base of the hill.

Samuel's cousin Eliza Ann Peirson was also there. She wrote to her sister, Susan, in Massachusetts: "Uncle Levi's tent is pitched next ours, Uncle Phinehas and family have arrived from Mt. Pisgah where we left them and their tent is near, also Maria and her husband, so you need not suppose it very lonely in the wilderness."[26] Mary's journal tells of her joy at meeting friends again after the arduous journey.

She also mentions the call for five hundred men to join the Mormon Battalion on the sixteenth of June.[27] But Mary neglects at this time to mention that her eighteen-year-old brother-in-law, Joseph, volunteered to serve as a musician and drummer in Company A, under Captain Hart, after Uncle Willard told Joseph that it was his duty and that he must go.[28] The next day, the companies bade farewell to their families and marched eight miles to the river.

On Saturday, July 18, 1846, Phinehas recorded, "I went to the River to attend a Concert that evening, here I took Joseph by the hand, blessed him in the name of the Lord." That night, dancers at a farewell ball hard-packed the ground of the bowery as they whirled to music from William Pitt's band. According to Colonel Thomas Kane, the dancing continued until the "sun dipped below the Omaha Hills."

Although located outside the United States, the area of Council Bluffs was not unoccupied. The Potawatomi-Ottawa-Chippewa Federated Tribe of Indians resided on the Iowa side of the Missouri River, with 2,500 people living near the river and 2,250 in at least five other widely scattered villages. West of the river lived the Oto-Missouri and Omaha tribes. They had shared the area with an Indian trading post since 1804 and, by 1812, with army forts as well. Since 1819 steamboats from St. Louis made regular visits and the area served as a main point of overland departure for the West.

In 1824 Americans established a settlement complete with three stores at Trader's Point (Point Aux Poules), east across the river from the village of Bellevue. When the Mormons arrived, they found communities on both sides of the river, regular mail delivery, and many services and goods. Between 1846 and 1853, the Mormons added close to one hundred communities to the habitation of this area in southwest Iowa and eastern Nebraska. They also changed the face of the land, building bridges, ferries, roads, and mills and creating farms and schools.

Because the first settlement of Grand Encampment could not offer enough wood, grass, and water for the vast herds of livestock the Mormons brought with them, later arrivals had to move to other areas. They first organized Council Point in the middle Missouri Valley six miles west of the hill on Mosquito Creek where Parley P. Pratt and John Taylor lived and near where Mary first settled. This was the third largest of the Latter-day Saint communities on the Missouri River. It was also the site of the middle ferry, known as the Emigrant Landing, from 1849 through 1851, when 32,000 travelers passed through on their way to the Salt Lake Valley.

Bishop Henry W. Miller became one of the first to leave the Grand Encampment. He settled about six miles northeast near an old blockhouse that the U. S. Dragoons had built in 1837 to help the Potawatomi Indians.

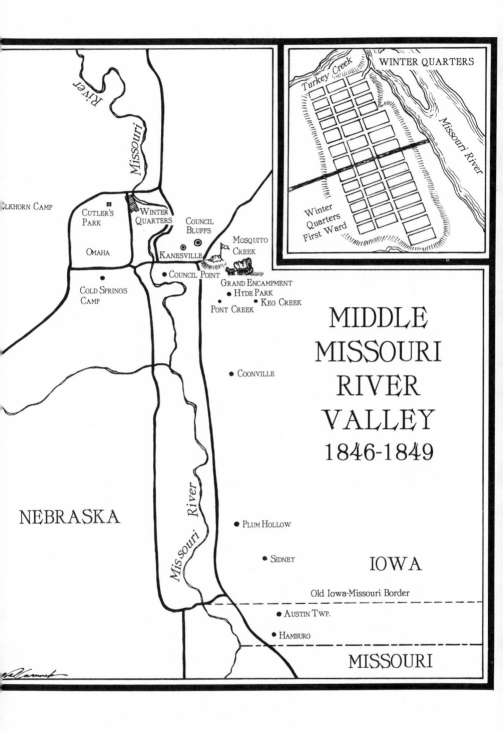

WINTER QUARTERS

Turkey Creek

Missouri River

Winter
Quarters
First Ward

.LKHORN CAMP

River

Missouri

Cutler's
Park

Winter
Quarters

Council
Bluffs

Omaha

Kanesville

Mosquito
Creek

• Council Point

Grand Encampment

• Hyde Park

• Keg Creek

Pony Creek

Cold Springs
Camp

• Coonville

MIDDLE
MISSOURI
RIVER
VALLEY
1846-1849

NEBRASKA

Missouri River

• Plum Hollow

• Sidney

IOWA

Old Iowa-Missouri Border

• Austin Twp.

• Hamburg

MISSOURI

In 1838 the blockhouse was converted into the St. Joseph Catholic Mission on Indian and Mosquito Creeks. The mission closed in 1841. Miller's subsequent settlement became known as Miller's Hollow. The name later changed to Kane. Then on April 8, 1848, Orson Hyde named the camp Kanesville, in honor of a non-member friend of the Mormons, Colonel Thomas L. Kane. The settlement finally took on its present name, Council Bluffs, in January 1853. At its peak, "Kanesville" was the largest of the Mormon communities, with seven to eight thousand persons.

Government officials had given Brigham Young permission to winter on the Potawatomi Indian land on the east side of the river; Kane advised him not to proceed farther west at that time. However, on July 1 Young decided to move the headquarters of the church across the river. Scouts had already explored the west side of the Missouri as far as the Elkhorn River, thirty-five miles to the west, and had established a small camping area at Cold Springs. This camp, situated around a large spring at the base of some rounded hills, served as the headquarters of the church until August 6 or 7, 1846. Women from the Cold Springs camp were among the first to call on Mary and Wealthy upon their arrival at Mosquito Creek.

The inevitable influx of emigrant wagons proved too much for the little camp at Cold Springs, and a new campsite, located on high ground fourteen miles to the north, absorbed excess travelers. Just three miles west of the river, this site was called Cutler's Park after Alpheus Cutler, who had discovered it. Once again the headquarters of the church moved with Brigham Young to the new area.

As soon as Phinehas joined the camp at Liberty Pole, or Mosquito Creek, Mary and Wealthy began the task of unpacking and settling in. Meanwhile, Phinehas and his son-in-law, Walter, returned to Mt. Pisgah to retrieve the remainder of their goods. They reached the camp on August 2 and found Saints ill in almost every house and tent. Franklin's wagon came in from the east the next day, carrying an extremely ill family and "a corps." Jane had given birth to an infant son shortly before reaching Mt. Pisgah. An hour later the baby died. The memoirs of Jane Snyder Richards detail her experience:

> exposure and anxiety hastened my illness and I was confined in the wagon on the twenty-third of the month. My baby, a little son, whom we named Isaac Phineas, died an hour after his birth. Our situation was pitiable, my little daughter was dangerously ill, I had no suitable food for her and nothing for myself for the past twenty-four hours—the severe rain prevented our having any fire for cooking, and we could scarcely keep the dampness out of the wagon. On the third day after my confinement we started again on our journey. I was very eager to reach Mt. Pisgah where I might bury my baby. We were now, on the twenty-third of July only sixty miles from our starting point.[29]

After anointing and administering to Jane and her three-year-old daughter Wealthy, who were not expected to live, Phinehas laid the baby to rest in the "burying place at Mt. Pisgah near a tree." Phinehas's wagon, Jane's wagon, driven by Philo Farnsworth, and her sister Sarah Jenne's wagon then started for the Bluffs.

Phinehas's plural wife, Mary Morse, refused to leave Mt. Pisgah with the rest of the family. She would find her own way to the Camp of Israel, and her marriage to Phinehas would be short lived. Wealthy Richards was very much opposed to polygamy and would not give her consent to any of the plural marriages that Phinehas contracted. Wealthy's unwelcome reception, coupled with Phinehas's stubbornness, probably helped most of his subsequent marriages to fail, including that to Mary Morse.

Somewhere Jane's wagon got separated from Phinehas's, and she arrived at the Liberty Pole camp two days later than her father-in-law. There she was taken into Mary's and Wealthy's care. They proceeded to nurse her back to health, even though at times it seemed that she was so ill she would not possibly live. However, ten days later, Jane had recovered sufficiently to leave her mother-in-law's family. Her mother, Lovisa Comstock Snyder, and others of her family were across the river living in Cutler's Park, so Jane and her wagon crossed on the ferry to be with them. Mary went also to continue her care for Jane.

At Cutler's Park, Brigham Young had established his camp on the south end of the settlement and Heber C. Kimball on the north. Both camps were divided into two large squares, marked along all four sides with locations to park incoming wagons in double rows. Tents were placed in rows between the wagons. Outside of the squares rectangular fences held the cattle. The first settlers of Cutler's Park began to dig wells, drain mires, build a meeting place, and cut and stack wild prairie grass for winter feed.

Knowing they were on Indian lands, the church authorities met first with the Omaha, then the Oto, Indians in council and obtained an agreement for two years' residence on the Indians' territory. Then, to satisfy demands from both Indian nations, President Young moved church headquarters again, to three miles northeast of Cutler's Park. Thousands of Saints soon began to spread across Iowa or swarm up the Missouri by steamboat. To oversee the dispersed settlements on the east side of the river, Young called eighty-eight bishops, lay leaders of local Mormon congregations, or wards. Most of the Mormon Battalion families settled on the Iowa side, as did a poor camp that arrived from Nauvoo in September that first year.[30]

Either Mary did not write a journal during the next three months (August 29 to November 28, 1846) or it has been lost. She indicated later in her writings that paper was scarce and noted her discomfort at having to borrow some to write a letter to Samuel. It is probable that in her haste to go with Jane, Mary left what paper she had behind and hesitated asking Jane for any.

Or she may simply not have found time to write. Jane's memoirs tell of the trials of this period. Little three-year-old Wealthy Lovisa died in the wagon, lying beside her mother, while Jane's sister-wife Elizabeth screamed from delirium in her nearby tent. Jane was still so weak that she had to be carried around. The tedious care of the ill fell to Mary, Jane's mother, and Amelia Peirson Richards.

On July 22, 1846, eleven days after Mary and Phinehas's family had arrived at Liberty Pole, the Mormon leaders appointed a High Council at Council Point. They named Isaac Morley president; George W. Harris, James Allred, Thomas Grover, Phinehas Richards, Heman Hyde, Andrew Perkins, William G. Perkins, Henry W. Miller, Jonathan Hale, Daniel Spencer and John Murdock made up the rest of the council. According to Phinehas, he and the others were called to transact business for the church in the absence of the Twelve. Because President Morley, like the Council of the Twelve, was away for a few weeks, Phinehas was appointed acting president. He held the council almost daily at Council Point.

Soon Phinehas moved his family the six miles to Council Point, where he planned to stay a short while until he could move across the river and settle with the rest of the High Council, church leaders, and his daughters-in-law at Cutler's Park. However, on September 11, 1846, the Twelve Apostles, who were living at Cutler's Park, officially chose a new headquarters site nearby on level ground on the second bluff above the river. They named the new town Winter Quarters. High bluffs on the north and west protected it from strong winds and unwelcome travelers. Creeks on the north and south made possible a water-powered flour mill. A second, horse-powered grist and flour mill was constructed later on Turkey Creek. During the winter of 1846-47, the Mormons built a six-foot picket fence from the river around three sides of Winter Quarters, in order to separate their town from the Indians.

When Mary wrote to Samuel on September 30, most of the Richards family had settled in the new town of Winter Quarters:

> the place where we have settled for winter quarters is one of the most beautyfull flats I ever see. it is about one mile square. the East side borders on the Mo river and most of the North & South. the West side is bounded. with a ridge or bluff. from the top of wich it decends graduley to the River. . . . we are about a quarter of a mile from the meeting ground. about ½ from Uncle W. & L. Father's folks are yet at Councel Point. but expect to move here. the fore part of next week.

Mary wrote six journals between May 1846 and May 1848. Apparently she wrote them at Samuel's urging as a way that they could later share experiences with each other.[31] The first journal covers the period crossing Iowa. The next journal was written while Mary camped on Mosquito Creek.

The last four journals cover her life at Winter Quarters and end just before Samuel arrived home from his mission. In addition, Mary wrote eleven known letters to Samuel during those two years; they provide detailed information than is not found in her journals.

These writings are a unique glimpse into the daily life of Winter Quarters. Mormon historian Kenneth Godfrey noted in 1980,

> It appears that for the most part this area of the Mormon experience in Winter Quarters had been neglected by church historians. Rather than documenting life in Winter Quarters as experienced by the less well-known Latter-day Saints, most historians have chosen to view life there through the eyes of Brigham Young, Orson Pratt, John D. Lee, Hosea Stout or other prominent leaders.[32]

Mary was one of these less well-known Latter-day Saints. Yet because of her close association with Uncle Willard Richards and Heber C. Kimball,[33] whom she often refers to simply as Heber, and her interaction with and acceptance into the circles of the church's leadership, she provides a distinctive point of view on the heirarchy's activities. She records friendly visits by members of the Council of the Twelve Apostles and notes their interest in her welfare. She tells of dancing with "Brother Brigham," and of crowding onto benches in the open bowery on Sunday mornings to listen to his fiery sermons. She records Apostle John Taylor's confession that he had difficulties visiting the wives of the British missionaries because they all fell in love with him. Mary's reply, "I expect it is some what dangerous . . . but I should be happy to have you bring Sister T with you when you come to see me. and if I should happen to fall in love with you' I will try to keep it to my self," shows an amiable relationship between this ordinary Latter-day Saint and her leaders.

Everyday life at Winter Quarters sometimes appears repetitive in Mary's accounts. She writes of washing, ironing, and sewing and describes the weather each day. Yet even in these accounts she paints a descriptive picture: "in the Morn Sister Barns came to help me wash Bed Cloths. we washed 6 Quilts 2 Blankets the Tent & Waggon Cover & 5 Woolen Sheets. 2 Bolster ticks & 4 Pillow Ticks. &C." Almost as an understatement, she adds, "we had a very heavy wash. and was very tired." Other household chores included baking bread, cleaning a hog's face and putting it on to boil, then making a pot pie for supper, boiling down pumpkin butter, cleaning the tent, scalding her bedstead and the logs around the bed to rid them of bedbugs, quilting, braiding straw for hats, and sewing and cooking for the family and others.

Although they say little specifically about it, Mary's journals give a sense of the physical form of the growing settlements. During October and November 1846, President Young asked the Saints to move to Winter Quarters. Soon five hundred houses had been built and another two hundred buildings started. The city plot showed thirty-eight blocks of five acres each, with five wells and twenty lots per block, for a total of 760 lots. There were sixteen named streets. Houses faced the streets, with gardens, yards, and outhouses in back. Some settlers established a large stockyard south of the city; others built bridges over Turkey Creek. Leaders encouraged all of the settlers to plant their own private gardens during the summers; many people also farmed larger lots outside the city.

At its zenith, Winter Quarters had eight hundred cabins, huts, caves, and sod homes and over four thousand inhabitants, making it the second largest of the Latter-day Saint communities in the area. The homes varied from large two-story houses to little cabins with no floors and only partial roofs. Most of the leaders of the church lived in substantial residences, but such houses usually had many more people living in them than more modest dwellings had. Willard Richards, one of the last leaders to build, constructed an octagonal-shaped house, which was also the post office, historian's office, and a council room (at least until a council house was built). His house was referred to in many journals as a "potato heap," "apple heap," "coal pit," "round house," or "the doctor's den" and was the site of many of Mary's visits. She asked his advice, received blessings, or "combed his head."

The smaller homes were usually twelve by twelve or twelve by eighteen feet wide and seven feet high, built of lynwood or cottonwood logs, and caulked inside with clay. They had dirt floors. Chimneys were either prairie sod, brick, or rock, but Mary often reported that "Janes chimney Smooked very bad. so that it kept the tears runing down my cheeks about all the time was very uncomfortable." A few families had stoves. Some had puncheon log roofs, made of oak timbers split into boards three inches thick and hewed on one side. Others used sod or shakes for their roofs. The doors were also made of shakes and fashioned with wooden hinges.

When Phinehas moved to Winter Quarters in November 1846, some of the other men promised to help with his house, but Phinehas was not content to put up a humble one-room dwelling. Instead, he began laying the foundation for two rooms, one to be used as a home and the other as a basket factory where he could have four or five women work with Wealthy. Unfortunately, Phinehas had not counted the cost of his projected home and was unable to complete construction. His family was forced to live throughout the bitter winter in their tent outside the city line. When the cold became unbearable, Wealthy moved in with her daughter Maria and Mary went back to Jane's. Phinehas and Henry continued to sleep in the tent but ate their meals within the shelter of Jane's or Maria's cabin.

It wasn't until the spring of 1847 that Phinehas bought a house on the south row. On May 1 Mary wrote,

> washed & scoured all the Tin ware knives &C also the sheets & boxes shelves & the floor. got all things fixt in order. I put on a clean dress

& sat down. and our little house seemed to me almost like a Palace
I rejoiced to think that after passing through such a dreary Winter
living in a Tent. and wandring from house to house to keep from
perishing with the Cold. suffering almost every inconveniance and
often very unpleasent feelings' I had once more a place I could call
my home.

The town of Winter Quarters had several stores, including a welfare store.
Small trade shops opened in the city as well as in the settlements on the east
of the river. Services included blacksmithing, woodworking, and crafting
chairs, tables, washboards, and other items. Women taught school, baby-
sat, spun yarn, worked in boarding houses, made and sold wine from
elderberries, and constructed baskets and flour sacks. The Seventies
Quorum established a willow basket factory that employed twenty or thirty
people. As Council Bluffs became a popular point of departure for emigrants
other than the Mormons, these services and industries benefitted them, as
they did outlying communities.

Mary and Wealthy braided hats[34] to use in exchange for store goods.
Braiding straw hats had been a prosperous industry in much of New
England. Wealthy and her sister-in-law Rhoda had brought the skills of
their trade with them. Phinehas's cousin Nancy Rockwood had been
president of the "Female Association for Manufacturing of Straw Bonnets,
Hats, and Straw Trimmings" in Nauvoo. Straw hats were a common head
covering for summer wear among frontier settlers. Although the methods
for making the hats in the Mormon settlements were simpler than those
used in New England, the results were quite similar. Mary's quick fingers,
already atuned to the weaving trade, easily picked up the rudiments and
techniques of braiding.

Mary and Wealthy were able to trade their hats at the store for items
such as a tea bottle, water pail, candle wicking, a wash board, quilt batting,
and material for clothing. Other hats were traded to individuals. Joseph
Richards sent home twenty dollars from his pay in the Mormon Battalion
to help the family. Mary also depended upon small monetary supplements
from Samuel (then in Scotland), money which Mary was able to use to
purchase meal and flour and to pay for her share of the herding fee. Often
Samuel and Franklin received donations of clothing and other items from
the Scottish Saints which were forwarded on to Mary, Jane, Wealthy, and
their families. Neighboring women often came in to do the laundry for the
Richards's household, sometimes in exchange for having a hat cleaned or
other favors. A few times, Mary moved in with friends while she sewed for
members of their family. This assured her of food to eat during that time
and also helped preserve Wealthy's larder. Mary also often sewed at home
for others.

Phinehas was appointed to organize and to preside over a fishing company which provided food for the poor Saints[35] and probably put fish on his table as well.

The first Mormon store was Newel Whitney's Bishop's Storehouse. It opened in December 1846 when Mormon Battalion families turned over large amounts of military pay from their men to the leaders of the church. Bishop Whitney, Jonathan Wright, and John Van Cott went to St. Louis for dry goods and other commodities to stock the store for the families. It operated until March 26, 1847, and carried a full line of food, textiles, hardware, household goods, and herbal medicines and some books. Many people came from as far away as Garden Grove and Mt. Pisgah to shop there. As the Saints had no paper money and very little coin, they bartered items to the store in exchange for goods. After the storehouse closed, a few privately owned stores opened and operated for a very short time, including one owned by a non-Mormon named Estill. However, the economy still revolved around interpersonal barter.

In a letter to Samuel dated June 8, 1847, Mary comments on one of these stores: "there is a Merchant here from St Louis who has brought up a large quantity of dry Good Groceris &C &C and opend a store in the Council House' they sell very resonable. Winter Quarters has quite the appearance of a City. and I never saw the Ladys dress half so well in Nauvoo as they do here."

In addition, the men in all of the Mormon settlements in Missouri and Iowa territory hired themselves out to the neighboring communities in order to earn means for their necessities. Some of the jobs available included planting, fencing, cutting logs, hauling wood, splitting rails, husking corn, plowing, making shingles, digging coal, plastering, doing brickwork, and building bridges, homes, barns, jails, and river locks. In this way, the Latter-day Saints unconsciously left their signature on the countryside.

The social climate of Winter Quarters is very much evidenced in Mary's writings. Mary writes of attending singing school under Stephen Goddard. William Pitt's band often went out and played for dances, some where Mary claims she was "a scouring that floor . . . danceng almost every figure & a mixing round at a great rate." At other dances she was more melancholy, keenly feeling the absence of her husband as she watched other couples enjoying themselves.

Although some of the church leaders, such as Alpheus Cutler and Wilford Woodruff, were opposed to dancing, Brigham Young knew that if he did not offer dancing at the Council House, the youth, especially, would go to the other settlements. He preferred to keep them at home. On February 5, 1847, he told his people, "For some weeks past I could not wake up at any time of the night but what I heard the axes at work. Some were building for the destitute and the widow; and now my feelings are, dance all night, if you desire to do so, for there is no harm in it."[36] The young people took him at his word, as many of Mary's reported dances lasted into the early hours of the morning.

One of the most significant contributions made by Mary's writing is her mention of almost five hundred individuals who wove in and out of her life. Maureen Beecher explains: "While men's documents recorded matters of state and the community, women, whose business is the domestic life which binds a people, chronicled life in its more everyday aspects."[37] In Mary's chronicle of the life around her, her associates loosely fit into one of five groups. The first consists of Richards family members, including extended relatives such as cousins Brigham and Joseph Young, Aunt Fanny Young Murray, John Haven's family, Albert Rockwood's family, and others. Also in this group are Mary's brothers, sisters, and father. During this time of dependance upon one another, family bonds intensified.

Mary provides, tucked into daily events, interesting portrayals of the relationships between Phinehas, Wealthy, Samuel's brother Henry, sister-in-law Jane, and herself. Phinehas appears as a stern, unbending authoritative figure, often hurting the feelings of others in the family. In one passage he argues with Mary over who had transgressed divine law, Adam or Eve. Later he tells Mary a secret to see if she will repeat it. And he locks horns with Jane but has to back down to retain peace in the family. Other sources, such as a letter from Walter Wilcox to Samuel,[38] suggest conflicts between Phinehas and his son-in-law.

Wealthy struggles with the hardships of cold, illness, a lack of finer comforts, Phinehas's insistence on practicing polygyny, and the absence of many of her children. She forms a close bond with Mary and writes to Samuel, "Mary is truly a great comfort to me. I don't know how I could content myself without her in our travels, I feel thankful she is in our family."

Henry appears to be a typical younger brother, usually very solicitous of Mary's feelings but at other times ornery. Mary mentions often her love for Jane and their close association, probably because both were without their husbands. Jane's teamster, Philo Farnsworth, and Maria and Walter Wilcox eventually moved to Missouri to find work.

Visiting was an important social function of the time and was usually gender oriented. Although female friendships functioned in other contemporary societies, Winter Quarters's isolation and the Saints' separation from homes and family made visiting a vital need. Maureen Beecher notes, "Women bonding to each other, drawing support from each other, was essential to survival in Mormon Winter Quarters and later to the creation of Mormonism's Utah society."[39]

As the women visited within the city and to and from the outlying settlements, they exchanged news about the status of other members. They learned of the sick and needy. They strengthened each other by sharing testimonies and faith-promoting experiences. They provided food and assisted with household chores. They gave a listening ear to stress and discouragement. This ritual of visiting is often evident in the journals.

The second group of associates in Mary's journals consists of Wealthy's friends, older women whom she knew from Massachusetts. They became Wealthy's link with the comfortable safe home she had once known and the primitive surroundings she now faced. Perhaps understanding her distress and trials, these women were able to support Wealthy through the ritual of visiting.

A third group in Mary's writings includes the many British Saints from Lancashire and other areas who were friends of the Parker family. Among this group was the family of James Smithies, whose wife, Ann, was Mary's first cousin.

The fourth group played a very important part in Mary's life. These are her young friends, male and female, married and single, with whom she shared confidences, attended dances, planned weddings, and visited. Whenever Mary felt she was not needed at home and could find a ride out into the settlements, she made extended visits to dear friends living outside Winter Quarters. Winter Quarters letters to Mary from friends Eliza Ann Haven, Rebecca Burton Jones, Abigail Abbott, and Elizabeth Fory add insight to these friendships.[40]

Another group of associates are neighbors who helped give blessings during illness, held quiltings, fought over cattle, shared poetry, and attended church meetings together. Finally, there are other individuals who Mary only mentions once or twice, with no hint as to a relationship.

The struggle to acknowledge and accept polygyny is another important element in Mary's writings. Although plural marriage was practiced secretly in Nauvoo, Winter Quarters residents openly entered into it. Many of Mary's closest friends were young plural wives. Mary's journals seem to indicate a positive attitude toward the life her friends had chosen, but her letters to Samuel reveal more hostility toward the practice. Often she wrote that Wealthy was unhappy because Phinehas was not at home with her. Prior to leaving for his mission, Samuel wrote from Nauvoo that a mutual friend, Ellen Wilding, had decided she made a mistake by marrying Edwin Woolley and wanted to leave him. Samuel asked Mary to talk to her. If Ellen chose to leave Woolley, Samuel wanted Mary to convince her to wait until he returned from his mission and marry him instead.[41] In a poignant reply, Mary replied that she had always tried to do as Samuel desired and that the love she had for him compelled her to accept his wishes, even though she knew that doing so would forever deprive her of all hopes of happiness. She then added, "if you had seen what I have seen. you would not wonder why I thus wrote for there is no such a thing as happiness known here where a man has more than one [wife]." She begged Samuel to wait at least until he came home and to allow them a year or two together before taking another wife. Mary would spend some time alone with Samuel, when he eventually returned, before she found herself sharing him with other wives, but she would not long have him entirely to herself.

Mary's dream of someday having a home where she and Samuel could live alone, of at least fixing dinner for Samuel and nobody else, is a theme continually found in her letters. At the time of their marriage, they had lived with one set or the other of their parents because they were planning to leave Nauvoo. Mary worried that Phinehas and Wealthy would convince Samuel to move in with them again when he returned. At one point, she even considered purchasing a small home in Winter Quarters so that she and Samuel could have a home of their own when he finished his mission. Mary's desire for a home is understandable in the light of her previous circumstances. As a young girl she had lived and worked outside the home. When her parents left for America, they took the security of their home, leaving Mary with her married siblings. Upon arriving in New York, Mary had to live with friends until they could regain their finances and continue west.

Mary also recorded the illness and death that constantly surrounded her.[42] Phinehas and Wealthy both got "black leg," which Mary described as an initial swelling in the feet, which eventually turned black.[43] The swelling and blackness then ascended the limbs. Phinehas was forced to use a cane after he recovered. Joseph, Mary's brother-in-law who was serving with the Mormon Battalion, died at Pueblo, Colorado, in November 1846. The exact cause was not known, but apparently the exposure and difficulty of the battalion's march was a primary factor. The family did not receive word of his death until the following February.

Mary was ill numerous times herself, with chills and fever, boils, or ague. Her preexisting health problems caused her to tire readily and made her susceptible to ailments. During one of her visits to friends on the east side of the Missouri, she became so ill that a group of endowed sisters anointed her and blessed her to regain her health. Mary tells of various medicines and treatments used to heal her, as well as of priesthood blessings.

Scattered among the hardships of Mary's life are references to her steadfast faith in God. She was happy to live among the leaders of her church, where she could obtain their instruction, "for," she wrote, "I think the water tastes much better to drink it from the founttain head. than it would after it had been carriad some distance through the hot Sun." When the family finally moved into a house after living for a year in the tent, Mary observed, "I kneeled down and thanked the Lord for the many blessing werewith he had blessed me." Earlier she had shared with Samuel her desire that they always walk uprightly so that they would have a name and a place with the chosen of God.

This abiding faith gave Mary hope for the future and helped her disregard her hardships, focus on the beauty around her instead of the ugliness, and feel love and friendship, not anger or bitterness. From repeated entries of "a beauty full day," to descriptions of the fledgling city with its "beauty full Gardins and extensive Fields' Clothed with the fast growing Corn and vegetables of every description' above all things pleasing to the Eyes of an Exile in the Wilderness of our afflictions," Mary basked in the beauty around her. Each time she traveled to the settlements she seemed overcome by the scenery. On one trip she wrote, in the romantic language of the period,

> the scene was beautifull. the Praira through which we traviled was dressed in a white Mantle of frost. while to our left was a range of Eternal Bluffs raising their Magestic Summits in solomn and confused grandure like the rooling Waves of the oacen. Beating before a tempestious Wind. while on our right to the West flowed the dark Waters of the Missouri.

This does not mean that Mary was always happy. She fought depression continually. Her letters, more than the journals, reveal her often deep despair. She keenly felt the distance between Winter Quarters and Scotland. With months between letters, she wondered sometimes if Samuel were dead or if he no longer loved her. His first letter to her from Scotland was written on New Year's Day, three and one-half months after his previous letter, written from New York, two and one-half months after he arrived in Liverpool. Until she received this letter, Mary had hoped and believed that Samuel was laboring in her native Lancashire, where he could be with her brothers and sisters. His announcement that he had been called as presiding elder over the Saints in Scotland was not good news to her, although he reported that he had been able to visit her family. Mary's illnesses fed her depressed spirit, which in turn, contributed to her continual physical ailments.

While the letters and journals often contain similar entries, they served different purposes. The letters carried more news of friends and relatives and more expressions of loneliness and of longing to see Samuel or hear from him. Some accounts are more detailed in the letters, others are more detailed in the journals. The journals record more day-to-day trivial and repetitive happenings. Since the letters were written sporadically when someone was in camp who could carry them east, the journals gave Mary a chance to communicate in some way with Samuel every day; they became a proxy for face-to-face conversation.

Mary wrote, besides her journals and letters, an additional account while in Winter Quarters. Entitled "The Memorandum of Mary H Parker," it is a record of her life in Chaigley, England, before emigrating to America. The memorandum tells of Mary's family, her childhood, and her conversion and baptism into the Church of Jesus Christ of Latter-day Saints. Apparently, Samuel asked her to write this account, along with her daily journals, while he was gone.[44] Mary only wrote in the memorandum when other duties were not pressing, and it was never completed. The last entry tells of sailing from the harbor at Liverpool and being terribly seasick. Unfortunately, the incomplete memorandum does not mention her activities or whereabouts after her arrival in America.

In 1848, as winter turned to spring, Mary and the Richards family received word that Samuel and Franklin would be coming home. Mary sent Samuel lists of supplies they would need for the trip west and gently chided him about the preparation they would need. She urged him not to tarry too long.

Samuel and Franklin arrived in New Orleans after a fifty-nine day passage from Liverpool. They boarded a steamer headed for St. Louis. There Samuel had a tearful reunion with his father-in-law, Old John Parker, who had despaired of living to see him return and who anxiously awaited word of his children remaining in England. There also, Samuel received his last letter from Mary. To his joy, it informed him that all was well in camp: "To think that I was once more so near my Mary and she well, with the hope of soon Meeting her, in health, filled my heart with grateful feeling to that God who had watched over us in our absence from each other."

There is a suggestion in Mary's last letter to Samuel that he was bringing home a substantial sum of money. Whether or not this was the case, he and Franklin brought trunks of clothing and household items with them, some they purchased and some which were given to them by the Saints in Scotland. Samuel's mission journal noted the many gifts received for him and Mary, which shows the appreciation and esteem he elicited from the members there. A few months prior to his departure, Samuel performed the marriage of fellow missionary Andrew Cahoon and Mary Carruth, after which Mary gave him a gold ring for Samuel's own "dear Mary" and Andrew gave Samuel money to buy a ring for himself. Samuel purchased his ring, which included a locket where he placed a lock of Mary's hair, and had the initials SW & MHR inscribed on both rings.[45] Samuel and Franklin also spent a day in St. Louis purchasing or trading for stoves, dry goods, hardware, groceries, and garden seeds.

The Richards brothers continued their journey up the Missouri on another steamer and arrived in Winter Quarters a little past noon on May 20, 1848. Winter Quarters was in a state of disarray. The church leadership had never intended the settlement to be a permanent home for the Saints; they considered it a springboard for emigration. When Samuel arrived, three large companies of Saints were making final preparations to leave for the year-old settlement in Utah, which they called Deseret. President Brigham Young planned to lead the first company, Heber C. Kimball, the second, and Willard Richards, the third. Phinehas, Wealthy, and Henry joined Willard's company.

Many families that were not ready to leave with any of these companies planned to move east across the river to live in Council Bluffs, which they called Kanesville. Others moved out into the small settlements spread across the loess bluffs of the Missouri or into the numerous branches of the church in Iowa. Additional Saints coming from Nauvoo or from England later stopped in these towns, adding to the branches of the church under the direction of the Pottawattamie High Council, with Orson Hyde as the presiding elder.

Samuel and Franklin quickly assessed their situations. Although they both had brought many goods from England and had purchased other necessary items in St. Louis, it was still doubtful that they could get a "fit out" ready in time to join the rest of the family on their trek. After they gave a report of their mission to Uncle Willard, he advised them both to remain at the Missouri River. Franklin, however, was able to make arrangements to join Willard's company, possibly because his teamster, Philo Farnsworth, had been working in Missouri and had arranged for a team and gear.

Samuel and Mary decided they could not accompany the rest of the family. Instead, Samuel rented a thirty-acre farm about four miles from Hunsaker's Ferry on the Nishnabotna River in what is now Fremont County, Iowa. At that time, though, the farm was in Atchison County, Missouri.[46] This was an area where Mary had previously visited Robert Burton and others of the Burton and Haven families. It was also the location of the Austin Post Office which served Winter Quarters during the first part of the Saints' sojourn there. The farm already sprouted wheat, corn, potatoes, and oats and had two houses, three cows, and a horse.

No journal accounts survive from Mary and Samuel's year on the Nishnabotna, but two important events happened to them there. In the farm house, Mary gave birth to their first baby, a little girl whom they named Mary Amelia. Born on April 22, 1849, she was named for her mother and for cousin Amelia Peirson Richards but was known as Amelia or "Minnie."

The other event was one of great importance to the Latter-day Saint church. This was a visit to Mary and Samuel by Oliver Cowdery, former church leader and one of the witnesses to the "golden plates," which the Saints believed Joseph Smith had translated into the scriptures called the Book of Mormon. It was during a bitter cold January day in 1849 that Cowdery and his wife, Elizabeth, set out from Kanesville to visit her brother David Whitmer in Richmond, Missouri. Stormy weather and almost impassable conditions compelled them to stop at a farm house along the way, and they discovered it to be the home of fellow Saints Samuel and Mary Richards. It was two weeks before the Cowderys could continue on their way, and they held many discussions with the Richards while sitting by the warmth of the fireplace. Mary probably welcomed news of friends who resided in Kanesville and surely was excited to have a female visitor to discuss her pregnancy and upcoming childbirth.

Samuel later recorded his delight in listening as Cowdery described Joseph Smith, the personalities of heavenly messengers he said conversed with Smith, and his extraordinary experience as scribe to Smith during translation of the golden plates. As the weather eased and Cowdery made plans to depart, Samuel asked him to write his testimony of the restoration through Smith of the priesthood of God. Cowdery signed the document and dated it January 13, 1849.[47] He and Elizabeth Cowdery then continued on their way to Richmond. Because of ill health, they remained there until Cowdery's death on March 3, 1850. His account to Samuel may well have been his last written testimony, an important document to believing Mormons.

Mary and Samuel were not without friends in their corner of Iowa. Nathaniel Jones returned from the Mormon Battalion in the fall of 1847, after serving as an escort to General S. F. Kearney during his return to Fort Leavenworth, Kansas. He joined his wife Rebecca in Atchison County, where their second child was born in May 1848. Like Samuel and Mary, they also emigrated to Salt Lake in 1849. Other friends, Mary and Samuel White, were still at their home in Keg Creek, Iowa, until 1850, and it is possible that the two couples visited.

Samuel's farm must have been financially successful because in the spring of 1849 he was able to buy the outfit he needed to go west.[48] This consisted of one wagon, four oxen, four cows, and two loose cattle. He would also carry one gun. Perhaps emigrants who were leaving Kanesville for the gold fields made it possible for him to earn good money off his crops. He, Mary, and Mary Amelia joined Silas Richards's company, which left the Elkhorn River on July 16.

Only one death, that of a child, occurred on the journey. The company also experienced very little illness. But it did encounter heat, cold, rain, and snow. Since they left late in the season, the Richards party had to push ahead as rapidly as possible. In one storm, at Willow Creek on the south of the Wind River Mountains, the snow fell eighteen inches deep and the company lost sixty-two head of cattle. Many pigs and chickens also froze to death. Samuel was fortunate not to lose any of his animals. After traveling for three months, he and Mary arrived in Salt Lake City, where they were given an allotment of land next to Phinehas and Franklin's lots, on the south side of Second South Street and between Main Street and First West.

In Salt Lake they discovered that Phinehas planned to leave for a mission to colonize the Sanpitch Valley,[49] so Samuel gave him his wagon. In return, Phinehas turned over the three rooms he owned in the pioneer fort, one of which Samuel sold for thirty dollars before moving into another.

By November, Samuel and his brother Henry had finished building a log cabin on Phinehas's lot and had moved into it with Mary and her baby. Samuel immediately began working for Willard to satisfy some debts. He often spent evenings visiting with Mary. She was happy to renew friendships, "regulate" her household goods, and show off baby Amelia. On Christmas day they attended a feast and dance at the Goddard home.

As soon as he could, Samuel expanded his holdings. He joined others in farming west of the Jordan River, in the southern part of the city. He planted potatoes, turnips, and garden seeds, sowed wheat, built fences, and hauled logs from the canyons. During the summer he rented the house of Robert Thompson, directly behind Franklin's property, and helped Henry build his home on a lot adjoining Phinehas's land. By the summer of 1851, Samuel and Mary were living in their own little cabin, and Samuel was constructing an additional room in the back.

Very little information is available on Mary in Salt Lake. Samuel's journals tell mostly of his activities in the new city. During the spring of 1850, he was appointed one of the regents of the University of the State of Deseret. He represented the Fourteenth Ward in choosing how to bring irrigation water to the ward and spent many hours digging the ditch. He was called on often for surveying assignments. In April 1851, Samuel was elected a member of the city council, and he was active in framing the ordinances of Salt Lake City. When the territory of Utah petitioned to become a state, Samuel was one of the members elected to frame a new constitution. The petition, however, was denied. Because of his involvement in civic affairs, Samuel usually had at least one hired man or boy living in the home to help with the farming, logging, or care of the animals.

Mary continued to have bouts with severe illness alternating with periods of only mild discomfort.[50] On occasion she would "faint for a long time" or was forced to spend time in bed. Samuel often recorded in his journal that he had given her a course of medicine. Once he drove her to the Warm Springs north of the city, where he baptized her for her health. He also showed his understanding of Mary's poor health by often having a girl or woman live with them to lighten her work load. Mary's second child and first son was born on December 16, 1850, and was named Samuel Parker.

Samuel was again called on a mission to England and left in November 1851. On his way east he stopped at St. Louis to see the John Parker family and Walter and Maria Wilcox. He then turned toward New England and his Richards relatives before boarding a ship for Liverpool. In England, at the age of twenty-six, he succeeded Franklin Richards as president of the British Mission. He also traveled among the French and Swiss branches of the church. As president of the mission, Samuel published and edited the *Millennial Star*, a Mormon church newspaper.

President Brigham Young authorized Samuel to act as the agent in Great Britain and adjoining countries of the Perpetual Emigration Fund, which used church donations to support the migrations of other members to Utah. In 1854, Samuel was summoned before a committee of the British

Mary Richards's children: Mary Amelia Richards, center, about ten years old; Samuel Parker Richards, right, about nine years old. Boy on left of picture is unidentified. Tintype from Roseabelle Streeper Gwynn collection.

Mary Richards's son Ianthus Parker Richards. Dorothy Streeper collection.

Mary Amelia Richards, age eighteen. Dorothy Streeper collection.

Samuel Parker Richards, May 1, 1878, age twenty-eight. Dorothy Streeper collection.

Parliament, which questioned him about the emigration system and adopted some of his suggestions.[51]

On February 14, 1852, without Samuel there to give her encouragement or help, Mary gave birth to her third child, Sylvester Alonzo. When he died eight months later, she buried him in the garden behind the house.

Two of Mary's letters to Samuel still exist from this time. In them, Mary admits that the days spent apart from Samuel were much easier during this second separation, even though he was gone a year longer than the first time. She confesses that the situation was easier because she was "more agreably situated" and because she had children to care for. Her living conditions were considerably better than they had been in Winter Quarters. However, they were not without problems: "the rain has been poreing profusely and were it not for the mud that has accompanied it through the roof. I should have enjoyed quite a shour Bath."

The letters also reveal Mary's despondency at the loss of her child. When she wrote of Amelia and Sammy singing and playing on the carpet and wished that Samuel could see them, she added, "then comes ever fresh before me. the vacant Place of him who has left us. for a better world."

In the spring of 1852, Mary's sisters, Ellen (married to William Corbridge) and Alice (married to Edward Corbridge), arrived in St. Louis. There they joined John Jr. and Ellen Parker and Father John Parker in preparing for a move to Salt Lake City. They bought a train of twelve wagons and complete outfits to transport all of the family west. John Jr. took along a threshing machine and set to work immediately upon arriving in the valley at the end of August. Samuel gave his brother-in-law the east third of his lot on Second South for a home site. Mary must have felt blessed to have her family around her again, especially her niece Mary Ann, who spent a great deal of time helping in Mary's home.

When Samuel arrived home from Great Britain on August 26, 1854, he again quickly assessed his family and work situations. He rode with Mary and the children to look at his five-acre lot in the Big Field.[52] He removed the roof of his house and made plans to add another story, enlarge the kitchen, and hire masons to come and adobe the house. He was also reelected to the city council. Meanwhile, his journal continued to report that Mary was very sick for long periods of time.

Although Mary had yearned for the time she and Samuel could live alone, she did not achieve that dream for long, as relatives and hired help continually moved in and out of the house. For the first years of their marriage, Samuel was able to grant Mary her wish not to practice polygamy, but that could not continue long. In December 1854, shortly after Samuel returned to Mary, President Brigham Young told him it was time to take a second wife. Samuel's thoughts went to the Isle of Man, where he had spent some time at the home of John and Elizabeth Robinson, and to their daughters, Helena and Jane. He also considered another young British woman, Mary Ann Taysum, as someone who would make him a good wife. During his first mission to Scotland, a "Sister Mary Craig" had been very much attracted to him and was willing to leave her father's house if she could go with him to the Camp of Israel. Samuel had responded that he hoped she would gather with him or "soon after."

During his two terms as a missionary, Samuel often found himself in situations where he had close relationships with young women, usually in his roles of counselor or mediator. However, he also spent many social hours, attending plays or parties.

There are no journals to describe Mary's feelings when Samuel told her that he would soon take a second wife. It isn't known whether they discussed the young women in England together. Considering Mary's abhorrence of plural marriage, the prospect of a sister-wife was surely traumatic to her. Samuel's choice of Mary's niece, Mary Ann Parker, as his new wife was, however, probably one Mary was able to accept. Mary Ann was already in and out of the home a great deal and cared for Amelia and Sammy during Mary's days of illness.

Although Ellen Briggs Parker approved of Samuel, she was not in favor of the marriage; her stepdaughter, Mary Ann, was only sixteen and still in grammar school. However, Samuel prevailed and married Mary Ann on February 14, 1855, in President Brigham Young's office.[53]

Samuel increased his land by drawing five acres east of the Jordan River and south of the city.[54] He then obtained forty-five acres in the Sugar House area southeast of the city, on Twenty-first East and Sixteenth South.[55] During 1855 and 1856 Samuel purchased lots in the Second, Fifth, and Sixth wards.[56] In conjunction with a friend, Joseph Cain, and others, he built a mill in Farmington, Davis County, about fifteen miles north of Salt Lake City, where he installed a carding machine brought from St. Louis. Again with Joseph Cain and other men, Samuel purchased land in Juab County, on which they ran cattle.

Mary's little home was too small for the growing family and Samuel made plans for a larger one. In June 1855, he wrote that two masons were laying up the foundation or basement of his new house, but he did not mention where it was. Presumably, it was being built on the same lot, as the family continued to reside in the Salt Lake Fourteenth Ward. Two months later, Samuel was shingling the roof of his adobe dwelling.

On July 2, 1855, Mary's second daughter was born. She was given the name of Iantha Adelia, after the ship *Ianthe*. In October 1854, Henry Richards had sailed on this ship from San Francisco to the Sandwich Islands, and the name must have interested Samuel and Mary.

That fall Samuel received a letter from Franklin in Liverpool telling him that Helena and Jane Robinson had sailed for America. Sailing on the same ship was an older widow named Ann Cash and her eleven-year old stepdaughter, Mary Ellen.[57] Ann had been the housekeeper for the British Mission under both Samuel and Franklin. Samuel sent a team east for the Robinson women to use. Then on September 2, he joined with other men from the city to meet the first company of Saints as they started up Big Mountain before descending into Salt Lake Valley. The machinery for his mill was with this company.

Mary must have realized that the family circle would soon be expanding as she watched Helena Robinson become increasingly involved in Samuel's activities. Helena was a beautiful, musically talented woman, obviously very much in love with Samuel. Her best friend was Elizabeth Whittaker Cain, the British wife of Samuel's partner, Joseph Cain. Observing Samuel's attentions to Helena had a devastating effect on Mary as she compared her own physical shortcomings and frailties. She lashed out angrily at Samuel over his betrayal of her feelings.

Available writings during this critical period include Samuel's journals and the letters written between Mary and Samuel while he was in Fillmore, Utah, with the territorial legislature.[58] Mary's letters depict Samuel as insensitive and inconsiderate, oblivious of the hurt he had inflicted on her and Mary Ann, and accuse him of building an unbreachable barrier between them. His letters talk of feeling lonely away from the warmth of his home and wives and of his love and concern for them.

Samuel may have been blind to the effect of his actions. He certainly was not purposely or maliciously cruel to Mary. Throughout his many journals, his concern for each member of his family shows clearly, whether for a wife, child, parent, sibling, in-law, or extended relative. Samuel seemed to feel so strongly about following the counsel of his church leaders concerning polygamy that he would obey regardless of the consequences. He may also have been so involved with his own affairs that he saw only what he wanted to see at home.

Mary's physical problems added to her depression, which at times caused a magnification of her weaknesses and a diminution of her worth in her mind. Her letters to him in Fillmore show the inconsistency of her feelings. In the first, she begins by wishing Samuel a Merry Christmas then tells him that he has built a wall between them which they will not easily breach. She accuses him of showing disrespect toward her in front of Helena, who would then act similarly. She then changes the subject to discuss the progression of their new house and ends with a few clipped sentences about the family, again revealing her emotional pain.

When Samuel wrote in return, promising to help her in the fight to overcome her trials and sorrows, she responded by thanking him because she felt "that I stood alone in the World. for he to whom I might na[t]uraly have looked for comfort. had not one kind look nor one encouraging word to give me. but those comforts for which my heart yearned were ever bestowed on another before my Eyes."

Mary refused Samuel's request to have Helena Robinson and Joseph and Elizabeth Cain in for tea. She tersely let him know that she was having a hard time at home without his help. Baby Iantha was teething and keeping her awake all night, the potatoes had frozen, and she was having to oversee the work on the house herself. Ann Cash, who was living with the family, was not well and had to be waited on. Young Mary Ellen Cash caused Mary ten times more trouble than her work was worth. Only Mary Ann was able to give Mary any relief and comfort. Mary suggested that Samuel might consider her ignorant, but she reminded him she was smart enough to know when she had been ill treated. Then after all this, she signed the letter "I am as ever your affectionate wife."

When Samuel returned home in January, he made plans for his marriage to Helena—and not only with her: he also called upon Mary Ann Taysum to discuss marriage. She declined his offer. He next proposed to Jane Elizabeth Mayer. Jane had a streak of independence but willingly accepted Samuel's proposal.

Thus it was that on Saturday, February 16, 1856, Samuel took Helena[59] as his third wife in President Brigham Young's office and then married Jane Mayer.[60] In attendance were Mary, Mary Ann, Joseph and Elizabeth Cain, Helena's sister Jane, and Jane Mayer's sister Henrietta Polydore. Wilford Woodruff, Daniel H. Wells, Albert Carrington, and George D. Watt acted as witnesses.

Samuel's journals indicate that he was still trying to finish his new home, having it whitewashed, building a table and bookcases, and shopping with Mary for furnishings. Because he did not write daily, it is unclear whether all of his family moved into the new house when it was completed or if some lived in the old one or on his other lots.[61] His family unit included four wives, Ann and Mary Ellen Cash, Mary's three children, and Mary Ann's month-old child. In addition, sometime during this period, another older woman, Mary Birch, lived with the family, as did one of Samuel's hired men. Eventually, Samuel installed one wife in Farmington at the mill, rotating her periodically with the others.

His journals present a glimpse into the family's activities. Some of his wives accompanied him to church meetings in the Fourteenth Ward and in the church's tabernacle on Salt Lake's Temple Square, to parties at the bath house, to dances, and to neighbors' houses for visits. Samuel was active in the Polysophical Society, which shared poetry, essays, music, and addresses.[62] He often presented his work or conducted meetings. Mary went with him occasionally, but no record indicates that she read any of her own poems or if she was still writing poetry. Samuel also invited some of his wives when he attended meetings of the Deseret Theological Society class. Mary and Mary Ann often visited a few days at a time with Mary Ann's brother William, who lived "over Jordan," or with Mary's sister Ellen Corbridge, who lived in Davis County. Helena and Jane also visited friends extensively, many times staying for days at a time. Once Helena took a long visit back to the Isle of Man to visit her family, and left her children, including a frail infant, in Mary Ann's care.

In March, Mary's baby daughter, Iantha, became ill with measles. After the measles subsided, she continued to grow worse with inflammation in her stomach despite all the doctoring that Samuel and Mary knew. They put spirits on her head and a poultice on her stomach. Finally a doctor was called who gave Iantha an injection to relieve her pain. Samuel's journal entry for April 25, 1856, reads:

> About half past 10 p.m. she seemed to look brighter than for some time before, and turned her eyes up to mine two or three times and gave me a pleasant but expressive look. A few moments after Mary took her into her lap and laid her down upon her stomach, soon after which she hove at the stomach and threw up a little. I immediately stepped around to her head and raised her up in my arms and found that her eyes were fixed. I sat down in my chair, and said, "she is gone" Iantha Adelia was dead. In a moment unexpectedly I was found with Mary and Mary Ann weeping and lamenting our departed child. The rest of the family had retired. Our grief seemed heavy for the moment— we were overwhelmed. This moment of anguish was unlooked for. That lovely child was indeed lifeless upon my knees, and Mary and Mary Ann were loudly sobbing while clinging to it. Such a moment I had never before witnessed—the death of one of my own family and the sorrow attendant upon such a mournful event.

The other family members were awakened, and Ann Cash prepared the little body for burial. Two days later, they laid Iantha in the Salt Lake Cemetery near Alonzo Sylvester, who had been disinterred from his burial spot in the family garden.

In 1857, Samuel again left on a brief mission to Great Britain, although this calling was much different from his previous missions. President Brigham Young had learned that the United States Government was sending a large army to Utah to subject it to military rule. He summoned Samuel to the president's office, where he commissioned him a lieutenant-colonel and gave him a special assignment to take a message to President Buchanan, informing him that Young would not allow the United States Army to enter Utah. Samuel left three days later with George Snyder. The two men covered the distance of nearly thirteen hundred miles in seventeen days, at an average of almost seventy-seven miles a day. They did not meet with the president personally, but entrusted the dispatch to Colonel Thomas Kane, who had interceded for the Mormons at other times. They then went to Boston and sailed for Europe to inform the missionaries that they could return home, if needed, to defend their families. Along the way, Samuel and George reported the number and nature of army units and supply trains they met. They returned home the following April.

While Samuel was gone, Mary gave birth to her fifth baby, Ianthus Parker Richards, who was born on September 6, 1857. Each time she gave birth while Samuel was gone, or watched without him as a little one died, Mary felt more isolated from her husband. Although the house was always full, only her children and her niece Mary Ann could lift her spirits.

After his return, Samuel entered into marriage two more times. On March 19, 1857, he was married to Ann Cash, twenty years his senior. On January 27, 1859, he married Elizabeth Cain, following the death of her husband Joseph.[63]

Throughout 1859, Samuel's journals indicate his concern for Mary's health:

> Mary not well today, <u>severe</u> sick-headache and chill which continued most of the day and left her feeble at night. . . . Mary continues quite unwell, and about midnight had a very low spell fainting &C which required very careful attention to keep an action in her system. . . . Gave my attention to Mary who had another low sinking spell, and continued very low through the day. Elizabeth came and cared for Mary. . . . Mary still sick only able to sit up part of the day. . . . Mary sitting up.

In the meantime, Jane Mayer Richards convinced Samuel to let her take their small son to visit her family. They were also members of the Mormon faith who had emigrated to America, but they had settled around New Orleans, Louisiana, and Hillsboro, Arkansas. Besides telling of her activities in Arkansas, Jane's letters[64] are dotted with references to her family in Utah. She often wished that Mary Ann or Helena could be with her to see the beautiful scenery. She chastised Helena for not writing when it was her turn. She especially delighted in receiving letters from young Amelia, who was learning to play the melodian from Helena and who, in her childish way, divulged family details the others' letters lacked. In every letter, Jane expressed concern for Mary's health.

One particular letter, dated November 27, 1859, Jane asked Samuel not to read aloud. This letter conveyed Jane's worry about Mary. She wrote,

> I think often and I may say sometimes trouble about Sister Mary. I wish she was a strong healthy person. I think in her situation it is necessary she should be. She has as I have no doubt she thinks much to bear, but I am sure you do every thing for her comfort. I tell you what it is I do believe she thinks too much of you for her to be happy

Mary Ann Parker Richards, Samuel
Richards's second wife and Mary's
niece. Rosabelle Streeper Gwynn
collection.

Helena Lydia Robinson Richards,
Samuel Richards's third wife.
Rosabelle Streeper Gwynn collection.

Ann Jones Valleley Cash Richards,
Samuel Richards's fifth wife.
Rosabelle Streeper Gwynn collection.

Elizabeth Whitaker Cain Richards,
Samuel Richards's sixth wife.
Rosabelle Streeper Gwynn collection.

and of course if she is not well in spirits she will not be in body. I wish she would write, she is very sparing of her letters. Please tell her.

In another letter to Samuel, Jane indicated that Mary needed to quit worrying whether Samuel loved another wife more than her. Jane confided that she herself had worried in the same manner for awhile, then had decided to accept what love he had for her, however strong it was.

These letters briefly describe Mary's physical and emotional condition at this time. They also suggest that none of the other wives could fully empathize with what Mary was experiencing. Undoubtedly, these other spouses at times felt jealousy and frustrations, but they had knowingly entered into plural marriage. Mary, on the other hand, had not bargained for having to share Samuel with other women. Her marriage had been a monogamous union, with her expectations of happiness centering on her husband and their life together. It is apparent that Mary's deteriorating health was directly tied to the matter of polygamy and to her relationship with Samuel.

By this time, Mary was pregnant with her sixth child. As she was almost totally bedridden throughout this pregnancy, the care of her three children fell to Mary Ann. Mary Ann also looked after Mary's needs, as she had during the previous five years.

Finally, the warp of Mary's spirit and the weft of her body wore out. On the evening of June 3, 1860, at the age of thirty-six, she passed away, taking with her a newborn son. At three o'clock the next afternoon, Orson Pratt and Franklin Richards spoke at Mary's funeral.[65] Then, with her baby in her arms, she was buried near Iantha and Alonzo Sylvester.

Among the tributes to Mary were the following. The first was written by Sarah DeArmon Pea Rich:

She was a dear friend of mine. Bless her, for she was a lovely sister. Brother Samuel loved her dearly. . . . We were intimate friends before her marriage. Her name was Mary Parker. I write this that my children may see I loved a good woman that was worthy of being loved, and I wish her name to be looked upon by them in honorable remembrance.[66]

Samuel wrote his final poem for Mary and included it with her obituary in the June 6 *Deseret News*:

Tis joy to think of those who've lived
Unblemished lives upon the earth;
Their loss on earth is gain in heaven,
A truly consolation given.

Her part "Well done," She's gone to rest,
In joys of home among the blest,

> Just spirits greet her welcome there
> A crown of endless life to wear.[67]

The short life of Mary Haskin Parker Richards was over. Her story is one of conflict between what was expected of her and what she wanted, perhaps expected. She struggled to accept plural marriage, believing it assured her salvation, yet knew she would never be happy again once Samuel began marrying other women. Other couples during that time made the choice for monogamy, against the pressures of the Mormon church, often because the wives made a firm stand. Mary's life may have turned out differently if she had not chosen to be a martyr to her faith.

Mary tried to be cheerful, but her mind was frequently wracked with despair. Persons with chemical depression often face similar challenges, being told that if they exercise enough faith, do good to others, and think positively, insecurities will magically vanish. Mary may have learned that people who have never been there have little patience with depression. Samuel, her beloved husband and dearest friend, the one who could have given her the most support, simply did not understand.

Mary's great desire was for a stable home life with her husband and children. Possibly the happiest time in her life was the year spent in the little log cabin on the Nishnabotna River living alone with Samuel, and later their daughter Amelia, with a few good friends close by. Except for that year and perhaps for the first year or two in the Salt Lake Valley, she never was granted her wish. The demands faith and the Mormon historical experience—the church's migrations, missions and colonizations, polygamy, and a subsequent life outside the law—placed on them left many Mormon women with unfulfilled dreams of stable and private home life, as they ran their households alone while their husbands were absent or shared them unwillingly with plural wives.

A letter written to her father after Mary had been at the Missouri River for one month showed her desire to be strong though she suffered in silence. She penned that at one time she would have thought it almost impossible to have lived in such circumstances as she was then living, with nothing but a tent to cover her head and exposed to all kinds of tempests, wind, and rain. She had found she could live in almost any situation. Moreover, she did not feel sorry to suffer thus, for she counted it a blessing to suffer with the Saints and hoped to gain her reward with them.

Mary's will to survive and to believe was often challenged, whether by polygamy, an ocean crossing without money, life in Winter Quarters in a tent, or her constant fight against the debilitating effects of illnesses. Survive she did, until, lacking the physical and psychological strength she needed, she could fight no more.

Her journal entries at Winter Quarters show only a small portion of Mary's life, a time when there was happiness amidst loneliness, illness, cold, dirt floors, hunger, and bedbugs. This was a time, more than any other period in her life, when friends were there. Even without Samuel, there were parties, dancing, singing, visiting, laughing, understanding, sharing, helping, and loving–in short, a community in which she had a role. The network of women surrounding Mary made her life bearable and even enjoyable.

Mary's life at Winter Quarters was not uncommon. Others also suffered through family dislocations and separations, bitter cold, lack of food, sickness, and death. Feelings of loneliness must have been widespread among the thousands of Mormon faithful and other emigrants who were uprooted from their homes and separated from loved ones. She experienced, with others, the thrill of living close to church leaders and the excitement of a growing community planning a westward migration to a new Zion. As did other women, she saw beauty in the towering bluffs, was the beneficiary of women's blessings, and kept a devout faith in her Lord.

Nevertheless, Mary's writings are special. Uninhibited and unreserved, Mary recorded life as she saw it and felt it. Her letters and journals are a valuable contribution, by a vital and personable young woman, to women's literature. Her candid words allow us to empathize with her while learning something of what it was to be British, Mormon, young, and female on the American frontier of the late 1840s.

Samuel Whitney Richards, ca. 1859, age 35. Rosabelle
Streeper Gwynn collection.

CHAPTER TWO

A Scribe for the Women:
The Journals and Letters

In the past few decades, scholars have come to realize that the western movement and frontier life were seen and experienced quite differently by women and men. The story of Mary Haskin Parker Richards, as told through her journals, memorandum, and letters, is of one Mormon woman's life from 1846 to 1848, with a partial account of her earlier years. Her writings describe the temporary Latter-day Saint camp at Winter Quarters (now Florence, Nebraska) from a female perspective.

Most journals from the Mormon settlements near the Missouri River, where Mary lived, focus on political, economic, and institutional developments. Mary saw her world through the eyes of a young, newly married woman. Although she was one of the unsung Mormons and will be unknown to most readers, Mary was married to a nephew of Church of Jesus Christ of Latter-day Saints leader Willard Richards and had been converted in Great Britain by others of the church hierarchy. Therefore, her associates were an interesting mix of personalities, from the famous to the obscure.

Her intimate accounts reveal both a complex and a simple world at Winter Quarters. The complexities of new marriage patterns, church organization, and an improvised social order contrasted with the simplicity of daily work, interaction with friends and family, and physical struggles. Unlike most male diaries, Mary's journals and letters are full of emotion. She vividly expresses happiness, sorrow, pain, gratitude, beauty, and love.

Her accounts are filled with the dedication and determination of a young British convert who is satisfying her desire to live with the Saints, no matter how hard the life. Mary also reveals her submission to the will of Mormon church leaders and of her husband, who made decisions that shaped her life.

Anyone who writes a firsthand account selectively chooses what to record and what to conceal; therefore, Mary's writings uniquely reflect her sifting of her feelings and perspectives. However, her experiences were common among the women living around her. Through her pen, Mary in many ways serves as a scribe for all of the women who lived contemporaneously in the Winter Quarters area.

The known 1846 to 1848 writings of Mary Haskin Parker Richards consist of six journals; one memorandum; eleven letters to her husband, Samuel Whitney Richards; and one partial letter to her father, John Parker Sr. Three additional pages or half pages written to Samuel are undated. They appear to be additions to particular letters and have been included with them.

Her original journals and letters are all deposited in the Historical Department of the Church of Jesus Christ of Latter-day Saints (LDS) Archives Division. One letter was donated to that institution by Mary's descendant Regina Slater. The other letters and the journals were donated by descendant Alton F. Richards. The memorandum is in the possession of the editor, Maurine Carr Ward; however, a microfilm copy is located in the Historical Department.

The journals were all made of folded and sewn sheets of paper, without binding boards. Mary wrote in blue or brown ink and in a small, cramped style. The writing usually covered the whole page, with no margin at the top, bottom, or sides. Only one book has ruled lines, and here Mary wrote two lines to one ruling. Some pages are torn, frayed, or missing. Two of the journals have had letters sewn on afterwards as a covering. Similarly, one journal uses a sheet of Mary's early poetry for a cover.

The spelling and punctuation in the writings have been retained. Editorial insertions, used for clarification, have been placed in brackets. Most of Mary's sentences do not end with periods or have spaces to indicate where a new sentence begins. Rather, she placed periods in the sentences in much the way others would use commas, perhaps indicating where she paused to think or where she re-inked her pen. Later in her writings, she also wrote apostrophes where commas should be. Paragraphs are rare, where they exist, are not indented, but begin on a new line. All paragraphs have been indented, however, in the printed transcript for ease in reading. Mary drew exclamation points upside down, but they have been transposed in the transcript. Her parentheses were written as { } but are also shown herein in standard form.

The dates in the first journals all end in *th* such as "2th" and "3th." Mary varied her treatment of *th*, underlining some with one line; some with two lines; some with a wavy, instead of straight, line; some with one wavy and one straight line; some with two or three dots; some with a combination of dots and lines. The first day of the month was usually written out by Mary as "first." All dates are reproduced here without showing lines or dots below the superscripts.

Mary's indiscriminate use of upper and lower case for word beginnings runs throughout the manuscripts. It is often difficult to differentiate between upper and lower case *S's* and *O's. O's* and *A's* are hard to tell apart. Many words which should be spelled with an *a*, such as Walter, consistently use an *o*, as "Wolter," possibly because of Mary's Lancashire accent. Her capital *L* has an extra final loop causing some earlier transcriptions to render it as "Le." She spelled some words inconsistently, perhaps because she was not sure of the correct form.

In some places Mary wrote the word *and* and at other times used the ampersand. She was fond of using *&C*, meaning et cetera, one, two, or even three times at the end of a sentence. She distinguished early morning as "morn" or "morning." "AM" meant the later morning, the period before noon; "PM" stood for afternoon; and "eve" or "evening" indicated nighttime. Abbreviations, such as "M^r," were often treated the same as dates, with lines under the superscript *r* or with a dot, dots, or even a colon after the word. In a few instances she wrote the plural for Misters as "M^{rs}."

Positive identification of individuals Mary mentioned is difficult for many reasons. She referred to most persons as "Brother . . ." or "Sister . . ." rather than using a given name, and there was often more than one man or woman in the area with the same surname. On occasions she changed to "Mr." or "Mrs.," perhaps indicating persons who were not members of the Mormon church. Because of polygamous marriages, in some references it is impossible to know which wife she means. Though she identified most plural wives with their maiden, not their married, names, this caused additional identification problems. At times she used an initial instead of the first name, or she abbreviated a name.

It also appears that Mary followed contemporary tradition in considering houses and other residences the property of husbands. This is apparent when she writes of visiting a Brother's home but then discusses a wife or daughter.

Approximately five hundred individuals are mentioned in Mary's writings. Where necessary for clarification, the identities of these persons are further specified in the text in brackets. They are listed as correctly as possible with identifying notes in a Biographical Register appended to the text.

Mary's letters are more difficult to read than the journals. They were usually written on large pieces of paper which were folded in half, then folded again to create self-contained envelopes addressed on the outside of the back page. Mary covered every blank spot of paper with minute writing. Left and right margins have addenda. The top of each page often has a sentence or two written upside down. In some of the letters, Mary turned the page around and wrote upside down between the original lines. Worn spots, fold lines, and areas sealed with wax have left illegible passages in the letters. Letters were written over an extended period of time until the entire pages were filled. Often, personal messages or additions to the main letters were written on smaller scraps and mailed with the letters.

These letters are more meaningful when read in conjunction with Samuel's letters to Mary, which are also deposited in the LDS Historical Department Archives Division. Often each correspondent's letter carries responses to a letter or letters received from the other.

CHAPTER THREE

"One of the most Beautyfull valeys"

Aboard the ferry leaving Kimball's landing in Nauvoo, Illinois, Mary Haskin Parker Richards began, on May 19, 1846, the crossing of the Mississippi River and her journey to a new home, an event reminiscent of her departure from Great Britain across the Atlantic Ocean some five years earlier. Then, young Mary had bade farewell to all of her brothers and sisters and to the land of her birth and sailed with family friends to America and a reunion with her parents. This time, Mary was leaving parents, husband, and friends to accompany her husband's family as it journeyed to an unknown land in search of a religious sanctuary.

At her husband's suggestion, Mary began recording her experiences and history in two small notebooks he provided for her. One became the first of at least six daily journals, which began with the river crossing. The other was a retrospective account of her life in England. While Mary kept her journals current, she only worked on the memorandum as time permitted and never completed it. However, the first seventeen years of Mary's life are vividly portrayed in her descriptive writing.

The Memorandum
September 8, 1823, Chaigley, Lancashire,
to December 25, 1840, aboard the *Alliance*

The Memorandum of Mary H Parker)[1] I Was Born in Chaidgley. In the County of Lancashire. England. Sept 8. 1825 [1823]. My Father. then ocupide a Small. Farm. Near the Foot of Mount Longridge. In one of the most Beautyfull valeys. that my Eyes Ever Beheld. It lay Between 2 mountains. that Extend East and West. in a Stright Line for Near 10 Miles. & are near 10 miles. From the Summit of One. to the Summit of the Other. Forming a Half Sircle.) In the Senter of the valey. is the River Other [Hodder]. Runing In the Same Derection With the Mountains) My Father's House was situwayted On the Main Road Between Preston. & Clithrow. Being 7 miles From the Nearest Town) The mountain Stream Ran Singing

The Memorandum of Mary
Parker, I Was Born in Chaidgley. In the
County of Leancashire. England. Sept 5.
1825. My Father. then Ocupide a Small.
Farm. Near the Foot of Mount Loongridge.
In One of the most Beautyfull valeys.
that My Eyes Ever Beheld. It lay Betwen
2 Mountans. that Extend East & West. in
a Stright Line For Near 10 Miles. & are near
10 Miles. From the Summit of One to the
Summit of the Other. Forming a Half
Sircle, In the Senter of the valey Is the
River Other. Runing In The Same Dereckt
With the Mountans, My Father's House was
Situurated On the Main Road Between
Preston. & Clithrow. Being 1 miles From the
Nearest Town, The Mountan Stram
Ran Singing By The Door. joind by the
Worbling notes. of unnumberd Birds

The first page of Mary Richards's memorandum of her early life in
Chaigley, Lancashire, England.

By The Door. joind by the Warbleing notes of unnumberd Birds Whose melody In the Spring & Samer together with other ajoining Beautys. made my Home apear Delightfull)

My Father had 5 sons and 5 Dauters of whom I was the youngest. when 4 years old I remember One Day standing By the Side of my Mother as She was Sowing the Seam of a garment thinking that I was able to saw as well as She. I Requested the Privalige. She then gave me a Piece of Old Cloth. witch affended me very mutch. She then left the room. so I thought I would try my hand upon her work. On retorning & seeing what I had don. She was very willing that I should continu. when 4 years & half old. I was larned to wind Bobins. my Brothers & Sisters. most of them. Being weavers. when 5 years old I could Earn 4 shilings in one week. wich is equel to one Dollar. I Continued to wind Bobings. until most 8 years old. when I was released From this work. Cops [?] being Instatuted In the Place thereof. I went to scool. to miss Jenneta Richards. until most 10 years old)

I then learned to weave. & Continued to do so. For one year. when mrs willson Prevailed with my Mother. to let me live with Her. I Stayed with her 2 months then not likeing Situwaytion I retorned Home. went to weaving again. until July 1837 when She again Prevailed with me to go Back & live another 2 months. I then retorned Home. Stayed one night. the next Day went to Mr Seeds. who was my [*blank space*] a very respectable man. they had one Sweet little babe to wich I Became Nurse. in the Spring of 1838 It was reported one Sunday that an Amarican. was to preach. at Mr Richards Chappal accordingly I went in the Evening & heard a discourse Deliverd by H C Kimball on the First ~~Princeapals~~ Principles of the gospel. Preached again on Monday & Tuesday Evenings. Babtised 6 Persons of whom my Brother John was one. the rev: mr Richards then Finding that He was loosing all His members Forbid them Preaching in his Chaple. Soon after I heard that my father and Brothe[r] Rodger was Babtised the next Sunday after them. my mother and sister Alice was Babtised also. after this the[y] held their meetings In my Father's House. mr Seeds was very mutch oposed to the Saints and therefore was not willing that I should go to my Fathers House on acount of the meetings. 2 months after this I went home to See my Friends. it being on Sunday the house was filled mr John Alston addrest the meeting. follod by several others. I was mutch Pleased with the meeting. & retorned Back with a detarmination to become one of their number On the 21 of July I left mr Seeds. and retorned Home. For the Porpose of Being Babtised. the[y] Said they were vary sory. that I was willful to join the Mormons. and if It had not been For that Reason. they could not have Parted with me.) On the 6: of aug [1838] I was Babtised Into the Church of Jesus ~~Crist~~ Christ of Lattarday Saints. By William Kay. On the 11 I was Confirmed by Elders Wilard Richards & Joseph Falding [Fielding]. acordingly I Continued to live at Home. & weave as usal. being Frequently visited by Bro W Richards. J.

John Parker Sr., father of Mary Haskin Parker Richards. Rosabelle Streeper Gwynn collection.

John Parker Jr., brother of Mary Haskin Parker Richards and father of Mary Ann Parker, second wife of Samuel Whitney Richards. Rosabelle Streeper Gwynn collection.

Richard Parker, brother of Mary Haskin Parker Richards; he remained in Lancashire, England. Rosabelle Streeper Gwynn collection.

Alice Parker Corbridge, sister of Mary Haskin Parker Richards. Rosabelle Streeper Gwynn collection.

Ellen Parker Corbridge, sister of Mary Haskin Parker Richards. Rosabelle Streeper Gwynn collection.

Fielding. F. Moon. & several others. from whom we Received good Instructions. & were strengthend From time to time. Being Now in the Church 3 months. I was visited by the Bev. [Rev.] mr. Aaron, a Church of England minister. who being very Desireous for the Wellfare of Souls. Came to Convince me of my delusion. asked seaveral questions Conserning Mormonism. One was did I Beleve In Babtism by Imersion. told Him yes. Asked for the Proff [proof] Refered to the 16 Chap of Mark also the 2 Chap of Acts this he said did not Prove that they Babtised by Imersion. I then Referd to the 6 Chap of Romans wich speaks of their being buryed with Christ By Babtism. he then said that those who were then Babtised all walked In Newness of life I said. it did not Read that the[y] did but rather that the[y] Should. He then asked me if we Beleved the Bible as it Read. tould him I did. Mary Said he you must not. I will Mr Aaron Said I. For I think if the Lord is not able to Speak His word as He Intends it to be. I shall not trust to men to mend it. Then taking me by the arm he exclaimed. Oh Mary-Mary-Mary. Let us Pray. after wich he exprest many good wishes for our wellfare & departed. he often visited us after this and although my Mother & Sister were always preasent. yet he always directed his conversasion to me. often wishing me to attend his Church and hear him preach. but I perfered to Spend my Sabaths. were the gospel was preached p̶ in its purety. on Sunday. morning. our meetings were held at brother James Corbridge's house 3 miles west. In the PM at my fathers and in the evening a bro W Bleasdales 2 miles west these I always attended when my health and the weather would permit.

In the Spring of 1840: bro H C Kimball. P P Pratt. O Pratt & O Hyde again retorned to Eng: 2 weeks after they arived. bro Kimball visited us. was quite unwell. Said he had come. porpose for sister Alice & my self to nurse him. Staid with us One week. in wich time I took mutch comfrt washin his feet. & administering to his wants. he often gave me good instrucsions. & pronounced many blessings on my head. during this sumer he often viseted & preached at my fathers house. it being the most conveneant house for meeting. he was often invited to Stay with the rest of the breathren yet with about 2 excepsions he allways stayed with us. One time wile washing his feet. he laid his hand upon my head & said. Mary. it Shall be said of you after many years. that you washed the feet of the Searvants of the Lord and administerd to their wants. o̶f̶ ̶t̶h̶e̶ & the Lord Sayes that whosoever Shall give unto one of my Servants a drink of cold water shall in no wise loose his reward. Mary. you Shall See the day. when the rememberance of what you are now doing. shall be a consolasion to you. for there is great blessings laid up for you if you will be faithfull & adhere to my counsal. for I know you love to do anything for the Saints, and you Shall be blest. yea I say it in the name of the Lord. you Shall have your reworde. another day having been left alone in the sitting room he called me from my work. & desired me to take a seat by his side. said he had some good counsal to give me if I would promis to receve & keep it. I told him I wold. he then told me that I must not get marid until I got to Nauvoo. brother Kimball said I. there is no danger of that ~~eve~~ I am ~~even to young~~ altogether to young even to think of sutch a thing. I know you are young. Mary said he. but remember you are growing older every day. and I should not be surprised if you were tryed more than once or twise before you reach Nauvoo. but if you will do as I say you shall have the desire of your heart. and you shall enjoy greater b[l]essings than you can even think of or immaging. you shall have a great porsion of the Spirit of the Lord and you shall praise God because of the counsel wich I give you. Sister Mary said he I wish you were with my wife. I know she would love you and take good care of you. and I am sure you could not help but love her. aboute the first of March Sister Mary Bleasdal and myself went to Preston to visit some of our friends arived there aboute 9 oclock in the morn spent the day very Pleasant & in the evening took a walk with my cousen Robert Huntington. Sister M[ary] with my cousen John. they took us through some of the most pleasent parts of the town. gave us some preasents &C had a very pleasent walk. the next day attended meetting at the Temperance Hall receved an interoduction to miss Ellen Wilding. In the evening retorned home acompanyed by my cousens R and J. also 2 other young men. one by the name of W Potter who was very ancious to become acqueanted with me. 2 weeks afterwords he rote me a letter desiring my company. promising to visit me on Easter Sunday. But having receved. an invitation from the sisters in Chadborn. to visit them. I accordinly went on Saturday and spent the eve. at mr Burns. the next morn attended meetting at Downham. a large company of the Sisters went with me. my Brother John & also Bro E Corbridge came to accompany me home. had a good meeting in the afternoon attended meeting at Bro Halls in Chadborn in the Evening retorned home. Sister Alice told me mr P. had been and was very mutch disapointed at not finding me at home. he sent me another message by my cousen to wich I replyed after wich he trubled me no more. Soon after this a young man named William Willson. solisited my company. and apeared very unwilling to be refused. One Saboth about the middle of June I went to Wadington in company with W Kay. attended meeting there in the AM & in the PM attended meeting at the Mills 8 miles from Chaidgley. in the evening retorned home. had a p[l]easant time. about the 3 of September [1840] my Parents commenced to make preparations to go to Amarica. On the 5th took leve of the house where the[y] had lived for forty two years and their native Country. Sister Alice. and my self accompanyed them to Preston. and at nine oclock. bade them goodbye. it was a very dark Night. after we lost sight of them. sister Alice fainted and it was for some time before we could bring her to. it was indeed a gloomy night to us booth. stayed the night at Bro T [or Y] Richardsons. I was very sick all the night. the next morn

I took the railway Car to Longridge 8 miles then walked 6 miles was very sick all the way. reached home about 5 in the eve. after this was sick 4 weeks with the typ[h]us fever. for 3 weeks was ~~quite~~ not expected to live. after wich the fever torned and I soon began to ammend. during my sickness. I was kindly taken care of by my dear Sister Alice. who administerd day & night to my wants for wich kindness may god reward her. about the 6 of October I went to visit my Sister Ellen. Sister Alice wept. & said she felt as though we should never live together more. Stayed with Ellen 3 weeks then went to visit Sister Isabella at Blackburn 12 miles from Chaidgley. Stayed with [her] 1 week then retorned to get some things. expecting to live with her through the winter. went ~~then~~ back. & stayed with her 3 weeks. On the 7th of December. [1840] my Brother Rodger. & George Rhodas[2] come to see me. the latter informed me that he together with Bro Bleasdales folkes[3] intended to sail for America on the 12. he tould me if I would go with them he would fournish me whatsoever means I might be lacking to cary me to Nauvoo. My Bro & the Bretheren of the Church Counceled me to go. so I took leave of my sister Isabella on the 8th [December 1840]. about 8 in the morn traviled about 4 miles & came to mellerbrook. found my Sister Ann. and stayed with her 2 hours. then after taking some refreshment took leve of her and her dear family. who wept much at my departure. travild 8 miles on foot and about 5 in the eve came to my Sister Ellens house. found her with a little Daughter near 3 weeks old herself very sick and also her Husband. Stayed & took care of them that night and til noon the next day. then went to see my Bro Richards folks about 2 miles East. Stayed with them till eve then went to Chipping. 3 miles N.W. to see my Bro Roberts folks. acampanyed by my sister Alice and Bro E Corbridge visited with them about 2 houres. then bid the family good bye. Bro. R came with me about a mile. he not being a saint I gave him my testmony in regard to my faith in the work wich I had imbraced and desird him to join the Church. & to gather with the Saints that I might hope. that one day ere long I might see his face again. I then bade him good bye & left him in tears. with but little hope that [I] should ever See his face more. got to Bro Johns about 11 oclock & slept that night with Sister Alice. the next day viseted among my friends. and at Evening. attended a Prayer meeting at Bro Johns house wich had been called on acount of my being coming away. there was a number of Bretheren & Sisters who spoke & promised us their Prayers for our wellfare. we had a good meeting, at the latter part of wich I sung a few verses wich I had Composed as a farewell song to my Brothers & Sisters. Spent that night it being the last. with Sister Alice. the next morning took leave of Brother Richards family also Bro Johns family. traviled one mile and took leave of the spot that gave me birth. called to see our nearest naighbor Mrs Tayler. who came with me about a quarter of a mile and wept most bitterly to part with me about 10 oclock came to sister Ellens found her and William My

Brother in law still very sick. at 9 PM took leave of Brother Rodger and his family also William and Ellen and their dear Infant.

[*space of about four lines before the next sentence begins*]

Nevver shall I forget the feeling that shriled through my Bosem this day. while parting with all my dear Brothers & Sisters. and all my kindred who were near & dear to me by the ties of nature. and expecialy my Dear Sick Sister and her companion. who needed my assistance. to travil to a distant Port. from there to venture upon the wide Expanded Ocean. behind wich to wander in a strange Land in wich I should be a stranger. hope at intervales would glimer in my bosem. there dwells my Dear Parents. but what if God should please to take them to himself. E'er I be permitted to see them. I must bid an everlasting adue to my native Land and to that dear spot that gave me birth. wich had been the dwelling Place of my dear Parents for more than 40 years also of my forefathers for many years before them. 'tis true I was going with a family who had promised to befriend me. but what if they should forget their covanant and leave me a Stranger. in a Strange Land. the trial of parting with my Friends. together with these reflections. caused me to give vent to my tears. wich until this time I had endeaverd to conseal.

Past through Preston at Sundown the Night was very cold. about 5 the next morn came to Longton. put up at an Inn and took some refreshments. at 7 again proceeded past through several Villiges and at 6 in the eve arived in Liverpool. put up at a Taveran for the night. expecting to go on board a ship the next day. next morn Bro Bleasdale learned from the man with whom he had engaged our pashige one week before that he intended to charge us for the same each 10 shillings more than we had ingaged to pay. to this Bro B would not agree. and left the ship. Went forthwith and engaged our pashige on bord the ~~El~~ Ealians [*Alliance*] bound for New York published to sail on the 23th [December]

then went and hired a room. of Mr. Birkinnight. where we lived 11 days. Bro Taylor was at this time delivering a Course of Lectures in the Music Hall L[iverpool] I attended several of them and was highly Interested. while here became acquainted with several of the Saints whom I found to be agreeable. The 21st December was a general fast day here among the Saints and I fasted with them. After the AM service' I went with Sister Brikinnight to a brothers house to see a sister Curtis who had lately arrived from America. She was the first American Woman. I ever saw.

to day I received an invetation' from 2 young Sisters' who had lived together in a Gentlemans family for 4 years. to visit them the next day' with Sister Bir. next day came' and sis B and myself went and made our visit. enjoyed ourselfs exceeding well. found the young ladys interesting & Amiable. they treated us very kindly' presented me with some Books' and requested me to keep them on rememberance of the giver. we stayed with them until 8 oclock in the evening. talking about the good things of the kingdom of our God. when after receiving many kind wishes for my wellfare and a promis of their prayers I took a kind leave of them & left them in tears. Bro William Taffingder having spent the eve with us. now very kindly accompanyed me to the Ship and conducted me to that part of it that was destined to be my future home or rather my abode for a time all was dark and Gloomy. my freinds also seemed sorrowfull and degected on enquiring the cause I was told that Bro Rhodes had been out in Town' and had got Robed of all the Money he had–this brought a change upon our future prospects. he was the only one among us' that possessed means. & he had promised to defray our expenses from NY to Nauvoo but now our hopes were Plighted

Sister Bleasdale says Mary the Ship will sail in the mornin' what shall we do. I replied our Passage is paid. our provisions are on Board. let us go to NY the Lord is just as able to sustain us there' as he is' if we should remain here. and so long as we walk uprightly before him' we shall have no cause to fear. for he has promised that he will never forsake those who put their trust in him.

On the 23rd [December] about 10 oclock we drew Angker and set sail. we were tawed out by a steam Boat. about 2 miles. which then left us.

it was with feelings of no ordinary kind' that I took (my I) a last look upon my native shore' which was now fast fading away' in the distance. and Launched out' upon the broad Atlantic Oacen we had a fair wind and our Gallant Ship' bore us on Magesticly' at the rate of 8 knots per hour. Six Oclock Eve about this time most of the Passangers were sick mysilf among the rest. Nevertheless I rested tollerable good through the 24th sister Bleasdale and myself both sick. nevertheless we made out to prepair our food' and Bros Rhoads and Bleasdale. took it on deck to the fire' and tended it while it was Cooking. but 'twas little food I eat

25 Christmas day. pyes & Puddings were made' and eat' in all quarters of the Ship. but Mary cared nothing about them for she was to sick to eat.

the next Berth to mine was ocuped by two young Ladys' who were following their intended husbands to America. one of them was proud and haughty. the other was pleasant and amiable. the latter be came my Companion during the voige. and was always very kind to me when sick. she always accompanyed me on dect' and when there' remained by my side' & assisted me to walk from one place to another. her name was Ann.

our Captin was an American. and was very kind. to us. he would often bring a cuple of Chairs out of the Cabin' for Ann' and me' to sat on. in the Portch of the Cabin door. and would then give each of us a rope from the Mast wich stood in front of us' to ballance ourselfs by. and would then Ask us if we ever enjoyed a nicer Rocking than we was then taking.

I used to ask him then if he did wish his [*manuscript ends abruptly*]

Nauvoo Temple on the hill, as seen from the river flats. Daguerreotype probably taken by Lucian Foster in the early spring of 1846; courtesy of LDS Historical Department.

CHAPTER FOUR

"Weept about an houre & . . . felt some better"

From Montrose to Sugar Creek, from Richardson's Point to Mt. Pisgah, and from there through the Potawatomi Indian camp to the encampment of John Taylor and Parley P. Pratt on Mosquito Creek, Mary's first journal covers the crossing of Iowa. Within its pages, she shares her sorrow and loneliness at parting with Samuel, the hardships of wagon travel, her reunion with dear friends at Mt. Pisgah, and her dance with Brigham Young at the bowery before the Mormon Battalion men departed.

Journal One
Tuesday, May 19, 1846, Nauvoo, Illinois,
to Friday, July 17, 1846, Mosquito Creek, Iowa[1]

Tue May 19th   In the AM was making a shirt for my Husband. and at one oclock in the PM. took my departure with my Father in laws famaly for the west parted with my Father at Hyrum Kimballs[2] landing. had a pleasent sail acoross the Mississippy River. and arived at the Camp about one mile from the landing in the Ioway a little after 5 went to Bro Vancotts tent with my Husband. and took suppor. slept that night in Bro W Wilcocks wagon.

Weds 20th   was sawing on my Husbands shirt. &C In the evening had a tremendious rain storm. stayed in Bro V C tent until 10 oclock then slept in the wagon.

Thursday 21th   Spent most of the day in the wagon with my Husband. hearing him read. braiding a rislet. convarsing with him &C. injoyed my self very much. in the evening had another rain storm.

Friday 22th   Took a walk with my Husband in the morning. half past 9 in and at half past 9 again proceded on our jorny for the west. past throu montrose. in the PM got stuck One of our wagons got stuck in a slue. had a hard time getting it out. my Husband. & Bro V C went in to the water &

63

pryed it up it took 4 yoke of oxen to draw it out. past several very muddy p[l]ace & about 5 o clock broke one of our wagon tonges. went on for about 1 mile then campt for the night. having traviled about ten miles.

Saturday 23.   This morning My Dear Husband left me. to retorn to Nauvoo. to prepare for his mission to England. this indeed was one of the most trying Scenes that I ever witnessed. To part with him to whome alonee I look for protection & comfort. & who alone is the most dear to my heart. to wander for hundereds of miles in a dreary wildernss wile he is traviling for thousands of miles in another direction is a trial beyond decription. I parted with him about ½ past 8 in the AM. & after riding about ½ a mile lost sight of him & the place w[h]ere we stayed. the road being rough. I then got out & walked ~~in~~ aboute ½ a mile & came to Charlston. from thence I rode with Bro Vancott in his carige. to Shuger Creek. about 2 miles. we there stoped to do some washing &C. Spent most of the after noon writeing in my journal. in the eveing was quite unwell. slept in the wagon had a good nights rest.

Sunday 24ᵗʰ   In the morn was writeing in my journal. In the PM was reading. In the evening was ruther unwell.

Monday 25ᵗʰ   Left Suger creek at 5 in the morn. went 2 miles then stopt & took breakfast. aboute one oclock we came to Farmington. found bro Palmers famaley. & took dinner with them. we there crossed the dessmoin River at 6 o clock came to a Grove were we campt. for the night. having traviled 12 miles through woods & perairy. being nowe 25 miles from Nauvoo.

Tuesday 26   left the grove at 8 in the morn. traviled 15. miles. the weather veary hot. the road pretty good. campt that night on the Priara.

Wednsdy 27ᵗʰ   In the morn rwrote a letter to my husband. & sent it to him by Bro Vancott. at 8 oclock AM proceded on our jorney. at one oclock came to Richardsons point. found a number of the saints encampt there. pitched our tent to await bro Vs retorn. in the PM cut out 2 garments for my self & worked on one.

Thursday 28ᵗʰ   was sawing on my garment.[3] in the evening went to see Bro littles [Edwin S. Little] grave.[4]

Friday 29ᵗʰ   at 5 in the morn. was much rejoic'd to receve a letter from my husband. wich was read by me with much satisfaction. was much pleased to see Aunt Rody [Rhoda Richards]. and Aunt Sariah [Sarah Griffith Richards]. who had reach'd the camp in the night. after this was writing in my jornal. In the PM finished making my garment & commenced to work on another. spent the evening in Bro VCs tent.

Saturday 30ᵗʰ   In the AM was sawing on my garment. In the PM finished it. & took a walk with Eliza A. P. [Eliza Ann Peirson]

Sunday 31ᵗʰ   left Richardsons point a[t] 8 in the AM. travel'd for sever'l miles through a beautyfull Priara. the weather Pleasent until 5. in the PM when the rain began to poure down in torents. waited til the storm began to abate. then went about one mile & stopt for the night. the weather very uncomforttable. th[r]ough the day was rather unhappy.

Monday June 1ˢᵗ   went 2 miles then stopt.⁵ the roads being very muddy in the AM was knitting. & also in the PM.

Tuesday 2ᵗʰ   Proce'ded on our journey at 8 in the morn traveled about 23 miles through a beautyfull country. then campt for the night. the weather very Pleasent until 8 in the evening. when it commenced to rain. & continued to do so most of the night.

Wednesday 3ᵗʰ   a rainey morn. the creeks so high we cannot cross them. In the morn was writing in my journal. in the AM was sewing. about 2 in the PM again proceeded on our journey went about 8 mils then stopt for the night. the roads very roughs.

Thursday 4ᵗʰ   In the morn commenced writing a letter to my husband. at 8 again went on. went about 7 miles. the road very rough & muddy. had to dubble team 1. ½ mile at a time.⁶ the weather vea[r]y cold. in the eve was writing in my letter.

Friday 5ᵗʰ   in the morn got breakfast & washed the dishes &C. at 8 oclock again proce'ded on our journey. Traviled about 10 mils then campt for the night. in the eve was writing.⁷

Saturday 6ᵗʰ   In the morn finished writing my letter. & sent to Nauvoo. by Bro. John Huntington. who said he wold try to see my husband & give it to him. at 8 again started on our journey. traviled about 14 miles then stopt for the night. the roads very good the weather very pleasent.

Sunday 7ᵗʰ   in the morn was writing in my journal and at ½ past 8 left the place were we campt. went about 4 miles then stopt to do some washing. air our cloths. see to our provisions. &C In the PM assisted the folks. to spred out the crakers. found some of them spoiling. attend'd to drying them &C. felt very unhappy through the day. went into the woods twice. sat down under an oak tree. Offerd up a prayer to the lord. weept about an houre & retorned. in the evening felt some better took a walk with cousin Eliza & A[bigail] abbot.

Monday 8ᵗʰ   In the morning got breakfast. washed the dishes. did some washing. &C. at ½ past 12. again proceed went about 5 miles then campt for the night. the weather very pleast.

Tuesday 9ᵗʰ   In the morn ~~got breakfast~~ wrote a letter to my husband & at 8 again Proceeded on our journey. traviled about 12 miles then campt for the night. the weather very pleasent. the roads very good.

Wednesday 01ᵗʰ   In the morn got breakfast and at 7 proceed'd. went about 13 miles. good traviling. then stopt for the night.

Thursday 11ᵗʰ   assisted mother in the morn. and at 9 again proceeded. the weather & roads being good. we t[r]aviled about 12 miles. and at 5 in the PM arived within 3 miles of the camp. having understood that there was not much feed for our Cattle near the camp. we stayed here for the night. In the eve was writing in my journal & sewing.

Friday 12[th]   In the morn was sewing & at ½ past 9 again proceeded on our journy arived at the Camp on Mount Pizga at 12. went to Bro Riches tent with Cousen Eliza. Sister [Lucy Lavinia Sackett] VanCott. Mother & miss [Abigail] abot. at 2 PM. bro Van Cott uncle Levi and all those who came with us. crost the River. Bro vc left us one wagon & 2 yoke of oxen. was very sory to part with them. felt very lonesome all day. about 4 Melissa Burton came to see me. was much pleas'd to see her in the Eve called to see sister wille [Samantha Call Willey]

Saturday 13th   In the morn got breakfast in the AM asistted mother to do some washing. in the PM was sawing & went with mo[ther] to see sister [Pamela Andrus] Benson. [h]ad a pleasent walk. wrote a letter to my husband. and sent by the post. felt very lonly all the day.

Sunday 14th   in the AM went to meetting. good instructions were given by Bros [William] Huntington. [Isaac] Morly. and [Charles C.] Rich.[8] in the PM went with Maria [Maria Haven Burton] & Rebecka [Rebecca Burton Jones]. to their tent on the other side of the River. about one mile from Mount Pizgah. stayed with them all night

Monday 15th   at Bro [Samuel] Burtons. til six in the eve. then retorned home. had a good visit. found Fathers folks had moved to another place. Mother had made a tent out of our wagon covers & they had were living in it. was rather unwell all day

Tuesday 16th   was sewing most of the day. felt quite unwell. about 11 oclock Wolters folkes [Walter and Maria Richards Wilcox] arived at our tent in the eve was writing. then had a viset from sister benson

Wednesday 17th   at 6 in the morn receved a letter from my Husband bearing date June 4 9 & 10 It gave me much joy to hear from him who though abscant in body is always Present in mind. in the PM was sewing. & in the PM also. did some writing &C. in the eve visited at bro E Barrows. was quite unwell all the day.

Thursday 18th   In the AM viseted was sawing. & in the PM viseted at Bro Riches with R[ebecca] Jones. Maria. & Melissa Burton. had a good visit. in the eve went with them to see the grave yard. it now contains 5 Bodys.

Friday 19th   In the AM did some washing spent the PM with sister Jacobs. was quite unwell.

Saturday 20th   In the AM was Irining in the PM was sawing felt quite unwell

Sunday 21th   at AM went to meeting heard an exelant discorse deliverd by Bro W Woodrufe. commenced by saying. that he rejoyced to see this day. for it was a day. that he had long desird to see when he could meet with his Brethren away from what is now called the Christian World. said he had never seen the time when he felt better. adviced the bretheren by alway al means to adhear to counsel. & not rush on. to get ahead of those who were apointed to lead them. but seek councel of those who were apointed by the athority of the chorch to give it said he had always been subject to counsel was ready to go when the councel said go & come when they say come &C. was followd Bro's Huntington [Ezra T.] Benson Rich & Shearwood. had a good meeting. in the PM was writing. at ½ past 6 Father receved a letter from uncle Wilard. in wich he says tell Jane [Jane Snyder Richards]. & Mary to take corige all will go well. the boys will come back. urged us to come on as soon as we can.

Monday 22nd   was sewing. made me one sh. &C in the eve visited at Bro Bensons. had a good visit.

Tuesday 23th   In the AM was sewing finished making another Sh. at 2 PM recieved a line from R Jones to attend Melissa Burton wedding. at 4. accordinly I prepared myself and at 3 left for the wedding. arived in time. they were maried 15 minutes before 5 by Bro Rich. had a good supper. some singing &C. spent the eve very pleasingly

Wednesday 24th   a rainy day was at Bro Burtons until ½ past 5 in the eve. then was brought home by the Bridegroom & Bride Mr & Mrs. Cory [William Coray and Melissa Burton]. in a coverd wagon. they intended to start for the west the next morning.

Thursday 25th   In the AM was sewing. also in the PM. did some writing in my journal. at 5 comme[n]ced to rain very heavy. & continued to do so most of the night went to bed. coverd my self with a quilt & slept sound.

Friday 26th   a wet gloomy morn. felt very lonely. made the skirt to a new dress. put out my things to dry. assisted in raising our chests from the groun[d] &C.

Saturday 27th   a beautifull morn asisted Mother about the work at 2 oclock went to viset Maria about 1 mile &C. Melinda [Malinda Wilcox Wood] cut & basted my dress for me. had a pleasent viset & retorned home in the eve. was very ~~lonely~~ tired.

Sunday 28th   had a very high wind in the morn. and appearance of rain about 2 it cleard away. and we had an excellant meeting. Bro Benson. first addresst us. was followed by Bro Rich & Huntington & Woodroff. I was much cheered by thir remarks I received a letter from Cousen Eliza Peirson 10021 [121] mil west from Mount Pisgah. in the PM rote an ansure. and sent it by bro [William] Clayton. was a very wet afternoon & evening. and I felt as gloomy as the times.

Monday 29th   in the Morn put out our things to dry. then went to washing. had a large washing. the weather very hot.

Tuesday 30th   in the AM was irining. in the PM was sewing &C. the weather still continued to be very hot and my self very weak stayed all night with Sister Barrows

Wednesday 1st of July.   in the AM unpacked my new Chest. & put out my things to air. found them all in order. was very [*blank space*] alday packing up & preparing to take our departure the next day for the west. in the PM

Bro Parly [P. Pratt] arived at Mount pisgah on a mision to rais a Pioneer Company to gard the Twelve across the rockey mountains. called a meeting at ½ past 5 for that pourpose. at wich time I sat down and rote a letter to Elizabeth Fory & sent it by Bro Johnson.

Thursday 2th   finished packing our things & loading our waggon. and at 11 AM took leve of Mount Pisgah. crost grand River at 12 traveled about 8 miles then camped for night. [h]ad pleasent weather & good roads.

Friday 3th   got breakfast washed the dishes and at 6 in the morn Proceeded on our journey crost several creeks along wich ran a narrow strip of wood. had good roads with the exception of 2 slews where we had to unload all our loos things. to lighten our load. traveled about 16 miles then stopt for the night

Saturday 4th   took an early start before breakfast at 5 in the morn. stoped at 7 & took breakfast. at 8 proceeded crost a roveing Praira with intervening slews. fell in company with Bro Stevens got stuck twice he assisted us with his oxen. the weather was very warm but pleasent.[9] stopt at 8 had a tremendious thunder storm. lasted most of the night. I took some cold.[10]

Sunday 5th   started at 7 traveled till 11 then stopt to let our Cattle rest at one met Bro Brigham [Brigham Young] Heber [Heber C. Kimball] & ~~uncle~~ Benson. & Uncle Willard. Retorning to Mount Pisgah to raise a company of 500 men to go into the cervice of the United States. for year. Bro Brigham asked me if my Husband had gon to Eng. tould him I expected he was. he had left me for that porpose. he said that was good. asked me if it wo'nt hard to part with him. and how I stood it. tould him it was hard. and I stood it the best I could being satisfide that I had to endure it I did the best I knew how bro Kimball also tould me he was glad that he was gone said he was a good boy. tould me to be a good girl and it would only be a little while before I should meet him on the other side of the rockey mountains. Uncle Willard came to our waggon & made us quite a visit. spoke to him of my trials sacrefice &C asked him for a blessing. to wich he replied. you have got your hearts desire and there is every blessing in the world for you and what do you ask more. gave us much instructions and at 4 took leave of us and we proceded. went 7 mils crost a large creek & at 8 stop for the night. this day the weather was very hot. had pretty good ~~roads~~ roads. felt pretty well

Monday 6th   started at 5 in the morn stopt at ½ past 6 an[d] took breakfast. & proceded at ½ past 7. at 12 crost a river passed through the Potawhatame vilage. it is situwated between Rivers on a bluff. Traviled about 3 miles then camped on the Praira for the night.

Tuesday 7th   again haveing no wood. we started before breakfast. went 1 mile found wood. & stopt to take refreshments after wich we proceded. crost several bad slews and hard hills. the weather being very hot we rested from 11 till 3 met about 40 Indians. traviled til Sun down

Wednesday 8th   proceded at 7 in the morn. the weather being very hot we again rested from 12 til 3 went on till dark.

Thursday 9th   traviled about 10 miles. & arived within 8 miles of the Camp had very hot weather & tolarable good roads.

Friday 10th   Traviled 2 miles then took breakfast. about 2 more then father lef us & went on to the Camp. in one houre more come to Wolters tent. in another to Burtons camp. met the folks all well. went another mile. & met Father retorning. waited here til Sundown for Father to go back & see Wolter on buisness. We then preceeded about 1 mile. When it began to rain & we camped for the Night.

Saturday 11th   Started at 5 in the morn at ½ past 6 crost the Miscato creak. at 7 arived ~~arive~~ at Bro. VanCotts tent. found all the folks well except Aunt Rhoda. She was quite sick. mother and myself took breakfast with the former. we pitched our tent close by them. helped Mother some and did some sewing. felt some wery after my jorney.

Sunday 12th   went to meeting in the 10 AM. was first addrest by Bro Woodroff who gave an account of his Mission to Eng. the progress of the work of the Lord in that Country. &C said if 50 good Elders would go there who would know. or teach nothing but Christ and him Crucified. for that was all the[y] had aught to teach. that would find a plenty to do. & their labors would be blest with success. was followed by bro P.P.P. & [John] Taylor. who spoke chiefly on the buisness of the day. wich was to rais a Company of 500 men to go into the Army ~~of the~~ for one year. in the PM was writing in my journal. felt comfortable.

Monday 13th   in the morn received a letter from my Husband. bearing date June 26 7 & ~~7~~th It was handed to me by ~~Bro Wilard~~ Uncle Willard. & brought from Nauvoo by Bro. [Jesse C.] Litlle. It gave me much pleasure to hear of his well fare. and to feel & know that I was rememberd by him. Whom I love Above all others. after breakfast it comenced to rain and I got up into the waggon and commenced to write an ansure to my letter. wrote 2 pages. at 6 o'clock in the PM received an invetation from Bro VanCott. to attend a dance with him & his family at the bower went with them. in a few minutes after I got there Bro Brigham came and introduced. Bro Little to me and desired me to dance with him. I did so. danced also with Robert Burton enjoyed myself pretty well.

Tuesday 14th   Washed a suit of Clothes for Uncle Willard and Ironed them. in the [PM] attended another dance at the Bower with Bro v danced with Bro W[illiam] Cory. W[illiam] Hyde. W[illiam] Kimball. and last of all with Bro Brigham e[n]joyed my self as well as might be expected. considering that he whose presence ever made the Circle of Sociaty to me appear perfect. was far absent from me.

Wednesday 15th   In the AM was sewing. in the PM was quite unwell wrote one page in my letter

Thursday 16[th]   Wrote some in my letter. in the PM was quite Sick. took some composion. Spice & bitters. Night slept in Wolters waggon.

Friday 17th   In the AM was Sewing. had quite number of Ladys from the other side of the River[11] call to see me. First Mary Kimball & H. Sanders [Helen Sanders Kimball]. then Vilate Young & Nancy Green next Hellen [Mar Kimball] Whitney & another lady whose name I do not remember.

Letters to Samuel Richards, May to July 1846

Tuesday Morn May 25 1846 4 miles from Farmington
Evening on the Praira 40 miles from Nauvoo[12]
My Dear Husband
    as I understand that Bro Vancott is going back to Nauvoo to morrow or next day I thought I would improve the op[ortu]nity to send you a few lines. as I expect you will be glad to hear from me. although b[eing] but a short time since I parted with you. but dear Samuel the time seems long [to] me. although I have indured the trial better than I could have expected. y[e]t my Dear you are never abstant from my mind. we broke our wagon tounge soon after you left us. stopt at suger creek til monday morn at 5. then proc[eeded] on our journey Stopt at Farmington. were we found Sister [Mary Ellen Haven] Pa[l]mer & took [di]nner with her. they are all well. we then crost the desmoin River[13] & after traveling 4 miles campt for the night. we have come 15 miles to day the roads are genaraly pretty good.
    Wednsday morn 26 Dear Samuel I dreamed I was with you this morn. it is indeed pleasent to dream of you. but is not so to awake & find it a mistake. my health is improving every day. the Lord be praised for it. I do feel thankfull for that blessing & pray God it may continue. I sincerly trust this letter will find you injoying the same blessing. not onley that. but every other blessing wich your heart desires in ritouness. Oh my Deary I am lonley withought you & were it not that I have all confidence in your Love & affection [I co]uld never indure the tryel Oh Samuel do write as often as you can. I do [wan]t to hear from you. I wish I would see your Face once more before yo[u go] Pray for me my dear I know you will. & be asured you are allways remembered by me Mother & the folks are all very kind to me. mother apears as usual. Joseph's feet truble him some. the rest of the famely area all well. Bro. vancott is about to start & I just come to a close. excuse the imperfect maner in wich it is written I remain your ever affectionate wife
        Mary H. Richards
[*addressed to*]
Samuel W. Richards
Nauvoo Ill

Thursday June 3th on the Praira about 100 miles from Nauvoo[14]
My Ever Dear Husband
    having a few minutes of leasure time. I have chosen to spend them in writing a few lines to you. wich I sincerely trust will find you injoying health & strenth. as I am happy to say it leaves us at the present. I received your

kind and unexpected letter. from Bro Van Cott. on sat. the 30 at 5 in the morn. I was exceeding glad to hear from you and espacialy to hear that you was well. wish I could hear from you every morn. though would much rather be with you. you said you never thought of me only all the time. and I have never thought of you only once since you left me. so you see that what ever measure you mete. shall be measured to you again

I have been trying to decline friendship with mrs grief & make a friend of miss Patiance. have succeeded in some degree. though the former seems unwilling to leave me having become so well acquainted with me. I am sory to hear that Bro Franklins prospects are so dull. would rather hear that you was ready to start seeing it is so that you have to go. Oh! would it had been my lot to have gone with you. me thinks I would gladly have past through the perils of the ocan & the trials through wich I might have been called to pass. could I only have been Blest with your sociaty. but alass! for me- Providance has provided it otherwise. and I must submit to my lonely fate. but forgive me. for why should I thus complain seeing I am among Friends. who are always ready to adminster to my wants & who are interessted for my wellfare. do not think me dear Samuel. unmindfull of the things that you have to suffer. for it is not the case. you know I have crost the sea my self. and know something what it is to be a stranger in a strange land. & can therefore sympathise with those that are doomed to the same fate. & it would be my greatest satisfaction. could I only be with you in the hour of your afflection. to sooth your grief and adminster to your wants. But since I can not may the Lord bless & preserve you from the evels of temptation of this wicked world. & from the power of the adversary of your soul. that he may not be able to afflect you but that you may be able to go forth. and accomplich the work that is for you to accomplich. be a usefull instrument in the hand of God. in doing a great work. & may the time soon come when you shall retorn to the bosem of your anxious friends. is the sincere prayer of companion. Tis a beautyfull evening. wish you was here to take a walk with me. 'Tis to dark to write Samuel so good night

[*page 2*] Thursday eve 4th at ½ past 5. Dear Samuel we have traviled about 8 miles today. the roads exceeding muddy. very hard traviling. the weather cold. wore my shawl & cloak. all day. and have never felt worm til now. we can see nothing but Praira for several miles. we had a tremendious storm last Sun eve. & allso on Tus night. beat through our covers & wet our bed clothes. did not any of us take cold. dear Samuel I have rememberd your councel. have taken good care of number one. when we stopd imploy my self sawing. knitting. writing. &C help mother a little sometimes. I made my garments[15] wile bro V C. was going to & retorning from nauvoo. have worn them since Sat. morn. have written a jornal since the time I left Nauvoo up to this morn have written some in my other & intend to complete it. as soon as time & sircumstances will admit. mother says give my love to Samuel. tell him I never forget him. I am sory to say that she appears unhappy. but it is not without reason. fa[ther] has not eat with us but once for more than a week. the former has been my bed fellow ever since you left. Joseph says tell Samuel I feel pagyue [?] tired to night. have waded 2 miles to day up to the knees in mud. wold sent him a letter full of love. only I am afraid. the[re] would not be room. the folks are all well I mean the camp. are very Pleasent. treat me with much respect. there is nothing lacking. but your Presance to make me happy. the sun is gone down. mother says Mary come to supper. so dear Samuel. good night.

Friday eve. dear Samuel we have come about nine miles to day. the 3 first the road was very muddy. the remainder pretty good. met Bro Genne [Benjamin Prince Jenne] retorning to fetch his famley. Sister G [Sarah Comstock Snyder Jenne] told us She did not intend to go west & leave sister Jane. tel Jane I do want to see her. give my love to all inquiring friends and especialy to my aged Father. tel him not to think that I have for got him. I did not mention him in my last letter because I had not time. I intend to write to them soon after I reach the camp. tel Elizabeth Fory I often wish she was with me when I view the Romantic scens of the west. where is Ellen [Wilding Woolley]. is there any prospect of her coming west. I intended to have given you a kiss for each of my sisters but forgot. give each of them one for me and tel them if the[y] love me. to take good care of you for my sake. If you can I wish you would send mother one pound of brimstone I shall want my bonet bleached & she has not got any. I had almost forgot to tel you that uncle Levys folks was [*page 3*] with us we waited for them at Richardsons point. it is allmost dark wish I had a little longer time to write. but there is a man just came from the camp bound for Nauvoo and I want to send this with him. I do'nt know that you will be able to read it. but do the best you can. it is dark I must come to an end. The Lord bless you my Dearest Friend beleve me I am forever your affectionate wife

     Mary H. Richards

Saterday morn 6

P.S. Oh my dear. do not forget to write to me as often as you can & let me know all perticulars you know I shall ever be wishing to hear from you. I am very glad to hear that you are going to send me your likeness though would mutch rather see the Boy that wears the curl.[16] but since I cannot see him I shall be glad to see the other. I have got sunburnt alittle. the folks say just enough to make me look healthy & good have had no visiter[17] as yet cannot tel wheathe[r] I shall or not

Oh were it not for that sweet hope
That says we soon shall meet again
My Soul would sink beneth the load
<u>and</u> seek in death repose to gain
that cheering hope. Still says to me

the trials that you now endure
when you your friends again shall see
Shall like a dream of yore appear
Samuel I long to see the houre
When you and I shall meet once more
When this fond heart shall once again find rest
Beneth thy kind thy soothing breast.

good bye dear Samuel. I shall write again when you desire me to pray
for me. Mary R.
[*across the bottom of page 3*] Thank you Samuel for the kiss you sent me and
here is kisses [*dotted line drawn around the word kisses*] for you. I have kissed
them and you may do the same.

[*on the outside of the letter, page 4, along with the address*]
how weary do the houres pass by
since your sweet face no more I see
Remember dear my dreary lot
and let me never be forgot

[*addressed to*]
Mr Samuel W. Richards
Nauvoo Ill.
Care of Mr. J. Huntington

Camp of Isral June 9th 10060 [160] miles from Nauvoo 50 from the camp[18]
My Dear Husband having an oppertunity to send you a line I though I
wold imprve it. I sent a letter to you last Saturday by a bro. John Huntington
who said he wold try to find you. & give it to you. I am happy to say we are
all well. I hope this letter will find you enjoying the same Blessing. Bro A.
[Amos] Felding stayed most of the AM with us yesterday. was retorning from
the camp. expects to go directly to eng.. met Bro Jacobs. last Saturday eve.
retorning for the same porpose. met R. [Robert Taylor] Burton & N[athaniel]
P [Very] Jones yesterday. going out into the settlements. Bro R said he had
been with the Counsel before they started. heard nothing said concerning
his going to Eng. do's not expect to go at present. said Maria. Malissa & all
the folks was well. if you can just just as well as not. I should be glad to have
you send me a few wafers. so that I may have something to seal my letters
with lest I should give some one the same truble that I did Bro. V. C. dear
Samuel I think last Sunday was the gloomyest day to me that I have seen
since you left me. we stopt at noon to do some washing. see to our things
&C in the PM I went into the woods twice. oferd up a prayer to the Lord.
& gave vent to my Tears. I cant help but feel bad some times. but I allways
feel better when I get over it. remember me in your Prayers & also my our

dear [fa]ther [*or* mother] & all the folks. be asured dear Samuel that you are
ever rememberd and adored by me. I'm glad your going to send me your
likeness. I do wishe you had mine. to take with you. Mother says give my
love to Samuel tel him I think it would be a great addision to my happyness.
if he was here give my Love to all the folks. and take a good porsion of it to
your self. Cousen Eliza says ~~give~~ remember [her] to Samuel. uncle Levi has
been rather [*page 2*] [ill] for the last 2 days feels some better. now my dear
be sure to imnprove every oppertunity to write to me. the Lord bless you
forever my dear Companion. good bye for he present
from your ever affectionate wife Mary H. Richards
[*addressed to*]
Mr. Samuel W. Richards.
Nauvoo Hancock County. Ill.
Care of Joseph Young.

Camp of Israel Councel Bluffs on the Mo River July 13 1846[19]
My Dear Samuel and Ever Beloved Husband.
   I had the pleasure this morn of re[ce]iveing from the hand of Uncle
Willard. a kind letter. wich you sent to me by Bro Little. it gave me much
pleasure to hear from you and espacialy to hear that you was well. and I feel
greatfull to my Heavenly Father. that I can say once more my health is good.
& also that of the family. Uncle Willard & Bro Little took breakfast with us
this morn. the latter kindly ofer'd to carry a line back to [you] for me if I
wished to send one. so I have got up in the waggon to try to write one but
it rains so fast. & the wind blows so hard. that I find it almost imposable. the
things are piled so high in the waggon that I cannot sit upright & you can
well will see that the rain blotches every mark I try to make. We arived at
Mount Pisgah on the 12th of June. Bro Van Cott & Uncle Levi left the next
day for the Bluffs. the perticulars of wich I wrote you the the same day &
sent by Post but it appears you have not re[ce]ived it. we did expect then.
we should have to stay there this season. but received a letter from Uncle
Willar[d] to come forthwith. so Father concluded that as we have but One
waggon he would take the family & what things he could and go to the Bluffs
& leave the rest with Sister Morse until he could retorn with waggon & get
them. so we left Mount Pisgah. on the 2 of July and arived at Bro VanCotts
tent on the 11th about 8 in the morn. I attended meeting yesterday at the
bouer [bowery] was first addrest by Bro Woodroff who gave an account of
his mission to Eng. spoke of the prosperity of the Church there said if 50
good Elders would go there. who would know or teach nothing by Christ
and him Crusifide for was all they had aught to teach that they would find
plenty to do & their labors would be blest with success. said that many by
trying to teach great things. and things they were forbid to teach had
destroyed them ~~sel~~ selfs & been the cause of destroying many others. was

followed by Bro P Pratt & Taylor who spoke cheifly on the buisness now before them that is to raise a Company of 500 men to go in to the service of the United States one year. met Bro Brigham Heber & Uncle Willard on the 5th retorning to Mount Pisgah for that Porpose Bro Brigham asked where you was tould him I did not know. asked if you was gon to Eng. said I expected you was thats right. said he. twas pretty hard was 'nt it. it was said I. well how do you get along. well Bro B. said I I get along just as well as I know how. I am satisfiede that I have got to bear it and I do the best I can. that [is] right said he you shall be blest for it. Br Heber then said. Samuel is gon is he he is Said I well said he I am glad to hear it he's a good boy and you be a good girl and [*page 2*] twill only be a little wile before he will meet you on the other side of the rockey mountains Uncle Willard was the next one to enquire spoke after the same maner as the others came to our waggon and made us quite a visit said if you had not gon to Eng he would now have sent you & Franklin into the army. I addrest him in the manner that you desired me to & he told me that I had got my hearts desire and what did I ask more said I there was every blessing in the world for me &C &C gave Joseph a mision to go in to the States service for one year as a drummer he will start ~~he will~~ as soon as they can get the company ready. made Mother feel bad to think she had got to part with her boys so fast. they retorned from ~~the~~ Mount Pisgah last night with Bro Little. the Companys are now peraiding before our tent. Bro E T Benson is apointed one of the 12 in the place of John E. Page he is camped on our right hand Wolter ~~&~~ on our left. uncle Levi J Van Cott Parley & J Cott all in a stright line at our rear is Taylors & Woodruffs encampment Brigham & Hebers fameileys are over the river Uncle Willards about 2 miles from this place have not seen Amelia [Peirson Richards] yet. I understand she is well I have taken much comfort with Eliza She & Melinda Wood are well found aunt Rhoda quite sick but she is much better Father intends to start back for his things ~~for~~ on thursday will go into Mo. to traide of some of them for provisions as soon as he retorns. we then intend to go on with the Church to grand Island this fall if posable. pray for us My dear that the Lord may prosper & prepair our way before us. that we may be where the 12 is. for there is the fountain of wisdom. the weather is very hot this PM the rain cleard away about 9. I have just been to see aunt Rhoda. told her I was writing to you. She says give my love to Samuel & Franklin. tell them I think a great deal about them. & their familys. & always remember them in my prayers I want to see Jane [Snyder Richards] very much. it seems to be my lot to inform you that Melissa Burton is no more. I received a line from Rebecca on the 23 of June wich read as follows dear Mary. you are reguested to come over here this PM and take your last leave of Melissa Burton. I attended. & she now sleeps in the arms of William Cory every night when she can get the chance. we had an excellant Supper. but the infare is to be when you retorn. at the same time when we have our

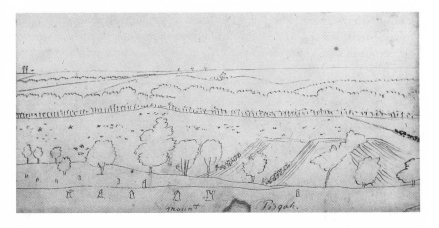

Mt. Pisgah, Iowa. Copy of original sketch in the Heber C. Kimball Journals of 1846, probably drawn by Peter Hansen; courtesy of LDS Historical Department.

Mormon Battalion Ball, near Mosquito Creek, Iowa, July 1846. From an oil-on-canvas painting by C. C. A. Christensen; courtesy of LDS Historical Department.

wedding the family are about 2 miles from us are all well. I think you will think by this time I am full of news but I have wrote pretty much all the news I have go[t] uncle Willard & Bro L. are coming to supper so I must go and help Mother

[*page 3*] July 15 instead of helping Mother the other night. I excepted an invitation from Bro VanCott to attend a dance at the Bower. when I had been there about 5 minuts Bro Brigham came & interoduced Bro Little to me. & desired me to dance with him. I did so. danced also with Robert Burton. this is the first time I have danced since I danced with my Samuel in the House of the Lord. I attended last night also with the same danced with William Cory W Hyde & W Kimball the Twelve did not dance till the last figure. Bro Brigham took me for a partner. we danced the hopa [?] reel. I expect by this time you will think I am getting rude. but though there might a smile have dwelt opon my countinance—yet there was a gloom [t]hat overshadowed this heart. and espacialy when I would look around & see Rebecca. Maria. & Melissa. all enjoying them selfs with their Companions. then Oh my dear. I felt like a lone dove. the recreations in wich others enjoy themselfs afford but little comfort to me wile he whom I love above all others is abcent from me. as regardes the reguest you asked of me concerning Ellen [Wilding Woolley][20] you know my dear. I have ever tryed to do all that you desired me to. yea the ~~love~~ affection that dwells in this bosem to wards you compells me to do it although it deprives me of the hopes of happyness for ever. I was in hopes that after your retorn you would have been contented to have lived with me alone for a little season. A comfort wich I have never yet been permitted to enjoy although it has been the greatest desire of my heart. Oh! my Husband. yea—more My <u>Lord</u> shall I not after suffering all that I have got to suffer. I now Suffer and have got to Suffer trials wich I must keep with in my own bosem. at last till you retorn. shall I not oh! my companion merit this boon from you are we not young. if we live according~~ly~~ to that wich seems to be our privalige is there not time enough for us to enjoy ourselfs alittle e'er you have another to share in your affections. if in writing my feelings thus I have exposed my weekness it is to you I have don[e] it. if I have said any thing that is wrong it is to you I look for instructions. me thinks. if you had seen what I have seen. you would not wonder why I thus wrote for there is no such a thing as happiness known here where a man has more than one &C it realy seems to me that this is a day in wich Woman is destined to misery. it is true if I have got to have another to share with me in your affections I would as soon have Ellen as any other. I am also concious of the benifet she would be to us on account of her kindered [I] shall do as you disire me to You ask if my visiter [*upside down on page 3*] is faithfull with me. She has viseted me twice is with me now and has been since last Friday. I sopose you will feel disapointed but surely not more than I do. gladly would I have enjured [endured] it. not only for your sake. but also for my own. I expect the seed was planted but am sory to say it is best why it should have been so I know not. for I have taken the best care of number one that I posably could but oh my dear it is hard to take care where we have to be so much exposed. I fancied I should have taken much comfort could I only have been blest according to our desire. it would have been something by wich I could always have rememberd you. but I have no reflections on my mind for I am sure I have done the best I knew how and if it had pleased God it should not be so. I feel to submit to his will. Oh my Dear it does give me so much pleasure to read your kind letters. and I when I write it seems as if I had conversed with you. for a season.

I am glad you remember me so well and write so often. this letter will [be] unexpected as I did not expect to hear from you till I saw [J]ane. I hope my Dear you ever be so mindfull of me. and rest asured your love will ever be reciprocated by me. it is in vain for me to try to express my feelings towards you. I cannot find words to do it you know I love you. Yea and my love increases the more I think of you. do not fail to write before you leave New York and as many times more as you ~~plai~~ can. pleas. and when you get to Eng. be sure and write as often as you can. Father says tell Samuel & Franklin I have send them my love and good wishes & blessing and when I get settled as I can I intend to write to them. I have left room for mother She wishes to write a line to you Maria & Melinda wishes to be rememberd. the former expects to be sick[21] every day. Eliza Ann & Henry and all the friends wish me to give their love to you. give my kind love to Franklin tell him when I see Jane I intend to do the best I can to comfort her. give my love to my brothers and sisters and their familys tell them they little know. while liveing in their good houses what I have to suffer. while traviling in the wilderness with nothing but a cotton covering for my home. yet I would not exchange my home ~~for~~ for theirs. for I considder ~~that~~ 'tis better to suffer with the saints and enjoy the blessings with them than to be ignorant of the things [*upside down on page 2*] that pertain to my salvation. accept my kindest love to your self and be asured that you are always rememberd by me. and my prayers shall ever be for your wellfare. and prosperity and that you may in safety retorn to my bosom. having labord like a faithfull Servant in your [*illegible*] may you retorn in honer. loaded with the frutes of you labor. it seems as thoug there was every body here but you they most all of them tell me I look the most natural of any person they see ~~only the~~ Sun July 16th I think my self that your Mary looks some as she used to only the Sun has given her a higher coler. I wonder if Samuel looks the same wish I could see him. I would love to rest my head alittle wile on his bosom. and hear from his lips the soothing words wich he would speak me thinks it would seem as a cordial to my soul. Oh! Samuel. shall I ever enjoy this blessing. oh! yes I trust the Lord will percerve [preserve] your life. yea and also that the garments that you wear will be a precervation to you until you retorn to me.

Bro A Limon [Amasa M. Lyman] caled to see me this morn. said he had come after me. asked what I had done with that boy. he gave [me] to. I told him I took the best care of him I could. wile he stayed with me. but he had left me and I had every reason to beleve that this the 12 had been the cause of it. and I thought it was me if any one that aught to ask where he was. asked if you was gon to Eng. I said you left me for that porpose. Said he was glad &C. made me quite a visit. Samuel I have been scribling for a long time dont know half what I have writton at any rate I think 'twill try your patiance to read it. it is wrote under all maner of sircumstances So I I am sure there can be no regulation about it. Joseph is gone I have just bid him good bye. tis a little more news Sister Hendrix expects to be confined every day. I must close for the present. accept this line excuse all mistakes and beleve me to be as ever your affectionate wife Mary H Richards

> [*A difficult to read poem is written upside down on page 1*]
> Oh! am I then remembered still
> by him I love is ~~clear~~ well
> The pleasure that this thought doth give
> Is more than tounge can tell
> Say does the flowers apear as sweet
> The woodline walkes as dear
> Or does the moon thy evens cheer
> As in the days of yore
> Or does her bright and silvery rays
> Cause the think with ~~glad~~ gloom
> repose [?] the happy hours
> when you with Mary use to rome
> The flowers though blooming all around
> Have lost their sweets to me
> I seek no more the shady bower
> except to pray for thee
> And when I look upon the Moon
> It calls a tear from me
> T[o] think how changed has been the scene
> Since last I romed with thee

As regards [*blank space*] I Derby [Erastus Derby][22] & mrs Whitmarch I do'nt know what has become of them. Maria Burton tould me that Mrs. W told Brigham that she wished to have a [*blank space*] &C by derby. he tould her she might go a head an that he told the boys to watch them &C I understand they did so and when they saw D get into the waggon they torned it over and exposed them in the very act. after this she mistrusted a young man and blinded him by throwing a cup of boiling water in his face she is no more brighams and I thinks she had aught to be no ones else. Mary H. R.

July 7th I have concluded twice & still begin again. Oh! Samuel I was so glad this morn to receive from the hand of uncle Willard another Sweet letter wich you sent by Mother [Agnes] Taylor. you must know it is a great trial for me to receive so many letters from you but if you will only send me 2 in one week. I will try to bear it with patiance and look forward to your retorn for a day of deliverance to come and glad to hear you are well. may you enjoy this blessing forever Samuel there is so many calls to see me it takes me all the time to tend to them. had some ladys from the other side of the river today. M[ary] Kimball & H[elen Mar Kimball] Whitney. [?] Young & Nancy Greene and H Sanders [Helen Sanders Kimball] and others to [*illegible*] to mension. I think I have wrote you all the new I can. it presents not much blank papper in this letter will write to you again in about 3 months if you desire me to and [*illegible*] E. [Edward] Corbridge. Tell my friends bro James Smithes [Smithies] and family are well. R. [Richard] Slater and George Rhodes are here goodbye MHR

[*On the back page is a letter from Wealthy, followed by this postscript from Mary*] our little heifer is doing first rate. shes all the pet I have got here with me. July 19 have been to meeting Parly deliverd excellant address. wish I had room to write more but this must sofice for the present.
[*addressed to*]
For Mr. Samuel W. Richards
Care of Edward. Corbridge
Chipping, Lancashir
England
recd Oct 20th 1846

Phinehas Richards, father of Samuel Whitney Richards. J. Grant Stevenson collection.

Wealthy Dewey Richards, mother of Samuel Whitney Richards. Rosabelle Streeper Gwynn collection.

Willard Richards, member of the Latter-day Saints Quorum of the Twelve Apostles, later second counselor to President Brigham Young, and younger brother of Phinehas Richards. J. Grant Stevenson collection.

Franklin Dewey Richards, older brother of Samuel Whitney Richards. He accompanied Samuel on a mission in Great Britain, 1846-1848. J. Grant Stevenson collection.

CHAPTER FIVE

Sleeping on the "soft side of a bord"

Giving birth in a wagon, amid crackling thunder, flashes of lightening, pelting rain, and wind strong enough to level tents, Maria Richards Wilcox delivered her first child. Her sister-in-law, Mary Richards, assisted her. Mary led a life of service to her husband's family during her two-year sojourn at the Missouri. She sewed a tent from a wagon cover, helped to raise it, then set out the trunks and aired the soggy contents. With Wealthy, she continued her care of Maria and the baby, often sitting up all night. She rubbed Aunt Rhoda, washed for Uncle Levi's family, and slept on the "soft side of a bord" when visitors took her bed. Mary tenderly cared for her sister-in-law and dear friend, Jane Snyder Richards, who was critically ill, and moved with her, first to Council Point, then across the river to Cutler's Park, where members of Jane's family were camped.

Journal Two
Wednesday, July 22, 1846, to Friday, August 28, 1846
John Taylor and Parley P. Pratt's camp above Mosquito
Creek, which Phinehas called Liberty Pole[1]

[*page 5*]
. . . and how I used to wait upon him.[2] said he had always thought more of me than any girl that ever left Eng and if it should ever be in his power to raise to me to be a queen. or to gain me honer in this church. he intended to do it. I thanked him for that promise. & also for what he had already done. ~~he~~ he said he had tould Samuel. to marry me because he new me to be a good Girl. and he intended to do more for me yet. than he ever had done. gave us some good instruction in regard to addoption.[3] Said if he had 12 Daughters. he would give them to 12 good men alowing it should be their choice. then if these men should become 12 Kings he would have connection with 12 Kingdoms. and they would be under oblegations to Sostain him. said that those who were so over ancious to have their family all piled in one

little corner together would by & by find themselfs the lesser number. said many other things wich time will not permit me to write aboute noon the rain cleard away & we had a pleasent PM. did some sewing &C spent some time with Amelia

Thursday 23th   after breakfast went to work to make a tent. out of one of our waggon covers & [*illegible number*] sheets. was sewing most of the day. made a short viset with abigal Abott.

Friday 25th   [*sic*] in the morn helped Mother about the work sewed some loops on our tent. &C in the PM was writing in my journal. until 4 oclock. then got supper. washed the dishes. made our beds. fixed the tent for the night &C in the eve visited with aunt Rhoda.

Saturday 25th   In the AM was sewing. in the PM was prepareing our tent to be raised. about 4 oclock she was hoisted. I then went to work & swept off our green Earth Carpet. brought in some blocks to set our trunks upon. helped to carry them in & fix them to sute my own notion. I then sat down & thought my home although but a tent. appeared pleasent in the eve made my bed in Wolter's waggon. & lay down to take a sweet repose. about one oclock I was aroused from my slumber. by the wind having blowed in our sheet wich we had for a front door to our waggon. I arose and replaced it. & lay down again. but was not permited to lay long. the wind began to blow most tremendious. the lightning eluminated the whole Country. had one of the heavyest cracks of thunder that I ever heard. had to hould down the sheet in the front of the waggon during the storm wich lasted more than an houre. this took all the strenth I could summons. having nothing on but my night clothes. I got very wet. about the middle of the storm our tent blowed down. & Wolter's also. Maria was obliged to make her way throw the storm. to the waggon. barefoot & in her night clothes. soon after she was taken very Sick. & kept getting worse. I got Wolter to make a fire. & prepair'd for what might follow. I attended apon her all the night.

Sunday 26th   25 minuts before 7 Maria gave birth to a fine little Daughter. made her bed for her. & then left her in the care of her 2 mothers. & went to examing our tent found it had tore from end to the other. sat down & sewed it. the sun was very hot gave me severe head ace. about 10 oclock I lay down & rested til 3. I then got up & washed me & sat down in Maria's a little wile. then father unloaded the waggon. raised the tent. & I helped him all I could. this night slept in Wolters tent.

Monday 27th   in the morn got breakfast. & washed the dises. baked a pise of meet for father to take with him. went to work & regalated our boxes so as to be comfortable for a bed stead. caryed out our crackers. & spred them on a sheet to sun did the same by our straw. packed up Fathers provisions to take with him. about 12 he started for Mount Pisgah. in the PM I was working very hard. both at home and at Marias. in the eve felt very tired. made up a bed in our tent and slept very comfortable.

RHODA RICHARDS
1784-1879

DR. LEVI RICHARDS
1799-1876

Rhoda Richards, older sister of Phinehas Richards. J. Grant Stevenson collection.

Levi Richards, older brother of Phinehas Richards. J. Grant Stevenson collection.

Henry Phinehas Richards, younger brother of Samuel Whitney Richards. J. Grant Stevenson collection.

Maria Wealthy Richards Wilcox, sister of Samuel Whitney Richards. J. Grant Stevenson collection.

Tuesday 28th   in the morn got breakfast, washed & scoured up all our tin ware. Baked a peice of meet. parched some barly Coffee &C fixed our tent so as to appear quite comfortable. about 3. in the PM. it began to rain very hard. beat through our tent and also Wolters. had to move Maria out of her bed. found about 2 quarts of water in the place were she lay I held an umberella over her. while the storm lasted. wich was about an houre. & I then took a bed. wich had kept dry. & got her into it. fixed her as comfortable as I could. then came home and got supper. evening the weather still haveing the appearance of rain. at dark we lay down but did not undress. about 11 oclock we was aroused from a sweet sleep by another tremendious storm blew down Wolters tent.[4] was obiged to move Maria into ours. & put her in our bed. our bed clothes being most all wet Mother. or myself was obliged to sit up all night. so I prevailed with mother to lay down. and I took care of Maria & the babe. til Sunrise. I then lay down about 2 houres but could not sleep. got up & took breakfast & did up the work. went & helped Malinda to fix the tent sewed it in several places. then we & Mother Williams raised it. I then spred out every thing I could find. wet to dry. about 4 in the PM Mother got a man to cary Maria back to her own tent. I then got her supper for her. then came home & made our bed an sat down & wrote a little wile in my journal. then took supper & retired.

Thursday 30th   In the morn got up. felt first rate got breakfast & went ~~to went~~ to washing. about 11 oclock Bro P P Pratt called to see us. was on his way to England. past some jokes with him about seeing my Husband. said he should not have thought that I had got a husband. Mother told him that I was her ~~Daughter~~ Daughter. said he was very sory for he should have liked to have had me for a daughter himself &C &C finished washing about noon. then went to take a hat to Bro Horns [Joseph Horne]. but did not find them at home. Bro P P P came in as soon as I got there had another short visit with him. called to see Sister Willey & met Bro Little. called also to see Bro Okaleys folks then came home & prepaired for an aproching storm. in the eve Uncle Willard and Bro Little came to see us. had quite a good visit with them about 11 they left to go to their lodging. as soon as they was gone. the wind & rain. began to beat upon us. blew down Wolters tent & broke the ridge pole and one of the end poles. had to bring Maria again into our tent. as soon as that was done. Uncle W & Bro L again retorned. & stayed all night with Us. the wind seased to blow in about one hour. but the rain continued most of the night. I lay down on the soft side of a bord & slept for 2 hours & ½.[5]

Friday 31th   about daybreak Bro L[ittle] went & got us a little stove & made us a fire. I then got breakfast. Bro L and Uncle W. took breakfast then the former bade us good bye. and started together with Bros. Taylor. [Orson] Hyde. & [Parley P.] Pratt. on there mission.[6] Eastward. went by way of the Mo River. the AM was very lowery. but it cleard away about noon so as to give us a chance to dry our clothes. in the PM was waiting on Maria writing in my journal. knitting &C had the head ace. very hard got Uncle W to lay hands upon me. he gave me a good blessing. P Prayad also for my Husband. his wellfare. prosperity. & safe retorn. at night made our bed on the ground and had a good rest. all night

Saturday February [August] First   did the work so as to give mother a chance to go braiding. in the PM. Aunt Rhoda sent for me to come and rub her. found her in much pain. rubed her from head. to foot. got her some warm drink. & toast. at eve made her bed for her. also Aunt Sarahs. about ½ past 9 Bro Benson and Gooddel [Isaac N. Goodale]. came & stayed all night with us. the former made a good prayer. after he rose from his knees. said the Spirit of the Lord was under our tent. and he knew it. and what was that. the Spirit of peace and Love. Mother & I gave them our bed and we spred a quilt on the soft side of a bord and slept there

Sunday 2th   in the morn helped mother do the work and at ½ 10 oclock went to meeting. Bro G A Smith called to see us. and informed us of the death of Hyrum Spencer, at meeting. Preached to us first & gave us some good instructions was followed by Bro Benson who did the same. had a firstrate meeting. in the PM went with Melinda Wood to see Bro King's little sick Child. came home & enjoyed a good viset with aunt Rhoda in the eve was writing in my journal. this day the weather was very worm.

Monday 3th   in the morn got breakfast. did up the work. & went to washing. washed a dress & some other things for aunt Rhoda and a vest for Uncle Levi. together with our own washing. finished about 2 in the PM. the wether was very worm and after washing myself I lay down & rested. then foulded my clothes. got supper &C in the eve had a sweet visit with aunt Rhoda.

Tuesday 4th   after breakfast went to ironing. ironed 3 shirts for Uncle Levi. also the things I had washed for aunt Rhoda. in the PM took care of Maria. & the babe [Cynthia Maria Wilcox]. awile then Aunt Rhoda. being sick. she sent for me to come & rub her with some spirits. I did so. also made her bed and Aunt Sariahs also.

Wednesday 5th   In the morn baked 3 loafs of bread for Uncle Levis folks. & one for our selfs. helped mother do the work. & assisted Uncle Levis folks to prepair for their departure to the other side of the River. the weather was very hot. myself rather unwell.[7]

Thursday 6th   got breakfast & did up the work. then went to help aunt Rhoda. about ½ past 9. recieved her blessing and a promise that she would pray for me & my Companion. and bid her good bye. together with Uncle Levis folks. came home & swept our tent. washed myself. and sat down to sew. made me a touel wich was presented to me by aunt Rhoda. did some patching &C. in the eve took a walk with Melinda Wood. came home & went to bed. but the misskateos haveing taken possesion of our tent we was [not] permited to sleep all night.

Friday 7th   helped mother get breakfast. after wich she went to see Danial Spencers folks they being sick. after doing up the work. I sat down to writing in my journal. then wrote one page in a letter to my Father. the weather was very hot. all day eve got supper. made the beds &C was kept awake most all night by the misskateos

Saturday 8th   morn got up early & got breakfast before Mother got up. washed the dishes made a dutch Chese. baked 3 loaves of bread. swept the tent washed ~~the~~ my self & sat down to sew. through the day the weather was very hot. the eve quite pleasent. night had a good rest

Sunday 9th   morn got breakfast did up the work. washed & drest myself. then took a walk down between 2 bluffs. found a shade and kneelt down and oferd up a prayer to the Lord. retorned home and wrote a few verces. as a memorial. of the birthday of my companion. then filled up the letter I had commenced to write to my Father the weather was hotter today than I had ever felt it before this season. the eve was pleasent night was kept awake again by the miskateos.

Monday 10th   in the morn helped about the work. AM was writing in my journal the weather very hot. in the PM did some sewing for mother. washed some dishes for sister Stevens and assisted her to pack up for a removal. while doing this Bro [Edwin D.] Woolly's Camp came in. & camped close by us. after I got through I went to see them. spent the eve with Ellen. had a very plesent Chat with her

Tuesday 11th   In the morn helped get breakfast. & washed the dishes. then went with Melinda Wood into the woods to get some Grapes.[8] went by way of the cold spring. about 2 miles East. to get a young Girl to go with us. spent some time in the woods. found the grapes very [s]carce. got about 3 quarts & arived home at ½ past one in the PM then washed me & got dinner and did some sewing for mother. got supper & spent the eve at Bro Woollys. this day. the weather was more comfortable

Wednesday 12th   morning helped get breakfast. and did up the work in the AM Ellen Wilding came to see me. went with her to see Bro [William] Felshews folks. & spent the AM with them. came home and got dinner. & did up the work. PM was writing in my journal. did some sewing for mother. the weather was very Pleasent.

Thursay 13th   morning got breakfast. and did up the work. AM made mother a cap. PM Commenced to braid & braided 3 yards for a beginning. the first I ever braided. this PM Wolter arived back from Mount Pisgah. eve Ellen Wilding. came to see me.

Friday 14th   in the morn got breakfast. washed the dishes. swept the tent &C then went to writing in journal. PM went to see Bro Woolley folks. stayed there about 2 hours combed Ellens hair for her. & assisted her to fit a dress. While doing this father arived home from Mount Pisgah and I retorned to see him. had been 18 days on the journey was well but tired. after this Braided 2 yards of straw this was a very Pleasent day.

Saturday 15ᵗʰ in the morn assisted mother about getting Breakfast, and did up the work. Braided another yard of straw. in the PM made me an apron. and did some other sewing. Ellen came to see me had a good visit in the waggon with her and Melinda Wood. the [weather] still very Pleasent.

~~Saturday~~ Sunday 16ᵗʰ in the morn. helped mother do the work. recieved an invetation from Sister [Elizabeth Price] Bentley to take a ride with her to Councel Point. got permision to take Melida Wood with me. about 10 in the AM Bro [William] Price [Jr.] came and waited upon us to the Carrige. it was a beautifull morn. we had a pleasant ride. the distance was about 5 miles we went into the woods & got quite a number of grapes. came back to sister Bs. tent & made a little viset we then came home. Bro [Richard] B[entley] came with us & carried our grapes for us stayed an made us quite a little viset about 6 in the eve Bro Franklin's waggon came in sight. on the top of a large bluff.⁹ I went & picked over some grapes & put them to cook then went to meet Jane. meet with her very sick also little Wealthy [Lovisa Richards]. & Elizabeth [McFate Richards]. brought them into our tent and got supper for them. after supper I made Janes bed for her & Father assisted her to get back to the waggon. after washing the dishes. and doing what was nessasry to be done. I went & sat down and talked with Jane about 1 houre then retired. never was I more rejoiced to meet with a friend than I was to meet with Sister Jane, although it grieved me to the heart to see her. & her child. so much afflicted. I tould her if it was her wish. it was my intention to take care of her. til she got better and that that was the desire & request of my Samuel. she seemd very gratefull and willing to accept my offer. we talked over many of the scens that had past during our abcance from each other. rejoiced in each others wellfare. & sympathised with each other sorrows. exprest many a wish for the wellfare of our companions &C &C this night I slept alone in Fathers waggon.

Monday 17ᵗʰ helped do the work. in the morn. then went washing. had 2 weeks wash. washed a few thing for Jane & Wealthy. did most all of it alone 'twas a pleasent day felt pretty well

Tuesday 18ᵗʰ a gloomy morn got breakfast. did up the work &C it then commenced to rain & rained most of the day. I sat in our waggon with J[ane] & worked on a garment for Philo [Dibble] spent the day very pleasently was well

Wednesday 19ᵗʰ in the morn assisted Mother to do the Work. then Ironed in the PM finished making P[hilo] Garment. and commenced to write a letter to my Husband. the weather more comfortable myself pretty well.

Thursday 20ᵗʰ assisted about the work at home also at Wolters. whose family were all sick in the PM I went with Jane [to] her waggon while there she was taken very sick and was obliged to remain she lay on Salleys bed while Philo and my self. cleand out the waggon. I washed it. helped replace the chests. made her bed as comfortable as posable and got her on to it. got her some supper &C stayed with her all night.

Friday 21ᵗʰ   was very buizey all day. attending to Wolters. sick folks. also to Jane & Wealthy who was very sick. staid with them that Night got up with Jane 7 times.

Saturday 22ᵗʰ   attended upon Jane & W the former continued worse all the time we Doctord her with such things as we thought best for her was very sick all night. got up with her 9 times.

Sunday 23ᵗʰ   remaind waighting on Jane who was so much worse that we almost despaird of life. evening Bro Brigham & Heber called to see her and administerd to her & W promising that they should recover. spoke many comforting words to us both said they was glad. that I was with Jane to take care of her. advised me to remain with her I asked them to pray I might enjoy [h]ealth, to wich they replyed that I should not get sick said I would hold them to there promis watched with Jane all night

Monday 24ᵗʰ   still attending on Sister Jane Who was still very sick in the PM Uncle Willard came to see us. spoke many comforting words to us both and promissed to be a father to us. laid hands on Jane & W. night Watched with Jane

Tuesday 25ᵗʰ   with Jane till 9 in the AM then laid down til one in the PM had a sweet sleep then got up and washed me. and went back to Janes Waggon to take care of her about 4 Uncle W called again was very kind and consoling With him we feasted on water & musk mellons. a very unexpected treat in the Willderness he laid hands on Jane and W blest us all and departed night attended on Jane who was still very sick today Wealthy had a Chill

Wednesday 26ᵗʰ   Jane a little more comfortable, having told father that 'twas Samuels desire that I should go and take care of Jane when she came. if she needed my assistance. and thinking that she would never need it more than at the present I obtained his consent and about 2 oclock left Council Bluffs in company with Jane and family for the Point. father mooved there the same day. the distance was about 6 miles. the weather pleasant. we arrived about sundown today I felt quite unwell. night attended on Jane

Thursday 27ᵗʰ   to day our cattle having strayed today we was unable to proceed any farther I felt quite unwell through the day attended upon Jane & Wealthy who were still very Sick. at Night Sister Jane said I should go to fathers and take a nights rest, as I had had no rest for several nights. accordingly I went. found the folks had retired to bed in the Waggon. so I made my bed on a cupple of quilts in the Tent. and had a sweet sleep

Friday 28ᵗʰ   a beautyfull day

Letter to Samuel Richards, September to October 1846

Camp of Israel, Ommehas Nation. Winter Quarters. 30 miles North of the mouth of Platt River. West side of the Mo[10]
Sep 30th 1846.

My Dear though far absent Husband 'tis with pleasure. I once more take my penn in hand to address a few lines to you. wich I trust my dear will find you enjoying health peace and the Spirit of God. to comfort & strenthen you in the discharge of every duty. until you shall have completed your mission and retorned in safty to your home. although I know not where you will find it. but I trust it 'twill be according to your prayers. that is—in the bosem of your Mary. Oh! my dear. I do ever think of you. and as I cannot be with you. I pray my Heavenly Father to preserve our lives. and permit us once more to enjoy each others society. it has pleased him to bless me with health for wich I feel truly gratefull I think I have gaind with intrest all the flesh I lost during my Illness before you left me. I recieved your kind letter bearing date June 26 & 7th also another bearing date July first & 2th the former on the 13th of July the latter on the 17th. I wrote you a long letter in ansure to them and sent it by Bro Taylor. dedrected to you in care of our Bro E[dward] Corbridge. wich I trust by this time you have recieved. in it I wrote you some of the perticulars concerning our journey our arival at the Bluffs our situwation &C also that there had been a Company of 500 men. sent into service of the U S for one year. that Joseph had gone. we got a letter from [him] on the 15th of Aug. he had had the chills. but was getting better. also that Melissa B. had changed her name to Cory. they are gon into the army. Bro Franklin's folks arived at the Bluffs. aug the 15th was greatley rejoiced to meet with Jane who I think has indeed come up through great tribulation. She lost a little Son on the 23th of July who lived but a ½ an houre. his name was Franklin Snider [Isaac Phinehas Richards]. She brought him to Mount Pisgah were She met with Father who had retorned there to get a load of his things wich we were obliged to leave having but one waggon he buryed little F S. Jane & dear little W[ealthy] L[ovisa] had been sick most of the way but was much better when they arived Elizabeth had had the chills lightley. ever since the 14th of July. on the 21th of Aug. Jane was ~~go again~~ taken sick. with the flux. suffered the severest affliction. until the ~~23~~ 26. I attended upon her. day. and night. as far as my strenth would admit. on the 23th Bro Brigham and Heber came to see her and administerd to her & W[ealthy] Lovisa]. said they was glad that I was with her and Councld me to remain with [*page 2*] her said if I would I should be Blest with health the next morning Bro Woodruff called to see her. he also layed hands on Jane & W L. in the PM

Uncle Willard came and made quite a visit. told us what to do for Jane. &C spoke many comforting words to us both. prayed for Jane & WL. this day we ~~had a~~ feasted on water & musk mellons. in the AM WL had a chill on the 26th I left the Bluffs in company with Jane & family. traviled 4 miles to Council Point. fathers folkes moved there. the same day. the 12 & the main body of the Church had crost the Mo. and were encamped 20 miles up the River Janes Bro & mother being all in the main camp. She was counceld to go there also. So on the 26 we took leve of fathers folks. & started for the main Camp. crost the Mo. and on the 31 arived at Brigham's encampment. Jane was much better but W L grew worse all [the] time. uncle Levi attended upon her. uncle W came almost every day to see her we tried with all our strenth & faith to save her but I am sory to say. it was all to no porpose. she still continued to grow worse. until the 19 when about one oclock She departed this life. Peacefull her gentle Spirit fled. The Heavenly Corts to addorn. Her body slumbers with the deat To wait the resurrection morn. Wealthys sickness was the diarrhoea and canker.

Jane is writing to Franklin. all the perticulars concerning her death. so I forbear. as you will be able to larn from him. Oh! my dear 'twas a distresing sight to see the afflection or sorrow that Jane endured at the death of her only Child. it would be imposable for me to decribe it. you must judge for your self. on [t]he 15th Uncle W came with his Carige and carrid us to the grave. W L was the first one laid in the new burying ground. uncle W took us home with him to his own tent. were we visited until the 20th. Uncle W is very kind told me I was welcome to his table & home. untill you retorned. he claims Jane and myself for his childeren has promised to be a father to us both seems to feel quite interessted for us. have had the chance to talk with him on many subgects have learned consi[d]erable. one thing is that it is the calculation at present. for us to remain here until you retorn. wich to use his own expresion. he said he new no reason why you could not retorn to accompany us accross the mountains one year from next Spring

Jane is writing on the other side of the table. She sayes it will be 2 years to her. next spring. so she will expect Franklin then.

another thing was that the 12 & all the men that are able are expecting to ~~cross~~ leave their familys and cross the mountains next spring

October first. the place where we have settled for winter quarters is one of the most beautyfull flatts I ever see. it is about one mile square. the East side borders on the Mo River and most of the North & South. the West side is bounded. with a ridge or bluff. from the top of wich it decends graduley to the River. to the North is a view of several bluffs ½ grass & ½ timber. the scene is quite Romantic. the City is devided into quarter Acre lots each family possessing a lot. there is 20 lots in one block 10 fronting on each Street. the streets run the same way as they did in nauvoo Janes lot is about the senter of the City. fathers lot is joining to it but fronts on another street.

the one next to it is reserved for Chester [Snyder] who is not here yet but is expeted soon. Bro Jenne has the next lot left of Jane. Sally [Sarah Jenne] took care of Jane all the way to the Mo River. there she was taken sick has been sick ever since. but is now recovering. next to them is Jesse. next to him Father Jacobs we are about a quarter of a mile from the meeting ground. about ½ from Uncle W & L. Father's folks are yet at Councel Point. but expect to move here. the fore part of next week. I heard from them yesterday. Father & mother were well Henry has been quite sick but is much better. Maria was blest with a little Daughter. on Sun the 26th of July. she is handsom Child her name is Synthe Maria. Maria & Melind[a] have both been very sick but are getting better. mother Willcox about the 9th of aug was taken sick with the chills & fever. she died on the 20th. Bro Danial Hendrexs wife died on the 25 of july. left a littl daughter 2 weeks old who died 10 days afterwards. Mary spencer died about the first of aug. lost a babe Hyrum Spencer died about the middle of July between nauvoo & mount Pisgah.

[*page 3*] father's [Samuel] Bent & Huntington. died about the first of Aug. the former ~~about~~ at garden Grove. the latter at mount Pisgah. father Colten [John Coltrin]. died on the 31 of Aug. Squer. [Daniel H.] Wells. & William Cuttler arived here on the 26th aug in 6 days from Nauvoo. bringing information concerning a battle fought in that City on the 19th between 100 of the Bretheren and ten 100 of the mob. The former had 5 Cannons. the mob 6 the battle lasted one houre and 20 minets in wich time the Brethern fired 36 Cannon. mob 42. the mob retreated to their Camp. Bro <u>Henderson</u> & his Son [Captain William Anderson and his son, Augustus][11] were <u>slain</u> in the war. also <u>Bro Noris</u> [David Norris] the number slain among [the] mob is yet unknown. the[y] are trying to keep it secret one Sister saw them throw 16 into one Waggon. Bro Cormick being sick got into his seller they brought some & laid them by his well curbe. the battle was fought in the rear of Boscos store. report says in the St. Louis papers that the mormons killed [*illegible*] men on the 18 by fireing into the mobs Camp & that they killed one of the mormons. the Bre fired upon the mob. but knew not how many they had killed. until they told the story themselfs the statement that the[y] had killed one of the bretheren is fals. they fired 3 Cannons at Squ. Wells. house one took the hat from a boys head. & past over the house. the other struck the barn. the other the well curbe. the[y] also fired several at Bro Barlow locust grove. & cut it all down soposeing the Bre was hid there. at the same time the Bre was fireing upon them from another direction. I have wrote the above as near as I can remember. as I heard it from Uncle Willards mouth.

Oct. 2 My dear Samuel if you can read & make sence. of what I have writton I shall feel glad. but it is writton in such & [an] unconnected maner. I fear 'twill be almost imposable. but as you know I ~~am~~ham unlarned I hope you will bear with my imperfections and excuse all my misstakes. you wrote to me that I might go and assist Jane. if she stood in need of me. I have been with her ever since the 21 of Aug. I have watched by her by day & by night when it has seemed almost. imposable for her to live. also my dear little Wealthy. I have spent some happy hours with her. and many gloomy ones during her & Ws sickness give my love to Franklin. tell him when he prays for Jane to remember me. and I will try to comfort her all I can. and keep her alive if posable for a comfort for me and also for him when he retorns. I do not know how long I shall remain with her. I sopose fathers folks will expect me to live with them when they come but 'twill be so near. 'twill be almost the same. I expect I shall sleep with her this winter. fathers folks have sold all their feather beds save one. when we got [to] Farmington our load was so heavy. father sold one bed. & left another. unsold another at mount Pisgah. I was glad I left my bed. for we could not have carred it. Jane got a letter wich Franklin wrote to Bro Clard [Clark] bearing date July 14th on the 20th of Sep. this was the last time I heard from you. have long been looking. for one from you but have looked in vain. almost begin to despair Oh! Samuel deary have you forgot me. Surely not. but why should that letter that brings intelligence from you my dearest. be delayed so long. I was glad to hear that you had got some new Clothes. my prayers shall be for the wellfare of those. who administer to your nessessitys. but how was it my dear. that you had to go so long without eating. can it be there was one so unfeeling. as to enjoy food & withhold it from you. was also exeeding glad to hear that you was well & that prosperity attended you which blessings I pray may ever abide with you.

Oct. 3th. Samuel dear. recieve my thanks. for the preasents you sent me by Jane. and espacialy for the one that bears your likeness. 'tis a comfort to see any thing that resembles you. though I sometimes say 'tis an aggrevation for I would much rather see the Original. but forgive me. I love to gaze upon it. though it retorns a ell cool & sober look. they folks say if you had been looking at Mary when it was taken you would have looked much more pleasent. wish it could have been so I often thought after you left us. had I been well nothing would have induced me to have left before you. but I expect 'twas all for the best. I try to think so and endeaver to live for your sake until you retorn

[*page 4*] give my love to all my Brothers & Sisters. tell Edward Alice [Edward and Alice Parker Corbridge] William and Ellen [William and Ellen Parker Corbridge] that I say if they do not come. before or when you come. I shall begin to think they never mean to. Robert [Parker] Richard [Parker] Isabella [Parker Cottam] Ann [Parker Watson] and their Children Familys I would love to see but hope is almost forbid me. tell them for me if the[y] love me. and ever wish to do any thing that would add to my comfort they must comfort & take good care of my Samuel. for should I ever larn that they treated him with disrespect. it would almost break my heart. but I have

too much confidence in them. to beleve they would ever ill treat my
Husband. I would dearly love to see all my nephews and neices and hear
them say Uncle Samuel and Aunt Mary. how pleasant 'twould seem to have
all my Fathers Children with their children. planted together in some
pleasant spot. they could call their own. & that spot in the midst of the Saints.
they all ~~they all~~ bileveing in the truth and my aged Father in their midst. if
wishing or praying could ever bring us all together. I would never seace
cease. there is many things I would love to write concerning them but have
no room. I leave them in the hands of him who rules our destiny. hope in
all things will work together for our good. and I have all confidance that my
Samuel will do his part. deary I enjoy myself as well as you can expect yet
there is no solid happyness. for me without you I find your place is vacant
where e'er I go Jane says give my love to Samuel ask him for me. if you may
live with me ~~if you may~~ till he retorns Samuel accept my kindest love and
bleve me I remain as ever

Your affectionate wife, Mary H. Richards

[*In the bottom left corner of the page is a poem*]
That love that never knows to change
For you in Marys bosem reigns
Though years & space may us devide
It ever shall for you abide

[*upside down across pages 2 and 3 and in the margins*] Sunday [*date illegible*]
Samuel I have been to meeting to day heard Bro O Pratt Preach on the
resurrection redempion and Salvation of the body. his decorce was very
intressting. after meeting. I went to Uncle Willards. Aunt Amelia appeard
very glad to see me. she is well. Eliza Ann was there. she has been quite
unwell for several days both wish to be kindly rememberd to you & Franklin.
Sarah is not very well. though she keeps to work. took supper with Uncle
Levis folks Aunt Sarahs health is quite poor. Aunt Rhoda is quite unwell.
they desire me to give their love to you. Bro VanCot is gon to St Louis his
family are well.

[*upside down on front page*] our dear Cousin Eliza Ann Peirson died on the
12th of Oct. with the chills & Fever have not room to write the perticulars I
was with her when she died. Ellen you wrote was coming with Bro [Edward]
Hunter. instead of that she came with Bro Woolly. they arived at the Bluffs
aug. 10th camped for 2 weeks close by us. used to be with her almost every
day. had sevarel long talks with her in wich she exprest herself to me much
the same as to you. She spoke of being freed. when she saw Brig. to wich I
replyed I have larned that those who were sealed over the alter must in the
same maner be unsealed. I sopose you can seperate by mutual agreement
and I dont know but what you Covnant to be sealed to another. but I should
judge that you could not be freed. until there is another Temple completed.

I gave her some what I would call good instructions. about being so ficcle minded. and trued [tried] to persuad her to have a mind of her own. and not be torned about by every body say so she is still with W. they appear to live quit[e] comfortable together now to what they used too. her health is pretty good I have just heard that Wolters folks have crost the River. Maria for some reason. has weaned her babe I have not learned what. they are camped. about 2 miles from us with Bro Joseph Youngs folks. Cousen John Young has been very sick. but is getting better. there is one favor I ask of you. which if you love me you will certainly grant. that is. that you let no oppertunity ~~pass~~ of writing pass by you unimproved. Bro Pratt will retorn in the spring. if you cannot send me a letter before he retorns do not fail to write then. pleas to write me all the perticulars about your journey your prosperity your meeting with my friends &C &C it seems almost a year since I had a letter from your own hand. hope I shall hear from you soon. deary I do want to hear from you. you know I love you yea rest asured forever that you have the sincere affections of you Mary H Richards goodbye

[*back page in the margin*] 19ᵗʰ [*tear*] learnd that Bro O Spencer ~~for~~ leave for Eng tomorrow he will carry this to New York. so will just say. we are all well and in tolerable good spirets. still with Jane father is not yet come. Samuel good Bye

[*addressed to*]
Mr. Samuel W. Richards
Liverpool England
To remain in the Stranger office till called for
rec'd Jan 26 1847

[*scrap of paper*] Oct 10ᵗʰ dear Samuel as we have not yet had a chance to send our letters. I thought I would write a scrap to let you know that we are still well. on the eve of the 7ᵗʰ Uncle W sent for me to come to watch with E A Peirson. who was very sick. taken sick while there on a visit. while there had the pleasure of reading a letter which you wrote to Bro Paine in Nauvoo. dated on the 31ˢᵗ of Aug. which he sent to Uncle W. it gave me much comfort to hear from you although I often wonder why it is. that I cannot have a letter from you as well as others. I am sure if you thought half as much about me. as I do about you. or felt half so lonely. you could not forbear writing so long. I would just as soon you had wrote 6 letters before you sailed. as to have waited till the last day it would not have hort my feelings the least mite.

[*back of the scrap*] but perhaps I am finding fault without cause. you may have wrote to me. if so I ask your forgiveness. and will try to wait patiantly for the proof of your rememberance. Bro Everit. is hear brought our dog. watch[12] with them. father has got him. Bro [Almon W.] Babit is here on an express from Nauvoo. Says the mob has taken possession of the Temple have cut a hole through the Font. & broken the horns of[f] the oxen cut the floor & disfigured the inner part &C &C will not the Lord pity his Saints. and do unto them that have injured his House even as they have done unto it I do not think of any more news to write to you at preasent. though though if you was here I could tell you many things wich I cannot write. but this must sofise. May the blessings of heaven attend you were e'er your lot is cast. Oh may that Angel who has garded you unto the present time never forsake you but watch over you by day & by night. & comfort you under all your trials & Sorrows untill I Shall again behold your face and injoy your sweet sociaty. M H R

Cutler's Park, Nebraska. Copy of original sketch in the Heber C. Kimball Journals of 1846, probably drawn by Peter Hansen. The journal page was not long enough to capture the whole scene, so the right half of the campsite is drawn on the bottom of the page. Courtesy of LDS Historical Department.

Winter Quarters, 1846-1847. From an oil-on-canvas painting by C. C. A. Christensen; courtesy of LDS Historical Department.

CHAPTER SIX

"Our Tent was crowded all day with folks coming in"

In September, Mormon church leaders selected the site for the town of Winter Quarters, urging all the Saints to move there. Jane and Mary obeyed counsel, as did Phinehas and Wealthy. By this time Jane was well enough for Mary to return to the tent of Phinehas, which became her home until the following spring. Throughout the bitter cold winter, Mary visited from house to house to keep warm, baked on borrowed stoves, and washed over her friends' fires. Her spirit was warm, however, as she went to singing school, attended church meetings, and visited friends. Some of these visits were into the neighboring settlements and lasted many days. When she finally moved to a house on the South Row, Mary dropped to her knees and thanked the Lord for the many blessings bestowed upon her and her loved ones.

Journal Three
Saturday, November 28, 1846, to Wednesday, May 19, 1847
Winter Quarters, Nebraska[1]

A Journal & Memorandom of Mary H Richards commencing Saturday November 28th 1846   In the PM went to Bro Smithes.[2] expecting to get a letter from my father. but was disapointed. called at Uncle Willards. and talked with him about 20 minutes. got a letter for mother and a paper for Sister Jane. called to see Aunt Rhoda & spent a few minutes with her and Uncle Levis folks. next called to see Bro Bensons folks. he having just retorned from his mission to the East. the Evening before. from him I got considerable information concerning my Husband. he also brought me some presents which he sent me. a work box in which was 2 letters. a Sattin ribon. & flowers. for a bonet. smelling bottle. 2 white An [handkerchiefs] [*blank space*] & a Silk one for Henry. and a purse containing 10 dollars. Sister B[enson] took of bonnet & shawl. and made me stay and make a visit took supper & spent the eve with them enjoyed my self much. it was indeed a day of rejoicing to me to hear of the prosperity an wellbeing of my dear companion. may Heavens ritchest blessing attend him. weree're he romes & retorn him in safty to my bosem

Sunday 29th   in the AM went to meeting. was addrest by Bro Kimball. who gave us some good instructions how we Aught to walk &C was followed by Bro Benson who gave us an interressting account of his mission to the East. the state of the different branches. the down fall of aposstacy &C &C in the PM Aunt Amelia [Peirson Richards] and R[hoda] visited with us, & read 5 letters which she had just recieved from Richmond mass. Maria & Jane also visited with us. we had a joy full time.

Monday 30th   the weather some what comfortable. after doing up my work in the morn. I sat down and mended Fathers over coat. and a dress for my self. after supper went with Mother to Bro Van Cotts. & spent the eve. had a pleasent visit

Tuesday December first   windy day after breakfast Mrs Rebecca M Jones & babe from Mo. called to see me. was in great hast. I accompanyed her to the River from whence she retorns to Mo on my retorn called at Bro Wolleys. and spent the day had a good visit Ellen and Mrs Smith accompanied [me] home

Wednesday 2th   a cold day was makeing me a hood. spent the eve at Bro W[m] Youngs enjoyed my self much

Thursday 3th   the weather cold helped do the Work and finished making my hood.

·Friday 4th   a cold day was sewing in the AM and in the PM baked 3 ~~loaf~~ loaves of bread in Bro W[m] Youngs eve was knitting.

Saturday 5th   the weather comfortable. fixed Mothers hood for her & mended a dress for my self. in the eve read about an hour in the bible[3]

Sunday 6th   the weather cold in the morning got breakfast &C was no meeting. went out to see some of my friends. called at Bro Van Cotts. to see his wife & mother. they having been sick. found them comfortable. spent about & hour with them. eat some ~~bred~~ bread & butter. honey & chese &C. Next went to Sister Noons. [Sarah Peak Noon Kimball] to carry home a hood which I had borrowed. spent a few minutes with them. Next called to see Ellen Wilding. at Bro Wolleys had the pleasure of spending about & houre with her alone in the waggon. Next called at Uncle Levis found them well Aunt Rhoda having kept her waggon for near 4 weeks ~~I went~~ on account of sickness I went into her humble abode to see her. found Amelia with her. spent a ~~few~~ short time with them. Next called at Uncle Willards house to see Bros [Thomas] Bullock and [John] Rushtons families who had just arrived. found Sister R morning the loss of her Child [Isabella Hannah Rushton] she having died the day before. stayed a short time with them. then called to see Maria. & spent a few minutes with them. &C from there I went about ½ mile ~~East~~ South to see Sister Jane found her suffering with face Ace and canker spent the eve and Nigh[t] with her had a good supper &C

Monday 7th   a very cold day stayed till eve with Jane. she read her letters for me &C spent the evening writting in my Journal. knitting. &C

Tuesday 8th   a cold day was sewing. knitting. reading & cooking &C

Wednesday 9th   the weather a little more comfortable. in the AM Sister Maria came to see us. got her to fit the lining in my black silck dress. I cut the waist and sewed on it the rest of the day eve was knitting

Thursday 10th   a pleasant day. was sewing on my dress all day. and in the [eve] was knitting

~~Saturday~~ Friday 11th   a lovely day ~~was~~ was sewing on my dress. eve was knitting

Saturday 12th   a beauty full day sister Jane and my self went out to do some buisness. in the first place went to the Store. which was very much. crouded. stayed a while bought some Cotton. &C. then called to see Bro Smithes folks & made a short stay with them next called at Uncle Willards house. were we had the pleasure. of being present at a Council held between the Twelve & the Natives. there was present 10 Indians two Chiefs & two interpiters.[4] one a french Man or half breed we was quite interessted to hear them talk & see them act. after Council was dismissed had some talk with W and asked him which way he thought Samuel & F would retorn. said he did not know. but he soposed they would come back by this place. said we might make our selfs contented. all things should go right. after leaving there. we called to see Bro Bensons family. & spent a few minutes with them. On our way home called to see Bro Fielding & family. who seemed quite glad to see us. stayed and conversed with him about 2 hours. then came to Janes house & took supper with her wich I enjoyed. & soon after had the pleasure of seeing Bro [Stephen H.] Godard direct from Nauvoo in the eve he accompanyed us to Bro H Grows were we spent about 2 hours. and then retorned home. had quite a pleasant conversation with Bro G who brought to remembrance by gone days.

Sunday 13th   the weather comfortable. after getting breakfast. washing dishes. &C went to meetting. heard a raugh discourse. delivered by Bro [Cornelius Peter] Lot, and afew remarks by Bro Brigham. spent the rest of the day at home. reading, &C

Monday 14th   had a little snow. this morning the first I have seen this year. but it melted as soon as the Sun was out. and was very pleasent today I commenced writing a letter to my Husband. and in eve was knitting reading &C

Tuesday 15th   had a little more Snow the weather rather cold. went to Janes & baked a loaf of bread. PM was writing in my letter. eve sewing &C

Wednesday 16th   a cold day. in the morn cut a garment for Henry. was cooking writing in my letter &C

Thursday 17ᵗʰ   a cold day. was writing in my letter. eve Jane came to
~~stay~~ stay with me I being a lone. she was writing a letter to Franklin, and I
was writing in my Journal. She read me her letter, and I read her most of mine

Friday 18ᵗʰ   a very cold day was sewing & wrting in my ~~eitha~~ letter eve
borrowed a penn at sister Pratts and finished it Mother & father went out to
spend the eve at Bro [Elias] Hart's. Henry & I was all alone

Saturday 19ᵗʰ   the weather please[n]t had the head Ache all day. felt
Sober in the morn Sister [Margaret Phillips] Obanks came to learn to make
baskets could not get room to sit down near Stove. So I went to Sisters Janes
and sewed on my dress. & baked a loaf of bread. they were washing. eve
wrong & hung out some of her cloths. then came home spent the rest of the
night knitting

Sunday 20ᵗʰ   in the morn got breakfast. washed the dishes, swept the
Tent. washed me, changed my dress and sat down & commenced to write
a [s]crap to put in my letter. in about ten minutes after the Temple bell rung
for meeting. got ready and went Bro Brigham preached a sermon that I
think will be long rememberd by all who heard it. he began by speaking
of several Evils exsisting in the Camp. such as. swearing. stealing. eveil
speaking. &C said if they did not repent and leave of their Eveil doings.
The ~~keys~~ door of knwledge should be shut up against them. and they should
be wasted by sickness. by Pestilance. and by the Sword. and those who
were found righteous. among them. should be taken out of their midst. and
they should perish with their dead. said many [things] that were interessting.
had & excellant meeting. Evening. father & Mother went to spend the eve
at Bro Rights [Jonathan Calkins Wright]. and sister Jane came to spend it
with me. we were each writing a [s]crap to put in our letters. 'twas a beauty
full day.

Monday 21ˢᵗ   a cold day in the AM was sewing. in the PM went to visit
Bro Grows [Henry Grow Jr.] family. who appeared Glad to see me. we talked
of by gone days. and of things that had trancepired during our absence from
Each other had a very pleasent visit. & stayed all night

Tuesday 22ᵗʰ   the weather cold in the morn Bro Grow started for Mo.
spent the day with his family. in the AM was sewing on my black silck dress.
PM made an Apron for Sister [Mary Moyer] Grow &C while there had the
pleasure of seeing Sister Fairbanks and received an Introduction to Sister
[Nancy Elliott] Veach. at Sun down retorned to Sister Janes house and spend
the eve. & Night with her

Wednesday 23ᵗʰ   the weather more comfortable. was at home all day
sewing helping Mother &C at dusk went with her to Bro Willys and spent
the Eve. had a very pleasent Visit.

Thursday 24ᵗʰ   a pleasent day in the morn. Jane came & said if I wished
to wash to day. I might have the privelige to do so in her house. if not she
wanted father Mother. & my self. to go & make her a visit. father & mother

consented to do the latter & I aggreed to do both. so after breakfast. I went down to her house & washed me out 4 dresses. & as many Aprons & some other things. put them out to dry then washed of the floor. wich is the first time I have washed a floor since the first of Aprial. father & mother came. we had an excellant Supper Sister Jenne was with us also. we staid the Eve. talked of several things that had passed since our leaving Nauvoo. father spoke some things that hort Jane's feelings. but she spoke noble in her own defence. and made father draw in his horns. and they parted still freinds I remained with Jane all night

Friday 25th   a beauty full day in the morn went home an getherd together a large washing of clothes and retorned to Jane's to spend Christmass over the wash tub. was washing with all my might til dark then put my clothes ~~to~~ in water til morning eve went with Jane to Bro Phinehas Youngs. to see about getting some flower. on our retorn. called on Maria. & spent about 2 hours with them. ate supper with her &C had a pleasent little visit and retorned home spent the night with Jane

Saturday 26th   another fine day in the morn went home & getherd ~~y~~ up all the clothes I could find. that needed washing. and retorned again to Janes. to finish my washing. rung out my clothes I had put to soak the night before and hung them out to dry. then washed the remainder of my clothes. Had a considerable large wash. finished about dark. washed of the floor & took supper. in the evening foulded my cloths and put them out of the folks way. felt very tired staid all night with Jane.

Sunday 27th   The weather pleasent took breakfast with Jane then came home changed my dress and at 12 oclock went to meeting. was addrest by Orson Pratt. on the Policy of removal of the Church in the spring. said they intended to send out a company as early as posable in the Spring. to put in a crop at the foot of the mountains on the banks of the Yellow Stone. they also intended to send a company accross the mountains to put in a crop of w[h]eat in the fall. he was followed by Bro Benson on the same subgect he told the brethren that none of them should leave this place to go any further without receiving council to do so. desired them to fix their waggons & hold themselfs in readyness. so that if they were called upon to go the[y] might be ready. to do so &C exorted the Saints to be faithfull and reform from all there Eavil doings &C &C had a good meeting. came home & read a while in the book of Mormon & helped mother get supper. after wich Elcy Snyder called to go to singing Scool with me. On our way there called on Abigal Abott. & took her with us. Bro Godard ~~was~~ led the Coir for the first time since the Dedecation of the [Nauvoo] Temple. we had a good sing enjoyed ourselfs much. went & slept that night with sister Jane

Monday 28th   the weather still good took breakfast with Jane then Ironed my cloths finished about dark. after supper took my knitting and went with Jane to spend the eve at Bro Samuel Snyders

Tuesday 29ᵗʰ   the weather cold spent the day with Jane sewing. in the eve was reading until 8 oclock. then Jane Elcy [Elsie Snyder] & myself spent about two hours trying to see which could Compose the best Poetry. then retired to bed

Wednesday 30ᵗʰ   a cold day in the AM was at Jane's sewing for my self. in the PM went with her to Bro Bakers had a good visit. and an excellant Supper spent the eve and retorned home with Jane & stayed all night with her

Thursday 31ˢᵗ   a very cold day in the morn. went with Jane to Uncle Willards to help them do some sewing. made an Apron for Amelia & 2 handkerchiefs for Uncle W and helped sew on his garment after we dismissed our work. Uncle W sat down to eat some supper. Asked me if I was grown proud. I said if I was it was unknown to me. then said he come & Eat some supper with me. I did so. & eat of from his plate while conversing with him. Aunt Rhoda came & kneeled down by him & said she had bowed down on her benders to recieve a blessing he then took the word Benders for a text & preached a sermon from it. about an half houre long. on false modesty. after this. I went to Uncle Levis & slept with Aunt R. had a good nights rest

Friday Janawary first 1847   A Cold day after wishing & being wished. a happy New Year by Uncle L. & family I retorned to Uncle Ws to spend the day. sewing for them. helped make a garment for Uncle W. & a Apron for Ellen [Partington]. &C &C

Saturday 2ᵗʰ   a very cold day took breakfast at Uncle Ws. then retorned to Janes house to get some things. from there I went to Bro Everits to make a visit. spent the day very pleasently conversing. reading &C stayed all night

Sunday 3ᵗʰ   the weather cold went with Sister E to meeting at Bro Scots [John Scott]. was addrest by H C Kimball. on the duty of familys. exorted Husbands to watch over their wives & Children. & too instrut them. in the knowledge. & fear of the Lord. not with severity but with meekness. & forbearance. Wives to be subject to their husbands. & to watch over their Children & set before them an example worthy of imitation. he desired the Saints to reform from all their Wickedness, & put away all their contracted feelings, &C &C after meeting retorned to Bro Everits & took dinner. while there Ellen Wilding came & staid a short time. then accompanyed Sister E and my self to Bro Willcoxs were we staid about & hour & ½. had a pleasent coversation with walter & Maria on diferant points of doctring from there sister E and I went to singing Scool and had a very good sing bro Godard was present. then went & staid all night with Jane

Monday 4ᵗʰ   a cold day took breakfast with Jane. then retorned home home and did some sewing. & wrote a little in my journal &C &C

Tuesday 5ᵗʰ   a cold day after getting breakfast, I went with Mother to the Store. were she was going to trade out a bill. got me cloth for a pair of garments on our way home call to see Maria [Wilcox]. after I got home. I cut out a garment for mother then went to Bro [Alfred B.] Lambsons to make a visit met with a very warm reception. Sister Robins who had lately arived from Nauvoo finding I was there came & spent the PM with us. then perswaided Mrs. La. [Melissa Jane Bigler Lambson] to let me go and Eat supper with her. which I did. as she lived the next house. after this we retorned to Bro L & spent the Eve very pleasently. then Br L accompanid me home. the Snow had been falling all the PM & eve and was now quite deep

Wednesday 6th a very cold day got breakfast. then cut out a garment for Mother & 2 for my self. Eve was sewing

Thursday 7th an exceeding cold day. had only wood enough to make one fire. got breakfast. which took us til noon then being froze out with the cold. I went to sister Janes. when I got there my hands & feet ached severely. felt quite unwell all day from the effects of the cold. was reading spent the night with Jane[5]

Friday 8th a bitter cold day staid with Jane. in the AM Mother came & brought some bread to bake. in the eve Jane & myself got supper. when it was ready father & Henry came. and we all took supper together. after which we washed the dishes and spent the eve reading

Saturday 9th a very cold day in the morn baked a corn cake & sent it to fathers for their breakfast. then spent the day makeing a garment. eve finished it

Sunday 10th the weather still very cold. took breakfast with Jane. then went to meeting at Bro [Daniel] Russels. was addrest by Bishop [Thomas] Lang. Br Rusel. & father. had a good meeting. after wich I called to see Br Harts folks & spent about an hour with them then retorned to Janes & took supper. after wich she accompanied me to singing Scool were we spent the eve very pleasently, then retorned home

Monday 11th a very cold day still with Jane. in the morn got breakfast for father & Henry. in the PM helped Jane to fix a dress. then got supper for F. & H. eve went with Jane to Bro Fildings' [Joseph Fielding] were we spent the eve very pleasently. after which Bro Filding accompanied us home

Tuesday 12th the weather a little more comfortable in the morn got breakfast for Father & Henry. washed the dishes & then then sat down & wrote a few lines in my Journal. PM baked a shoulder of a Lamb. got supper &C father & H eat with us, Mother having been for 3 days with Maria. eve I went with Jane & H to a meeting at Bro Allens house were we was addressed by Elder W Woodruff. who gave us some good instructions in relation to the resurrection of the dead. &C &C Said if there was any under the sound of his voise who felt as if the journey was to great for them. or the trials to hard for them to endure. his advice too such would be. to go into their Waggons & shut themselfs up. as the[y] had no closets. & pray the Lord to take away their lives. & grant them a burial with the Saints of of God. as their death would prove a blessing to their posterity. who would ever beleve that their fathers died in full belief of the Gospel of Christ. and when the servants of God should retorn to the places were they had buryed their dead. in the morn of the Resurrection. & sound the Trumpit. that should shake the Earth and call them from their slumbering tombs. then they also would receve a resurrection & come forth. wereas. if they should go into Missouri. & be buryed there. he did not know who would be to the truble to go there and hunt them up for the[y] would never once think that a Saint of God would be buryed [there].

Wednesday 13th a fair day in the morn got breakfast. washed the dishes. made the bed &C sewed a little on my garment. PM baked a loaf of breads & cleaned a hogs face and put it to boil. & made a pot pye for supper then washed the dishes. & spent the Eve sewing

Thursday 14th a pleasent day in the morn. got breakfast. washed the dishes. scoured the table. &C then carried in some clay to make a new hearth. and pounded it ~~til~~ about an hour. PM Bro ~~Huntington~~ Hunter called to see us. & staid about an hour. had a pleasent talk with him after wich I took supper at Br Jennes. it being the next door. & Mother Jacob there on a visit we had a good supper I then helped to do up the work. then assisted Jane a little about her washing. Eve went with her to Bro Scrodshams. one of the neighbors were we spent it sewing. and had a social conversation with them

Friday 15th a cold stormy snowey day^6 morn got breakfast &C then went to Bro Chesters Snyders. & bought 10 pounds of flower for which I paid 31 cents. then retorned home & hung out some Cloths on the line for Jane. wich froze before I could get them on the line. tried to sew on my garment. but was anable to accomplish much for the cold. Eve helped bring in the cloths & wood

Saturday 16th the weather cold after cooking breakfast. washing dishes &C &C Jane & my self went to Bro Smithes to make a visit we spent the day very pleasently had an excellent Supper. and at 9 oclock was accompanied home by Bro S.

Sunday 17th a very cold day after doing up my work in the morning. I went with Sister Jane to Uncle Willards. were we spent the PM & took Supper. then retorned home on our way called at Bro Grants Scool room. expecting to have a sing. but was disapointed. While at Uncle Ws today Amelia loaned me a Josey to wear through the Winter which had belong to Elize Ann

Monday 18th an exeeding cold day got breakfast as usual. then sewed on a garment for Mother. eve got Supper &C then sat down and read

Tuesday 19th the weather still cold after getting breakfast. washing dishes. making the bed &C I accompanied Jane to Maria's were we spent the day very pleasently. Mother was still with them I was marking a garment for her we had a good Supper. in the eve Maria played several tunes on her Accordian. about 9 oclock we returned home

Wednesday 20th the weather more comfortable. did my Work as usual. then sat down and wrote a short time in my journal. PM baked a loaf of bread and got Supper. Eve went to Meeting and Bro VanCotts accompanied by Elsia Snyder had a very good Meeting

Thursday 21th the weather Moderate. after doing up my Work Sat down and wrote awhile in my Journal. PM was sewing. also in the eve.

Friday 22st the weather cold was cooking. cleaning house. sewing. &C eve Abagil Abott came to inform me that Bro Van Cott had brought a letter for me from Mo. so I retorned with A to Br V Cs got my letter. and found it was from my Bro Johns Wife [Ellen Briggs Douglass Parker] informing me that they were well & prospering. I spent the eve & enjoyed my self much. before I left Sister V C made me drink Tea & eat Gingebread. wich was quite a treat.

Saturday 23th the weather cold was sewing. &C &C the house smooked so bad that it was amost imposable to keep any fire

Sunday 23 4th the weather still cold went to meeting in Bro Curtis Ward had a good meeting PM I was writing eve was reading

Monday 25th a cold day was sewing most of the day. eve was knitting

Tuesday 25 6th the weather comfortable early in the morn Sister Chester Snyder [Katherine Montgomery] sent for Jane and my self to come to her house to a quilting. we went stayed a little while then Henry came and informed me that Bro Godard had come to invite me to a party at the Counsel house. Sister Snyder excused me and I went up to our tent. found Bro G waiting for me. so I got ready as quick as posable and accompanid him called at Bro Hendrixs and got his wife. and about 4 oclock enterd the Councel house. Bro G took me on to the floor the first dance. here for the first time I joined with those who praised God in the dance when this figure was formed it being the first. and Bro [Albert P.] Rockwood being at the head. according to order. we all kneeled down and he offerd up a prayer. we then arose & danced the figure. and so praised God in the dance.[7] I danced with Bros Dewsette [Edward P. Duzette] W[illiam F.] Cahoon & G Grant. and others. and once with Bro Brigham the mony musk[8] had a very pleasent party and some good refreshments. about 11 oclock every man took his partner or partners & marched 3 times round the room. we were then dismised with the blessings of God. Bro G accompanied me to sister Janes were I spent the nigh[t].

Wednesday 27th & Thursday 28th Moderate weather was sewing kniting &C &C

Friday 29 we had a little snow after getting my breakfast & doing up my work I went up to our Tent. found a good fire in the stove was there all alone for several hours, writing a letter to my far absent husband. felt very lonely although it seemed good to be alone awhile communicating my thoughts to that absent freind who is dearer to me yes far dearer than all others about 5 in PM I returned to Janes. got supper &C then went with Elsy Snyder to ~~Sin~~ the Singing Scool on our way called at Maria's. found her about ready so we all went together. there were more of Coir tonight at the Councel house than had been seen together since we left Nauvoo. we sung for about an hour & ½ then danced til ½ past 11 I danced with Godard bros Duzette. Chatman [Welcome Chapman] and others. and once with little Brigham Young, and 3 Couple of little Children it was the Anniversary of that night I was Marrid and I told ~~the~~ some of the Sisters that I was celebrating it &C we had a very pleasent time. but my thoughts were wandering on by gone day & I could not help recalling to mind the many changes that had taken place since that night [a] year ago. then was I happy in the Sociaty of the only one I ever loved but now more than 5000 miles separates us from each other. and the ever restless oacian rools between us but hope still Wispers we shall meet again. about 12 oclock I came to Sister Janes were I spent the night

Saturday 30th   the weather somewhat comfortable. after doing my mornings work I again went up to the Tent and spent ~~the~~ the day writing evening returned to Janes. and got supper &C after which I was knitting

Sunday 31st   wather cold went with Jane to meeting in her ward. Brother Curtis preached to us. & said we were now enjoying a day of Jublee. but days of truble were yet before us. in which we should be tried in every thing. but if we endured our trials patiantly. our reward would be great. his sermone was very interessting. in the PM we went to the Council House were we were addresst by Bro Majer [William W. Major] A Bro from London Bro Brigham bore testemony to what Bro M had said the decourse was very interessting after meeting I called at Wolters. were I stayed and took supper. I then called to see Sister Benson and staid afew minutes with her had a pleasent little chat. afterwards Maria & myself went to Singing Scool which was held at Bro G Grants scool room. we had a very good sing. after which I went with E Snyder to Janes were I spent the night

Monday Febuary first   a cold day Janes chimney Smooked very bad. so that it kept the tears runing down my cheeks about all the time was very uncomfortable did a little sewing. and in the eve was knitting.

Tuesday 2nd & Wednesday 3rd   the weather still cold. did some writing sewing &C the smook trubbled us considerable.

Thursday 4th   a Cold day I was writing in my journal. eveing went to meeting at Bro VanCotts had a very good meeting

Friday 5th & Saturday 6th   the weather cold was writing some in my letter. sewing. knitting. Cooking. &C &C.

Sunday 7th   the weather comfortable went with Jane to meetting in her ward from there we went to the Councel House to meeting. where we were addrest by Bro Zebedee Colten, followed by several of the Bretheren on the subject of the Saints being united showing the nesseessity of their being so. I then went to Bro James Smithises were I ~~spent~~ spent the night

Monday 8th the weather comfortable. I cut & fitted a dress for Sister S and spent the day sewing on it. eve I visited with Sister [Vilate Murray] Kimball and had a sweet ~~with~~ talk with her. saw her little Son Solomon who was then but a few days old. night slept with Sister [Tamson Parshley] Egan.

Tuesday 9th the weather cold was at Bro Smithes sewing on Sister Ann's dress. eve I went with them to the Council House were there was a party assembled this eve I danced with Bros Grant Duzette & [William] Pitt & once a Kethlian [cotillion] with Bro Brigham and when he took me to my seat he said Sister Mary you have learned me I am very much obliged to you. &C. we spent the evning very pleasently and about 12 oclock returned home. I spent the rest of the night. with Sister Egan

Wednesday 10th the weather cold spent the day at Brother Smithes sewing on her dress. eve I visited at Bro Orson Whitney's had a very pleasent visit with Ellen [Helen Mar Kimball Whitney] she repeated or said over some verses to me that her Mother Sister [Vilate] Kimball had composed the next morn after her little Son Solomon was born. the first verse is all I remember. it is as follows The Lord has blessed us with another Son Which is the seventh I have Born May he be the father of many lives. But not the Husband of many Wives.[9] before I left. Bro O orderd a bowl of hot Punch to be made. and made us all drink of it freely. I then went to Sister Egans where I spent the night.

Thursday 11th a cold day was at Bro Smithes sewing for ~~for~~ them about 2 oclock in the PM Bro William Cahoon called to take Sister Mary Casson who was then there on a visit to the Council House. he gave me an invitation to go in the eve. as his Wife was going then. so I agreed to go. accordingly they called and I went with them. I danced with Bro Wiliam & Danial Cahoon G Grant and others. spent the eve pleasently. and about 12th oclock returned to Bro Smithes where I spent the night.

Friday 12th the weather cold in the AM was sewing for Sister S [Ann Knowles Smithies] and in the PM I visited with Sister Noon K. I alterd a dress for Betsy [Elizabeth Ann Noon] her daughter. Sister S came and took tea with us and I had a very pleasent visit with them and departed about nine in the eve. after receiving many pressing invetation to repeat my visits. this night I slept with Sister Egan

Saturday 13th the weather warm was sewing ~~with~~ for Sister S. took dinner with David Smith and spent part of the PM with her [Phoebe Bowley Smith]. she combed my hair for me &C &C Sister Noon made me promis to go with her & Bro S to the Councel House in the eve said she wished to go but would not go except I did. so I went with them. we had a very nice party. I danced with Bros Smithes O[rson] Whitney G Grant Duzette and others. about 12th oclock I returned to Bro Smithes where I spent the night

Sunday 14th the weather warm in the AM I went with Br & Sister Smithes to Bro Kimballs to a family Meetting. Bro K was quite unwell. but arose & spoke to us in a very interesting maner. he spoke of the dutys of his Children & family. towards him as their father and <u>Head</u>, which was that they should love honor and obey him. and do every thing that lay in their power for his wellfare & prosperity. that they should uphold him by their prayers continualy that he might live long on the Earth to be a blessing and comfort to them all. that they should love his Wife. & do all they could for her comfort. for she was a good woman and whorthy their love & esteem and whomsoever honerd & loved her honerd & loved himself. he also spoke of his own feelings towards his family and his anxiaty for their wellfare &C &C was followed by Bro Whitney on the same subject who spoke very well. after which Bro K commenced a conversation somewhat as follows. There is one. of the best girls that ever crossed the Sea. pointing them to me. I have been to her father's house. many a day & night and I was always wellcome and they always did all they could for my comfort. Mary she was then but a little girl and I used to call her My pet. She used to take pleasure in doing any thing for me. She would step around as quick & as light as a feather and would seem glad when she could get a chance to do any thing for me. it was from her I learned how to understand the differant dialects the[y] speak there & her Sister Jennette R. I would ask Mary questions & she would explain them to me so that I could understand about all they said but Bro Hyde never could understand them he would sit & look at them. and I had to interpit for him I shall never forget Sister Richards kindness to me. and she shall be blessed for it. I mean Sister Mary there she ~~eits~~ sits. Bro Samuel Richards wife he is gone to England on a mision &C after this we sung a hymn and we dismised with the Blessings of the Lord I then took dinner with Bro S folks and in the PM went to meeting at the councel House were we were addressed by Bro O Pratt who had just returned from visiting Mt Pisgah garden Grove and all the scatterd Branches between here ~~he~~ and there. had been there to instruct them in regard to their future proseedings and teach them the word of the Lord &C he said they were all glad to see him and manyfested a good Spirit &C after meetting I went to Sister Marias and took supper then called in to see Sister Benson a few Minutes after which I returned to Marias and staid all night.

Monday 15th   comfortable weather took breakfast with Maria then went to Bro Smithes to do some more sewing for them I took much comfort with Bro Sm folks they were so very kind to me. besides they were the only cousens I have in this country in the AM Bro Kimball came in and I had a good long talk with him. he asked me some questions about Mother & Sister [Mary Vail] Morse if they agreed when they lived together so on. I told him I had never heard them quaril and I thought any one that undertook to quaril with Mother would have to do their own quariling. but she used to feel bad sometimes when they lived together. but she said she could not help her feelings. why said he did any one think she could help her feelings Whell said I I have heard a pearson say that woman could help feeling bad if they were only a mind to. & there was no use in their feeling &C pa-shaw said he there is not one respectable Woman in this church but what would feel bad under such sircumstances. and I know there is no Woman can ever feel worse than my Wife has done. and she is just as good a Woman as ever lived. and I never blamed her for feeling bad but loved her the more about noon father came & told me that father Burton was in town and wanted very much to have me go home with him and make them a visit. said they intended to come up to the City again in about 2 weeks and I could then return if I wished. father seemed to be willing that I should go. & so I concluded to do so. I took my leave of Bro Smithes folks and returned home to prepair for my departure called at sister Janes to get some things that I had left there bid her and Elizabeth good bye. she was quite lame. I spent the rest of the day prepairing my cloths &C

Tuesday 16th   the weather comfortable. about nine oclock in the AM I bid goodbye to father Mother & Henry. and started with father [Samuel Burton] and Charles [Burton]. to visit their home.[10] we traviled about 4 miles through the bottoms. then crossed the Missouri River on the Ice. we traviled along through wood and prarira and about 2 oclock arrived at the pony cr[eek] Indian Village were we stayed all night at a Bro [James] McLellens I think. with whom I had a confab about keeping council & following the Church. he thought 'twas best for every one to live ~~where~~ where he could get the most to Eat and keep his family the most comfortable and I contended that it was better to saccrefice and suffer with the Saints for then we possessed a hope that e'er long we should enjoy the blessings with them. but those who ~~those~~ lived in luxury could not expect to enjoy the blessing that they enjoyed untill like them they had sufferd &C there was many other thing that we spoke about but I cannot write them

Wednesday 17th   the weather pleasent. took breakfast and proseeded on our [way] about 8 oclock. bro B was walking and & Indian who had got some lickure took hold of him and would not let him go untill I turned back and loosand his hands and made him let go his hold we then traviled along through some woods & passed severa[l] Indians & their Wigwams. & several houses that were inhabited by our brethren and a cross a long praira and about Sun down came to Bro [Libbeus T.] Coons[11] where we put up for the night. Sister C [Mary Ann Williamson Coons] got supper for us. after which I went a Sister [*blank space*] to a prayer meeting about ½ mile we had a very good meeting I spoke a few words and told them what good meetings we had in the Camp and what good instructions were given &C they all seemed to rejoice and many of them seemed anxious to be in the camp I received several invitations to come and visit them after which I returned with Sister [*blank space*] to her house were I spent the night. she kept me awake about 2 hours talking about the things of the kingdom

Thursday 18th   a pleasant morn took Breakfast and about ½ past 7 proseeded on our journey to day the scene was beautifull. the Praira through which we traviled was dressed in a white Mantle of frost. while to our left was a range of Eternal Bluffs raising their Magestic Summits in solomn and confused grandure like the rooling Waves of the oacen. Beating before a tempestious Wind. while on our right to the West flowed the dark Waters of the Missouri we past several houses inhabited by our Brethren and about Sundown came to a bed of Willows which were about 2 miles through it and about one hour after arrived at our place of destination was courdialy received both by fathers Burton and [John] Havens folks. they asked many questions which I ansurd according to the best of my knowlige after which I retired with E A

Friday 19th   the weather cloudey and cold made two handkerchiefs for father & Mother [Hannah Shipley Burton] B. played with little Clara [Lucinda Jones] who is a sweet little dear read some &C in the Eve I was introoduced to 3 Jents as Miss Richards a young lady just from the Camp. we Rebecca [Burton Jones] & myself sung 2 or 3 songs while Robert [T. Burton] played on his fiddle.

Saturday 20th   a stormey day the snow fell so as to be very deep was reading sewing playing with Clara &C[12]

Sunday 21st   a cold stormry day was reading picking out Wallnut meets & eating them talking &C &C &C

Monday 22nd   a cold day in the morn heard that Bro Meeks had got a letter from the Army in it was written that Brother Joseph was dead[13] I felt very uneasey to know if it was so. and it hapend so that Uncle [John] & Aunt [Judith W. Temple] Haven were going there with an Ox team so I rode up with them. and heard the letter read. that of it that spoke of Josephs death was about as follows please tell Bro Phinehas Richards that his Son Joseph is dead. he died of a lingering sickness. I helped to wash him and lay him out, and convey him to him to his narrow home.[14] the letter was written by a Bro Wilkey [David Wilkin] after hearing the letter we returned home. the place were we went was about 4 miles I then went with R & M to a Methotest Meeting expecting to witness the funral of Mormonism. as the man that was expected to preach had said he was going to put a end to it. but I supose he began to think he was not competant to do it. and so never come near. after this a M[r] Severage came with a sleigh and invited us all to take a ride. so Rebecca. EA [Eliza Ann]. R[obert] M[aria]. C[harles] and myself all went. we went to M[r] [William] Slushers about 4 miles then came back and went again. we then went to M[r] Cornays, got Mrs Wells and took her home about 2 miles further we then returned to Brother [Priddy] Meeks were we took supper. after which the[y] had a dance there were about 8 Mormon girls and about 5 gentile gents. I danced some 2 & or 3 times but it was no enjoyment to me for my heart was weighed down with grief. for the loss of our beloved

Brother Joseph. about 10 oclock Rebecca and myself prevailed with Charls to take us home and so we went and left the rest all there who staid til day light

Tuesday 23rd   the weather cold took breakfast with father Haven folks

Wednesday 24th   was sewing reading &C I went out each day to the Corn Crib[15] and offerd up a prayer to my Heavenly father that he would preserve the life of my dear companion and permit us again to meet and enjoy each others sociaty &C &C &C

Thursday 25th Friday 26th   the weather still cold

Saturday 27th   was making a night dress for my self reading taking care of little Clara &C &C

Sunday 28th   the weather cold took breakfast with Father Havens folks and was reading most of the day

Monday March First   a cold day

Tuesday 2nd   the weather cold took breakfast with Father Havens folks was sewing reading &C. received an invetation. to attend a party at M[r] Wells, on the 4th

Wednesday 3rd   a cold day Maria cut an fitted the lining to a dress that I received as a present from my Husband before we were marrid was sewing

Thursday 4th   the weather cold was sewing on my dress. evening went with R M Reb EA & Ch to the party at M[r] Ws [Wells] while there was made acquainted with M[r] Tutle [Thomas E. Tootle], Mercant & Post Master at Auston PO, also M[rs] [misters] Huntsucker [Daniel or Isaac] and [A. J.] Singleton.[16] I danced with them. & M[r] Wells R C & R was the fiddler. Reb & my self tryed to have C take us home about 12 oclock by he would not and so we had to stay till 4 in the morn

Friday 5th Saturday 6th   the weather still cold took breakfast with father Havens folks was sewing on my dress reading &C

Sunday 7th   the weather cold was eating Walnuts & reading most of the day

Monday 8th

Tuesday 9th   very cold weather was sewing on my dress reading taking care of Clara &C &C

Wednesday 10th   the weather cold

Thursday 11th   felt quite unwell. both days was sewing reading &C

~~Thursday~~ Friday 12th   a very cold day staid in father Havens in the AM & took some Salts &C felt quite sick all day was reading

Saturday 13th   the weather cold I was still sick. sewed a little and was reading

Sunday 14th   the weather very cold I spent some of the day reading but felt bad

Monday 15th Tuesday 16th   the weather still cold was reading & sewing but still felt quite poorly

Wednesday 17th   a cold day began to be afflicted with Boils on my limbs

Thursday 18ᵗʰ Friday 19ᵗʰ   the weather cold I was very much afflicted the number of boils kept increasing and became very painfull¹⁷

Saturday 20ᵗʰ   had the appearance of rain in the morn. About ~~10 oclock R & M started to go to Oregon for flower, about 80 miles. I sent for some things by them~~ was reading and sufferd considerabl pain had to lay down

Sunday 21ˢᵗ   the weather pleasent ~~a very cold windy day was on the bed most of the time~~ felt a little better was writing some poetry for Reb and Eliza A walked with them to Bro Williams who lived near by to see his wife who was very sick eat some walnuts and read alittle in the PM Mʳˢ [misters] Tutle & Hunsucker came to see the family. I enquired of Mʳ T if any letters had yet come to the ofice for me. he said there had not. R proposed in case there should not one come by the next mail that T should [write] one for he thought it was a pity that I should enquire every week for letters and still be disapointed so he agreed to do so

Monday 22ⁿᵈ   the weather comfortable was very unwell all day night took sulpher and anointed with sulpher and lard &C

Tuesday 23ʳᵈ   the weather modarate felt quite poorly lay down most of the day night took sulpher and anointed

Wednesday 24ᵗʰ & Thursday 25ᵗʰ   the weather moderate felt some better was reading &C night slept with Rebecca and had a good long talk about our Husbands

Friday 26ᵗʰ   the weather moderate and my health seemed to be improving was reading. and received an invetation to attend a party at Senore, about 8 miles distance on the 30th

Saturday 27ᵗʰ   the weather warm made a little Apron for Clara

Sunday 28ᵗʰ   a pleasent day took a walk with Rebecca R M & EA to the River about ½ mile. We talked much about Samuel & Nathanial and wished often that they were with us. after we returned home Reb & myself went and sat down in the waggon were we had a long talk and enjoyed our selfs much. talking about our dear companions. who now were far from us. and sympathizing with each other &C &C I received a letter from Mʳ Tutle stating that there was no letter in the Ofice for me

Monday 29ᵗʰ   the weather warm I made a little white Apron for Clara in the eve attended a party at Bro Swamlys danced with Charls Robert and Bro Duel and Mr Gass. and about 11 oclock returned home again with Bro Duel to take me to the point to s[t]art the next day

Tuesday 30ᵗʰ   a pleasent day made a sun Bonnet for Rebecca they were all expecting to go to the party but could not get horses to go with I sold Mothers shawl to day & went to Mr Cornays an got the pay in soap pork lard potatoes

Wednesday 31ˢᵗ   the weather pleasent packed up my things and prepaird to take my departure for the Camp father Burtons folks all said they were sorry that I was going and tried to have me stay til the first of June when they expected to go to the Camp. Robert said I was welcome to come when I wishes to and stay just as long as I was a mind to. said he would be glad to have me stay all Summer with them when I was well I enjoyed myself much while there. and when I was sick they took the best of care of me they were all very kind to me about 3 Oclock a little boy came to inform me that Bro Duel was waiting for me about ½ mile of and wished me to go me to go as soon as I could so the boy took my bundle. and I bid good bye to all the folks except Rebecca & Eliza Ann who accompanid me to the Waggon. I there parted with them. after receiving many Invetations to visit them again and promising to write to them. I found Bro Duels family to be very kind and sociable the[y] treated me with the greatest respect. we traviled about 4 miles and at night camped by the Lake

Thursday April first   a fine day I helped Sister D get breakfast & wash the dishes and about 7 oclock we proceeded on our journey. we traviled through a praira found the road pretty good though a little soft in some places I read to them a book called the Golden marri[a]g[e] or Anne the orphan of St. Mary. we traviled about 24 miles to day and at night camped by a Bro Allens were there were quite a settlement of the Brethern. after supper I took a short walk from the waggon. and kneeled down under a tree and offerd up a prayer

Friday 2nd warm but windy. Bro Ds little girl had a chill in the morning which prevented us from starting till 10 oclock we then proceeded ~~and~~ about 4 miles and crossed Cag Creek were there were quite a number of familys belonging to the Church. we traviled about 16 miles & about 5 in the eve incamped by a widdow Smiths house were there were another settlement of Mormons after supper we being sorounded by larg trees. I went and kneeled down under one of them pourd out my soul in prayer to my Heavenly Father that he would protect and preserve Me and my dear Samuel from every danger and permit us to live long upon the earth and do much good in our day and Generation. and be blessed with all things that our hearts should desire in righteousness.

Saturday 3rd a pleasant day started early in the morning. past several Indians and their wigwaams also one of their burying grounds got out of the waggon to se it. one grave was coverd with logs laid in the form of a small crib The bones was laid on the out side of the ground. while passing one of the wigwaams an Indian peaked out. & called to me and said say Squaw come in. say Squaw come in. to day I read in a book called Elonza & Melissa. about 3 oclock we met Bro [Reuben] W Allred going to Cag Creek in a Carriga expecting to come back the next day. so I agreed with him to call at Bro Birds for me and take me home. Bro D told him he did not think he would think it much truble to take me home. for if he was going 500 miles he should be glad to have me go with them for the sake of having my company. &C about 5 oclock I bid good bye to Sister D gave her 2 little girls

10 cents. Bro D took me to Bro Birds and introduced [me] to the family and made arrangements for my nights loging &C he would take nothing for bringing me up only a promis that I would visit them whenever I could he then left me. Bro Birds folks got supper for me. and I spent the night very pleasently

Sunday 4th   a pleasent day in the AM had meeting at Bro Birds Bro Moordock preached a very interessting Sermon after meeting was out Bro Allred arrived. and I proceeded for home. we passed through a bed of Willows. along by the Mo River. and about 3 oclock in the PM arrived at the ferry opposite the Camp the Boat was on the other side of the River and we had to wait untill 5 before we could cross I went home with Bro Allred and took supper I then left my bundle there and started to go home met with Bro Joseph Straton who told me that he had brought up 2 letters for me and had given them to Sister Jane. he gave me an introduction to his Wife &C &C I called at Sister Janes and got my letters she told me that Elizebeth had died one week before she went up to the Tent with me I was Gladly received by Mother who had been quite sick for about 3 Weeks and was still feeble. I then read my letters. found that one of them was one that Samuel had writon to fathers folks in St Louis. and they infoulded in another and sent it to me. I was glad to have one line more from my dear Absent Husband for near six months had past since I had a line from him. I then went home with Jane & stayed all night

Monday 5th   it rained all the AM and until 4 in the PM. I did my Cooking &C and braided 5 yards. I then went to see Uncle Willards folks and spent the evening and night with them. in the eve Amelia and my self went into the ofice and heard a letter read' that the Twelve had writton to Mother [Lucy Mack] Smith which was very interesting. after hearing it. we rose to leave the room but Uncle W bid us stay. said he wanted to have a talk with me. he asked me several questions about fathers Burtons & Havens folks which I answerd according to the b[e]st of my knowlidge. he then spoke about Franklin said he was a good man quick of understanding. and a usefull Man in the Work. but George [Spencer Richards]18 had the brightest Intellect of any of the family. said he was a reall go ahead boy. if he was passing through a wood and should meet with a tree in his path. he would up and cut it down while others would be thinking how to get arround it. Samuel was as good a boy as any of the rest. but he had not had as much experience. Joseph [William Richards] he said would have been a man of deep thought. and sound judgement. but he would not have been a Man of many words. Henry said he is a good boy. in fact they are all good Children and now Mary said he you have been a good Girl you have not come a whining arround because your Husband is gone but you have endured his absence patiantly and you shall be blessed for it. I know your desires are to do right. and to do whatsoever is right in the Sight of God. ~~and~~ and now I will tell you some thing that will comfort your heart. I have been thinking of sendng for Samuel to come home this fall. shall speak to Bro Brigham about it to night. and will tell you before you go home what we intend to do. I told him I was very [glad] to hear of his intendtions. for as yet I had had no knowlidge when he would return. but I hoped when he did he would return in houner having done his duty in the sight of God and Man. for rather than he should do any thing that would injure the Cause of God or put a stain upon his own Character. and thereby have to be called home to give an account of him self. I would rather he would stay ten years. although said I the time seems long. and I want to see him so bad I scarcely know how to wait. til the time comes. but I trust the Lord will give me strenth and patiance to endure all thing through which I may be called to pass. he will Mary said he and I bless you in his name and you shall be blessed both now hence forth and forever. I talked about an hour with him. in which time he told me many things that were very comforting. said he had spent more time [with] me than he had with all his family within two weeks &C &C I then retired with Amelia to her bed Chamber were she read some letters to me &C joust before we retired to bed Uncle W came into the room and told me he had been talking with Brigham and they had desided to give Samuel permision to came home this fall.[19] I asked some questions about F. he said he might have the same privelige in case he was not so engaged as to make it hard for him to leave &C he then laid his hands on my head. and blessed, and kissed me and bid good night.

Tuesday 6th   the weather pleasent took breakfast with Amelia then went to Bro Rockwoods to deliver a messige from Bro Havens folks to them from there I called to see Bro Smithes. also Bro Egans folks to make some enquires for Rebecca. from there I came home' drest and went to Conferance were we had a good time there were 8 of the Twelve present. Bro Brigham spoke of the buisness of the day. after which it was voted and carred that the Twelve be sostained in their place. also the high councel. father was apointed as one of the latter.[20] Bro B & Kimball gave us much good instruction. in regard to the future proceeding of the Camp in this place. &C after which we were dismissed with the Blessings of the Lord. after meeting Maria went home with me and took supper in the eve I was braiding

Wednesday 7th   the weather comfortable. in the AM Bros Benson & L[yman] O Littlefield called in our Tent. the latter told me that he intended to start for England in a few days. and would carry letters or any thing that I wished to send. I told him I should be happy to avail my self of his promis and would write. he said he [would] call and get my letter. the rest of the day I spent Braiding and spent the nigth with Jane

Thursday 8th   a fair day after doing up my work in the Morn I took my braid and went to Bro Smithes to spend a few hours. on my way there I called at Uncles Willards. found him about ready to start for the west in

Company with the rest of the Twelve to search out a resting place for the Saints.[21] he said he had been writing a letter to England and had writton our Samuel to come home this fall. &C I had a very good visit with Sister Smithes and in the eve returned home and was braiding

Friday 9th   the weather pleasent I commenced writing a letter to my Husband and was writing all the time I could get from my work. and from paying attention to the many ladys who called to see us for after we had retired Mother counted 9 that had called to see us. to day Bro [Parley P.] Pratt arrived and I went to see him in hope of getting a letter but was disapointed He said samuel was well[22]

Saturday 10th   a pleasant day &C I gave our tent a regular Cleaning out after which I was writing in my letter and in the eve was braiding

Sunday 11th   the weather pleasent went to meeting. was addressed by Bro Pratt who gave us a history of his travils to England Scotland & Wales.

Monday 12th   the weather pleasent was writing in the eve was braiding

Tuesday 13th   Bro [John] Taylor arrived[23] but got no letters eve Amelia came to see us

Wednesday 14th   the weather pleasent though Windy was ~~writing Braiding &C~~ washing evenings slept with J

Thursday 15th   the weather comfortable was ~~writing & braiding~~ Ironing braiding &C spent the night with Ja

Friday 16th   the weather comfortable in the AM was writing. and in the PM visited at Bro W Millers. with fathher and Mother. and had a very pleasent visit. in the eve Bro Andrew Lamroux [Lamoreaux] came and soliseted me to attend a party with him at the Councal House. said it was the last night Bro Littlefield would be with us. and that he' was very anxious that I should attend &C so he waited upon me there then returned. and waited upon Jane there also. I danced with Bro Lamroux. & twice with Bro Littlefield once as he said for himself. and once he danced proxy for Samuel I also danced once with Bros Joseph Young. ~~& one~~ Right [Jonathan Wright] and another young man whose name I do not remember about 12 oclock we were dismissed with the Blessings of the Lord and Bro Lamroux attended upon us home. this eve I enjoyed myself pretty well had a good talk with Bro Littlefield

Saturday 17th   the weather comfortable. in the AM was cleaning scouring &C in the PM was writing eve was braiding to day gave Father one dollar to buy flower with

Sunday 18th   the weather pleasent in the AM went to meeting was addressed by Bro Taylor who also gave us a history of his journey and Mision to Eng. Stated how the Churches in that Country were being drained of all the money they could spare. by the joint stock Association under pretence that it was to assist them to Emigrate to this Country. While the founders of the Association were apropreating the funds of the same to their own use. and Benifit He also stated how [Reuben] Hedlock Absconded and how they dissolved & put an end to the Association. their future prospects of Emigration. &C &C his discourse was very interesting. after meeting I went to Uncle Levis to enquire of him and Aunt Rhoda. if they had anything they wished me to write to for them to Samuel I gave the latter the privelige to write a scrap to put in my letter but she thought she would not have time I Eat dinner with Uncle L then started to go home on my way called at Sister Maria and Bro VanCotts. also Bro [Lewis] Abotts. Miss Abigill then went home with with me and spent the PM. she braided a ristlet for me of my own hair which I sent to my Husband. eve Bro Littlefield came and invited me to walk to sister Janes with him. witch I did and spent the evening very plesently I tried to appear as happy as possable so that he might carry the news to my Samuel. thinking perhaps it might add to his comfort to know that I was well and appearing happy. I told Bro L many things to tell him. & promised to remember him in my prayers. he then walked home with me. while going he asked me if I did not wish it was Samuel I was walking with instead of himself I told him I would if it was not that it was a vain wish. but as it was' as it was. I was very well satisfide with my company &C &C

Monday 19th   the weather comfortable was Braiding most of the day. in the PM went down to Sister Janes and sat a while with her. heard that Bro [Joseph] Cain who had charge of our letters [h]ad arrived on the other side of the River

Tuesday 20th   The weather rather windy In the AM was sewing. to day Maria [Wilcox] & her babe came to visit us. about 11 oclock Henry came in and said Bro Cain was at Janes. and that he had helped carry a Chest of things there that belonged to Jane & myself.[24] Maria and I then went down to see Bro C and the things. but found the Chest was locked and the Key was yet on the other side of the River. and so was still unable to get our letters. which was the greatest disapointment we met with father and Mother soon followed us. and and we all enjoyed a real feast. talking with Bro Cain about Samuel & Franklin. I think he told us all he could think of about them their wellfare. what they had been doing and how they were beloved by the Brethren and Sisters. and how much they were thought of by Bros Taylor [Orson] Hyde & [P. P.] Pratt. which was no little he assured us. after spending about 2 hours with us he took his leave and we went to the Tent & I got supper after which I went part way home with M to help her carry her Babe. met with Jane and brought her home with me to get supper. she told me she had the letters was 3 for me I wished her to say nothing about them as I desired to have the privelige of reading them myself before any one else heard them. so after washing the dishes I went down and read them. then looked over our things. found all that was mensioned in the letter except my Cloak which was missing. this took us till 11 oclock so I stayed all night

Wednesday 21ˢᵗ   the weather warm in the morn took up my letters and read 2 of them to the family. told H[enry] to go to Janes and get the parsel & fathers the shoes &C then presented Mother with boots and one handkerchief and one dollar in mony for her own comfort. I also gave father a half Sovering in Gold and one handkerchief. after breakfast Sister Jane sent me word that Bro Cain was at her house. so I went to see & talk with him about my Cloak. but he could give no account of it. but said he would make inquires about it and hoped it would yet be found. he stayed about an hour we had another good talk with him about Samuel & F and he seemed to take pleasure in talking to us about them. after he was gone Maria & Amelia came to hear the news and see the presents. I presented Maria with the or a half Sovering which my dear Husband had sent her she seemed much pleased at receiving it. and said she would write to Samuel and F[ranklin]. M[aria], E[lizabeth Whittaker Cain] & J[ane] then went to the Tent with [me] and [I] read them my letters. Our Tent was crowded all day with folks coming in to hear the news see about hats &C today Evaline Potter and her sister Edney Henman [Edna Sarah Hinman] called to see us. I was writing braiding packing away my things &C.

Thursday 22ⁿᵈ   the weather warm commenced writing another letter to my mu[c]h beloved Husband and was writing most of the day. & spent the eve at Bro Millers braiding. to day received a letter that Samuel wrote to Br [Alexander] Badlum in Boston

Friday 23ʳᵈ   the weather pleasent was writing to my Husband eve was braiding Mother was still lame but able to sit & Sew.

Saturday 24ᵗʰ   fair weather was writing in my letter eve was braiding

Sunday 25ᵗʰ   a windy day had a short biusness meeting Bros Taylor and pratt were there and spoke their instructions were very good PM went to Bro Smithis and spent a short time with them then called to see Maria. from there I came home and spent the eve reading

Monday 26ᵗʰ   ~~w~~ a warm day wrote a scrap to put in my letter and sealed them up expecting Bro L to call to day and get them. but he came not. was sewing

Tuesday 27ᵗʰ   the weather pleasent AM was sewing PM visited at Bro VanCotts with mother. I read them one letter that Samuel wrote to me and the one he wrote to Bro Badlam we had a very pleasent visit. after which Mother went home and I went to see Maria on my way there met with Jane and Bro Cain. Jane told me that B[r]other Walter had returned from St Louis and gave me a letter that he had brought from my Brother in that City. in it was one doller which his Children had sent as a present to me. Bro Cain gave me one of Josephs Plates Preaching to the Indians. I then called at Walters & had a good Chatt with him and M. I then returned home. and read my letter and felt very glad to hear that the folks were well.

Wednesday 28ᵗʰ   rather windy was sewing Cooking &C eve was braiding

Thursday 29th AM was very windy was bakeing sewing &C PM Mother went a visiting to Bro Heringtons [Leonard Harrington]. I did not go with her because I had to call at Bro Taylors first and get some letter Papper which my Husband has sent me by him he told me he had promised all the Elders that in Eng that he would go and see their Wives when he got back to the Camp but they had not given him a chance to go and see them for they had all come to see him. except me said I for I came to day to see Sister Taylor and shall live in hopes that you will redeem your word and come and see me. if Sister T [Leonora Cannon Taylor] has no objections. well said he I feel some affraid of going to see the Sisters for the truble is they all fall in love with me. I expect it is some what dangerous said I. but I should be happy to have you bring Sister T with you when you come to see me. and if I should happen to fall in love with you' I will try to keep it to my self. Yes said sister T but they all ask him and never say one word to me about going with him &C & so on. from there I went to Bro Heringtons. & father came and took supper with us. and I spent the eve braiding

Friday 30th a pleasent day was helping to pack up the things for Mooving helped to take down the Tent &C Bro W[illiam] Kay mooved us and our tent to a house on the South line,[25] which is the first house we have lived in since we left Nauvoo on the 19th of May 1846 Bro W[illiam] Miller helped W to load the Waggon also helped Hen[ry] to pull down the house that father had put up in the fall. and we had the timber taken to the house to fence with. after I got to the house I got dinner and Bro K eat with ~~with~~ us. after which I helped cord the bedstead move the bed. and regulated some of the things felt some tired

Saturday May first the weather Windy. washed & scoured all the Tin ware knives &C also the sheets & boxes shelves & the floor. got all things fixt in order. I put on a clean dress & sat down. and our little house seemed to me almost like a Palace I rejoiced to think that after passing through such a dreary Winter living in a Tent. and wandring from house to house to keep from perishing with the Cold. suffering almost every inconveniance and often very unpleasent feelings' I had once more a place I could call my home. after this I took a walk to Bro Grows who lived but a little distance from us. took supper and spent the eve knitting Bro & Sister G accompanied me home found the folks in bed. I kneeled down and thanked the Lord fl for the many blessing werewith he had blessed me and also for the many Blessings he had bestowed upon My dear Companion. and all our friends. and implored his future care & protection. for our Safty & wellfare. told him my desire was to do good. to walk uprightly. to live long upon the Earth. and be usefull in my day & jeneration. I prayed for strenth & patiance to endure to the end. that I might share the reward what was laid up for the faithfull &C &C

Sunday 2nd a very Windy day went to meeting. Bro Pratt arose and said I do not know what I shall preach about for I have got no text to preach from but I want the Brethren to take care of their Cattle. and not lett the Indians kill them all off.[26] to build up the pickets round the City to prevent them from coming in to your houses and insulting your Woman & Children or robing your tables while they are out tending their gardians &C &C Bro Taylor then spoke much after the same the Maner. some other business was attended to after which we were dismissed by father Morley. Bro Littlefield then came and spoke to me. and I told him I had one boon to Ask of him which was that he would come and see me once before he left us for Eng. for I wanted him to tell my Husband that he had seen me living in a house that belonged to our family. he said he would go with me now if I wished. I said I should be happy to have him do so. so he accompanid me home I then went to work & got dinner. he seemed to enjoy it much said he would tell Samuel that he Eat dinner with his father Mother and Wife on that day. and that we talked about him most of the time. he spent the PM with us. I let him read 2 or 3 of my letters and he let me read. and read to me a number several peices of Poetry. we had a pleasent visit with him in the PM. after which I walked with him to Sister Janes. he there left me. and I went on to see Bro Smithes folkes and read them My Brothers letters &C &C I took supper with them, then called to see & spent a few minutes with Ellen Wilding. the she came afew steps with me. and we met sisters West & Parry while speaking with them. Bro Littlefield rode up in a Carrige. and Asked if I did not wish to ride home I told him I had no objections so he assisted me into the Carrige there were 3 ladys in before me. I took a seat by the side of Aunt Fanny Morry who kissed and Carraced me. Bro L took a seat on my lap and so we rode home to day I gave Bro Littlefield my letters and bid him good bye as I thought for the last time till he returned from Eng. the eve I spent with Bro Lennard & his wife.

Monday 3rd & Tuesday 4th   the weather comfortable. did my Cooking &C and alterd me a dress that my Husband sent me from Scotland

Wednesday 5th & Thursday 6th   the weather pleasent did my work as usual. and was writing in my Journal [memorandum?]. had not writton aline in it before since the 28 January

Friday 7th   a pleasent day in the AM Bro Jesse Haven came to see us and I had a good long visit with him his Wife [Martha Spring Hall Haven] was yet at Mount Pisgah in the PM was writing in my Jurnal eve was braiding

Saturday 8th   warm weather AM I cleaned & (s)Crubed the house. PM father took an emmettic. & Sister O Banks [Margaret Phillips OBanks] attended upon him. about 5 oclock Maria & Amelia called to see & spent about an hour with us. Walter was taking Melinda [Malinda Wood] out to ride for her health she having been sick for several Months they also stoped to see us. I walked to sister Janes with M[aria] & A[melia] and got some thread to make a Cape for Sister Snyder. I then returned home and in the evening made it.

Sunday 9th the weather pleasent after doing up my Work in the morning I went to Meeting. Bro Pratt arose and said I had no text to Preach from last Sunday. but today I have got one. he then read a letter that the Twelve had written who were ahead had writton to the Saints in this City. advising them what course to persue this season. after reading which he said' I have heard that some of the Brethren here say that Bro Taylor & Myself. give differant Council than what Bro Brigham & the rest of the Twelve did. they say that we say kill the Indians. but Bro Brigham said we should not kill the Indians. no one has ever heard me say kill the Indians or Bro T either we never said it. but we say you shall not kill them. neither shall you let them come in to the City and kill off all your Cattle or the Cattle of them belonging to the Wives of those who have gone in the Army Army or the Widdows who are among you last Thursday they came and killed off 9 of your Cattle and you let them carry them off with out resistance. and said to them in your acttions if not in words' come again and get all you wish we will not hinder you. we sent out men to follow them and take the Cattle away from them. but they either did nothing or else they were ashamed of what they did at any rate they never made any report of what they did. we told them if they caught any of them to give them a good Whipping. which would do far more good than it would to kill them he then spoke of a Sister (whose husband was in the Army) who was trying to drive in one of her Cattle that had been asstray. she was meeting a herd of Cattle when hers got away from her and joined them she asked one of the Men to assist her to get it back. but he refused and bid her get it back herself and mind her own buisness &C. were is Brotherly love said he. or your feelings one for another that you can thus treat a Woman. whose <u>husband</u> has been called to leave her and is gone to fight your Battles. a man that can do this aught to be <u>Coursed</u> and <u>he will</u> be <u>Coursed</u> he then spoke of the nessessity of the Citys being Picketed in. also a field being fenced in the Plowing being done &C after which he gave way for Bro Taylor to Preach. who arrose and said he did not know how much Preaching he should do but he would tell us a story. said he I once heard of 2 men going to a man to hire to do some work for him. he asked the first what he could do. he said he could do every thing. he then asked the 2nd what he could do. and he said nothing why what did you come here to hire for why I came to hire to work. but this man says he can do every thing. if so the and I thought there would be nothing left for me to do. so I think Bro Pratt has done all that is nessary to be done at this time so I will sit down. we had a very interesting meeting. Bro Pratt seemed to be filled with the good spirit to overflowing. in the intermision I went home with sister Lenard. and took dinner. had a sweet little visit with her. after which we went to the PM meeting. Bro Pratt then arose and said he was going to put some things to vote and he wanted every man & woman to vote for or against so that he might know what to do the first vote was to know whither they Saints were willing to keep Council & follow the heads of the Church carrid it was then voted that none leave this City to go West till the City was Picketed in. and the fencing done. and the Plowing. those who were going on were to labor as much as those who stayed here. and those who stayed by the stuff. should be equel with those who went forth to the war. &C considerable Buisness was done after which the Meeting was dismissed I then went to Bro Smithes to see his Wife as I had understood she was sick. on my way I called at Bro Packs and saw his Wife this was the first time I had been in their house in Winter Quarters. I spent a short time with Bro Smithes folks after which I returned to sister Janes and spent the night

Monday 10th   the weather pleasent had the head ache. Bro Littlefield who I started for Eng. one week before stopped in a Buggy to see me. he for some purpuse or other ha best known to him self having had to return back to the City. I asked him several questions about his journey how he found and left the folks in England if my Husband was well. if he had got letters for me &C &C to which he smiled and answerd as if he knew all about them. he desired me to meet him that evening at Sister Janes as he wished to spend the eve with us both in the AM I was writing in my Journals and in the PM went with Mother a made a visit at sister Levetts. Bro Burrows & his family having just returned [from] Mo I called to see them. they appeard much rejoyced to see me and was very unwilling to let me leave them that PM but I beged off. I had a very pleasent visit at Sister Ls [Levett's] and saw Bro [Stephen M.] Farnsworths folks just from Loup Creek. I then went and spent the eve with Sister Jane & Bro Littlefield. we had a very pleasent visit with him and told him a great many things to tell our Husbands which he said he would remember to do. he wished us if we felt like it. to remember him when we wrote to our Husbands. my headache continued to worse and I requested him to lay his hands on my head and pray for me. this he did & offerd up a most excellent prayer. in my behalf and the behalf of my Husband dear after which he laid his hands upon Jane and prayed for her and F also he then arrose to take his leave. when Jane proposed that we each send a Kiss by him to our Husbands which he seemed pleased to convey. and asked permision to take one for him self. which we permited him to do. we then bid him farewell till he returned from England and wished him a prosperous journey and many enjouments

Tuesday 11th & Wednesday 12th   the weather comfortable attended to my domestic affairs as usual and was writing in my journal. Thursday PM visited with Maria and sent for some things by Walter from St. Josephs.

Thursday 13th   a pleasent day day did a very heavy Washing and got my cloths all dry. & about 5 PM took my sewing and went and spent the eve at Bro Burrows and had a very good talk with them. after which he accompanyed me home

Friday 14th   the weather pleasent I washed a very large washing of fine Cloths & Calico. after which I sprinkled & folded what I had washed the day before. Maria came in the PM and spent about an houre & ½ I was mending me a garment and felt very tired

Saturday 15th   a fine day in the AM was scouring a[n]d cleaning the tin ware chests Boxs &C &C gave the house a good Cleaning PM was Ironing felt very heavy and dull. sister Matson one of our neighbors came in and eat a while with us. in the evening I cut out some blocks of Calico for a bed Quelt

Sunday 16th   a wet rainey day in the AM was reading and wrote a little in my journal. about 2 in the PM I went to sister Janes and took supper at sister Jennes. after which I ~~took Supper~~ went with with with Jane to see her Mother who was very sick & had no one but her Husband to do any thing for her. I washed her dishes &C for her while Jane did something else for her. while there Bro Hyrum Clark came in to pray for her and I had a long talk with him. I had not spoken with him before since he visited my fathers house in England. how much an interview like this, brings to rememberance by gone days after this I returned home with J and spent about an hour then George Snyder accompanied me home.

Monday 17th   the weather windy in the AM cleaned up after the rain. washed the floor &C PM & eve was sewing cutting out Calico &C

Tuesday 18th   ~~the~~ pleasent weather in the Morn Sister Barns came to help me wash Bed Cloths. we washed 6 Quilts 2 Blankets the Tent & Waggon Cover & 5 Woolen Sheets. 2 Bolster ticks & 4 Pillow Ticks. &C &C. we had a very heavy wash. and was very tired. I put the Tent waggon cover & 2 Quilts to soak over night. eve I went to Bro Barrows and borrowed some Coffee for Mother.

Wednesday 19th   the weather pleasent in the morn put out the Quilts Tent &C to dry. then cleaned the house Stewed some apples. made a pye Custerd &C. PM Sisters Jane R. Salley Snyder. & Mary Grow. came and made us a visit. sisters [Henrietta Wheeler] Douglas. Gourdian & Greenalch [Mary Clough Greenalgh] made us a call and spent a short time with us. I had a very severe head Ache most of the day. but enjoyed my company much. eve I walked home with J & S and helped the latter cary her Babe. after I returned home.

Letters to Samuel Richards, January to April 1847

Camp of Israel, Winter Quarters, Ommahas Nation[27]
Jan 29th 1847
 My Dear & Well rememberd Husband. after sitting for some time in silence, meditating upon the many changes' that have taken place since this day Year ago. & contrasting my then happy condition. to my now lonely Situation.[28] at the same time wishing that I could now sit down by your Side. & hear you relate the history of your travils. during our absence from each other. while I in retorn would tell of my sojourn in the Willderness. & finding myself deprived of that happy privelidge. I have now sat down to communicate to you by the penn those things that I would take pleasure in telling you were you but present. In the first place I would say for your comfort. as well as my own. that my health is very good. & has been ever Since I last wrote wich was about the 20th Dec. in answer to yours of the 20th Sep wich I received together with the presents you sent me by Bro Benson on the 28th Nov. I sincerly trust my Dear' that this letter will find you in the full enjoyment. of health. wich is one of Heavens ritchest blessings. together with all the nessary comforts of life. I must say my dear Samuel that it has indeed been a scorce of great comfort to me to hear that our Heavenly Father has been mindfull of you & has blessed you with those desireable Blessings. and my most sincere prayer is to him who holds our destany. is that these blessings may continu [with] you. & that our lives may be preserved. & we permited once more to enjoy each others Sociaty. The health of the family is genealy good' although I cannot write under as pleasent Sircumstances as I could wish for your sake that I could. In my last letter I wrote' that I expected we should have a house the following week. but in that we were disapointed. and have no house yet. on the 7th of this month the weather was so exceeding cold that we were Obli~~d~~ged to leave our Tent. since then I have been living with Jane. Mother has been & is living with Maria. Father comes to Eat with me sometimes. the rest of the time I cannot tell were he stays' only that Henry & he sleep in the Tent H[enry] Eats with me all the time. The weather this season has been remarkably dry although it has been very cold with the exception of a few days. today it is pleasent ~~althou~~ although the Snow is about 3 In deep. itis the deepest Snow we have had this year So I have come up to the Tent. to spend the PM writing to you. I am <u>alone</u> & were is my Samuel! I wonder if he is now thinking of me. or if he at all remembers that this is the ~~day~~ Anniversary of the <u>Day</u> that Sealed our Union then was I for the first time acknowlidged as the Bride yea the happy Bride. of one whom I had long loved Dearer than Myself yea & all

the World beside. yes dear Samuel and the very rememberance of your love & kindness. cheers many an hour of Solitude. then was I indeed happy but was permited to enjoy happyness but a short time e'er the hand of affliction fell upon me. and had it not been for your faith & attention. I must have yealded to it's withering blast. never can I forget the kindess. the Sympathy. & the unceaseing attention with wich you watched over me in that hour of affliction wich often drew the tears from mine Eyes. & caused my Heart to flow with gratitude to my <u>Heavenly Father</u> that he had blessed me with a companion who felt such intrest in my wellfare. & by whose faith I still live. although I had Scarcely Scaled the summit of affliction e'er I was torn from your scoothing Bosem and every day bore me farther from it's carraces. and now 8 months & 6 days have past since I have seen your <u>face</u> and now more than 5 Thousand miles sepperates you from my sight while the wide Expanded Ocean rools between us. & heaves its unsceasing bosem as if prowd to seperate us. from each other. but I must cease this strain. lest I weary your patiance. and if I have already done it I hope you will forgive me' and let me indulge this once in writing my simple thoughts. & the feelings of my heart. it seems & is a long time since I had a letter from you. not any of latter date than the 20th of Sep I have been hoping for some time to receive one from you. but as yet have hoped in vain. Sisters [Leonora Cannon] Taylor & [Nancy Marinda Johnson] Hyde. have had letters from their Husbands in England some weeks go stating that they had incounterd a dreadfull storm. this my dear gave me some uneaseness. but hope kept me from despair. last Monday I had the pleasure of reading the October Number of the Mellenial Star. wich gave me much pleasure to hear that you had arrived in safty to your destined Shore I was surprised to read that you were appointed to go to Scotland ~~did~~ was it agreable to your feelings. I fear you have not had the privelige of visiting my Freinds but if you have I hope you have writton me all the perticulars about them

[*page 2*] last Tuesday I called to see Bro & Sister Fory. who have lately arrived from Nashvill. the[y] were in'tollarable health. from them I learned that Sister Syrus Weellock died about 3 weeks ago. before her death she put her Arms around her mothers neck several times. & Kissed her. saying them was for Syrus. in the PM & eve I viseted with Ellen at Bro Woollys she was well & wished me to write her kind love to you. I must tell you that the Lord has once more rememberd his servants & favord them with a revalation of his will. showing the order wich the Saints must observe on there next journey. Commanding the Saints to be Orgonize in Companies of hundreds fiftys & tens with their Captians each apointing Bros Benson & E[rastus] Snow. to lead a Company Brs Woodruff & O Pratt another. & Brs A[masa] Liman & G A Smith a third the Saints must covenant to keep the Law of the Lord and no Thief is to be permited to have place in our midst. there is a great deal of matter contained in it. & good instructions' and will be of great worth to the Saints who observe & do as it directs it is entitled the word of the Lord there has been quite a reformation this winter amongst the Saints in the Camp. the Twelve have been worning them as I stated in my last letter' to leave of all their Eveil habits an torn unto the Lord and I am happy to inform you that their instructions have taken affect. and that Peace & unity raiyns in our midst. and the Spiret of God is prevelant amongst us. and a good feeling prevails through the Camp. The Seventy's have been building a Councel House it was finished an dedecated last Saturday eve by Bro Brigham. & the Brethren knocked the first slivers of from the floor. this week has been a kind of Jubilee amongst us. last Tuesday the first Company of those that build the House met with their Wives to Scour the floor. on ~~Thursday~~ Wednes the 2ᵗʰ Company met to do likewise. I accepted an invetation from Bro Godard and attended in the PM here for the first time I learned the the way to praise God in Dance. I must give you a little description of it. When the first figure is formed. the one who stands as first makes a few remarks then they all kneel down. & he offers up a prayer they then arise & dance the figure. &C &C the last performance every Man takes his partner or partners. & marches 3 times round the room. & ~~this~~ so praise God in the march. on Thursday the 3ᵗʰ Company met also this day I viseted at Bro Joseph Youngs & had a very pleasent visit

Saturday 30ᵗʰ the weather is pleasent and I am once more alone in the Tent writing to My dear Samuel although I know not were he is or were these lines will find him but I trust just were the Lord would have him be. & just were I would have him be could I but be with him and now I must tell you a little something about your Mary. The last night she went to Singing Scool. & behaved her self pretty well. til after they got through Singing and then if you could only have seen her. a scouring that floor. you would have Surely thought that She felt better than. she did when she was sick. she was danceng almost every figure and a mixing round at a great rate. she danced with Bro Brigham. & when he took her to her seat. he said Sister Mary you have learned me. I am very much oblide to you. dont you think she must have felt well! I will tel you how well she felt. she scarce ever sat down but she was asked why she looked so sober. She told them it was no wonder that she looked sober for that was the Anniversary of her wedding day. & she had no Husband here' to cheer her with his presence. and simelar expresions. so much for Mary. she felt sober dear Samuel. although you might think she felt happy in such a place. but I can Asure you that that is the time that I always miss you for your presence always was the life of all recreations to me and without you I am lonely Oh! when when my dear shall I again be permited to see you. the time seems very long both the past & the future. I feel as an exile an wanderer. although I am sorounded with freinds on every side' who make me welcome & seem to feel intrested in my welfare yet there is no one who can sooth greif. or cheer up my drooping

spirets to be compard with my dear Samuel may the Lord bless you my dear
& prosper you in all your undertakings. labor like a good Steward for your
Master and you shall ~~have~~ have my prayers both night & day. and I feel
satisfide that he will reword you bountifully. do not feel uneasy about me
my dear for I have a father who has watched over [me] from the earlyest
period of my existance unto the present time and who blesses me from day
to day with strenth' & patiance to endure all the trials through wich I am
called to pass and to him be all the glory for ever I have been writing in the
dark for some time so good night my dearest

[*page 3*] Monday Febuary first. a beautifull day almost like Spring I am
at Sister Janes house. yesterday AM I attended a meeting in this Ward. PM
at the Councel house were we were addrest by Bro Woodruff. I should think
from [*wax seal*] preaching now a days. that this ~~Generation~~ Nation had nearly
filled up the Cup of her Inequety and that there must be a dreadfull Crisis'
near at hand. the Lord says fear not your Enemys for they are in my hands
and me thinks he would not say this if there was no cause for fear again he
says fear them not. for they ~~are~~ can ~~my hands~~ not stop my work I should be
glad to write you a coppy of the revalation. if I could obtain one & find it
wisdom to do so. I saw Br Smithes family. last night. they were well and are
doing first rate. they wished to be kindly rememberd to you also that you
would remember them kindly to all their freinds. I must now tell you that
we have got a new Cousen. he arrived in the World on the 19th of January.
he is the Son of Uncle Willard & Aunt Sarah [Langstroth]. his name is Willard
Brigham and a fine little Gent he is. Amelia & all the family are well. also
Aunt Rhoda & Uncle Levis family I asked Mother with I should write for
her. she said give my best love to my dear boys. & tell them I do want to see
them Wolter & Maria. said I might write you lotts of love for them and te[ll]
[*edge of page torn for about nineteen lines, asumptions made as to parts missing are
shown in brackets*] you that little Synthe was doing firstrate and that she was
the fin[est] little neice you had got. she is a sweet pretty Child. Melinda h[as]
had the Ague for nearly 5 months. but is now complaining of being [*tear*]tter
all the time. she wished me to write you' her rememberance. Si[ster] Jennetta
Bleasdale sends her kind respects. Sister Jane says she has n[othing] very
special to say to Samuel at present. only that she wishes him as [*tear*] as she
ever did and she hopes you will remember Jane the promise that was [*tear*]
for her when you did for me. She enjoys pretty good health says she d[oes]
not know but what she is now realizeing that you have done as you [a]greed.
she is about to write to Franklin so I expect he will hear f[rom] her by the
time you get this Philo is gone to Work down in MO. E[lizabe]th [McFate
Richards] has been living with her father for some weeks but returned
[home] on Saturday she is not very well. Mr Claudius' Spencer was mar[ried]
the 24 of Jan to Miss Antoinette Spencer. so poor Andrew has re[*tear*] her.
I have almost forgot to tell you that we had got a Splended [m]ill on the

North Creek nearly Completed. this I have no doubt [will] be of great benifit to the Camp you would be surprized to see [*wax seal*] a large City we have got and so many good houses in so Short a [time] Sidney Rigdon we hear has gone back to the good old Cambleite Church Charles Tomson who joined Strang. has written to the Twelve for admittance into the Church again. compairs himself to a Sheep out side of the fould bleating for admitance. Bro Brigham has got fathers name together with Uncles Willard & Levis in his Company for the west but wether we shall be able to go or not I am quite unprepaird to tell you at present. but I intend to write again in about 3 months then I hope to be able to let you know all the perticulars. I rejoice my dear that it is my lot to be with the Church. seeing I could not accompany you. for I think the water tastes much better to drink it from the founttain head. than it would after it had been carriad some distance through the hot Sun. I received a letter from fathers folks in St Louis on the 30th of Jan dated on the 20th of Dec stating that they were all well & doing so. also that they had received a line from you also that they had writton one for you & sent to Eng. and how you had blessed them with a parting blessing. I think I have told you all the news I can think of at present excepting that there is a company called the Silver Grays. to meet next Friday at the Council House to have a picnic. Fathers [Isaac] Morly. & John Smith the Patriarch. are apointed to Manage & Conduct the affairs of the same. I must now go & get supper for Henry. & myself. wish it was for Samuel & I. I think I should much rather do it but it cannot be. so again good night my dear Companion

Feb 2th PM the weather is very cold & I feel lonely. me thinks if I could only get a letter form you. that said you was well & prospering I should feel more happy. can it be you did not write soon after you arrived. Oh! yes I cannot think you could be so unfeeling' as to do otherwise seeing you could not help knowing that I should feel very ancious to hear that you had arrived in safty. have you visited my freinds. how did they receive you. how are they all. when do they talk of coming West. and what are their prospects. do please to write me all the perticulars. my dear & usue your Influance both by writing. & instructions to have them gather withe the Saints of God. to the place where he in his Wisdom shall seem fit to apoint as a resting place for his people. Give my love to them all & tel them my desires

[*page 4*] tell them they need not be afraid to come out into the Willderness. for their is the place. to learn to serve the Lord acceptable. and there my dear is the place where all those who will not serve him aceptable will meet with a very Unealthy Climate' that will soon wear out their existance. for the time has come all that Inequety must be cleanzed out of Isreal. I pray dear Samuel that you & I m[a]y ever be found among those that walk uprightly that we may have a name and a place with the chosen of God. for what good would it do us to suffer all that we have sufferd should we for a moment ~~torn~~ turn aside from the path of our duty. we have heard nothing from Joseph for a long time but live in hopes that he is well father's Haven & Burtons familys are in Mo about 40 Miles from us I have not heard from them since I last wrote. Henry wishes to be rememberd to you with love &C

please excuse me for writing my letter so full and now good buy my dearest love tis from your lonely Mary H Richards

[*across the bottom of page 4*] the Girl [Elizabeth Caroline Hutchins] that was sealed to Br Jacob Gates about a year ago. died 3 weeks ago & left a small babe. Sofrone Harmon [Sophronia Melinda Harmon Kimball] died last ~~last~~ Tuesday Bro Richard Procter is going to St Louis so I am in hast to finish this to send by him & intend to write one to send to fathers folks. please give my love to Bro Franklin. and tel him I live with his Jane at present. his name is very familiar with us. for it is Franklin & Samuel & Samuel & Franklin about all the time. when my dear shall I ~~hopp~~ hope to see you again or have you no Idea when you shall retorn. I do not want you to retorn til 'tis the will of the Lord that you should do so but I do long for the time to come when I shall again enjoy your sweet company. and when I can unbosem my feelings to you face to face. instead of being writing to you so far a way. I must now conclude praying Heavens choisest blessing may attend you til you return in safty to your lonely Mary beleve me my dear companion I remain as ever your sincere & affectionate Wife Mary H Richards

[*right margin of page 4*] father wishes me to give his best love to you. says he would say be a good boy but he thinks it is no use as he expects you know enough to be good. if you do not there are those among you who can learn you. so much from father. though I expect he did think I would write it all you will perhaps wonder why I did [not] in the fore part of my letter it was because I did not see him so as to have a chance to ask him what I should write for him. his health is some better though he is not very strong. I expect you will find some excellant Spelling in this letter. that will comport with the beautifull maner it is composed and placed to gether but as I have every reason to beleve you are high learned I have hopes you will be able to read it. do write to me often my dear if you love me I know you will. for it is all ways a pleasure for me to write to you. althoug I do not know that my letters are intresting to you. but my sheet is full and I must conclude Oh! that I could but get a letter from you when you write please direct to me in care of father or some one of the Twelve Huntsuckers ferry, Atchingson County, Mo. wishe you would write a letter to father some time when you can I think it would please him

[*left margin of page 1*] think not that you are forgot by me For every day my love grows stronger though between us rolls the restless sea And absence makes the heart grows fonder. the ~~not~~ knot that was tied between dady & sister Morse has slipt. so we find the key that locks will unlock

[*left margin of page 2*] I have said nothing very encoriging aboute our future prospects but I expect we shall all live though the winter to be sure 'tis not very pleasent to have our family sepperated but when we cannot do as we would then we do as we can some of the brethern have agreed to help father about his house when the weather will admit so we may [*left margin of page 3*] but if it should so be that we do not get one we can live as we now do until warm weather then we can live in our Tent Oh My dear do write to me often. I do want to hear from you. I may go where I cannot send letters to you but I shall always be were you can send letters to me then if you love me do write as often as you can.

[*at the bottom of page 2*] Elsie Snyder says give all due respects for her to Samuel Bro VanCotts folks often enquire after you & all wish to be kindly rememberd to you.

[*at the bottom of page 3*] Henry says Scotland as burning. Run for life Boys Run he is the same meray boy as ever

[*addressed to*]
Mr. Samuel W. Richards
Care of Mr. Orson Spencer Esq
No 6. Goree Piazza
Liverpool England
received April 17 1847

Camp of Isreal. Winter Quarters. Omehas Nation.[29]
In a Tent about 6 Rods West of the West Line of the City
April 15th 1847

My <u>Dear</u> an <u>well rememberd Husband</u>. Bros Benson & Littlefield called in our Tent yesterday to see us. the latter informed me that he intended to start for England in a few days. said he would carry letters or any thing that I might want to send to you. I tould him I should be happy to avail my self of his promis and I assure you itis with the greatest pleasure I improve this oppertunite to write to you. although I have written 3 letters. since the date of your last. which was Sep 30th near 8 long Months ago I wrote one in October & sent by Bro [Orson] Spencer. another in December Which Uncle W derected to be left in the Strangers Ofice Liverpool til called for. and a third on the 29th January directed to Goree Piazza liverpool. for four long Months I have Anxiously been looking for letters from you. but as yet have looked in vain. and had it not been that I was blessed with the privelige of reading the Mellenial Star. and learning there from that you had arrived to England in safty. I should long have been suffering that suspense which might be called Misery in the extream oh! my dear has your letters miscarrid or can it be that you have not written to me. if the latter why this neglect. has my Husband forgotten me has he no spare Moments to spend in communicating his thoughts & wishes to me. or have I indeed no claim upon your time or penn if so what have I done that you should consider me of so little consequence. oh my dear Samuel' had you but known' what we have had to pass through this Winter and how long and dreary it has seemed me. without a home save a Tent and without my greatest comfort. that is your sociaty. I am sure you would not have failed to have written to me. Oh! Samuel if you still love and respect me. do write often. I am sure it is the least you can do. if the Stars can come here in safty why not your letters. the above lines are a Specimen of the thoughts & enquires that have past through my mind this Winter. if you are inaccent of course they will not apply to you. and if they should in any ways seem unpleasent to your feelings I sincerly hope you will forgive me and I will try not to scold you any more for the preasent. but will try to write something that will sand [sound] more like sense I made mension in my last letter that I intended to visit father Burtons folcks in Mo. I started for that place the next day being Tuesday. and arrived on Thursday night. I stayed with them six weeks during which time they were all well with the exception of Aunt Haven who had the Ague. while there I was sick for about three weeks I was ~~af~~ afflicted I sopose somewhat after the maner of Job or at least with about 40 of his comforters I could neither stand or walk. sit down or lay down with the least degree of ease or comfort. like Job I tried to endure my afflicktions with Patance. and I expect it has saved me from a worse fate When I was well I enjoyed my self much. and when I was sick they did all they could for my comfort. My health is now quite good and has been for about 3 weeks. but when I retorned home one week ago last Sunday I found Mother had been sick for near 3 weeks. father also was taken sick about the time I got home. their illness is called the black leg this disease commences by the feet swelling' & turning black it continues to assend up into the limbs and if permited to reach the Stomach. it is considerd almost incurable. there has a great many been afflicted with this disease in the Camp. and many now sleep in the Arms of death among whom is Elizabeth Mcfate who died near 3 weeks ago also Mary Pierse. Joseph West's Widow [Lucinda Burton West] has already Chosen ~~B~~ Bro Benson as her future guardian. the black leg is said to arise from the want of Vegatables. Mother is getting much better is now sitting on the bed so as to give us more room in the Tent. she has finished sewing 2 hats which lay by her side' and is now to work on the 3th One of which I have braided since my retorn home. so you see we are not Idle I expect I shall have to work this sommer in order that I may eat. so I have chosen the straw buisiness as my ocupation. so I supose you will have no objections. father is still quite lame but I think he is some better he walks round considerable by the help of his cane. Henry is quite well is sitting on a Chest braiding. Maria & Synthe are well the latter is a sweet little dear. Melinda has been sick all Winter but appears to be getting better Wolter is gone to St Louis on Buisness. is expected back by the first of May. Jane was quite sick for a few days since my retorn but is now well. She is writing to Franklin. Uncle Levis folks & Aunt Rhoda & Uncle Willards folks are all well & send Love to you [*page 2*] if Franklin has received Janes last letter to him. you will doubtless have heard the Melloncholy news of the death of our beloved Brother Joseph' who left this World on the 19th of November a little while before his death he told a person who stood by that he was weary. and if they would call in the Elders to bless him he would lay down and rest. said he was glad that he was were he was that he felt satisfide he had done his duty & Obayed Council. it is said he was perfectly resigned to his fate. Samuel I loved bruther Joseph. he seemed. near & dear to me. I cannot tell why itis that so lovely a young Man should be taken away' in his bloom but 'tis good to be resigned to the Will of Heaven Oh! how much his death caused me to think of my Samuel and pray that his life might be spared to him. how gladly do I recieve & cherish the words' he still lives & is well. let them come from what scorce the[y] may. My dear do pray that we may both live to Meet again. I try to live for your sake and hope & pray that you will live to be a comfort and a blessing to me. for ever more I must now go and get supper' so good night My dear' & the Lord bless you

Friday 16th it is a pleasent morning. and may it be a happy one to my dear Samuel were e'er he may be. Samuel when you read this letter' I think you will be able to judge from the unconnected manner in which it is writton that my mind is in an unsettled state which I assure you it is at present but you will please look over my failings' and I will try to tell you the reason why it is so. I received a letter from fathers folks in St Louis on the 4th in which was infoalded a letter you wrote to them. the former was dated Feb 15 the latter was dated in Glasgow Nov 11th 1846. I was much rejoiced at recieving this letter although it was not written to me. but it was your writting and it gave my me much joy to hear. that you was well. and prospering. also that you had seen my Sisters and ~~One~~ Brothers. tell William & Ellen I feel to Sympathize with them in the loss of their little one. I should have been glad to have seen my little name sake. Richard still sticks to his old trad. I wonder if he would give me a Besum as he did Alice if I should come & see him I should have been glad to have heard from Ann. & Robert and Cousen Magdelene but I sopose you forgot to mension their names. fathers folks were all well. with the exception of Ellen [Briggs Douglass Parker]. She had been sick all Winter but was getting better they said nothing about coming here this Spring. and I think it is probable they will not come this season. they was waiting for a letter from me in order to Ansure yours. I sent one to them a about 2 months ago which I expect they would receive about the time I got theirs On Monday night the 5th I visited at Uncle Ws and had a good long talk with him alone & by his own request. he told me that they had been talking about you in the Council and had desided to give you permission to come home this fall. also that he intended to write a letter to you & F himself before he left the City giving both the same privelige in case F was not so engaged in buisness as to make it hard for him to leave but he said it was altogether for the best that you should come home and he wanted you should. said I had been a good girl. & had not Whined about your coming home. & so he had told me these things for my comfort. he said many things wich I would tel you if you was here but I cannot write them now before I retired he blessed me and said I should see you again for you should be blest and retorn in safty. since that I have seen him once and he told me he had writton to you. he left this City with the rest of the Twelve & the Pioneers on the 9th they are gone to seek in the far West a resting place for the Saints. on the 10 Bro P P Pratt arrived in the City. having left Bro Taylor in St. Louis he feard to come up the River lest it should cause the Missourians to go to the truble of feeding him on State expense. he found one of Brighams horses in St Louis and so rode up it upon it up to this Place. I saw him in the PM & made several enquires about you. he talked very freely with me. tould me he had seen you just nine Weeks before. that said you were well and in first rate Spirits. said you had sent letters and he bleved a parsel to me but the[y] were with Bro Taylor. &C &C Bro Taylor arrived here on the eve of the 13th and I waited as patiantly as I could' til the next day in the PM. so as to give them no reason to complain of my horrying them I then went to Bro Pratts and enquired about the letters. he informed me that their Bagage was at least 60 miles from this Place. that Bro Taylor left them in care of Bro Cane who is bringing them in on Ox Waggon and that they did not travil more than 10 knots a day so he did not expect they would reach this Place before next Sunday.

[*page 3*] I felt as though I could not begin to write til I had seen yours. but I feard I should not have time to write all I wished to write. after getting yours before Bro L[ittlefield] would go. I expect when you read this letter you will think I have mistaken the 3th page for the first. for you will not know were to find the beginning. and I do not know that you will the end I expect if I had your letter now. I should feel like putting this asside and writing a new one. for my Anxiaty is so great to see yours. that I scarcely know half the time. what I am writing. but I think you will have seen by this time why it is that my mind is in such a wandering condition. and I therefore hope that you will make allowances for all my wanderings. there is scarce a day passes. but what we receive ½ a dosen or more calls from the Sisters. and I have to stop and talk with them and so write when I can catch it. it is now time to prepair our evening meal so I must bid you good bye dear Samuel for the present

Saturday 17th this morning was very cold. with us but I pray it may greet you my dear in the full enjoyment of every needfull blessing. father has thought of writting to you & writing such things about the affairs of the Church as might interest you but he has just told [me] that he cannot write at present he feels sick. and I sopose his mind is weak in proportion with body. besides we are yet in our tent. and outside of the City line. & shall have to move in. so he prefers to wait a little while til we get moved &C when he intends [to] write. and hopes to do so under differant sircumstances he wishes me to write his love to you and Franklin. I just been trying to get Mother to write a few lines to you' herself and I think she will do so since writing the above. Amelia has been here. & brought me a letter. which you wrote to Br Alixander Badlam. dated Nov 13th & 25 he sent it to me by Bro J Little who has just arrived in the Camp. he was in such haste to join the Pioneers. that he had not time to call & see us. this letter speaks of F being sick also of your healths being poor. I am sorry to hear this. for it seems to me as though I would much rather suffer than to have you soffer. but I must submit to the will of <u>Heaven</u>. you also speak of Martin Harris being in Eng. Bro Pratt in the course of his Sermon last Sunday. said while in New Orleans he saw a letter. writon by a Reverant Gent. to [*hole*] he soposed to be his friend in that [*illegible*] after he [*hole*] in Eng. 2 Weeks. he had a Revalation to retorn home. [*hole*] said he got his Revalation from Bro Banks as it regards the [*hole*] the Camp. you will be able to learn more from Bro Littlefield [*hole*] can posabley write. the Twelve have left their familys and gone [to seek] a place for the Saints to gather to. but [*hole*] you [*hole*] you will no doubt have many chances to talk with them [*hole*]. Oh Samuel were I but sure that you would come home this [*hole*] one thinks the summer would pass away like [*hole*] but to [*hole*] forward to next Spring every month seems like a year [*hole*] but it is the will of the Twelve that you come home this fall and I hope you will. Samuel. as much as I love you was it not for the [*hole*] of the Twelve. I should be the last one to say to you come home. [*hole*] want you to do whatsoever is right in the sight of our Heavenly Father and as I said to Uncle W I now write that I would rather [*hole*] you should be absent from me 5 years. than that you should ever do anything. that would put a stain upon your Character. or do Ingury to the [*hole*] in which you are now ingaged. my prayer continualy is. that the Lord will bless you with his holy Spirit to gide and direct you into [*hole*] truth and make forever unto you all things which your heart des[ires] in Righteousness. that your life may be preacious in his sigh[t] and that you may live to do a great Work upon the Earth. do not think me cold and different dear Samuel because I write thus. itis far from me to be so.there is no Woman can think more of her <u>Husband</u> or <u>love</u> him <u>dearer</u>. than I do you itis imposable neighter is there any one that would love to be in the sociaty of their Companion better than myself. Monday 19th [*hole*] was so cold & windy yesterday. that we didnot have meeting Mother wrote one page a letter to you & F Father then commenced writing and is now filling up the sheet. I expect he will write you all the perticulars about the City. [*hole*] they are now doing. and what they intend to do this summer also the [be]seechings of the Church so I forbear as he has given me to understand that is [his] intention. I expect you would like to to hear something concerning the sircumstances of our family. as it regards useless things. we are [*hole*] to ritch for our comfort while [*washed out*] besides things that are [*hole*] to us others dont want to ~~buy buy~~ buy.

[*at the top of page 4*] provisions we have not had none for a long time except what we have bought I have paid out considerable Money already. and expect to do so long as I have any. Joseph sent 20 dollars to father wich has been a great help to us Mother has sold 5 hats this Spring and got good pay for them. but Henry dont love to braid. and I expect our own work is about all we have to depend upon. father is making great calculations about planting. but I am an unbelever in the Thery of counting Chickings before they are Atched. father laid the foundation for 2 houses last fall. or rather 2 large rooms joining together one he intended for a basket Factory and calculated to have 4 or 5 Women work there as an addision to mothers comfort by the bye. the other for us to live in. but I fear he forgot to count the cost before he commenced or at any rate he failed in doing either w[h]ere as if he had only been satisfide to have built one room as others had done. the Brethren would have torned out & helped to build it. and we migh[t] have been living in a comfortable house all winter. but it is past now. and I hope we shall all learn wisdom by the things we have sufferd. Sister Morse I wrote you is no longer counted as one of our family at present except my love to <u>your self</u> I am your Mary H R

[*at the bottom of page 4*] April 26th a few lines [*hole*] before I close my letter. yesterday was a very pleasent day we had meeting at the [*hole*] Brother Taylor preached us an interesting discourse and spoke of all [*hole*] England. in the highest terms. after meeting I went to see Aunt Rhoda on porpose to enquire if she had any thing to say to you & invited her to write a [s]crap to put in my letter. which she promised to do if she could get time. but desired me to tell you that she often thought of you & F and wished she could reach your [*hole*] wished you all the good you needed &C &C Aunt Sarah also wishes to be rememberd said she would write a note to you. Uncle Levi Says he feels [*hole*] Congratulate you in your high calling and Trusts you will prove your selfs Worthy of the Trusts commited to your Charge &C &C on my return home I called at Bro VanCots who enquired much about you & your [*illegible*] of which I told them considerable Mother V seemed to be very much interessted for you. I do think she thinks a great deal of you she wished very much to be rememberd. and also Sister VanCot. Oh my love I do love that <u>family</u> they are so <u>very kind</u> but I must [*hole*] to a close. and bid you good bye for the present and beleve me dear Samuel [to] be forever your affectionate Wife Mary H Richards

[*margin of page 4*] I expect when you return the folks will expect us to live ~~retorn to~~ with them as we did before you went. but if you should wish to know my mind on this subject I would much rather <u>live alone with you</u>. were I could do and have things to suite my own notion this is a matter dear to my heart. Samuel and I long to see the time when we shall enjoy it. I have heard the saying when youve got a wife you think youve gott all things. then you want every thing else but a Wife. you have got a wife my dear I am Glad to acknowledge but you know she is not posessed of riches aside from the ritches of the kingdom of God. So you can use your best judgement in what you bring. if you will direct letters to me. Auston Post Office near Huntsuckers ferry. Atchingson County Missour[i]. I am acquainted with Mr. Thomas Tutt[l]e who has charge of the Ofice and he has promised to forward direct to me. and do let me hear from you often I shall write to you again in about 2 months so no more

[*margin of page 1*] Bro & sister Smithes are well and wish to be rememberd to you and that you would remember them to their Brothers & Sisters and to all our friends I spent one week with them this winter. and enjoyed myself much. please to give my love to all my Brothers & sisters. tell them I often think of them all & wish to see them when you write again please to say how Ann is I would love to hear from her.

[*margins of pages 2 & 3*] I will here speak of the [*tear*] I spoke of in my other letter the Cloke you sent me I have not got & had thought to say nothing about this for the sake of Bro Cains feelings. but I saw him yesterday and he requested to write and let you know it. there was a sister who had charge of the keys for a few minutes. whom they mistrust having taken it out of the Chest. Bros Taylor & Pratt are going to write to her she is in St. Louis. so I expect when I write again I shall be able to tell you the result. if I should not get it I shall need another very much. as my Josey or Cloke I wrote you was milldewed and spoiled together with a number of other things. Last Summer the things you sent me are as usefull as as any things you could have sent. if you use as good judgement about all other things you will do well

[*addressed to*]
Mr. Samuel W. Richards
Care of Mr. Franklin D. Richards
6 Goree Piazza
Liverpool, England
received Sept 28th 1847

[*addition to the previous letter*][30]
Tuesday 27th My dear Samuel it is a pleasent morn and I expect Bro Littlefield ~~ey~~ every moment to call for my letters. but I thought While he lingerd I would write one more line to you. my health is very good. Mother is quite Smart. she has all the Straw work She can do. people flock in by the holsale to get hats made. Bonnets cleaned &C &C father seems to be gaining for [s]ame is in pretty good spirits. you ask who I take the most comfort [*hole*] with Mother when at home. and a great deal of comf[*hole*] [Jane] & kiss her often and tell her I could ten times rather [*hole*] have our jokes. to keep us from getting the Blues. I [*hole*] comfort with Maria and Melinda & Amelia.

A. has just got a [*hole*] Aunt Nancy [Nancy Richards Peirson]. and all the folks were well you speak of Merrym[ent] your Mary is such a merry Girl she ~~sh~~ takes Merryment with all her friends and would with you I expect if you were only here. for she used to take the most comfort with you of any one when you was here. My dear I often [think] of the time when we parted and wonder if you ~~think~~ look upon me as I then ~~as~~ felt. for I was a Child in feelings and more so' in Actions. I was weak in body and weak in mind and now do tell me if you look upon me in that light. and if I write or do any which you think is not right be free to tell me for I shall and do take comfort in doing any thing that is pleasing to you and want to do all I can for your comfort

[*page 2: a short poem in the left margin has a hole in most of it, so only the first part has been copied*]

> You cannot see me now my Dear
> Oh! no it cannot be
> But here is one lock of my hair
> View it and think of me. . . .

Jane has just been in our Tent and says I may give you a liberal portion of her love all she can spare from Franklin must so you will please accept it. and please to give a liberal portion of my love to F all I can Spare from you and the rest of my friends in <u>Eng</u>-tell him that I say Jane is a firstrate Girl. but I expect he knows it. Aunt Rhoda has just sent me word she cannot write now but wishes me to say she thinks more of you now than she ever did when you write again please say how Ann and her family is and Robert if you know any thing of them. and also dear Cousen Magdelene and all my freinds how do you like them was you much disapointed in them did they treat you well. & 40 11 questions I would be asking you if you were only here. I shall look for you home this fall. & please write what time you think you will start. good buy my love I am yours forever Mary H R

CHAPTER SEVEN

"These Hills are the Works
of thy hands"

Mary's ongoing illnesses became more frequent. She received various herbal treatments along with the spiritual treatment of laying on of hands. Despite her discouragement, her religious faith remained constant, as she continued to offer thankfulness to the Lord for his guidance, care, and protection. Her awareness of her own physical weaknesses gave her more understanding and concern when she heard that Samuel had smallpox, and Mary anguished that she was not there to watch by his bedside. Being able to appreciate beauty was solace during her trying times. Taking a walk on the bluffs with friends, Mary wrote of the "beauty full" gardens and extensive fields. The range of "projecting bluffs" towering almost "perpendicular" overhead, created a "romantic" scene as she rode to visit at Keg Creek, twenty miles from Winter Quarters. As a solemn awe overcame her at the beauty surrounding her, she uttered, "O God . . . these Hills are the Works of thy hands."

Journal Four
Thursday, May 20, 1847, to Tuesday, November 2, 1847
Winter Quarters, Nebraska[1]

Journal & Memorandon of Mary H Richards Commencing Thursday May 20th   this Morning it rained and seemed very Gloomy and my feelings were about as Gloomey as the weather. My head Ached and I felt sick after breakfast I lay down a little while. then got up and cut out a night dress and presented it to Mother. I then learned that Bro [Joseph A.] Stratton was going to preach Bro [Isaac] Davis Funeral Sermon so I got ready and went. Sister [Sarah DeArmon Pea] Rich called and went with me. just as I got seated Sister Jane came to the door & beckond me to come out she then went into the house and gave me a letter that Bro Hyde had brought me from My Husband. She told me that Bro H said that my Husband was very

Sick with the small Pox when he left England. had sent for Franklin to come and take care of him. but while he [Orson Hyde] was in New York he got a letter from F stating that he was getting better and was able to be arround. I then read my letter and found it was but 2 weeks latter date than my last. there was nothing in it about his sickness. he was then well and prospering. Oh! I <u>was</u> glad to receive this letter. but to hear that he was sick made me feel very very sorrowfull I <u>wished oh! -how much I wished-that</u> I could <u>fly</u> to <u>his assistance</u>. to watch by his bed and <u>comfort him</u> in the <u>hour of his affliction</u> Oh My Father in Heaven do thou look down upon him I but Intreat thee. in the Multitude of thy Mercy and forgive whatsoever thou mayest have seen amiss in him. and oh let it please thee to spare his life and permit him to return to me in safety. may he be one Whom thou wilt delight to honner and bless. and may he stand as a mighty Pillar in thy Kingdom. and may he be one that shall help spred it forth unto the ends of the Earth and may we both be blessed with the desire of our hearts in as much as our desires are in Rightousness before thee. hear and answer the prayer of thy handmaid I humbley ask thee in the Name of Jeses My redeemer Amen after I had read my letter I returned to the funral and heard bro Stratton preach his discourse was very interesting after I got home I reread my letter took dinner and in the PM went with Sister Mattison and made a visit at Bro [Edward] Hunters the ladys were sociable we had a very pleasent visit and an excellant Supper. & stayed till 8 oclock in the eve. when I got home the family had retired. and I bowed down and besought the Lord to spare the life of and bless my dear companion with every needfull blessing. &C &C

Friday 21st   the weather pleasent AM was sewing. PM went to make a visit at Bro Abbotts. but before I went in I went to the Store and bought me some Calico for Aprons. Cotton Cloth to line my dresses Candle weaking thread &C. called to see Sisters Smiths Douglass & Maria. While at Bro Abbotts in the PM I got acquainted with Sister Marthe [Monks] Pratt who had just arrived from England. eve I went into Bro P P Pratts and saw all his ladys and received a very pressing invetation to make them a visit. Marthe said I do love you Sister Richards because you came from My Country Abegill and myself then went into Bro Van Cotts and spent the evening I read them an extract from my letter. I then spent the night with Abegill we talked till 1 AM

Saturday 22nd   the weather fine in took breakfast and spent the AM at Bro Abbotts and after eating dinner Abegill went into Bro Van Cotts with me. I told Bro VC that I would make a hat for him if he would wear it. he told me he should be very Glad of to have a good strong hat but he could not wear such as we made because the[y] would not stand the Wind. but said he ba thanked me just as much as if he received one. for my kindness &C &C I had a very pleasent Visit with them for about one hour & ½ then Henry came and told me that Aunt Amelia and Jane had come to make us a Visit and desired me to come home so I obeyed him. when I got home found that Jane had presented Mother with a new dress and A and her was making it. little Rhoda Ann [Jennetta Richards] was with them also. I visited with and waited upon them in the PM got Supper &C. I enjoyed their company much although I ha had a very hard head ache. eve walked with them to Bro Redfields where I called and got 2 letters one from Rebecca Jones. and the other from Eliza Ann Haven. also some other things which I left behind me at father Burtons. which they sent by Bro Redfield. from there I went to Janes were I found H and whom I helped to carry home a peice of meat. after I got home I read my letters and felt glad to hear from my freinds

Tuesday 23th the weather seemed to threatton rain all day but it kept off till the evening. AM I went to meeting. it was one of Buisness. Bro Pratt reported to the Meeting that Bros [David] Boss & Sescians [Sessions] had withheld their Cattle from the plow field. that the former had 8 Yoke and the latter 5 he then told them of their Covnant the Sabath before. and reguested them to make known their reasons for keeping back their Cattle. Bro Taylor then arose and stated that Bro Boss according to his agreement had payed a Man for herding the Cattle. said as far as he had done right he should have Credit for it. Bro Boss then arose and told his reasons for not letting the Cattle work. said they were poor and he wanted them to get strenth so that he could go on West &C &C. Bro Pratt then said that no one should leave this City to go West untill they had got a certificut from those who were apointed to Manage the affairs of the same. Sa stating that they had done their plowing Picketing and every thing they had covnanted to do. said if any went without this they would have to go under the name of the Anti Plowing & Picketing Company Bro Taylor then asked the Congregation Why it was that they had to talk so much when you Covnant to do a thing said he why dont you do it. and act honerable like Men what need is there of so much talk day after day and sabath after Sabath. go to work and do as father Morley shall direct. Work together in unity as Brethren. for in unity there is Strenth. let evry Man do his duty and walk uprightly these and many other remarks were made after wich the meeting was dismised. I then went to Bro Rockwoods and told them I had heard from father Havens folks. and enguired if they had heard any thing from Sisters [Elizabeth Haven] Barlow & [Mary Ellen Haven] Palmer &C called to see Sister [Clarissa Aurilla Terry] Scofield were I met with Bro Jesse Haven and had an intersting visit with him. We talked of by gone days when we were in the <u>House</u> of the <u>Lord</u>. and rejoyced in the rememberance of what we then enjoyed. from there I went to Bro C Richs to enquire of him about Wm Burtons folk. he having just returned from Nauvoo. I there took supper and had a pleasent talk with his ladys after which I returned home and received a call from Sisters Lennard & Moses I then wrote a letter to Rebecca Jones and retired

Monday 24th a very rainey day was sewing most of the day and wrote a little in my journal. had the head Ache and felt very gloomy all day

Thuesday 25th the weather pleasent felt quite unwell in the morning got Breakfast after which Sister [Hulda] Barnes came to help me wash. we washed 2 weeks washing 3 large comforters & a bed Tick our work was very heavy today and made me feel very tired I also received a visit from Mrs Henryett Douglass

Wednesday 26th the weather pleasent AM Mother went to Marias to make a visit and I did a large Ironing. PM was sewing. &c &c

Thursday 27th the weather very warm I Ironed a very large Ironing of fine Cloths &C which I had Washed 2 weeks before. I felt very ill all day. Lovice & Olive Jenne came and made me a visit eve Sister Mattson came and sat a While with me.

Friday 28th the weather very heavy & and warm. was so hoarse with a cold that I ~~coul~~ could scarcely speek aloud. felt quite unwell through the day. AM did my work as usual and was sewing PM Cut & fitted a dress for Olive Jenne. wrote a little in my jounral &C then took my sewing and went and sat about 2 hours with Sisters Wilder & Matson they being our new neighbors. had an interesting ~~visit~~ talk with them about the Principals of the Gospil after which I came home got supper Molded some Candles &C to night Mother returned from her visit having been gone since Wednesday

Saturday 29th the weather louring and heavy. Scoured my Tins boxs &C and cleaned the house wrote some in my journal was sewing &C &C

Sunday 30th the weather windy ~~AM went to Meeting was addressed by Bro Hyde~~ and in the Morning it rained. after doing my mornings Work Washing the floor &C. Bro O Hyde called & spent about one hour with us. he told me my Husband was very sick with the Small Pox when he left Eng. and had sent for Franklin to come and take care of him but said he received a letter from F while in New York. stating that Samuel was Getting better and was able to be arround. this last inteligence gave me ~~me~~ much comfort. father then asked him if he thought the Boys were Competant to fill the Stations they were placed in. Bro Hunter then came in and interupted the conversation for a few minutes after which Br H spake as follows. in regard to the question you was asking me Bro Richards Said he I was very much disapointed in the Boys I always thought they were good Boys-but the fact is I found them to be far better than I ever expected. he then told me how much they were respected & beloved by the Saints said many things about them which were very comforting to me. said he considered them the most competant of any that was in the Old Country. to fill the place or Station in which the[y] were now placed. said there was some feeling amongst some of the Brethren about their being put there but he told them that the Wisperings of the Spirit to him was that they were the Ones to be put there. and in order that they might have no feelings about Bro Samuel he being

One of the Seventys I ordained him a high Priest he then asked me if I knew what the Twelve had writon to Eng. before their departure I told him that Uncle W told me that he had writon for Samuel and F to come home this fall. that he had Counciled with Brigham about it and they had decided that it was Wisdom for them to do so &C said he I promised the Brethren in Eng. that I would write to them after I got to the Camp and I wanted to know What the 12 had writon so that I need not write any thing differant from them. after he went away. I went to Sister Douglass to see her Child he having been very sick. I then called to see Maria and she walked with me to the Meeting. were we were addrest by Bro Hyde on differant Subjects which were very interesting. in the course of his sermon he said. Brethren the question is often asked when shall we rest from our labours. I will tell you it will be with you as with a labouring Man. Who comes home at Night weary and tired and lays down upon his bed to sleep. he rests from the labours of the day. awakes in the Morn refreshed but can scarcely realize that the Night is gone. so will you lay down in the Grave and rest from all your labours. and awake in the Morn of the Resurrection refreshed and full of vigure. and the time that you will sleep will appear to you as the sleep of the Night to the Weary Man. &C &C after Meeting I had a long talk with Sister Carter. then called to see Jane a few Minutes after which I returned home and ~~wrote~~ ~~a~~ spent the eve at Bro [John] Welchs

    Monday 31ˢᵗ   fine Weather AM washed a consideable large washing. PM braided 4 Yards. eve foulded up My Cloths &C

    Tuesday June first   a pleasent day AM did My Ironing PM Braided 5 Yards

    Wednesday 2ⁿᵈ   a very rainey day did my Work as usual and Braided 6 Yards about 2 oclock PM Bro Robert Burton called to see us having just arrived with his Wife Sister & Eliza Ann Haven from Mo to visit our City. he said the Girls were all very anxious to see me. I invited him to bring them all down and make me a visit he Promised to do so the next day. about 5 PM the rain seaced and I went up to sister Janes to see Rebecca & her Child stayed a little while with them then returned home. the Street was very Muddy.

    Thursday 3ʳᵈ   the weather pleasent morning I stewed some Apples. picked over some Goose Berrys and made a cupple of Pyes a Cracker Pudding &C AM R Burton and his Wife & Sister and EA Haven came and made me a visit. they talked Much about My dear Husband. & Wished Maney times that he was with us. I shewed them some of the Presents that My Husband sent me. read them some of his letters. & gave them Parleys love letter to his Wife[2] to read. they seemed to enjoy their visit Much. They took dinner with us. after which I went & visited with them at Bro William Kimballs. on our way there called to see Sisters Everit [Sarah Ann Everett] & [Catherine Walker] Fuller who were about to start on their journey to the

West. we had a pleasent visit good supper and enjoyed ourselfs Much. called in to see Sister Kimball and spend afew Minutes with them. also called to see bro Smithes folks. eve Rebecca came home with me and staid all night W K [William Kimball] and R B [Robert Burton] accompanied us home

Friday 4th   the weather very warm after getting Breakfast and doing up my work in the Morn I took my sewing and went with Rebecca to Sister Marias to make a visit. R[obert] M[aria] & E[liza] A[nn] soon joined us. and we enjoyed our selfs Much. PM we went into Store & traded. afterwards we went to the Mill and the Miller took & shewed us through every department of the same. it was then in Motion. we were well pleased with our visit there. we then went up on the West line and saw Sister Rice. after this Maria W[ilcox] Eliza A and Myself went down to the River & found the Ferry Boat about ready to start. Bro W[illiam] Young. invited us to take a sale across. Bro Wolter being on the other side we accepted the invetation and went. found Robert B there who returned with us to Sister Marias. Eliza Ann then went home with me and spent the night

Saturday 5th   the weather pleasent AM cleaned the house and Eliza made the scirt of my dress for me. PM she visited at W Kimballs and I went with Mother to the Store to trade off some hats which she did today I bought a tea bottle and a Water Pail from the store & went to Bro [Abel] Lambs and bought me a wash Board. from there returned to Wolters and received from him 5 dollers Worth of Groceries and Goods that he had brought me from St Louis. Henry carried them home for me. I then went to Bro Smithes and made a short visit eve called at the W Ks for Rebecca who came home with me and spent the night. on our way we called at Wolters and he accompanied us home. after we retired Rebecca & myself spent about 2 hours talking about our absent Companions oh May the Lord ever bless them and return them again to us in safty. tonight I received my Cloak that I thought was lost

Sunday 6th   the weather quite Windy after doing my Mornings Work I went with Rebecca to Bro Rockwoods were she dressed herself & child and we returned to meeting. were we were addressed by Bro Taylor in a very able and interesting Maner. he exorted the Saints to be deligant in doing their duty. and in keeping there sacred Covnants and walking uprightly before God. and keeping all his Righteous Commandments after Meeting I returned with R to Bro Rockwoods were we took dinner in company with Robert. Maria. & Eliza Ann. after dinner they bid us good bye and went down to the River expecting to start for home. after parting with them I called to see Sister Robings. and she accompanyed me to the Meeting were we were addrest by a Universalian Minester. he sang a hymn then Preached us quite a lenthy Sermon took his text in the 15th Chap of Mark 15th & 16th Vers after he got through Bro [Benjamin L.] Clap Answered to him in a very able maner. he then spoke again in Answer to Br C & Bro C in answer to him. the meeting was very interesting as it gave us oppertunity of judging

~~betwea~~ between light and darkness and stirred up our Pure Minds by way of rememberance. after Meeting I called to see Jane afew Minutes. then returned home. found Rebecca there she having been disapointed about crossing the River she stayed with us all night. to night father received a letter from my Husband

Monday 7th   it rained in the Morn and was very Muddy. after breakfast I accompanyed Rebecca to Bro Meeks were they waited for the Wind to cease in order that they might cross the River. here I bid them good bye and went to Bro Smithes and made a visit Mrs. Smith. Robings [Robbins]. & Miss Noon visited with me I Cut fited and made the Waist of a dress for Mary Smithes. we had a very Pleasent visit. evening I called in the Store with Mrs. Robings. and from there I proceded home

Tuesday 8th   the weather heavy and dull was writing in my journal sewing &C &C

Wednesday 9th   the weather very unsettled I commenced writing a letter to My Husband. eve was sewing

Thursday 10th   the weather pleasent AM was cleaning. sewing. &C PM ~~was writing on my letter~~ I visited at Sister Janes with Mrs Davis and Sophia Whitecar [Sophia Whitaker Taylor]. had a very Pleasent visit. also called and bid Sister Taylor good bye

Friday 11th   weather comfortable ~~was writing in my letter sewing~~ I took Breakfast with Jane. and about 2 oclock went to see Bro Smithes folks and bid them good bye they being about to start to the West. May the Lord bless them and bring them to the end of there journey in Peace and safty. I also called to see Bro Cains folks and bid them good bye. I then stoped a few minutes with Sister Jane and read some letters that Bro Cain had received from our Husbands. while there Amelia came, and after spending a ~~few~~ short time talking with her I returned home. and spent the rest of the day sewing had the head Ache very bad

Saturday 12th   the weather lowry & wet AM I cleaned the house &C &C PM I was writing in my letter. eve sewing

Sunday 13th   the weather pleasent AM I went to meeting it was one of buisness, after which I went to Bro Woollys and took dinner. while there Miss Susan One [Susanna Wann Hunter] called in and after staying a short time then she and myself started on our way home together. I called with her at the Post Ofice she then called with Me to see Sister Pratt who had just arrived from Nauvoo. had a short Pleasent talk with her. then called to see Sister Jane and spent a short time with her. after which we came to Samuels Woollys who is one of our nearest Neighbors and took Supper in company with Sister [Ann Stanley] Hunter. Sister H and Susan then came home with me and spent the eve

Monday 14th   the weather comfortable I did my work as usual and wrote a letter to My Father and Brother

Tuesday 15ᵗʰ   pleasent weather attended to my work as usual and wrote a scrap to put in my letter to my Husband also some in my letter. today I did not feel well.

Wednesday 16ᵗʰ   the weather pleasent I felt quite unwell all day was sewing writing &C

Thursday 17ᵗʰ   pleasent weather AM was braiding. today Wolter & Maria came to bid us good bye intending to start in the Morn for MO. where they intend to spend the Sommer and probabley the Winter. I finished and sealed My letter in hast. got Maria to put on the address and sent it by them to MO. the Lord bless and prosper them. & speed my letter to my dear Companion. Oh! may he be blessed with health and every good and be permited to return to Me soon and in safty to day I felt very unwell

Friday 18ᵗʰ   today it rained and was very stormey. I was braiding most of the day helped Mother about the Work. though I still felt quite ill.

Saturday 19ᵗʰ   the weather pleasent AM Cleaned the house Scoured the Tinware &C &C PM was braiding. still felt ill.

Sunday 20ᵗʰ   a pleasent day after doing up my work in the Morn I went to Meeting. Where we were addrest by Bro O Hyde. on varyous subjects. he spoke of the absence of the twelve and how he was now the only one left of his [*blank space*] to instruct and teach the Saints both on this & the other side of the River and now Brethren said he if I am to be your teacher & instructor. I want my word to be <u>Law</u> and an end of his [*blank space*] on all matters, and when I say to a Bro restore that Ox to its right owner I want that Bro should do it. &C and now said he if you would rather have any other one to lead you' you may appoint who ever you please (but I will be very sure to lead that man) and my word will have to be law to him.) It was then voted and carryed' that we accept Bro Hyde as our instructer and that his word be the law &C. he then stated that he was going to preach some strong Doctring. said there was a Man in the Congregation who had 40 dollars of Bogus Gold in his Pockit and who made his living by making it &C. now said he if that Man will come to me after the Close of the metting. and give me that Gold' and then go with me down to the River' and see me throw it just as far as I can into the River. and then promis that he will never handle the acorsed thing again his name shall not be exposed and he shall be forgiven. but if he does not do this his Priesthood shall be taken a way from him and he shall be Cut off from the Church. he then spoke of some of the Brethren who had been induced to join the Bogus makers. and had found themselves under Covnants not to expose them &C it was then Motioned and Carrid. that all such be released from these Covnants and from this time forth have full liberty to go and tell Bro Hyde the Perticulars of all such Secrets. He then spoke in regard to the Children of the Saints' being allowed to Profane the Name of the Most High in the Streets. he also said there was men who ~~had~~ held the Priesthood and who had Covnanted in the House of the Lord not to ~~take~~ take his Holy name in vain. who were heard to use Profane language. he then reguested the High Council to see to this matter. and when ever they heard a Bro Profane the name of Deiaty to take away his Priesthood and disfellowship him from the Church. said had aught to be Coursed and they would be Corsed. he then advised the Saints to have Scools' and send all their Children there to. and let them learn how to behave themselfs. and if their parents could not learn them behavour let them make it known to the Council. and let the[m] devise ways wereby they may be brought into Subjection &C &C his descourse was very interesting & much to the purpose. after meeting I called to Bro Millers & spent a few minutes then came Home felt very unwell and lay down. eve Sister Woolly came in and sat a while with us

Monday 21st the weather Pleasent in the Morn I felt very sick got up and Lay down again before breakfast. after breakfast I went to washing' thinking perhaps I could work off my illness' but this I failed to accomplish. PM I went to Bro Lennards and carryed home a hat that we had been making for him. staid and took supper with them. and sent for some cotten batten by them to Mo. eve returned home and was sick throug the night

Tuesday 22nd the weather very warm in the morning I was very much destressed with pain' and had not happitite to Eat. AM Sister O Banks Came and gave me an Emetic. before I took it I went into a Steam. also after my Emetic had opperated. also took 2 Injections. after I got through and rested a while I sat up and Braided One Yard. and Eat some supper. I then felt very tired and retired to bed. was along time before I could Get to Sleep it was so very warm and the bed bugs trubled me considerable. night rested tollarable

Wednesday 23rd weather very warm in the morn I was very Sick and suffering under severe pain. about 7 oclock I got father to call in the Elders and administer to me. which he did. Bro Covey anointed me' Bro Snyder. father and himself then laid hands upon' and prayed for me after which I felt some better. although was very sick through the day. and kept my bed most of the time. having little or no appitite for food I drank considerable Composision Ginger^3 &C to day Jane came and spent the PM with us night was very restless

Thursday 24th the weather Still very warm this morning. I was in Pain much the same as yesterday morn. and continued the Same until about noon when I began to feel a little more easey continued to drink Composision and take such things as I thought would be good for me Uncle Levi called in each day when going to. and coming from his work. I told him the nature of my desease and asked him what cour[s]e I should persue. he then asked me what I had taken. I told him. he then told [me] to take some Salerates water' and continue to take Composision Ginger &C which I did. night I exchanged beds with Henry rested some better

Friday 25th   a very warm day continued about the same. and felt very lonely. to day Sister Jenne came and made us a visit

Saturday 26th   AM. very warm PM it rained. I still continued about the same having a steady Pain all the time through my bowels and and the lower part of my Back. Oh how Much through these days of suffering did I miss the kindly look. and Sympathizing words of my beloved Companion. true I had a kind Mother who seemed willing to do all she could for me. but she needed to be waited upon' rather than to attend upon me. and the thought that she had so much to do' rather added to' than deminished my Suffering. but thanks be to the Lord who still continues to bless me with Patiance. & Strenth to endure all my trials. and oh! that I may ever continue to find favor in his sight.

Sunday 27th   the weather very pleasent and I felt a little better AM the family all went to Meeting' and I remained alone. Sister [Catherine Elizabeth Mehring] Woolly came in and sat a while with me. Sisters Noon Smith Coalflesh [Harriet Wollerton Dillworth Colflesh]and Ellen W[ilding Woolley] then called to see me. they all gave me very pressing invetations to go and see then as soon as I recoverd. PM there were several others called in to see me and Mother

Monday 28th   spent the PM with Sister Woolly

Tuesday 29th   the weather pleasent felt myself recovering though very Slowly spent the PM with Sisters Dillworth & Coalflesh sewing on my dress

Wednesday 30th   the weather quite warm I continued to amend and to day Braided 2 Yards

Thursday July first   the weather very warm I felt better though very weak. I braided 4 yards. to day Mother went to prayer meeting' and to see Jane who had been very Sick with teeth ache

Friday 2nd   the weather very warm to day I commenced writing a letter to my Husband-wrote one Page' braided 2 Yards. and helped Mother about the Work. felt Comfortable

Saturday 3rd   the weather pleasent helped Mother clean the House. wrote some in my letter. cut out Peices for my quilt &C &C

Sunday 4th   the weather very warm AM went to Meeting. was addrest by Bro Morley and Magor [William W. Major] on various subjects. stayed till I got very tired then went to see Sister Jane. found her some better she was writing to Franklin stayed a short time with her. then called to see Sister Jenne who was very sick & spent a few Minutes with her. I then called to see Br Millers folks were I was obliged to stay most of the PM as the Rain desended in torents. I took supper with them had Roast Veal Black Berrys and Goose Berrys &C &C. spent the PM very pleasently Bro Miller then tried to get a horse & Buggy to bring me home but was disapointed of the former. he and his wife then prevailed upon me to get into the Buggy and permit Br Miller to draw me across the St it being very muddy this he did and conducted me most home. and thus I spent the day of Independence. My Health still improving

Monday 5th the weather comfortable was writing in my letter. and braided 3 yards.

Tuesday 6th the weather pleasent to day I finished my letter and sent to St Josephs by Samuel Snyder. helped mother a little about the work. and braided 2 yards &C &C

Wednesday 7th the weather quite warm I took my bed & beding out of doors. Scalded the bedstead and the logs around my bed' and washed the floor. on account of having previously been very much troubled with bed Bugs. I sewed several Blocks of Calico and in the eve replaced my bed. and felt very tired

Thursday 8th the weather pleasent AM washed. after which I felt very tired. PM was in Mrs. Coalfleshs a while reading News papers. the rest of the time was sewing

Friday 9th the weather pleasent Morn I Ironed' then went to Uncle Willards on a visit. on my way called on Jane expecting her she would accompany me. but found her indesposed. was kindly received by the family had string Beans for dinner the first I had seen for 2 years. went into Uncle Levis and had a good Chatt with Aunt Rhoda. after which Amelia Ellen & myself took a walk on to the Bluff where we gazed with delight upon our City of 8 months groweth its beauty full Gardins and extensive Fields' Clothed with the fast growing Corn and vegetables of every description' above all things pleasing to the Eyes of an Exile in the Wilderness of our afflictions we then returned and on our way home called at Sister Bullocks were we spent the eve and had a first rate sing. night I could not sleep for the bed bugs

Saturday 10th the weather pleasent morn took breakfast with Uncle Levis folks. after which I drest Aunt Sarahs Hair and had quite a leanthy conversation with her spent the AM with them and took dinner. PM Amelia went with me to Bro Joseph Youngs saw Melinda Wood & Jennette Bleasdale and had a pleasent talk with them. as also with Br & Sister Young. Just as we were about [to] leave Bro O Hyde came in. he seemed much pleased to see us asked me several questions about my Husband myself the family &C after leaving there we went to Bro Pearts and spent a short time with them. then returned to Uncle Ws and took Supper. eve Amelia myself and several of the family went to Sister Bullocks and had a singing Scool. enjoyed ourselfs much. after which Br Camball accompanid Amelia and I to Sister Janes where we spent the night

Sunday 11th a pleasent day took breakfast with Jane. then returned home to dress for meeting. called to see Sister Matson who treated me with some Custerd. Jelley. & lemonade atended meeting and was addrest by bro Hyde whose descourse was very interesting after meeting I called and took dinner with Sister Mace and spent the PM very agreeably. about 5 in oclock returned home & received a call from Bro & Sister Haven [Jesse and Martha] I had not seen the latter for more than a Year and was much rejoiced to see her now' as also her Husband. enjoyed their call much after they had gone Mr Parsons his wife & daughter called to see us. and after them Br Miller and 4 of his ~~lay~~ ladys came and spent the eve

Monday 2 12ᵗʰ   the weather pleasent AM washed. PM was sewing felt very tired Eve went to Br Lennards and got some cotten batton that I had sent for by her to Mo. bought 40 weight of Flower of him

Tuesday 13ᵗʰ   the weather very warm this morning I paid out 3 dollars for Meal and Flower. and 36 cents for herding. AM I Ironed and about 10 oclock Sisters Stanley. Barns and [Henrietta Wheeler] Douglass came and made us a visit. got dinner for them. and in the PM Amelia came to spend a cupple of days with us. PM was Braiding and got Supper for our company. eve Amelia and I took a walk down by the line

Wednesday 14ᵗʰ   very warm and much trubled by the flys PM Amelia Jane and myself made a visit at Bro Barrows had a very good Supper and a good visit eve Amelia returned home with Jane

Thursday 15ᵗʰ   the weather very warm to day Mother was quite sick. I attended upon her and did the Work and wrote in my journal

Friday 16ᵗʰ   the weather quite warm attended to Mother and my domestic affears

Saturday 17ᵗʰ   weather as usual did my work as usual. to day Amelia came and gave Mother an <u>Emetic</u> Steam &C did well

Sunday 18ᵗʰ   morn it rained but soon cleared away. to day I stayed at home waited on Mother. did the work. and wrote a letter to my father. felt quite unwell all day

Monday 19ᵗʰ   the weather Pleasent Mother alittle better. baked. Churned &C &C

Tuesday 20ᵗʰ   weather Pleasent a little before day I awoke and felt very sick was relieved by vomiting 3 times. took some salleratus & Composision. AM felt some better. went into Mrs Coalflesh's and read a while in her Scrap Book. PM was writing in my journal

Wednesday 21ˢᵗ   the weather Pleasant I did my work as usual. PM visited at Bro [Henry Alonson] Clevelands. to day Braided 6 yards. Mother better

Thursday 22ⁿᵈ   weather very warm to day I washed. PM was sewing. spent the eve with Miss Boaley [Mary Ann Boley]. at Bro [Alonson] Ripely's. foulded the clothes &C

Friday 23ʳᵈ   the weather very warm AM I Ironed. and did the work braided 2 yards.

Saturday 24ᵗʰ   weather quite hot churned. Cleaned the house. baked and braided 1 yard.

Sunday 25ᵗʰ   very warm night it rained AM I went to Meeting. Bros Clap Morley & Mager [Major] spoke at some lenth and instructed the Saints to be faithfull in fullfilling their Covnants, and discharging the dutys required of them also to refrain from every evil habit & taking the Name of the Lord in vain. after meeting I went to see Mother Snyder who was very sick. eat some bread and butter with Sister Jenne. had an Interaduction to Sister Henmand [Aurelia Lewis Hinman]. Called to see Bro [William] Carmichals folks who had just arrived in the City, and had a short pleasent visit with them. then came home eve sat awhile with Sis Coalflesh reading

Monday 26th the weather pleasent in the morn I wrote a Scrap for my Husband to be inclosed in a letter that father was writing to him then washed got my Cloths dry and foulded them

Tuesday 27th weather very warm AM I ironed. PM braided 3 yards. sat awile with Sister [Grace Jane Ramsden] Mellen.

Wednesday 28th the weather as usual AM Churned. & braided 3 yards. PM went to the Store & bought me some cotten Cloth. Called to see Aunts Rhoda & Sarah [Griffith Richards] & Amelia. also Sisters Haven. Lamb. & Fielding received several invitations to visit them.

Thursday 29th a pleasent day commenced to sew together my quilt sewed most of the day

Friday 30th the weather pleasent helped about the work and sewed on my guilt

Saturday 31st very warm weather eve it rained I cleaned the house, baked and sewed on my quilt

Sunday August first The weather warm 'twas fast day. drest early and went to Singing Scool. on my way thither met Bro [Richard] Bentley from Bro [Orson] Hydes Camp who invited me very perticularly to call and see his wife [Elizabeth Price Bentley] & Sister in law M[rs] [Mary Ann Price] Hyde who were ~~then~~ on a visit at his sisters. which I did and was very kindly received by them. spent a short time with them. then went to the Council room was rather early for scool and called to see Jane a few minutes then returned to scool had a very good Sing then Marched to Meeting. we sung 2 twice. they then commenced to bless Children and continued to do so for about 3 hours. while this was going on I took a walk with Amelia to see Sisters Snyder & Jenne. and returned to meeting. after which I came home and ~~commenced to write a letter the father~~ did not feel well

Monday 2nd the weather warm to day I was sewing on my quilt and Baked

Tuesday 3rd the weather pleasent to day I finished peiceing my quilt. and helped about the work.

Wednesday 4th the weather pleasent AM was helping about the work. PM make a visit to Sister Robins with Jane and Amelia. called to see Bro Fieldings folks and found them Mourning the loss of their Infant Son [Hyrum Thomas Fielding] who had died that Morning. had a very pleasent visit and returned home in the eve. Jane & Amelia accompanyed me most home

Thursday 5th   weather very warm AM did a large washing. and PM took my sewing and visited at Sister Boaleys our near neighbor. eat some new potatoes the first I have tasted for 2 years. eve foulded the Cloths I had washed to day.

Friday 6th   weather still very warm AM I Ironed &C. PM was sewing

Saturday 7th   weather very warm was Cleaning house Baking. sewing & writing in my journal

Sunday 8th   weather pleasent in the morn I went to see Jane and spent a short time with her then went to meeting. where we received some good Instructions from Bros Joseph Young. Magor. & Clapp. after meeting I returned home and commenced writing a letter to my Father received a call from Sisters Fielding & Greenalch with 4 children. also Bro & Sis Davis [Elisha Hildebrand and Mary Ann Mitchell Davis] and Bro Neph

Monday 9th   the weather pleasent Morning finished my letter to father & sent it to St Louis by Bro Covey. AM did our washing. eve was sewing and writing in my Journal.

> This day 23 years ago, My Husband dear was born
> Oh! May he live with Joy to hail.
> A thousand Anniversary Morns
>
> Live to thy praise Oh Heavenly King
> Upright and pure without a Stain.
> To do the work which thou designs
> And in thy presense favour find
>
> O may he as a Husband e'er
> In love and kindness act his part
> The failings of his Mary bear
> For true he clings arround my heart

Tuesday 10th   weather pleasent to day I ironed. Baked. and scalded my bed stead. sewed &C

Wednesday 11th   weather pleasent morn got Breakfast and did up the work Mother went to Janes to visit. to day I commenced writing a letter to my Brothers & Sisters and wrote 2 pages

Thursday 12th   weather pleasent I helped about the work & was writing in my letter

Friday 13th   weather very pleasent AM Cleaned up the house. made a sweet Cake. & stewed some dryed Apples. PM Sisters Elisha [Mary Ann Mitchell Davis] & Edeth Davis came and made me a visit. I enjoyed it much got Supper and did some sewing

Saturday 14th   the weather pleasent to day I finished my letter to Brothers &C and wrote a scrap to my Husband and enclosed it also wrote in my journal

Sunday 15th weather very warm Morn called to see Robings & sent my letter to St Louis by a Sister Potter. also called to see Sister Jane and spent about an hour with her then attended meeting was addrest by Bros Joseph Young, Clapp Magor and others. they gave much good instructions to Parents in regard to bringing up the Children in the way they should go &C &C after Meeting I went to Bro W Millers and took dinner. at 4 oclock I went with him and his ladys to another meeting at the Stand. composed of Seventys and their wifes. heard a very interesting descourse deliverd by Pres J Young after which a Bro from Bro Brigham farm arose and told in a most touching manner of the afflictions of the Saints in that Place. who were maney of them sick. and suffering for want of the necessasary Comforts of life. he appealed to the Sympathys of the Brethren here to let them have such things as they now needed and when their Crops were ripe he said they should have their pay. he said allready 5 had been laid under the Sod and others must soon follow if some thing was [not] done soon for their rescue. many tears were shed in the Congregation and some money was donated for their releive. after meeting I called to see Bro Carmichials family. then returned home

Monday 16th weather pleasent felt very ill all day. in the morn got y up but was obliged to lay down again. AM helped Mother a little about washing. got dinner. did up the work. and baked a sweet Cake and some Cukes [cookies] expecting to morrow to have a guilting was very sick all night

Tuesday 17th weather very warm to day Jane came and aassisted mother to give me an Emetic and Steam which opperated well. night rested tollerable well.

Wednesday 18th the weather pleasent to day I felt worse and sufferd much pain took some Composision pepper &C put a draft of horse redish leaves on my Stomick[4] from which I found reliefe night slept but little

Thursday 19th the weather very warm was very sick all day had the Elders come and lay hands on' and pray for me. spent restless night

Friday 20th the weather pleasent

Saturday 21st continued much about the same sent for Uncle Levi who came to see me he asked me what I had done I told him. he said I must continue to do as I had done and send to him and he would send me some pills which he did I took them and beleve they did me good

Sunday 22nd the weather pleasent was alone most of the day as the folks all went to meeting. I felt a little better. had quite number of Sisters call to see me. got very tired

Monday 23rd the comfortable weather

also Tuesday 24th felt my health improving tho very slowly. my Appitite a little better to day I received a letter from my husband by Br [David] Candland

Wednesday 25th the weather pleasent

Thursday 26   my hea[l]th gaining slowly began to sew a little and read continued to take warm drinks every day

Friday 27th   the weather pleasent to day I visited with Ellen and Sisters [Nancy Marinda Johnson] Hyde and Browit [Martha Rebecca Browett Hyde]

Saturday 28th   I still continue to grow better to day Jane came to see me and I walked down to Bro [Stephen] Farnsworths with her it being but a short distance felt quite low spirited. Mothers health had now been quite poor for several day[s] and still no better to day I wrote a ½ page in a letter to Samuel

Sunday 29th   the weather pleasent I went to meeting after that to see Jane

Monday 30th   the weather pleasent I put my bed quilt into the Frames on the AM and PM quilted had it out in the back Room.

Tuesday 31st   the weather pleasent was guilting most of the day. PM Miss Noon came and made me a visit and helped me quilt eve washed out few garments

Wednesday September first   a pleasent day AM baked some pyes and a sweet Cake &C&C and Cleaned the house. to day I had a quilting. had Sisters Jane. Amelia. Robings. Lennard. and Hardy had a very pleasent time indeed. and my company all seemed to enjoy them selves very much

Thursday 2nd   weather very pleasent AM was cooking Cleaning &C PM had another quilting had Sisters Coalflesh. [Lucinda Almeda Merritt] Hartwell. and [*blank space*] invited Miss [Edith] Davis. and Miss [Mary Ann] Boaley but they did not attend[5] to day my company seemed to enjoy them selves well and we had a very agreeable visit together evening it rained and I was obliged to bring my quilt into the house eve was reading

Friday 3rd   a rainey day. was quilting in the house PM Mother and Miss Hardy helped me eve was reading

Saturday 4th   very muddy and the weather very lourey. AM was quilting mother helped me and Henry and I had some plain talk he having been very cross and snapish with me of late' and I having born it as long as I could. and not being willing to retain such unpleasent feelings I considerd it best to talk it over and so have and end put to them. just as we got through talking a Bro [John Griggs] White from keg Creek came in and brought me 2 letters. one from Rebecca Jones. and the other from Mary [Hannah Burton] White. I had quite a good long talk with him as I had not seen him for 2 Years. I invited him to fetch his Wife [Lucy Maranda Bailey White] (She being in Town) and come and take dinner with us which he did. I got my quilt finished (or rather finished quilting about ½ past 11 oclock. got dinner and cleaned the house Bro and Sister White gave me an invitation to accompany them home the next day said Sister Mary White had sent for me. she also wrote for me to came back with them. eve I was sewing

Sunday 5ᵗʰ   the weather pleasent about 8 oclock Bro White made his appearance and desired to know if I had concluded to go with them I told him I had he then wished me to make hast as they intended to start forthwith. I did so and about 9 oclock took my departure from home we called at Bro [James] Davenports where we were joined by his Wife [Lucy Bailey White] and their Son Joel. we then crossed the River which was very calm and pleasent and on the oppisite side found his horses and Carriage in waiting. we then rode about 3 miles across the flats and here came to a Road that ran or lay beneath a Range of projecting Bluffs here the scene was quite Romantic on our right hand the magestic Bluffs stood towering almost Perpendicular above our heads. on the left it seems as levil as a becalmed Oacen we persued this road to where it turns on to the Praira. past several florishing Farms and 2 or 3 Viliges all of which had been built by our Brethren within one Year about 4 oclock we arrived at Bro Whites farm 20 Miles from Winter Quarters took supper with the Old people. and spent the night with his son Samuel [Dennis White] and family very agreeabley we not having seen one another since my Marrige. though lived neighbors before I was Marride. today I enjoyed my ride very much and my company was very scocible

Monday 6ᵗʰ   the weather pleasent to day I visited with Bro Samuels folks and enjoyed myself much was sewing. reading. Nursing their little Babe [Mary Elizabeth White] which was 9 months old and a very interesting little one and my namesake &C &C

Tuesday 7ᵗʰ   the weather cold and windy in the morning Mother W sent for me to come and take Breakfast with them' which I did spent a short time with them then return to his Sons were I spent the rest of the day (they lived near neighbors

Wednesday 8ᵗʰ   the weather pleasent AM father W[hite] came and invited me to take a ride with him over to the Village were He was going to take a sick woman out to ride for her health. I accepted the invitation and went found several their with whom I was acquainted the Vill[age] was composed of from 14 to 18 houses built on a very ruff hilley peice of land but near a beautyfull spring of Water. Bro W brought the sick lady home with him were she spent the night Her name was Whitaker a Widow I took dinner with Father Ws folks and spent the remainder of the day with Sister Mary W and thus I selebrated the Anniversary of my Birth day

Thursday 9ᵗʰ   the weather very windy I spent the day with Mary W very agreeably sewing. reading. &C &C PM went a Pluming & got half a bushel

Friday 10ᵗʰ   the weather cold & rather windy visited with the 2 familys was sewing reading and cut up about a Peck of Plums and put them out to dry Today Bro W went down into Mo.

Saturday 11ᵗʰ   the weather pleasent took breakfast with father Ws folks after which I took a ride with the afore said Jentleman to another Village which was a very pretty location about 2 Miles from Bro Ws farm called at the house of a Bro Chenne [Elijah Cheney] and spent ½ an hour talking about the things of the Kingdom we then returned back had a very pleasent ride I spent the remainder of the day with Sister Mary W sewing reading playing with the baby &C

Sunday 12ᵗʰ   the weather very pleasent rode with Father w and his folks to meeting at the Grove or rather the Village we visited yesterday. 'twas fast day was quite a number at the meeting. but we had rather a dull time. when we returned home sister P Dunn rode with us' and gave me a very special invataion to visit them before I returned home which I promised to do. I spent the rest of the day with Sister Mary W talking of by gone days and reading by turn in the History of the U. S.

Monday 13ᵗʰ   the weather somewhat windy was with Sister Mary all day sewing reading &C received a call from father [James] Dunn he came to talk with me about his Son [Crandall Dunn] who is in Eng he urged me very much to go and make a visit. today Mrs Smith made Sister W a visit. She has been about six Months' and is now but 43 years of Age and is very small of her Age.

Tuesday 14ᵗʰ   the weather pleasent AM I went out with Mother White and Joel and gatherd Elderberys after I got home I tied them in bunches and put them out to dry I spent the remainder of the day with Sister Mary and helped her make a dress for her little Girl. eve I was reading in the History of the U S

Wednesday 15ᵗʰ   the weather rather windy today I helped Sister Mary quilt a Cradle quilt and enjoyed ourselfs much talking about the things of the Kingdom of our God, &C &C

Thursday 16ᵗʰ   the [weather] pleasent AM I went with Mother W to gether Hops the distance of about a ½ Mile through a Corn field here we came to Bro [Merlin] Plums' and Sister P [Elizabeth Cleopatra Bellows Plumb] accompanyed us to a place were there was a number of Plum Trees all loaded with with unripe Plums except one or 2 from them I gethered my Apron full and eat all I wished to. Mrs P then went & got a Muskmellon and treated us with that. we then returned home & I took dinner Mother W. PM Sister Mary and I went to Father Dunns and made a visit. we enjoyed ourselfs much talking about our absent freinds. and the ~~Princal~~ Principles of the Gospil. about 4 oclock, the wind began to blow a perfect hurricane and the rain pored down in torents untill about 5 when it ceased. then having had an excellent supper we left for home. the distance was about a quarter of a mile which we had to walk through the wet our freinds regretted much that we had to walk but their horses being out on the Praira it seemed imposable to obtain them however we got home much better than we could have e[x]pected. we found the Children crying with impatiance for our return no fire and the floor all wet with the rain that had beat through the roof. but we soon had a good fire & all things put to right and spent the eve reading

Friday 17[th]   the weather very pleasent took breakfast with Sister Mary made the nessasary prepairations to return home today. knowing my anxiety to return to my folks. father White said he would take his horses and Carrage and conduct me home in person accordingly about 9 oclock I took leave of my freinds here who imbraced and wished me many good wishes pored their blessings upon my head we returned back the same way we had come crossed a beautyfull roaling Praira which extended as far as the Eye could penatrate and although Autumn's Chilling Blasts had began to make its depredations among the Trees that appeard at intervails' yet the Praira seemed dected in a rich livery of flowers and presented to the Eye a scene truely pleasing and interesting. about 12 oclock we came to the Bluffs whose towering Summits as I have before described' presented a very Rromantic appearnce. a solmn awa came o'er my feelings as I gazed upon these magestic Piles. and my Soul exclaimed Oh! how wonderfull are thy works O God' and how unsearchable is thy Wisdom & knowledge and thy ways are past finding out. for thou didst lay the foundations of the Earth and these Hills are the Works of thy hands. Oh that I may ever have thy Spirit to enable me to give unto Thee the Praises' that is due ~~th~~ to thy most Holy name. about 3 Oclock we came to the Ferry opposite WQ found the River so low that on this side apart of the Stream was sepperated from the main Channel by means of a sand bar. this we had to cross in a Cannoo which was very muddy and no place for us to sit down came very near being capsized got my cloths quite muddy. we then walked across the Sand bar. and crossed the River in a Sciff. had a pleasent Sail. and arived home about 4 oclock. found the family all well and met with a warm reception. after Eating Supper I went with Father White to see Sister Jane he having been acquainted with her brother Robert [Snyder] he now wished to become acquainted with her also we found Amelia there spent the evening very pleasantly and about 9 oclock returned home. father W spent the night with us

Saturday 18th   the weather pleasent Bro White took breakfast with us in the morning and then returned home. to day I cleaned the house and took all my clothes out of my Chest and aired them did some sewing &C spent the evening and night with Sister Jane and enjoyed myself much talking with her

Sunday 19th   the weather pleasent AM Jane and I went to singing Scool and from thence to Meeting where we were addrest by Bros Cutler. Magor, and President J Young. on different Subjects. which were very good and interesting. went home and took dinner with Jane and spent the PM with her. then returned home and went to see Sister Barrows her children 3 in number being all sick stayed with her about an hour and returned home

Monday 20th   the weather comfortable hilped Mother about the work. borrowed a ~~pair~~ set of quilting frames and put on a scirt and quilted' in the back room &C &C

Tuesday 21ˢᵗ   the weather pleasent to day Miss Hardy came and washed for Mother to pay her for cleaning her Bonnet. I assisted Mother about the work and quilted a little

Wednesday 22ⁿᵈ   the weather pleasent AM was cooking cleaning &C PM Sister Williams and Sister Jane came and made us a visit and helped me quilt were very sociable and we had an interesting time eve was sewing

Thursday 23ʳᵈ   the weather pleasent AM I Ironed. PM I washed me & Mother some dresses &C Mother went to Janes and made a visit

Friday 24ᵗʰ   the weather loury & cold did the housework and made my quilt to day sister Jane came to see us. eve I was sewing

Saturday 25ᵗʰ   the weather pleasent today I was at Sister Janes helping ~~help~~ her sew Amelia was there a part of the day. I had a first rate visit with Jane and spent the night with her and we take much comfort together

Sunday 26ᵗʰ   the weather comfortable was reading &C until 10 oclock. then Jane and myself went to meeting. was adrest by Bros B Clapp. Cutler. & J. Young. who gave us some good instructions. very appropriate to our present sircumstances the[y] desired the Saints to walk in union one with another to leave off evil speaking Swearing Stealing and all maner of wickedness. they also reminded them of the Covnants they had made in the Temple of the Lord and entreated them to be faithfull in fullfilling all their covnants and agreements &C &C after meeting I went home and took dinner with Jane' after which I went with her to Bro Cutlers to get a letter from Philo her addopted Son. which she did. we then called to see Sis Scovil who was sick with the quincy. while there Bro Candland came along and said he was going to Janes to see the Star. so we went with him. he then invited us to go with him to the Seventys Scool. which invitation we accepted. and called and got Sister Robings who went with us. met Amelia took her with us also. the principals to be discused this eve was humility. first. Self Government 2nd and the Government of familys 3rd. each subject was discussed by 3 differant persons. it was desided that humility consisted in a persons being in perfect submission to the will of heaven' and to all the powers that be, &C &C that self government consisted in a Man's having perfect Cont[r]ole over all his Passions both mentel. Morel. & Physical. and over ~~all~~ his happytites &C &C. that the goverment of the familys consisted in a man ruling over his family in meekness. love. and forbearance that to be fulley competant to do this he must possess self goverment in its fullness. these were allustrated by figures and made plain to the understanding. and were indeed instructive and interesting. Bro Hyde who had been a very attentive observer tho mostly unobserved now made his appearance in our midst and exprest his approbation of the preseedings of the meeting' in a very feeting and interesting manner' blessed the assembley and advised them to continue their meetings. said it would be the means of prepairing their minds for the great work of God in which they were to be instrumental in bearing to the ends of the Earth. &C Pres J Young then spoke in continuation of the same subject and was filled with the Spirit of the Lord. yea and the whole house was filled with a Spirit also. never have I enjoyed such a meeting since I was in the House of the Lord. every countenance beamed with delight and oh how good it was to be there. my soul longs for another such a feast. I spent the night with Jane. and my sleep was sweet and peacefull

Monday 27th   the weather pleasent took breakfast with Jane. and about 9 oclock returned home and commenced writing a letter to my brother Rodger. helped Mother about the work and evening was sewing & reading

Tuesday 28th   the weather pleasent today I finished writing my letter. received an invitation from Bro [Joseph] Knight to attend a dance at the Council House that was got up for the benefit of the poor. evening. Henry and I went and took Sister Jane with us. when we got there the latter and myself got seated in an obscure part of the room and took all comfort we could annimadverting[6] upon everything that we saw fit. I danced one figure with the martial. about 12 oclock we returned home

Wednesday 29th   the weather comfortable AM helped about the work did some sewing PM went to Bro Jesse Havens and made a visit. we talked over the sceens of by gone days and enjoyed ourselfs much. had a good vegetables Supper and spent the eve. Bro Haven then accompanyed me home. he made me a present of a pail of tomatos

Thursday 30th   the weather pleasent helped mother about the work and did some sewing

friday October   first the weather pleasent I scalded our Bedsteads. cleaned the house and sewed on my quilt

Saturday 2nd   the weather pleasent to day mother went to Sister Greens and made a visit. I colored my 2 quilt linings and washed them out. also cooked meat & pumkins and cleaned the house. eve was sewing

Sunday 3rd   the weather ~~pleasent~~ rather windy AM went to Singing Scool. called to see Uncle Willards folks. Amelia went with me to meeting Bro Phinehas Young who arrived to day from the Pioneers came upon the Stand and gave us a description of his travils during his absense. the Country he had visited what he had seen s&C &C he had not visited the Valey' but brought a very favorable report of the Country. his discourse was very interesting. after meeting I went to Sister Jane's but she was not at home. the dust having blowed much during meeting I washed my self. and returned to wards home. called at Sister Jennes' where I found Jane. who accompanied me home. after eating dinner I went with her to Bro Barrow's were we each received a cupple of green Apples. after returning home we learned that Bro Scovil had arrived home. and being anxious to hear from our beloved Husbands we (Jane and myself) went to see him and received each 2 letters from them. and had an interesting conversation with him. about them and the affairs in the Old Country. we then returned to Janes to read our letters' was overtaken by Sister Melinda Wood who came and spent the eve with us. after her departure Father Mother and Henry came and spent the evening with us 'to hear our letters &C 'twas a time of rejoicing. yea, and I am sure that no one' unless like us they are deprived of the sociaty of their companions' can know how we prize a line from the dear absent ones. it is Indeed a scourse of comfort that is indescribeable I spent the night with sister Jane

Monday 4th   the weather pleasent took breakfast with Jane. then went to Bro Scovils and received from his hands 3 Soverigns pounds which my husband had sent to me by him. also got a parsel which my Sister in Law [Ellen Briggs Douglass Parker] sent by him to her daughter in Law [Henrietta Wheeler Douglass] and a letter. went and carryed it to her' and read the letter. after which I returned home and commenced writing a letter to my Brothers & Sisters in Eng. &C &C

Tuesday 5th   the weather pleasent got breakfast. AM put my quilt into the frames and Mother and I received an invetation to attend a quilting at Sister G Williams [Hannah Maria Andrews Williams] in the PM which we did. 2 of O Spencers Daughters [Aurelia Reed and Ellen Curtis] was there. Mrs [Henrietta Rushton] Bullock and a young lady whose name I don't remember. we had a very pleasent viset and a good Supper and returned home in the eve. expected to have some music but was disapointed. Sister Jane came down expecting to hear. I went home with her and helped Lovica quilt a Skirt and stayed all night

Wednesday 6th   the weather pleasent AM I made some pyes &C &C PM 2 Miss Spencers visited me and helped me quilt. eve I went to Janes and spent the night

Thursday 7th   the weather pleasent AM I cleaned the house and quilted on my quilt. PM Sisters Haven. Rockwood. and Jane viseted with me. spent the afternoon very agreeabley. was sewing and got supper. eve was sewing & reading

Friday 8th   the weather pleasent AM was cooking &C. PM had a quilting. had 2 Sister Welches [Eliza Billington Welch and Elizabeth Briggs Welch]. Sisters [Ann Welch] Crookston and Hmma Wayley [Emma Whaley Scovil] just from Eng. Had a very pleasaent time. they spent the eve and had some singing. this eve Sister Jane sent for me to attend a party at her house. so after my company were gone I went and took Miss Wayley with me. they danced until about 12 oclock then dispersed but Miss W and myself spent the night

Saturday 9th   the weather pleasent AM I finished quilting my quilt. PM and eve I cleaned the house and was sewing & reading

Sunday 10th   the weather pleasent AM went to meeting was addrest by Bro Scovil who gave us an account of his mission to Eng how he left all the Brethren who were there on missions where they were stationed &C &C his discourse was quite interesting. after meeting I went to Sister Janes and took dinner. spent part of the PM and returned home Lovica & Olive Jenne walked down home with me. on our way we called at Br Elsworths and got some tomatos when we got home we found Jane and Amelia there' having just brought Mother a letter from Maria was glad to hear that she was well. eve I spent in Bro Welches.

Monday 11th   to day it rained and Mother was quite unwell. I did the work. and finished writing my letter to Brothers & Sisters.

Tuesday 12th & Wednesday 13th   the weather windey and unpleasent. Mother quite sick did the work and attended upon her. sewed a little &C

Thursday 14th   the weather windy to day Sister Rollins came and did our washing I did the work and helped her alittle. eve was sewing

Friday 15   the weather more pleasent in the morn got breakfast. then wroung out all the Clothes out of the Renching [rinsing] water and put them out to dry. this morn Bro Joseph Young called to see us. I did my work as usual. and did some sewing. foulded the Clothes &C was boiling down Molasses

Saturday 16th   the weather pleasent did a large Ironing cleaned the house did the cooking &C PM went to see Bro Barrows folks and took Supper with them. eve Sister Jane sent for me to go and see her as she was going to start for Mo in the morn. so I went. and spent the night with her. we stayed up until nearly one oclock and I cut out peices for a quilt for her. and had a very agreeable viset with her.

Sunday 17th   the weather pleasent Mother still unwell. AM Jane came to see us and took dinner. I wrote a scrap to Samuel for her to put in her letter to Franklin. I then walked up to Sister Jennes with her and there bid her good bye. and returned home. there found a pair of mits that she had left which I knew she would need on her journey and carryed them in hast to her house. was joust in time to see her go I felt sorry to part with her for so short a period as 5 weeks. returned home and received a call from Bro Barrows & Bro Crookston his wife and Miss Waley. read them some Poetry that my husband composed on Bro Joseph's death. spent part of the eve in Bro Welches. the rest at home reading

Monday 18th   the weather pleasent did the house work as usual. was making molasses. sewing. &C

Tuesday 19th   the weather pleasent AM did the work. PM I viseted at Bro Crookstons with Sisters Waley & Turner we had an excellent Supper. & some first rate Singing. in short we had a good viset eve Bro C Sisters W & T came home with me to hear some music as we had 3 fiddlers viz Bros Macantire. McGray. & D Cahoon. had some good music and treated them with Cake and mellons &C &C

Wednesday 20th   the weather pleasent did the work. and PM went to Bro [Jacob] Pearts & bought me a P̶ Bake kettle & lid and some Tallow eve Henry and I fetched them home. I did some sewing &C

Thursday 21ˢᵗ   the weather comfortable

Friday 22ⁿᵈ   I did the work. tended to boiling down Molasses. sewed. read &C &C had a hard cold

Saturday 23ʳᵈ   the weather pleasent AM I cleaned the house did the cooking &C PM I went to the Store and bought some Sugar Tea Cotton batton and some little notions. saw Bro [Truman Root] Barlow just from Farmington with the corps of Mother Barton. in his wagon. called to see Uncles Willards and Levis folks. and took Supper with the latter. had a good visit with Aunt Rhoda Amelia then accompaneyed me on my way home as far as Sister Jennes. after I got home father and mother went out to spend the evening I felt very cold and sore and had considerable Pain in my limbs. about 9 oclock I had a la Chill' got me some composision and bathed my feet. went to bed and had a raging Fevor through the night

Sunday 24ᵗʰ   the weather windy and cold AM went to meeting. was addrest by Bro [John] Pack who had just returned from the Pioneers. he gave us a descripion of the valey and the sorounding Country. and numerous objects that he had seen the hot warm and cold Springs. the Salt Lake &C his discourse was quite interesting. during the meeting I sufferd much pain in my back and limbs. as soon as he got through Preaching I left and came to Bro Millers. and spent a few minutes with them. then went into Bro Maces across the St from them and spent the PM and took Supper with them. and had a very interesting viset with them. it being the first time I had seen Bro M since I left Nauvoo. eve I returned home and spent about 2 hours in Bro Welches

Monday 25ᵗʰ   the weather cold and windy morning helped mother get Breakfast and do up the work and about 10 oclock AM went to bed with a Chill. after which I had a very high fevor and felt very Sick all day. told Father if he could spare time to attend to me I should be glad to take an Emetic. he said he would try to do so in the evening. but was absent. Mother though weary undertook the task. and gave me a steam. and waited upon me with hot Breaks [bricks] in the bed. hot drinks &C. but just as she was about to give me the Lobelia' Uncle Levi came and orderd her to give me Boneset which she did twice over but was unable to keep it down anytime. after this I took the Lobelia which opperated pretty well. I then changed my garment and lay down was very weary. and soon sunk into a sleep rested tollerable well

Tuesday 26ᵗʰ   the weather moderate for a short time in the morn I though[t] I was better but soon my fever came on and spoiled it all. was very sick all day. eve got Father to call in Bros Crookston & Welch and pray for me. I told them I had prepared myself by works and desired to try what virtue there was in faith father anointed and prayed for me. after which I felt some better for which blessing I felt to give God the Glory. I rested tollerable well to night.

Wednesday 27th   the weather cold and windy this morn felt somewhat comfortable but at noon had a hard Chill after which I had a high fever the remainder of the day and felt very Ill. sufferd much pain in my head, Back and Limbs. night was very restless. and my bed seemed like a prison it being so narrow and hard

Thursday 28th   the weather moderate this morn as soon as father and mother left their bed I got onto it. and was very Sick all day. had a chill and a raging fever and sufferd much pain. eve got father & Bro [John] Welsh to pray for me after which I got up and had the bed made for me. to night I laid in Mothers bed and past a restless night

Friday 29th   the weather cold and windy past a very sick day had a very high fever and felt very weak. having had no appitite to Eat since I was first taken. past a weary some night

Saturday 30th   the weather more pleasent I sent for Olive Jenne who came and Combed my hair for me. it not having been combed before since Sunday. after this I had a very hard Chill and a high fevor. PM Sister Waley & Turner came to see me and spent about an hour. after them Ellen Wilding called to see me. I talked with them till I was very tired eve sent and got some quinine and about 10 oclock my fever having abated I took some Pills, but past a very restless night

Sunday 31st   tollerable weather was very sick all day. eve took quinine. today Uncle Willard & the Twelve arrived home from the west. was much rejoiced to hear of it Uncle W sent me words to be comforted and I should soon be well &C &C

Monday November first   windy weather AM Uncle W sent Bro Camball to invite us all to go and spend the day with him so father mother & Henry all went and Lovisa Jenne came and staid with me. PM a young Man named John Riston [John Price Clifford/Wriston] who took care of Brother Joseph when sick & helped bury him' called to see us and took supper with whom I had an interesting conversation and learned much about Joseph. I missed my Chill today' and felt a little more comfortable

Tuesday 2nd   weather cold & windy AM bro [Robert Lang] Camball came again and invited our family to attend a family meeting at Uncle Ws in the evening. he told me that Uncle W said he should expect to see me there among the rest' and he (C) knew that he W was in earnest from the maner in Which he spoke. I told him' if Uncle W only knew that I had not left my bed for more than a week' I thought he would have no such expectations. he said Uncle W had heard how sick I was. I then asked him in a joke if he would come and fetch me in a Wheelbarrow he said he would do anything I wished if I would only go. I then told him I would go if he would come for me with a waggon &C Mother was much surprized that I should think of such a thing' and asked me if I would dare go out, after being confined so long' I told her if Uncle W said I could go there' I was willing to try. so about 3 oclock PM I got up' and by exerting myself all I could endure I got ready by Six. at which time Bro Camball came with a Waggon & Oxen and carrid us up to Uncle Ws. he carrid me in his arms from the Waggon into the house were there was quite a number assembled' Uncle W them received me from him and led me into his bed room & made me lay down on his bed. he then kneeled down beside me and talke[d] awhile. blessed me. and kissed twice. once he said was for Samuel. and asked if 'twas not as good as if from him &C &C we had an excellent meeting. Uncle W father & Uncle Levi laid hands on me. the first offerd up a beautifull Prayer for me and my husban[d].

[*One half page is blank here*]

Being very sick on the night of the 27th and being alone on my bed. I composed the following lines

So on a hart[7] and narrow bed
Alone and sleepless hear I lay
No freind to ease my pillow for my head
Or moist my lips which now are parched and dry

Oh! Samuel dear 'twas not so
When thou was by my side
For thou didst seek my wants to know
And hasten to suply

Thy words how comforting were the[y].
Thy Smiles would chase my tears away,
My pain was ease'y to endure
When thou My dearest Love was near.

But now my love thou't far away
Yet still me thinks thou prays for me
Our God I trust the same will hear
And I shall live thy face to see

Letters to Samuel Richards, June to August 1847

Camp of Isreal, Winter Quarters. Omehas Nation[8]
June 8th 1847

My Dear Samuel or dearly beloved Husband it is with a degree of pleasure and satisfaction that I sit down this morning to write a few lines to you. and I sincerely pray that they may greet you' <u>injoying</u> as <u>I do</u> this day' the blessings of health and strength. together with evry other needfull blessing. I received your kind & Interesting letter by Bro Hyde on the 20th of May. This would have been a great Comfort to me. had I not received with it the Painfull Inteligence of your Sickness' with that most disagreeable of all sickness the <u>Small Pox</u>. it is in vain my dear for me to undertake to describe my feelings at the reception of this unexpected inteligence. for my heart was grieved' and the yearnings of my Soul was & is <u>Oh</u>! that I <u>could have been with you</u> in that <u>hour</u> of <u>pain</u> and <u>affliction</u>. to have watched over you through the dreary watches of the Nights and to have pored out my Soul in prayer to our Heavenly Father in your behalf for your speedy recovery &C &C Many and various have been the thoughts that have passed through my mind since hearing the above' for I knew not when to hope for another letter from you. for if I should judge from those that you have writon I should be led to beleve that you looked upon us as being behond the reach of letters. but to releve me from this sospence' father received your almost unexpected but most wellcome letter bearing date March 16th which gave us all great joy to hear from you. and it was indeed a great satisfaction to read from your own Pen an account of your Sickness and recovery. I ~~was~~ am glad it was so that Franklin could be with you. but am sory to hear his health is so poor. I trust that long e'er this you are both enjoying good health. I <u>pray</u> the <u>Lord may bless</u> all my brethren and Sisters who have administerd to you. and reward them for their kindness. my prayers shall ever be for the wellfare of those who show kindness to my dear Husband especialy when he is far from me. please remember me kindly to Mother Kerr and Sister Catharine Kennedy. tell them they have my thanks and blessing and a rememberance in my Prayers (dear Samuel did you ever wish to see me when sick) Oh! I long for the time to come when I shall again be permited to <u>see</u> and <u>enjoy</u> your <u>sweet sociaty</u>. had I the Wings of the morning I would <u>fly</u> to <u>your arms</u>. and <u>enjoy</u> a <u>repose</u> upon that <u>beloved bosem</u>. but it cannot be now Mother is making Henry a pair of pants. her health is pretty good excepting that she has a little truble with her feet. the black leg or Scurvy so called has left them weak. fathers health is pretty good also. he seems to have plenty of buisness. but I must leave him to tell you what it is when he writes. Henry enjoys first

Front page of letter from Mary to Samuel Richards, June 8, 1847. Glued to the letter are small green stickers. Courtesy of LDS Historical Department.

rate health. Maria looks some what poorer than she used to but enjoys tollerable health Wolter has just returned from St Joseph where he has been to get a load of provisions &C. that he left there on his way from St Louis. his health has not been very good this winter but he is now well. little Syntha grows finely' she is a sweet pretty Child has Eyes just like Uncle Samuel. Melinda has not yet fully recoverd her health but is much better and the is She will soon be well. Aunts Rhoda and Amelia were here last friday and made us a visit they are well as is also Uncle Levi and family. and Uncle Willards family. they all wish me to write you their love and rememberance and say you have their blessing.

Wednesday morn Jun 9th yesterday PM sister Elisha Davis from London came and made me a visit they live nearby us. she seems to be a pretty little woman. I will now tell you something about our situation on friday the last of April we moved with our Tent from the West to the South Line of the City w[h]ere we are now living in a House that father bought of a bro William Patton. and paid for with one of Bro Josephs Coats and one dollar in money it has a good Punsion floor in it Brick hearth and fire place. has a good Roof & floor over head. we have a well close by the door have good neighbors. and in short we are well pleased with our home for the present. our room is not very large. but there is sofficiant space between the back of [t]he house and the Pickets to build another room as large. it can be done with very little truble. as the Pickets will serve for one wall. father has got the rafters on and as soon as he gets through planting intends to finish it. we have got but little planting done yet excepting our gardian. father has got land were he intends [to] plant Corn and saw [sow] buck weat. Bro William Clark is plowing for us to day his wife died about 2 weeks ago. there is a noble large field plowed and part planted. and the brethren are plowing and planting every day when the weather will admit. they have covnanted not to make short furroughs. or furrows in order for every man to plough his own piese of land. but to commence on one side of the fild and plough through to the other. no matter wither it be their own land or their Bretherens for we ar all one family. those who are gone and going West have had to plough all they posably could before going. as much so as if they were going to stay here. and none are permited to go until they have done so. and received a letter of commendation & permision from their respective Bishops to show that they have done so. and also a part of the Pickiting had you my dear been deprived of Vegetables as we have for the last year you would no doubt be better able to judge. how pleasing the prospect of again enjoying those blessings appears to us. I expect itis necesary that we should sometimes be deprived of the fruits of the Earth in order that we may know how to <u>prize their worth</u>. I never enjoyed the prospect of fields and gardens and the fruts of the Earth as much as I do this year. for it itis truly Cheering and reviving I expect when you come home in the fall. you will find us enjoying those things which we now hope for. I want you to write as soon as you receive this and let me know how soon you intend to start. and weather you intend to ~~come~~ come by New York or New Orleans. My dear as you now see that letters can come direct to us. do please write often. I have sent 2 letters to you by mail which I sopose you have never received. & have also sent 2 letters by Bro Littlefield which I trust will safely reach you. if he dilivers what I gave him to give to you. please receive it as from me and forgive all imprudance on my part. please give my kind respects to him and tel him he is not forgotten in my prayers. Oh Samuel if the affection of a fond wife is any addision to the happyness of a man. me thinks you enjoy one comfort that Br Littlefield does not. he left this City on the 11th of May.

June 10th it is a lovely Morn. all is Calm and sorene Nature is dected in the beauty of Spring and nothing is lacking but your presence to make all things appear pleasing and delightfull. yesterday PM Sisters Jane Ellen & Permelia Hatch were here and made us a visit they are all well. since last Saturday Bros P P Pratt. J Taylor. Van Cott. & a large number of others with their familys have left this City for the far West. and a large number of others are prepairing and intend to start this week. Jane has bought Bro VanCotts House & mooved into it last Monday' itis about as good a house as there is in the City. has a good floor. Chamber. Sellor & a well near by the door. I think Frankln will be well pleased with the situation when he returns. Bro Pratt says he told the brethren before leaving England to come home if the Climate did not agree with them no matter wither they were sent for or not. for he did not want the Brethren to stay there and die. if Bro Franklins health is still poor' I hope he will receive this adminision as to him self' and bear it in mind. please remember me kindly to him. and tell him his Jane is well and smarter and prettyer than I ever saw her. I get a good sweet Kiss from her every once and again' but she says she would ten times rather Kiss him than me but she dont gain any thing by that for I tell her that I would rather have one Kiss from you' than one 100 from her. you must alow us to have our Jokes for the greatest comfort that is left to us is to talk about you and F and hope and pray' that we may all <u>live</u> to <u>meet again</u> and our God and preserver shall have the Glory forever more. for he is Worthy. Bro Hunter⁹ will leave for the west tomorrow. and Bro Hyde has got his house and is going to live in it this Summer. itis on the South line and but a few steps from us. he called to [see] us on the 30 of last month and we had a good visit with him. he talked much about you and F. and said. he was very much disapointed in you both. Said he had always thought you were <u>good Boys</u>' but the fact was he found you were better than he ever expected. &C &C he told me he was going to write to the Brethren in England and Asked me if I knew what had been writton I told that Uncle Willard told me. that he had writon for you and F to come <u>home</u> this <u>fall</u> that he had been talking with Brigham about it and they had concluded that it was for the best &C &C he said he did not like the Idea of changing so mutch at the head of affairs. but he wanted [to] know what his Brethren had writon so that he need not do any thing different from what they had writon or Counciled. I do not know what Bro Hyde has writon' but in Compliance to what ~~Bro~~ Uncle W said I shall <u>look for you home</u> this <u>Fall</u>. for he <u>said you would be here then</u>.

June 12th last Thursday PM I visited at Sister Janes with Sisters Elisha Davis and Sophia Whitaker and had a pleasent visit. Bro & Sis D desire a rememberance to you. Bro Cain his wife [Elizabeth Whitaker Cain] & the sister Ws [Sophia Whitaker Taylor and Harriet Whitaker] started yesterday on their journey to to the West. they send their respects love & blessing to you. Miss Walker [Diontia Walker Lyman] & Monks [Martha Monks Pratt]. have gone in <u>Parlys family</u>. Sophia W in Taylors family

[*page 3*] Bro Van Cott and family wished very perticularly to be rememberd. to you & F say they hope that in little more than one year you and I will be out there and made me promis that we would go and make them a good visit. he has lost quite a number of his Cattle since being here had one yoke drowned & others died &C he has been Compelled through nessessity' to take the Cattle and waggons he loaned lent to us & Uncle Levis folks. so you will see we are left without either. the old Cow died last winter. and our little heiffer is all the Cow we now possess but she gives a fine mess of milk and is doing firstrate. I would like much to go on next Season. if we could conveniantly but I feel very contented about it. for I expect the means will have to come through my Samuel and I know he will do the best he can. at any rate I shall be Satisfide to be were he is. wither it be here or the Land of promis. but here is one thing my dear I could not feel satifide with. and that is to think that we must always live with fathers folks. that is in the same house. for although they are' and doubtless would be kind to me. yet I could not feel as happy as I should to live in a <u>house</u> by <u>our selfs</u>. I know itwill be their desires that we should live with them but shall we not. my dear' after being <u>seperated</u> so <u>long</u>. live were we can enjoy ourself the most. for if I should look upon the <u>time past</u> since our <u>marrige</u> as a tipical of our years in future. I should be led to conclude that there was not any to much <u>happyness</u> laid up for <u>me</u> in this <u>life</u>' let me <u>enjoy it</u> the best way <u>I</u> <u>could</u> but enough of this last week on thursday Robert Burton his wife. Rebecca & Eliza A. Hav[en] arrived from Mo on a visit. they all took dinner with us that day & PM I visited with them at W Kimballs. next day at Wolters and Sunday Rebecca stayed with me 3 nights Eliza Ann one. we enjoyed ourselfs much together. talked about you most of the time. they all exprest a <u>hope</u> that they <u>would next fall</u> have the <u>pleasure</u> of <u>eating with you</u> and <u>Mary</u> they all wished me to give their kind respects to you R said I might tell you he was staying to rais Corn &C for me and for you also when you return says he feels himself under some obligation to take care of your Wife when you are doing just as he had aught to do I told him I soposed he thought that was sofisiant excuse. but said I[t] 'twill be Samuels turn next to stay and plant Corn. and you will have to go and perhaps plough the Oacen as he has done & so he will be that far ahead of you &C &C Rebecca has got a fine little <u>girl</u> the Image [of] Nathan[iel]. we hear that the Mormon Battanion have arrived in California. but we hear nothing from our friends who are with them of late. it seem as though I can scarcely endure to think about them since Joseph is ~~gone~~ no more. father says I may tel you he intends to begin to write you in about one Week. I think you may epect a line from Mother also. they wrote you one letter by Bro Littlefield. Henry says I may give you his [re]spects or his love if that will sute me any better. says he will try to be good enough to merit a piece of Sugar Candy against you[r] return I have no news to write you at present. that would be interesting. only that Nauvoo and other parts of the US there is a Merchant here from St Louis who has brought up a large quantity of dry Good Groceris &C &C and opend a store in the Council House' they sell very resonable. Winter Quarters has quite the appearance of a City. and I never saw the Ladys dress half so well in Nauvoo as they do here. we have a firstrate Mill here and in fact it is quite a buisness City.

> Forget thee-Samuel can it be-
> Such words-did emminate from thee-
> Say does one thought e'er cross thy mind
> that Mary is to thee unkind
> For Til Fishes live upon dry land
> And Birds shall cease to scim the Air
> Til the rolling Ocean cease to Move
> And Blooming Springs return no More
> <u>Til then</u>. and <u>not Til then</u> So <u>grief forego</u>. can I <u>Forget thee no</u>
>   <u>love No</u>

[*page 4*] the last letter I received from Fathers folks was dated Feb 15th they were then all enjoying good health except Ellen [Briggs Douglass Parker] her health had been poor all Winter but she was then able to do her work. I shall write to them tomorrow if the Lord permit. am now expecting a letter from them. they are expecting to come here this fall. I am glad to hear that father enjoys such good health I sopose you have not visited the friends in Eng but once since your arrival I wonder why they never write to me or fathers folks I should be glad to have a letter from them. I have intended to write a letter to them for some time been to busy. I shall write to you again in about 3 three Weeks which will be the last I sopose that can posably reach you before you return. after that I shall write to them. please remember me kindly to them. and tel them they are ever rememberd by me. I should like much to hear from Ann please give a porsion of my love to her. her Husband and family espacialy Ellen. I cannot see what there is

[in] Eng to enduce those who are in the Church to remain there so long. would they were all here

[*upside down at the bottom of the page*] I spent yesterday PM with Bro Smithes folks they are all well excepting Ann she has not enjoyed very good health for some time but the prospect is she will be better before many weeks. they will start to day' for the Rockey Mountains they send their love to all their friends and in a perticular maner to Cousin Magdelene they wished oh how much that she was with them. and I feel to join them sincerely. they are good people I have enjoyed myself in their sociaty this Winter. please tell Edward and William. C[orbridge] that sister Ann [Corbridge] Slater and her family are all well. Richard is in the Army. Ann wishes very much to have her folks send her some little presents by Edward when he comes as a token of rememberance. I have writton this by her request. Elizebeth Corbridge is marrid to Bro Walker and is doing well. George Rhodes & Child are living in Br Kimballs family and is doing firstrate they all wish to be rememberd to their freinds. My sheet is about full and I must draw it to a close I pray it may soon and safely reach you. the Lord bless you my dear Companion and preserve you spotlass unto the day of his appearing and may we soon be permited to meet again is the desire of my heart wich may the Lord ever grant may be our lot. good bye my dear for the present. this from your Wife Mary H Richards

[*left margin of page 1*] Bros Sheets Willy have sold their houses which were very Comfortable for 5 dollars each. I told the former if I had known before he sold his house that he was going to sell it. I would have bought it of him. he said he wished he had known that I wanted to bye one and I should have had it I had a good long talk with him one day [*left margin of page 2*] would you have been displeased if I had paid out 5 dollers and got a good house for it it would save you the truble of building one if we should need one. Oh how I should love to keep house for you. it is you know some thing love I have never done. but hope to e'er long [*left margin of page 3*] Oh my dear Samuel how long the time seems since I saw you. I wonder if it seems as long to you why do you always appear so cold and distant to me. when I see you in my dreams. is it because you feel so or do dreams sometimes go by contary my dear. you always seem as though you was in great hast[e] and I can scarce get a chance to speak to you. I expect this is because you you have so much to do is it not my love. good bye for the present write soon as you can & let me enjoy the pleasure of hearing from you

      Mary

[*upside down on page 3*] I have received all the money you sent me by Benson Taylor Hyde. if I except one Pound which it cost to pay the expences of the things you sent me by Bro Cain. I have given father 5 dollars out of it Mother one Henry a ½ dol[lar] Maria a ½ Sovring. and the Rest I have used as we have needed for provisions. and other things for our comfort. all excepting about Six dollars and I expect there will soon be call for that. one thing is certian and that is that my Purse will be the topic so long as there is any thing in it.

[*addressed to*]

Mr. Samuel W. Richards
6 Goree Piazza
Liverpool Eng.
Care of Franklin D. Richards
received Aug 21st 1847

[*addition to the previous letter*][10]

I will here agreeable to your request' write you a list of such things as will be most usefull and nessasary for you to bring with you when you return and will leave you my love to use your own judgement wither you bring them or not. do not feel that you are obliged to bring them because I write them. for if you return to me as destetude as you went from me. you will be just as <u>welcome as though you brought you weight in Gold</u> but I wish for your sake it may be other wise.

one <u>Spider and lid</u> a meal Siv

one puding Cettle and one Tin Cettle to boil Cloths in. I have got a Tea Cettle

a set of Kives & Forks

a cupple of German Silver Table Spoons and some Iron ones

a Candle Stick

a Coffee Boiler that will be good to make herbe tea in when we keep the word Wisdom

a Pair of small Shears or large Scisors

a pair of Tongs and Shoval and a small pair Bellows these things will be usefull were ever we go.

Cotten Cloth will be the most usefull for the family

I should be glad to have you bring me a pair of Slippers. No 3 Mother I expect would be glad of a pair also. She needs a Cap to wear you know when father says if Franklin and you will bring him a lining for his Cloak he will be much pleased if it should be so that you can get Cloth for Pants I expect 'twould be very acceptable to father. you know what would be most usefull for them I would be glad if you would bring me a few pounds Cotten batten for Quilts a Bottle of Ink & some Pens I have been very much trubled to get either. I was disaponted about getting Thread from the sister Witecars.[11] they said they had not got enough for their own use. if you can I should be much pleased to have you bring me & Mother a sopply of differant kinds also some needles. the things you sent me by Bro Cain were just such things as I needed. I think you are good at gessing. I sopose you will remember my Parasole. and the Vail & Crivatte or small Silk handkercheif to wear on <u>my neck</u> that you Promised to bring me before you went away. I would also like a pair of black Worsted Stockings. I do not expect you will bring all these from Eng if you bring them at all for I beleve you know just as well about that matter and doubtless a little better. a pair of Blankits would be very acceptable to me and also a <u>cheap Counter Pain</u>[12] or Cover lid I do no know what you would call it. I will leave you my dear now to bring just what else you please you have done well so far and I can trust to your judgement

[*upside down on front page*] if my sisters wish to send or bring a present to me I would be Glad to have them bring me some lace or Edgeing and ribon to trim a Cap. for they are become quite fasonable here. tell our neice Alice Cottom I want her to sent me a pepper Box or Caster and I will keep it for her sake if any of the rest of my neices wish to send me a keepsake they will be just as kindly received or my nephews either please give Aunt Marys respects to them all and my love to my dear Samuel

[*page 2*] Amelia has lately received a letter from her mother the freind[s] were all well. it brings tidings of Edwins [cousin Edwin Dwight Peirson] Marrige to a Young Lady in North Adams by the name of Clamanze U Wells I think they are intending to move and settle in Michagan the freind there most always send love to me

Monday 14th yesterday I saw and talked [with] Sister Simeon Carter [Lydia Kenyon Carter] if you should see or can send to her husband please tell him she is Well. but wants to see him very much she would be glad to have him come home this fall if he can consistantly for she has no home of her own except with another family. Sister Jacobs is here & is well Sister Scovil is allso. I think Bro Martins Wife [Julia Priscilla Smith Martin] is not yet arrived but expected dayly his Sisters are well. Bro Spencers family are well they live not far from us. Bro Danial Ss family are gone to the west. you will consider Hyrums family as being with them. for D has marrid the Widdow & C Antenette. I got the letter you sent by Sister Baylis but she is back at or near Farmington. I wrote you that the Cloak you sent me was lost. but am happy to inform you that itis now found. it had got ~~along~~ amongst Sister Jacobs things it is only one week since I received it I beleve I have got every thing now that you sent me Sister P P P arrived here last friday from Nauvoo I saw her yesterday She has been very sick before coming out here. and her health is still poor. I think she is a very unhappy Woman and a very good one also. if you can read all my scriblings without having your patiance tried I shall think you have pretty patience. and' as you have studyed the Science of. Phonogrophy I am in hopes you will be able to understand all my Spelling Wolter Maria & the babe will I expect start to morrow for Westren Missouri. were they expect to spend the Summer. I shall send this to St Joseph by them. June 16th Walter & Maria are here now will start in the morn they wish me to give their love & Respects to you and tel you they often think of you they are going ~~to~~ with the intent to try to fit themself out. for the Mountains and go on next Spring. father Mother and all the family join me in love to you we are all well. I pray these few lines may safly reach you and find you in the enjoyment of every good I must now bid good bye and seal up my letter please excuse all misstakes and accept my Sincere wishes for your wellfare & prosperity and beleve me to be forever you affectionate Wife ~~for~~ fare thee Well My love and God Bless thee

      Mary H Richards

Camp of Isreal. Winter Quarters[13]
Thursday August 12th 1847

    My dear Samuel I have taken up my Pen to write afew lines to you although I have not much Idea that you will ever get them. as you will I hope have left Eng. before they can get there. but should sircumstances detain you longer than we could hope' I do not feel willing that you should be obliged to remain there with out any inteligence from us. for I cannot help but feel vain enough to think that you will be pleased to hear from me as well as all the rest of the family. but should you be in America when this arrives in Eng I shall have no objections. for I want to see you. how is your health My love (would I knew) I pray that you may ever enjoy good health' and be blessed abbundantly with Heavens choisest blesings and oh that the ~~lord~~ Lord may ever preserve you as in the hollow of his hand. from every danger & deliver you from every temptation and trial though which you may be called to Pass. during the Spring my health was very poor as I have writton to you in former letters. but thanks be to my Heavenly father itis now very good and has been for about 3 weeks. father had a Chill on Tuesday. has had another to day but is now up and around. Mothers health is pretty good at present though she is [t]rubled at times with the Palpatation of the heart. Henry enjoys firstrate health. Wolter & Maria are down in Mo to work have not heard from them for some time. Jane's health is not very good though she does her work and keeps around Mother was there yesterday and spent the day with her I spent last Saturday night with her. and dreamed that you returned home and I was so glad to see you' but I awoke in the morn and found 'twas but a dream. Oh how long will it be before I awake & find it so in reality Jane wrote a letter to Franklin last Sunday (but did not tell me she was going to. so I thought to be even with her I would write one to you now and not tell her of it ~~after~~ all in good part) she is a good girl. pleas remember me to Bro Franklin. Bro [Thomas] Bullock who has gone with the Twelve or Pioneers. has sent back to his wife a journal of their travils from this City to Fort Laramy on the Sweet Waters. which was read last T[*hole*]day at the meeting itwas very interesting. they have seen a great many Buffalow and Deer had all the meat they wanted to eat. were about 500 & 50 miles from this City all well and in firstrate Spirits. they were here met by our Brethren of the Army who had winter'd at Perbelour [Pueblo] (where <u>Joseph died</u>) and who has all joined them as Pioneers with the exception of 5 who have returned to this

City. & who met the last Company that went out (the first of July) on the North Fork of the Platt about 362 miles from this Place. they had met with no misfortune except the loss of some Cattle from Br Grants Co but not sofisient to detain them as their places were filled out of other Companys. I had a letter from Miss [Abigail] Abbott[14] which says that Bro VanCott and family are or were all well. the Camp were in firstrate spirits and generaly in good health. the health of the Camp is not so good as it has been. there has been several <u>deaths</u> of late. Many Children but I know of none among Persons of years. Uncles Willards & Levis folks are about as well as is comon for them. you know Aunts Rhoda & Sarahs healths are not very good at the Best and Amelia has been somewhat complaining of late. our Crops look exceeding well and we now begin to realize the good of our gardins we have had some green Corn that was brought us from da[l]tons farm and tomorrow expect to have some of our own. wish you were here to share with us' Samuel I hope you will let no unnessecessary thing detain you from coming home as soon as sircumstances will admit. for although I am willing' that you should remain as long as 'tis the Lords will that you should. yet I am none the less willing' that you should come home. as soon as his Servants gives you permission to do so. and for my own part I think 'tis all right that you should if 'twas' not me thinks Uncle W would be the last one to say so. the Sun has gone down my dear and I must bid you good night & sweet rest

 Saturday 14th good morn my dear. one more line before I close my letter. Bro W[illiam] Huntington is here from St Louis and I hear is about to return to thither. so I thought I would not let so good oppertunity pass unimproved as I expect he will be willing to take it I do not know when he will start but I though[t] I would have it ready. I shall seal up this Scrap and enclose it in a letter that I have writon to my Bros & Sisters and request them to send it to you as soon as possable. if you are yet there if not to destroy it. at the same time telling them that what I write to you' I write for you <u>alone</u> am willing they should take the hint that I was not any to well Pleased' that they took the liberty to open the one I directed to their charge. I can think of no more news to write you at present' that will be likely to interest you only that mother [*at the top of page 2*] Bleasdale has got a little Son 5 Months old that weighs 12 Pounds. you may be Anxious to know how we get along in family matters' I would say for your comfort that we have not yet lact'd or wanted for food' and also that I do not entertain any fears that we are going to. although at times the prospect looks rather dull. but you know it is said that the darkest hour is just before the day breaks. yet a continual droping tis said will wear away stone. father sent you 2 letters by one Mail about 3 weeks ago <u>I think</u> he is <u>very kind to you</u> & F. now when he thinks you are about ready to start for home (no matter about the long intervail which Silence has rained) you are about to come home now. [*illegible*] you' want you to bring a little honey with you. 'twill all be very acceptable. there is always Policy in War. 'tis all right I sopose. father has got another Chill to day but 'tis not so hard as his other 2 was I gave him money to get him some of Richardsons Bitters. he thinks they will have the desired affect. and I hope they will. he dont seem to have much fever keeps arround about all the time and eats pretty well I hear there are several that have Ague in the Camp. I was in hopes we should have left it behind.

[*at the bottom of page 2*] the Place were we now are is not very healthy. I pray we may not have to remain here long. I long to go to a place were the Air is pure' and the Climate healthy but I desire to remain here til you come to go with me. for I <u>never</u> want to travil again in your absence. I Oh I wish you were here there are so many things I have got to tell you. and so many questions I wish to Ask you. I sometimes wish you could come home and stay a week without any one knowing it for I know just as quick as 'tis known you have come the house will be crouded from morn until night. and I do wish they would have maners enough to keep away til I have had a chance to speak with you. (I think I had aught to have that Privelige after so long an absence dont you think I had) please look over my folley. and dont judge me harshly. for I try to be patiant' and do the best I can. but my Scrap is getting full and I must bring it to a close. accept my dearest love my sincere and unceasing wishes for your Wellfare. Prosperity and <u>safe Return</u> and beleve me to be as ever your affectionate Wife

    Mary H Richards

[*margin of page 2*] Sister Elicha Davis and her sister in law were here yesterday and made me a visit. Sister Davis is a very frendly agreeable Woman. I have been peicing me a quilt' and next Tuesday am going to have a quilting. would be much pleased to have you for my right hand man at the Table. Sister Scovil has had a letter from her husband that stated that Bro Candlen started for home about the first of June and that he himself intended to start in a month after wards by them I am expecting letters from you. shall my expecations be realized. I think the[y] will. for I cannot think that my Samuel would be so unkind as to neglect to write to me' when so favorable opportunity of sending letters presented itself to him. I read a Star that Br Spencr sent to his family Published May 15th from which I learned that you was able to attend a Conferance and speek. this gave me reason to beleve you was well. was much pleased to hear so much. the Lord ~~you~~ bless you ~~for~~ for ever more

    from <u>your</u> Mary

[*addressed to*]
Mr. Samuel W. Richards
6 Goree Piazza
Liverpool England
Care of Mr. Franklin D. Richards
received in Chipping Jan 19th 1848

CHAPTER EIGHT

"Tis when I am Sick' that I miss you the most"

The separation from Samuel grew more difficult for Mary as she watched other couples around her. Although she attended dancing parties and socials with a cheerful countenance and the dances and visiting were welcome diversions, she grieved. Continued ill health compounded her unhappiness. Rumors of Samuel's imminent return intensified her preparations for the time she could take up housekeeping with him. Sewing, cutting quilt blocks, and boiling down pumpkin puree into butter helped to make the time pass more quickly.

Journal Five
Wednesday November 3, 1847, to Thursday March 30, 1848
Winter Quarters, Nebraska[1]

A Journal. and Memorandom. of Mary H Richards. Commencing Nov 3rd 1847 at Uncles Willards

to day the weather was very pleasant and my health much improved. I took a walk into the Gardin with Jane Hall and went into Uncle Levis. I spent the day very pleasently. though Uncle willard was most of it in Council. just before Sun down Bro Cam[p]ball brought me home in the Waggon. felt in good Spirits and rested good through the Night

Thursday 4th   the weather pleasent felt pretty comfortable. sewed a little and was reading

Friday 5th   the weather comfortable visited at Bro [Samuel] Woollys my next door Neighbor. and made me a Night Cap

Saturday 6th   the weather pleasent made me another Night Cap and read a little

Sunday 7th   the weather rather cool Bro Godard' who was one of the Pioneers came and spent the AM with us he told us many things. concerning the valley and their journey which were very interesting. and sung us some of the Journeying Songs &C PM I walked over to Mrs Shimers with Miss Bolding. called to see Miss Dillworth who was sick. also Mrs Jones. evening was reading

Monday 8ᵗʰ   this morning the ground was covered with Snow the first that we have had this fall AM I was writing in my journal PM I visited at Bro Mellons with Sister Luts [or Lnts]. Had a pleasent visit

Tuesday 9ᵗʰ   the weather comfortable. was writing in my journal. eve Sisters [Elizabeth Haven] Brarlow & [Mary Ellen Haven] Palmer made us a call. they have lately arrived in the City. I had [not] seen either of them for a year and a half. I was much pleased to see them here. father and Mother being gone to meeting at Uncle Willards. I had a pleasent visit with them alone

Wednesday 10ᵗʰ   the weather Moderate to day ~~Heny~~ Henry was diging a Sellar under the floor. and to escape from taking cold. I went and sat with Mrs Coalflesh. stayed and took Supper Bro J Scott took Supper with us. had a pleasent visit. eve Bro Richmond came and spent the evening with us had a good time bracking Nuts &C

Thursday 11ᵗʰ   the weather pleasent to day Mother and myself visited at Sister Lennards' was sewing and reading in some News Papers. eve Mother turned home but Sister L prevailed with me to stay all night.

Friday 12ᵗʰ   the weather comfortable stayed at Sister Lennards till 4 oclock in the PM then returned home had very pleasent visit indeed and enjoyed myself much. eve was sewing

Saturday 13ᵗʰ   the weather pleasent AM I cleaned up the house PM I went to Bro Barrows had a pleasent visit

Sunday 14ᵗʰ   the weather pleasent AM the family all went to meeting and Bro Richmond, one of ~~Uncle~~ Uncle willards boys visited with me he told me the history of his past life his sufferings in the Army[2] (from whence he had just returned) & his present calculations. I percieved he was a fickle minded youth. and gave him some instrucktions in regard to his future conduct. which he kindly accepted' and promised to prffit by it. I got dinner & he eat with us. Bro Rolf Douglass & his wife also called to see me I had not seen him before since he returned from the Army. PM Richmond went home' came again and spent the Eve

Monday 15ᵗʰ   weather rather cool was pressing the juice out of Pumpkins. and boiling it down to make Pumpkins Butter of or with it. I found it most to hard work for me' Eve felt very tired. but this weariness was forgotten about 9 oclock at which time I had the unspeakable pleasure of receiving a kind of letter from my dear Husband. which made my heart swell with gratetude to my Heavnly Father for all his goodness both to my Husband and me. Oh that his merces may continu toward us' so that we may be preserved to meet again. and enjoy the pleasure of knowing' that we have ~~the~~ his approbation in all we do and say. for oh Lord thou knowest it is my desire to do that which is pleassing in thy sight I read my letter. once to myself and once to the family. and retired to bed with a thankfull heart

Tuesday 16th   the weather pleasent went to the Store and bought some Sugar &C called to see Uncle Willard and Levis folks. Amelia I found with the latter being very sick with the Measels. I had scarcely got into the house. (of the last mentioned place) befor Aunt Sarah told me that she had just been wishing I was there so as to tip her hair for ~~hair~~ her as it was the old of the <u>Moon</u>.[3] and asked me if I would do it for her. I told her I was very tired. if I got rested I would try to do it for her so she kept reminding me of my promis about every 5 minutes, but Aunt Rhoda took my part. I read them a part of my letter after which good furtune brought Uncle W there & so I got released from being teased' and tiping hair that night. Uncle W asked me to let him read my letter' which I did Then he asked me if I was willing that Samuel should stay were he was 5 years. I told him yes if he would take me to him after this he told me in his own house' that he had no Idea that Samuel would cross the Mountains these 5 years. dont that comfort you said he. 'tis of a very comforting nature said I' I should think it would have a tendency to comfort me. but shall I infer from this' that you intend to keep Samuel over there 4 or 5 years longer. O no said he I expect he will come home in the Spring I don't intend to keep you sepperated quite all your life. well said I' do you intend to send me over the Mountains in the Spring' oh no I guess I'll let you stay were you can see Samuel every once in a while. do you want to go. No sir, said I' I never want to go another mile west without Samuel. I think it is hard enough to be here alone' were I can hear from [him] some times' without going over the Mounts were I can't have that privelige &C after this Aunt Sarah accompanyed me to Sister Jennes were I took supper and spent the Eve with Bro [Henry B.] Jacobs folks. he told me many things about the Saints in my Native Country. how he had seen my sister Ellen & her family &C had a very pleaset visit and returned home

Wednesday 17th   weather pleasent to day I commenced writing a letter to Samuel. Eve was reading

Thursday 18th   the weather moderate. I washed of the Shelvs. put my Pumpkins Butter in jars and packed it away. eve took some with some other notions to Sister Jennes' whose family was sick. evening writing in my letter

Friday 19th   having rained in the night it was quite muddy. AM Was writing in my letter About 11 oclock Bros G A Smith Phinehas Young. and T Bullock came in on business. Bro S told me. that he had heard a good report from Bro Samuel. said Bro Hyd[e] told him in Council that he did not know the worth of him and Frankklin until he proved them. I told him I hoped he would soon return and report himself. then having previsouly been requested by father I left the house' and went to Bro [Samuel] Woollys.

were I stayed about ½ hour then commenced to Chill. came home again' and took some hot drinks. and went to bed. was quite sick all day

Saturday 20th   weather moderate AM helped mother Clean house & commenced writing a letter to fathers folks. felt quite slim Eve was reading

Sunday 21st   the weather pleasent about 8 oclock in the morning I commenced to Chill. and continued to do so. till ½ past 11 when the fever took me. the family all went to meeting. and Bro Rodybacks little Girl came and stayed with me. I was very sick indeed all day about 3 oclock Jane Hall came to see me. Bro Richmon came home with our folks from meeting

Monday 22nd   weather moderate felt some better. was writing in my letter. PM Uncle Willard came to see me had a sweet little visit with him' and lent him 3 Dollars. eve I was reading

Tuesday 23rd   the weather Moderate today I had another Chill and felt very sick all day eve Jane came to see me

Wednesday 24th   weather calm was quite unwell. all day. but sat up and read a little

Thursday 25th   weather cold to day I had another Chill and felt very Ill. when my fever was on me I composed quite a lengthy piece of Poetry but not being able to write them down I soon forgot them Eve I sat up and wrote a Scrap to my Samuel. sealed my letters to him and father. tho I felt very unable to do so

Friday 26th   weather windy to day I felt very low Spirited and Ill. Eve I had a very hard Chill. & fever

Saturday 27th   weather moderate to day I felt more comfortable. made some Pills of Quinine and took some of them eve Bro Richmond was here[4]

Sunday 28th   weather moderate continued to feel more comfortable had several freinds call to see me.

Monday 29th   weather cold was sewing to day. PM I went and sat a while with Sister Woolley

Tuesday 30th   weather cold AM at home sewing. PM visited at Bro Mellons with Sister Woolley had a pleasent visit

Wednesday December first.   the weather rather windy. today I went [to] Sister Janes. called at Miss Spencers and rested awhile. at Sister Jennes and saw her little Child Brigham who had died but a few minutes before. here I found Sister Jane and went home with her' and helped her make the Shroud. stayed all Night

Thursday 2nd   a very cold day commenced to cut out my Cloak. Jane & Philo went to the funeral. eve Henry came there. and we had a lively time

Friday 3rd   the weather cold to day sewed on my Cloak and helped Jane a little. eve we had a very pleasent Party Bro Jacobs played the Violin. I danced 3 or 4 times

Saturday 4th   weather cold sewed on my Cloak and helped Jane. eve Richmond & Henry was there

Sunday 5th   having Snowed during the Night. 'twas very cold today. Mother who had been to Uncle Levis' to see little Levi who was very sick. called at Janes' on her way home' and took Supper with us Lovisa [Jenne] also was there and spent the day. as was also Henry. eve Henry and myself. and Philo and Jane went to Uncle Levis to see the little one. stayed about an hour and then went to J Youngs to see Melinda Wood who was afflicted with a ffellon⁵ on her finger. spent a short time with her and returned to Janes &C

Monday 6th   a very cold day was sewing on my Cloak. eve went with Jane to see Olive Jenne who was sick

Tuesday 7th   the weather cold Evening there was a prayer meeting at Janes. for that Ward Bro Right [Jonathan C. Wright] spoke and gave us some good instructions. had a good Meeting

Wednesday 8th   a cold day went and visited at Mother Snyders' and sewed for her. PM Sisters Lennard and Jane visited there also. eve the former sung some songs for us. had a very pleasent visit and I stayed Night

Thursday 9th   it snowed most all day. went to see Olive Jenne and returned to Janes. was sewing this eve Uncle W was here took supper

Friday 10th   the weather cold to day Robert Burton. and William Kimball called to see us. Jane was was[h]ing. I helped about the work &C Ellen Wilding called also & made me promis to go and stay with her awhile when she was sick which she soon expected to be. eve went to see Olive

Saturday 11th   the weather cold Jane washing again today. helped her again about the work & went to see Olive. attended a meeting at Bro Rights were Bro Benson Preached us a good sermon advizing the Saints to be faithfull in observing the Sacred Covnants and gave us much good instruction Uncle Leve spoke in an interesting maner for a short time. after which the meeting was dismissed this eve Jane was taken very sick with the face Ache.

Sunday 12th   very cold day Jane quite sick all day. took care of her and did the work

Monday 13th   weather more comfortable. Jane very sick did the work took care of her wrung out some Cloths. and put them out to dry. and had 2 visiters to supper. Mother & Henry came & spent the evening with [us] after 11 oclock we gave Jane a good steaming. this PM Uncle Willard was here & I combed his head for him for which he gave me a Kiss and the privelege of asking him as many questions as I pleased

Tuesday 14th   the weather moderate Jane much destressed. sent for Lovisa who came to help me. I cut out a dress for her & in the evenning made the sleeves went to meeting at Uncle Willards

Wednesday 15th   weather moderate Jane a little better. Lovica quite unwell. was in to see Sister Barns a short time did the work eve made the Sleevs of Lovisa dress

Thursday 16th   the weather cold Jane recovering. Lovisa most sick got breakfast &C AM had a Chill. PM went to bed wth a fever. eve Amelia and Jane Hall came to see us. latter part of the eve felt better

Friday 17th   the weather pleasent Jane better. myself very sick with the Chill and fever evening Bro Dalton had a party at Janes house I sat up and before the party was out I danced 2 or 3 times. they had a good time

Saturday 18th   weather moderate Lovisa sick with the measels and me with the Chill and fever. when in the Midst of the fever Henry came and took me home ~~on~~ seated on a load of <u>Wood</u>. evening took some quinine

Sunday 19th   the weather cold about 8 oclock in the morn Mr Tutle MP [Postmaster] from Austin PO called and brought me a letter from my Husband. I read about half a page and then Chilled so that I was obliged to leave off reading and go to bed. were I remained unable to read any more until 4 oclock PM then I read my letter. and felt myself revived by it. O how sweet it is to hear from those we love and espacily to hear that they are well. the Lord be prased for this and every other blessing' that he has bestowed upon me' and my dear Companion. and may he ever continue his goodness toward us. to day I was very sick with my chill & fever

Monday 20th   the weather cold

Tuesday 21st   do do [ditto] my Chills broke felt better did some sewing

Wednesday 22nd   weather moderate was sewing reading &C my health improving.

Thursday 23rd   the weather Pleasent AM went up to Sister Janes' and got her to fit and cut the lining to my dress. of tartin. had a pleasent visit Eve Bro Richmond came to see Jane and Jane anxious to have me stay the evening. Asked him if he would see me safe home which he kindly ofered to do. I accepted the ofer and at ½ past 9 arrived home

Friday 24th   the weather moderate to day Sister Jane came down and went with Mother and myself to make a Christamus visit at Sister Orsers We had a firstrate Supper. spent the eve was again treated with pye &C eve I called in to see Bro Fieldings folks as they lived near by Sister Os. found him confined to the house on account of having his foot Crushed by a log falling onto it. had a pleasent little chatt with the family. then came back to M^{rs} Os and from thence home we had quite a pleasent visit

Saturday 25th   the weather cold spent Christmas at home. was sewing reading &C

Sunday 26th   the weather moderate was at home reading. the family all went to meeting

Monday 27th   the weather pleasent went to Janes sewed on my Tarting ~~daress~~ dress had a pleasent visit

Tuesday 28th   weather pleasent to day I went to Bro E D Woolleys. to spend a few days. and assist in taking care of Ellen who had got a little Daughter [Sarah Woolley]. Eve Uncle Willard came on purpose he said to scold me for not letting him read my letter. I knelt down by his side & told him that I had' had no opportunity to let him read it. as yet, for he was gone to conferance[6] when I first got it. and since that I had been sick. and I thought if he wanted to hear it very much he would have comed to hear it. that I was willing he should hear from Samuel' but was not so anxious to have him read my letters' as to cause me to send them up there to be read. for I thought [they] were worth walking one ½ Mile to hear them read. &C he then told me that I might arise & he would forgive me' if I would do better for the future &C &C this night I did not sleep one hour the whole care of Ellen and her babe being left to me (though unexpectedly) & the latter fretted all night

Wednesday 29th   weather warm was busy all day waiting upon Ellen and her babe. Eve went to Uncle Willards were I met with Sisters Fielding & Wilding. Uncle W was very socible. had a pleasent visit. slept little to night again

Thursday 30th   pleasent weather took care of Ellen and the babe and night night never slept till after 8 oclock

Friday 31th   beauty full weather I worked hard until 4 oclock tending upon Ellen and the babe. then went home to fathers' and dressed myself and Henry waited upon me to a party at Sister Janes. were there was a very agreeable Company assembled Uncle Willard among the rest. the Bishop presided over the party and all things was done in order had a good supper past arround. the dance went of pleasently. I danced 4 or 5 times. danced the Old Year out' and New Year in with Henry. he then waited upon me to Brother Woolleys. I found the babe quite sick and was up all night with it. felt quite unwell myself on account of ~~being~~ missing my rest

Saturday January first 1848   the weather pleasent was waiting on Ellen and the babe. night the babe better. but Ellen nerveous & figity kept me awake untill after 2 oclock. when worn out I went to sleep

Sunday 2nd   the weather pleasent was kept busy all day. had a slight Chill and felt sick. eve I went to uncles Willards' with Sister Jane who had called to see me and spent about ½ an hour Slept little

Monday 3rd   fine weather tending to Ellen and the babe as usual. felt quite unwell. night slept but little

Tuesday 4th   pleasent weather morn I helped to take care of Ellen & the babe. about 10 oclock I commenced Chilling and was very sick all day with Chill and fever.

Wednesday 5th   weather pleasent morn dressed the babe and tended to her. got Ellen's ~~&C~~ breakfast &C at the usual time had a very hard Chill. followed by a burning fever I suffered much pain. Night I rested tollerable good

Thursday 6th   the weather pleasent morning I dressed the babe &C &C had another Chill & fever was very sick all day. eve brother Godard called to see me. night I rested pretty good

Friday 7th a pleasant day this morning father called to see me. AM Bro Young & Uncle Willard came to bless Ellen's babe. after which I asked them to pray for me' which they did Uncle W being mouth. they gave me a good blessing and a promis of health &C &C

I was then Chilling. PM I had a high fever and when in the midst of it Uncle Willard brought a Carrige to take me home. I had often wished to go home within the last 4 days but was not about to walk' and they was not willing to have me go. but now I got up out of bed and was assisted to the Carrige by Samuel Woolley. Jane Hall and Sister E Woolley being on the same seat with me I learned my head on Janes shoulder and so rode home in great speed. when assisting me out of the Carrige Uncle W asked me if I knew that I had come near fainting. I told him that I did. but the frest air I had received through our quick ride had prevented it. he replied that was all that you [got] from it. he then assisted me into the house' and on to the bed and told henry to make me some Composisiun father & Mother being gone to Bro S Woolleys next door to a party. were was all the Twelve with their wives. being left alone I got into a sleep and awoke quite refreshed. Sister B Young then came in with Mother and spent an hour with me which I enjoyed much Uncle W was in 3 times to see me and wished several times that I could take an Emetic that night. as my stomach he said was roiley. having thrown off every thing I had Eat the last four days. this night Uncle W was taken sick After 8 oclock Mother gave me an Emetic which opperated well

Saturday 8th a very stormey cold day. had a hard shake and fever suffered much pain. PM I got Henry to go and get me some Quinine and make me some pills. Eve I took 4 of them. and rested pretty good. to day Sister Woolly brought me some Turkey. Cake. Pye. &C

Sunday 9th the weather cold to day I missed my Chill and felt more comfortable. Bro Woodruff preached close by' and the family all went to meeting. and I was alone

Monday 10th the weather cold missed the Chill and felt better was reading

Tuesday 11th and Wednesday 12th the weather cold my health improving was reading, sewing &C

Thursday 13th and Friday 14   the weather moderate and my health still improving was sewing on my dress reading &C

Saturday 15th weather moderate was writing in my journal. sewing reading &C. PM Uncle Willard sent Ellen [Marie Partington]. with an invitation from him for me to go with his folks next morn at to the Jubilee 8 oclock to the Jubilee with a desire that I send back word wither I would go or not. I sent back word that I should love to go' but was afraid my health was not sofisint and my thanks for the invetation

Sunday 16th weather moderate ½ past 8 oclock Uncle Ws folks stoped on their way to the Jubilee to see if I was ready. and to tell me that Uncle

Willard said I must not go was sorry to learn from them that he was still very sick. this AM I went to meeting with father there were but six women and him and me there. he read 2 of O Spencers letters to Croel [Rev. W. Crowell][7] and gave us some instructions &C after meeting I called to see Sister Coal. ~~also sister~~ who was Sick also Sister Barlow. for whom I sewed a little on a dress she was going to wear to the Jubilee. about 4 oclock to Bros Grant. & Philo. & Sisters Jane. Grant. Lennard. and Lovisa called on their way to the Jubilee Eve Sisters E Davis and Boly came in to see us. about 7 oclock Philo returned back sick with a Collick. I got him some Composision. Pepper. hot drops. Tea. &C and doctored him according to the best of my abbility. about 10 oclock the whole Company returned back not knowing what was become of Philo and concluded to take a new start in the morning. Philo staid all night and the rest made quite a visit

Monday 17th   the weather cold was sewing on my dress. reading &C

Tuesday 18th   moderate weather father went to the Jubilee. I helped mother about the work. and finished making my Tartin dress. Eve I went to a Party at Bro [David] Brintons. one of our Neighbors father waited upon me then because I complained that I had no husband to wait upon me &C as soon as I got there' Mr burns asked me to dance with him but when we had danced through the first Change' the Poliece came in and told the Company that the Party was not according to Order that they had aught to have a Bishop to preside over them. and without one they must not dance &C some unpleasent words past between the poliece and the Company. but a Bishop was soon obtained and the party went on in order for a time. then the PO came again by order of ~~by~~ Bishop Knight[8] (the Bishop of this ward) to break up the party (the latter had been asked to come and preside but refused because they were not willing to give him 3 Bits a Couple) and also to inform Bishop Clark[9] that he was out of place (as this party was not in his ward. the Company was then dismised by Bishop Clark with good feelings toward him. whom they gave some reward for his service after which we had a good supper past arround in Stile. with warm sling[10] &C. Bro Danial Cahoon waited upon me home & stayed a short time' talking about my husband. and Andrew his brother

~~Monday 19th~~ Wednesday 19th   another cold yet pleasent. day was sewing. reading &C

Thursday 20th   weather moderate AM Mother was washing. I wash for myself 2 or 3 garments some handkerchiefs Caps &C while doing this' Bro Godard came and brought a letter he had just received from Sister Everett in the valley' half of wich was writton to me. he prest me very hard to go and make them a visit' which I promised to do the first oppertunity. PM Sister Jane and her Company returned from the jublee I had been wanting to go to Uncle Willards for some time. and so I wrode with them. found him still very sick. I called to see Sister Haven afew minutes. after which Uncle

W kept me' by his bed side untill after one oclock next AM. I had a very intersting visit with him indeed he got Sarah [Langstroth Richards] to get his blessings for me to read to him. also Aunt Jennittas. Hebers Js. Rhoda Anns. Ellens [Ellen Marie Partington]. Sarahs &C which I did excepting one or 2 which he read himself. after which I retired to bed but could not sleep

Friday 21st   weather pleasent while at Breakfast father came to inform me that Bro Barlow & his wife were going over the river to Br Godards. and if I wished to go I [could] ride with them soon after Henry came in to let me know they had come. so I bid good morning to the folks. Uncle W was yet asleep we had a fine ride across the River on the ice. and was wellcomed by Br Godards folks. but in the PM I had the Chill and fever. and was quite sick all the rest of the day about 9 oclock Evening Br & Sister Barlow went home. but they would not let me go so I stayed all night

Saturday 22nd   the weather pleasent to day I felt better. and had a pleasant visit all day. with Br & Sister Godard

Sunday 23rd   pleasent weather to day I had another Chill. felt very sick all day. PM Henry came over to see me. and brought some Composision. B G was over in the City till 10 oclock eve. when he brought with him some sweet Cake and a Box of Pills for me. wich he said would break the Chills. said he had once broke the Chills with that kind him self & they had rever [never] returned. this night I rested pretty good. Br G prayed for me

Monday 24th   weather pleasent to day Br Godard started to Mo to get a fitout. and see his freinds after assuring me that [I was] wellcome to stay as long as I wished and charging me to take the Pills and get well. I had to take ~~the~~ one every two hours. took six of them to day. was reading and visiting

Tuesday 25th   the weather pleasent to day I had a kind of dumb Ague and and felt sick. Eve the Sisters had a prayer meeting on my account. one of them sung in tongues. but we only got part of the interpitation. we had a good little meeting' and I felt that the spirit of the Lord was with us.[11]

Wednesday 26th   the weather pleasent to day I felt better and was reading and had an interesting Chatt with sister Godard whom I found to be a very Intilegent' interesting Woman

Thursday 27th   a pleasent day was not so well as yesterday was reading. and Cut out a dress for Sister Godard & sewed some upon it

Friday 28th   a pleasent day felt bitter [better] was sewing on sister Godards dress. and reading

Saturday 29th   a pleasent day and the 2nd Anniversary of my Wedding Day. both of which have been past in the absence of my Husband. who has now been gone One Year. Eight Months & Six days. Preaching the Everlasting Gospil in the Kingdom of Great Britton. Six Thousand Miles from me. Oh may he ever find favor in the Eyes of his Master Jesus Christ and be blessed of him continualy. and be preserved from every evil and danger and from death and the grave. may he do a mighty work in these last days. and his name be handed down to future generations' spotless and pure. is the prayer of his Mary H

> My bosim yearns
> To see his face again
> But he is labouring' in a good Cause
> And I must not complain
>
> Then grant me patience Gracious Lord
> That I may wait till he doth come
> In all thing' may I faithfull be
> And never murmer against thee

this PM I went with Sister Godard to Sister Janes on a visit eve we had a prayer meeting there and I stayed all night were no Brethren at the meeting. to day father came to see me. ~~I stayed all night and slept with Sister Tomson~~

Sunday 30th   a very cold Stormy day. Snowing all day. was at sister Godards reading and talking on the principles of the Gospil

Monday 31st   a cold day and deep snow. I cut and made the waist of a dress for Emmy Godard

Tuesday February first   weather moderate I fitted and nearly made the Waist of a dress for Arquly Godard and read a little

Wednesday 2nd   the weather pleasent AM I fitted a dress for Sister Louis and sewed upon it. PM I made a visit at William Mosss. when I got there Sister M was getting ready to come and see me afraid I was not going to visit her having heard I was sick. I had a very pleasent visit indeed. eve returned to Sister Godards and was sick all night. having taken a cold. ~~tho~~ tho was very carefull

Thursday 3rd   weather moderate felt better. finished the waist of Sister Louis dress and was reading.

Friday 4th   the weather pleasent about Noon to day I left Sister Godards for home. having spent 2 weeks with her and never was I more kindly treated. it seemed to me that the good Spirit of the Lord continualy dwelt under that Roof. and blest us with its cheering presence I was contented and happy for all arround me seemed happy and I could not be otherwise.

I rode home with Bro. Perry. We crossed the River on the Ice which cracked' and was broken in many places. but through the goodness of God we arrived home in safty and found the folks all well. eve I was sick with the dumb Ague but rested pretty good after 12 oclock

Saturday 5th   pleasent weather to day I commenced writing a letter to my Husband. to send to New Orleans by Bro Scovil. felt quite unwell. eve was reading

Sunday 6th   the weather pleasent was writing in my letter. Bro Woodruff preached at the scool house close by and and came home with our folks and took dinner with us. we had a very Interesting visit with him. he told us a good deal about what he had seen in London' and other parts of England. before he left us I told him' if he would pray for me. I felt the Ague would leave me. this he did' and gave me a good blessing said the Angles watched over me &C and that I should recover and enjoy health. Eve was reading.

Monday 7th weather moderate AM sewing PM went to Br Barlows' with father & Mother. were we met with Sisters Palmer. Ellen W. & [Mary Ann Huntley] Burnum. Eve Br [Joseph F.] Palmer came. we had an Excellant Supper' set out in fine order. had a pleasant visit' altho I was not very well

Tuesday 8th Weather rather cold AM Sister [Betsy Asenath Davis] Boaly came with 2 children and made us a visit. PM I visited at Sister Shimers' with Ellen W Woolly and had a good visit. spent the Eve

Wednesday 9th comfortable weather to day Mother visited visited at Mother Snyders. was writing sewing &C Eve Ellen W called to see me and we had quite a Chatt together

Thursday 10th weather rather cold was binding one of my bed quilts. finished it. Eve I rode up with Bro Barlows folks' to Bro Snyders party at Sister Janes house. I danced with Bros Jacobs. D Cahoon. & Dalton had quite a pleasant time. rode back with Bro B

Friday 11th the weather moderate to day Olive Smith visited with us. I felt quite unwell. was sewing & reading

Saturday 12th weather somewhat cold commenced writing a letter to my father. Eve was sewing & reading

Sunday 13th pleasent Weather to day there was a meeting out doors at the Stand' the first since last fall. Br Kimball preached. I was at home all day reading and writing. Eve father & Mother went to see Uncle Willard who is still very sick. and Amelia & Jane came to see me. and spent a short time with me which I enjoyed much

Monday 14   weather pleasent was writing in my journal. eve sewing and reading

Tuesday 15   pleasent weather to day Mother was washing. I washed a few things for my self. and helped Mother about the work' but was quite unwell

Wednesday 16th weather moderate AM I Ironed PM I visited at Miss Ellen Spencers. and had a very pleasent visit. Eve I called to see Sister Bullock. after which I returned home. were I was alone all the Evening our folks having gone to meeting was reading

Thursday 17th weather comfortable AM was sewing. PM writing in my journal. Jane and Amelia came in the Evening and brought me 2 letters. one from My Husband. and the other from my Brother Roger in PA whom I had not heard from' for more than 2 years. he wrote me a real Sectarian letter' inviting me to go back there' and live &C &C

but twas not so with my husbands letter. this breathing nothing but faithfullness love and desire to do good. I read it to the family and Amelia read Janes. and they were truly cheering and reviving. I think we all enjoyed a real feast before I retired I read my letters again and returned my sincere thanks to my Heavnly Father who had again permited me to hear from my dearest friends. and for all his kindness and unseacing goodness toward them' and me

Firday 18ᵗʰ wet morn but pleasent PM to day was writing in my journal by fathers request I read my letter to Bros Pulcipher and Camball. also read it to Sister Rhodyback. Eve was reading

Saturday 19ᵗʰ weather pleasent morn I rode with Bro Barlow' up to Uncle Willards. on a hay rack found Uncle W still very sick and unable to talk much. I went to Uncle Levis. with Aunt Rhoda' and took dinner. came back and took supper & spent the Eve at Uncles Ws. slept with Aunt Rhoda

Sunday 20ᵗʰ weather pleasent took breakfast at Uncles Levis. AM visited with 2 familys. PM I went to see Francis Swan' and tell her of the death of her mother' as my husband had requested me in his letter. this news grieved her much. O how much rather would I have been the bearer of more cheering tidings. after this I called to see Emaline Haris [Emmeline B. Wells] at Bishop Whitneys and got a Book of Poetry' her own Composition to read. with permision to write off a piece on true freindship. here I saw Brother Kimball and presented my husbands respects to him. as he had desired me to in his letter. I then called at Br E Woolleys were I Eat some Walnuts and my supper. after which I returned to Uncles Ws were I spent the Eve. slept with Aunt Rhoda

Monday 21ˢᵗ the weather pleasent was at Uncle Levis sewing for Aunt Sarah. had them (L & S) cite their lessons in Greek. to Br Phelps' who trancelated these words' and he received from God the Father honer Glory. which afterwards read' and he recived in presence of Gods' Father honer and Glory. Eve I took supper at Uncle Willards. while eating sister Jane came in. and she and Amelia and myself' went up to Br J Youngs' to see Melinda Wood. we stayed about an hour and then came back. after this I had a visit with Uncle W and Combed his head. slept Aunt Rhoda

Tuesday 22ⁿᵈ the weather fine. was sewing for Aunt Sarah. got Bro Camball to write off' the lines on True Frendship for me. Eve I went to the dancing Scool with him. and danced twice. after which I had another visit with Uncle W and Combed his head for him' while doing this he Preached me quite a sermon on Nerveousness said it was fear' and could be over come &C. slept Aunt R

Wednesday 23ʳᵈ fine weather AM took breakfast at Uncle Levis. took Miss [Emmeline] Haris book home & called at E Woollys. were I eat some bread & butter with Ellen. Sister Swan called to see me at Uncle Levis. PM I left Uncles. and visited at Sister Bensons' with Sisters PP and O Pratt. whom Sister B had invited to visit with me. I had a very pleasent visit indeed enjoyed it very much. after which I called at Br Scovils' to see Emmy who was sick' with the Lung fever I then went to Janes were I spent the Eve' and Night. enjoyed it much

Thursday 24th   weather moderate to day Sister Jane and I went to Sister Lennards & made a visit I stayed all night' and in the Eve Sister L and I was reading

Friday 25th   the weather pleasent AM I returned home' havind [having] enjoyed my visits all arround. PM I commenced writing a letter to my Husband. Eve was binding me another bed quilt

Saturday 26th   weather fair AM I helped Mother clean house. PM I visited with her and and Sister Green' at Bro Rhodybacks' and went with the latter and made a call at Br Barlows' where I saw Br Candland & his wife [Mary Ann Barton Candland]. Eve was sewing

Sunday 27th   weather moderate AM the folks all went to meeting. P̶M̶ I was reading' PM was writing in my letter. Eve was in Br Rhodybacks alittle while. after which I was reading

Monday 28th   the weather pleasent Mother washed and Ironed and I did the house work. and sewed Eve I was at a party at Br Mellons were we had some music and some good Singing. also refreshments past arround. this Eve I became acquainted with Br [John Streeter] Gleeson and his Wife [Desdemonia Chase Gleason]. was often asked if I had heard from my Husband lately and when he was coming home. I enjoyed myself pretty well although I always feel lonely at a party were I can see almost every W̶o̶m̶a̶n̶ Woman enjoying the Sociaty of her Husband except myself

Tuesday 29th   weather cold AM I helped Mother clean the house and Cook PM Sisters Ess and Green came and made us a visit. I entertained them' by reading them parts of my husbands letters I told them it was evident that my husband and I were One' from the fact' that I could not even entertain Company' without his assistance &C altho so far away. eve was in Samuel Woolleys writing off some Poetry¹²

Wednesday 3̶0̶th March first.   cold day AM was writing in my journal. PM Mother and myself visited with Brother Moses. their house smooked some which caused me to take cold we were treated very kindly. had a good supper. I received an invitation to visit at Sister Swans Eve I was at home' sewing & reading

Thursday 2nd   it snowed alday. and was very cold. was was writin in my Journal. I had a confab with father who undertook to make me beleve' that Adam never transgressed. but Eve had. and that the Woman alone' was under transgression. but the man was not. I then asked him why it was that Man was Cursed if he had not trangressed. he said man was not coursed but the Woman was. I then asked him why it was. that the Earth was coursed for mans sake and that he was to Eat of it in sorrow all the days of his life' and get his bread by the sweat of his face. he then read me a line from the Prophesy of Enock' were it says. the Man was not deceived' but the woman being deceived was in the tracegression. this says I does not prove to me that the Man was not under transgression. if you should tell me I must not Eat a sertin thing and I should go and <u>eat</u> that thing' would I not have transgressed your commands &C &C

I mean says I to ast Uncle W about these maters' he is always telling me to ask him questions.

you will remember (then) said he I did not tell you that man was not under transgression &C

I most certinly understood you so said I. Mother then Asked him a question' but instead of Answering her. he told her she had aught to ask Mary. that says I' is the same as to say. Mary seems to know everything ask her. but says I have made no pretentions. to knowledge that I am aware of. and I feer that I have merited no such Insinuation

I told you said he to Mother' to get Mary to ask Uncle W. as she was going to ask him some questions it seems said I. to be the hardest thing in the World' for us to understand one another' when we talk &C &C (This he acknowledged) this I said because I knew I was not mistaken. but he would have considered me ~~impetant~~ impertinant had I told him so. our debate lasted More than an hour. Eve was sewing

Friday 3rd   the snow very deep but the weather moderate was writing in my Journal. Eve spent an hour in Br Rodybacks. talking about the Gospil &C. finished binding my Quilt

Saturday 4th   the weather cold I helped Mother Clean house. then wrote in my Journal Eve I riped the waist of my white dress apart with the intention to alter it. more fasionable.

Sunday 5th   weather quite cold AM father and Mother went to meeting and stayed till 4 oclock PM I was writing until 2 PM in my Memerandom Sister Jane then came and spent the PM I got supper for her and me and we had an agreeable visit together. Eve I read the life of General Z Taylor in a Almanac and an account of the war in Mexico

Monday 6th   weather Pleasent helped mother do up the work and was writing in my Journal. eve Bro Candland was here' and spent one hour. I was sewing & reading

Tuesday 7th   AM weather warm PM windy was altering my white dress. Bro Joseph Fielding' was here & made quite a visit' is just recovering from a severe fit of sickness. we was talking about the Resurrection Melleneum &C Eve I visited at Br Woolleys' and had a good supper. was heming me a table Cloth

Wednesday 8th   weather moderate was sewing on my dress. Eve father and Mother went to prayer meeting I was at home sewing and reading Sister Rollins called to see me.

Thursday 9th   weather cold yet pleasent was sewing on my white dress ~~Eve PM I visited at Sister Mellon' and enjoyed my visit much Eve Bro~~

~~Cnadland spent one hour with us talking about the affairs~~ I spent the twilight with Sister Rhodyback

Friday 10th   the weather pleasent AM I helped mother about the work. PM I visited with Sister Mellon' and enjoyed myself much' had a good supper finished altering my dress. today Henry returned home from Brighams farm with 15 Bushels of corn. well and in good spirits. Eve a report reached our hears that Frankin & Samuel had arrived in New Orleans' and although we did not learn from whence it originated' ~~yet~~ and could only hope it was true. yet it seemed as tho it put new life with us' and caused our hearts to rejoice in the prospect of so soon being permited to enjoy the Sociaty. of those we so dearly love. Oh! Lord grant that the news may be true' and we soon see their mutch loved faces again in peace' and enjoy thy smiles.

Saturday 11th   weather pleasent till night then windy. AM Was cleaning house. cooking &C PM Sisters Hartwell and Slaid came and made us a visit with their 2 Babes. I enjoyed their Company much was sewing on my Scotch Calico dress eve I was reading in the St Louis Organ.

Sunday 12th   weather cold & windy AM the family all went to meeting. and I was at home writing in my journal PM Sister Orcer came home with the folks and took dinner with us. the two Sisters Bullocks [Henrietta Rushton Bullock and Lucy Caroline Clayton Bullock] was also here and drank a Cup of Coffee' and eat some pye. I had another dumb Ague and after their departure I went to bed' and was afflicted with the fever till Eve

Monday 13th   weather cold yet pleasent. felt pretty slim all day. mended me a couple of dresses. Eve went into Sis Woolleys and borrowed me a book to read. and was sewing and writing journal

Tuesday 14th   weather pleasant AM was reading and sewing. ~~PM~~ 12 oclock father brought in a Star just from England belonging to Sister Jane. I read it nearly through. then went and made a visit at Bro W Millers. I felt quite unwell with the Ague before I started from home and thought I would try for a change what affect a walk would have upon me. the Ague how ever kept pace with me. sister M prevailed ~~with~~ upon me to lay down on her bed and rest after which I felt much better. Eve I walked up to Sister Jennes' and spent the Night with her. had a good long talk with her

Wednesday 15th   weather pleasant tho somewhat windy. was at Sister Jennes until 11 oclock AM then went to see Uncle Willard' found him mutch better. I took dinner [with] him alone. he gave me a News Papper to read a story that was in it. which I did. I remained there until 3 PM. then left and came to Sister Janes. were I remained till Sun down' and had a very pleasent Conversation with her then returned home. on my way thither I called to see Sister Jenne who was upon the bed sick. when I got home I found the house alone the family being gone to Meeting. to day they had killed the Pig. Eve I was sewing.

this night a Young Bro by the name of Row. stayed with us. he was one of our dear Brother Joseph's Mess Mates' in whose Arms he lay' when his gentle Spirit took its departure to that being who gave it. he spoke much in praise of our dear departed Brother' said he was one of the best young Men he ever saw &C &C

Thursday 16th   weather very warm I was quite unwell all day. father was Cutting up' and Salting down his Meat Mother was trying [frying] out the Lard &C &C I helped about the work all I was able. today the house was thronged by about ½ a dossen Indians. we had also several of the Bre call to see us' as well as 2 or 3 sisters. PM Sister Jane came to see us and spent the Eve I enjoyed her visit much H[enry] went home with her. today I got a letter from Fathers folks

Friday 17th   weather very warm yet windy by spells. was helping Mother do the work. today Melinda Wood visited with us. I enjoyed her very much. altho she seemed somewhat low Spirited. I entertained her as well as I was able gave her some Poetry to read' also read to her some parts of my husbands letters. and had a pleasent tete tete with her. to day I commenced to turn Henrys Cap. Eve Brother Barlow was here and spent one hour. was sewing

Saturday 18th   the weather pleasent was helping about the work. and finished turning Henrys Cap. PM Br Mellen & Ormas Bates was in and spent some time talking on Prinsaples &C Eve I was cutting out Pieces' in the form of a Star for a Bed quilt

Sunday 19th   weather pleasent until Eve when we had some thunder. Lightning. and rain

at 12 oclock I went to meeting at the Stand where we were addrest by Bro O Pratt upon the Plurality of Gods he proved from Scripture that we are the Sons & Daughters of God (and that Jesus Christ was our Elder Brother' who through his birth right has become our Savour and our God) and as a Child grows up and be comes like his father. so we grow up like our Heavenly Father and pertake of all his Attributes' and in time shall become just like him Even Gods. he said that God himself was once Man like unto us. who was ameanable to a higher Power for his conduct. and had a Father &C &C

the question said he will naturaly arrise in your mind' were did the first God come from' and how was he Created. The Christian world in ~~geen~~ general' admit that he existed from all Eternity and there is only 2 ways

he must either have existed' from all Eternity. or otherwise have had a creation. and how could he have been Created as there was no living being. or Spirit in Existence. this would naturaly be soposed to be imposable I will tell you what my Cogitations are' but do not wish to consider that I teach it as doctring or beleve it as such.

he then gave us a view of what the World must have been E'er the Earth, &C &C was formed said the matter then Existed out of which all things were made that now exist. and he soposed that there was a kind of Intelligent

Matter' that had the Power of self Movement. and as Intelegence cleaveth to Intellegence' so one particle of intellegent Matter cleaveth to another' and at last a combination of this Matter' formed an <u>Intelegent Spirit</u> &C &C Bro Woodruff said he beleved what Bro Pratt had said was true. and that he had been well pleased with his remarks &C &C after which a Hymn was sung. and he dismised the meeting. I then went to see Sister Jenne who was sick' and told her what I could remember about what had been Preached. also read her the Epistle of the Twelve to all Nations.

then agreeable to Mother Snyders urgent request I went home with her and took Tea &C had quite a pleasent chatt with her' then returned home amidst drops of rain. Eve I was in Br Rodybacks alittle while after which I was reading and writing talking &C &C

Monday 20th   weather lowery and cold. was Making my Scotch dress of Blue. and helping Mother about her work' Who was making a Sociges. Eve was Cutting out Pieces. for a quilt

Tuesday 21st   weather moderate AM was prepairing to receive Company and at 12 oclock I had the unspeakable pleasure of receiving a letter from my Husband. Br Bullock brought it to me' and read it (the first time I ever permited any one to read one of my letter before reading it myself) then carried it back to Uncle Willard who was very impatiant to hear it. it gave me great joy as it always does to hear once more from my dearest freind' and espacialy to hear that he was soon to return. Oh! Our Father in Heaven do thou be pleased to preserve him as in the hollow of thy hand' from all danger both on Sea and Land and bring him speedly and safely to my Arms' for thou knowest that my Bosom yearns to see him once more and enjoy his sweet sociaty PM 3 of Wm Millers Ladys came and Made us a visit' also Sisters Barlow. and S Woolly. and very unexpectedly Jane Hall. or Richards. we got them as good a supper as we possabley could and was glad to see that they appeared to enjoy it. Eve father brought in Br [William P.] Mcantire (and his wife [Anna Patterson McIntire]) to play afew tunes for us on his violin these put the Spirit of dance into the company. and finely we danced 4 French 4s. after which a part of the company took their leave appearing well satisfied with their visit &C. Br Mcantire and his wife stayed longer and took some refreshments' talked about Br Joseph Smiths death and the results &C &C

Wednesday 22nd   a pleasent day Mother visited at Sister Jennes. I made a loaf of Bread. cooked Beans. scuched coffee. fed the Calf. washed dishes. cleaned the house. and eve sewed on my dress. Eve Sister Rollins came to see me about coming to work for me. made her Eat Supper with me after which I was writing in my Journal read my letter to Sister Rodyback. also Sister Rolins by Fathers request to day father told me a secret on purpose he said' to try or prove me wither I could keep one or not. said if he could find one who could keep one he would consider that person a prize &C

Thursday 23rd a cold windy day AM Aunt [Fanny Young] Murry. Sister Benson &C stoped in their Carrige to see us' and said they would come next Thursday and make us a visit. at 12 oclock Sister Haven came and spent the day with us. enjoyed her visit much' in my estimation she is one of the Choisest of Women' eve I walked with her as far as Sister Janes. she then invited Jane and myself to go and spend the next day with her. I spent the night with Jane very agreeably we talked until after midnight

Friday 24th weather pleasent AM went with Jane to see Sister Jenne. at noon went with her to Sister Havens' agreeable to former ingagements. and assisted Miss Sarah Hill to quilt a Quilt. (she being living with Sister Haven) Sister [Almira Merrill] Lamb also visited with us we had a very Plesant visit indeed. from there we went to dancing Scool (about 5 oclock) were I took a number among the rest' and danced several times. a few of the Brethren then hired the fid'ler to play a while longer' and Jane ane me accepted an Invetation from Br R Camball and stayed until 12 oclock' he and Henry then accompanied us home to night I injoyed tollerable well. danced just as much as I wanted. and stayed all night with Jane

Saturday 25th weather rather windy stayed with Jane till noon. then took leave of her and called to see Sister Jenne. from there I came to Sister Maces and spent the PM. with her and Elizabeth [Lydia Taft] Webb. enjoyed my visit much' and in the Eve returned home and Quilled [Quilted] a Cap for Mother. to day I hemmed some Insersion for Aunt Sarah

Sunday 26th weather pleasent was at home all day writing a letter to my Father. Eve Jane and Amelia came and spent the evening with us. was much pleased with their visit

Monday 27th weather very pleasent AM I assisted Mother do the work and cleard out my red Chest. and and put my things back in order again. filled up some Cracks in the floor' with Earth to prevent things from falling through. Moped [mopped] under my Bed &C PM was sewing on my new dress in Br Rodybacks. and spent the eve in Br Woolleys sewing.

Tuesday 28th a cold windy day AM I finished making my dress. PM I made a visit to Br Fielding in company with Sisters Cobb [or Coal] and E Wilding' saw Sister Hyrum Smith and enjoyed my visit much' was knitting Edging. Eve home writing journal.

Wednesday 29th AM weather pleasent PM windy. to day Sister Rollins did a large washing for us. I helped about the work allday and got so tired that I had a high fever. PM Amelia and Ellen Richards [Partington] came and made us a visit. Evening was cutting out Stars for quilt

Thursday 30th weather windy & cold AM was cleaning house' and preparing for Company. PM expecting Sisters Benson and [Fanny] Morrey but they did not come. I commenced to make me a new night dress. Evening was cutting out pieces

Letters to Samuel Richards, November 1847 to February 1848

Camp of Isreal. Winter Quarters. Omaha Nation. November 17th 1847[13]
My Dearest Freind' and beloved Husband.

I am once more Seated with my Desk upon my lap. and Pen in hand ~~to write~~ with the intention of writing a few more lines to you. which I sincerly pray' may reach you safely' and find you in the enjoyment of health' and all other needfull blessings. my health is tolerable good at present' father Mother & Henry are tolerable well also. the Lord be praised for this and every other blessing. for I think [we] have experianced enough ill health this Sommer to make us know how to appriciate a day of <u>health</u>' when it pleases our Heavenly father to bestow that blessing upon us. Mother and I have been taking turns in being Sick all Sommer. but have been so fortunate as not to be sick both at a time except once. and that only for 2 or 3 days. I have just recoverd from a very severe attact of the Chills and fever (the first time I ever was afflicted with that disease) had the first Chill on Saturday Oct 23th in the evening' soaked my feet. took composision and retired. had a very high fever through the night. Monday had another and was very Sick all day evening at my own request I went through a course of medecine in hopes that would have a tendancy to retart the progress of my desease' but every day this week found me worse and worse I have never endured so high a fever since in this Country. I sufferd a great deal though. I have seen the time that I sofferd more (viz just before we left Nauvoo.) but I sofferd all I wanted too I assure you. Oh Samuel 'tis when I am Sick' that I miss you the most when on a hard and narrow bed. alone and sleepless here I lay. No frend to ease my Pillow for my head. or moist my lips when parched and dry. O <u>Samuel dear</u> it was not so. <u>when thou was by</u> my <u>side</u>. for <u>thou didst seek</u> my <u>wants</u> to <u>know</u>. and <u>hasten</u> to <u>sopply</u>.

On Sunday the 30th Uncle Willard and the rest of the Twelve (PPP & Taylor excepted) arrived in the City. with the Pioneers. the former sent me his blessing (having heard that I was sick.) and said I should get well. next day the family all received an invetation and went and visited at Uncle Ws and Lovica Jenne came and stayed with me. eve Amelia came home home with them to see me. Uncle W sent me word that he should expect to see me at his house the next day. said he wanted to see me very much but was not able to come and see me. next morn Bro Cambell came to invite the family to a family meeting at uncle Ws in the eve said that uncle W said he should expect to see me among the rest and he knew he was in earnest from the manner in which he spoke. I could not help smiling at the Idea that he

could expect one who had not left her bed for Six days and nights. except
while it was made. to come a ½ mile to see him. and said in a joke to Bro C
will you bring a weelbarrow and take me there. he said he would do any
thing that I wished that was in his power if I would go. well said I if you will
I will go. Mother seemed quite Shocked at my presumption and asked if I
would think of such a thing after being so closely confind. I told her if Uncle
W said I could go I was willing to try. so he came at the apointed time with
a Carrige and I went. Bro C carrid me into the house. and uncle W received
me from his arms and led me into his bed room were I lay down on his bed.
he then kneeled down by the bedside. and I had a sweet little viset with him.
he told me I should be blessed for coming and be made whole. he kissed
me for you and Asked me if twas not just as good as though I had got it from
you. I told him it would answer very well for a substitute in the meeting he
uncle Levi and father laid hands upon me and Uncle W blessed and prayed
for me. Oh he offerd up such a sweet prayer for you there was just every
thing included in it that my fond heart could wish you to enjoy and I might
say the same in regard to that part of it that was ofer'd up in my behalf. we
enjoyed a very interesting meeting I stayed all night. and the next day went
into Uncle Ls and took a walk in the Gardin. had a good viset. and in the
eve' bro C brought me home again in the Carrige. Since that I have been
recovering' have had no Chills since and I pray God I may never have
another. but I think I have writon enough on that strain and as much as you
will want to hear.

last Monday I worked hard all day making Pumkin Butter. in hopes that
you would be here this fall or winter to help me eat it. but I sopose there is
no sic good luck for mary. about ½ past 9 Oclock in the evening I received
a letter from you which I can assure you was more than wellcome. althou it
did say that I had got to live alone another winter. [*page 2*] It was dated Sep
8th on that day I often wonderd if you rimemberd that 'twas my birth day
did not know you had chosen it as a day to communicate your thoughts to
me. you wonder if I rememberd the 9th of Aug to convince you that I did. I
will extract a few lines from my dayley journal writon on that day.

> This day 23 years ago
> My Husband dear was born
> O may he live with joy to hail
> A thousand Anniversary morns
> Live to Thy praise O heavenly King
> Upright and pure without a stain.
> To do the work that thou assigns
> And in thy Presence favor find.
> O may he as a Husband Act 'ere
> In love and wisdom Act his part

> The failings of his Mary bear
> For true he clings around my heart. &C & so on.

yes Samuel I remimberd it and like you contemplated the many and various scenes through which we both have been called to pass. since that day one year ago. and rejoiced to think that it was past even in the way it has. and the reccollection that we both have been endeavering to obay Council and do the will of our Heavenly Father caused a feeling of satisfaction to thrill through my bosem. and I felt to pray unto him that the end of every Year might find us both as earnestly engaged in the Path of our duty. although I cannot wish' that every year' should find us under the same sircumstances' for there is so much selfishness about me' that I think I should want to spend some of our <u>birth days in your</u> Sociaty. but go daft 'twill be few that I shall [have] the priveledge to enjoy

Thursday 18th 2 Oclock PM. I again resume my Pen. I wonder how my Samuel is today. I was sorry to hear that your health was not so good. my dear do try and be as carefull of your health as possable' and favour your self all you can and live for my sake' for in <u>you</u> is <u>reposed all my hopes</u> of <u>happyness. forever</u>. I never saw the time in all my <u>life</u> that I had so mutch <u>ambision</u> about <u>living</u>. if I get <u>sick</u> I must be <u>prayed for</u>' take <u>medicine</u> or some <u>thing must</u> be <u>done</u> to <u>hasten</u> my <u>recovery.</u> 'tis <u>all</u> for <u>your sake</u> and for your comfort and happyness that I wish to live. Oh! that I may ever be blessed with Patience and with the Spirit of the Lord. that I may ever find favour in your sight' and answer all your expectations. you say you hope I will not feel cast down' because I cannot see you as soon as I expeced &C I had fondly hoped to have seen you this <u>winter</u> but as it is as it is. I sopose I can possabley say as much as Bro P P P said his wife said-if-I must-! I can-! (endure your absence another Winter) I should have been very very happy I can assure you could it have been otherwish. but it is no [*illegible*] thing for me to be disapointed I have no doubt my love' but it will be for our best good. and I pray that you may be blessed with means sofisint to take us over the Mountains (altho I should not be muckle soprised if you and I should not see the Mountains for some years yet. but say nothing to any one) but I have found out to my satisfactions that some one^14 (who thinks he has a right to I supose) is looking some years into the future' and planning out <u>work</u> for <u>you</u>. twill all be right Samuel dear. but for my sake keep this within your own bosem! beleve me Samuel I do not want to do any thing that is wrong if I can help it. so if I should write you short sentences or even leave out something that you might think I could write just as well as not do not think it strange. (in that which follows as well as that wich is past.) I saw a Map of the Great Salt Lake City a few days ago I think there will not be mutch crowding there as there is an Achre & quarter alowed to each person for building spot and gardin. I saw writon on 3 Lots joining to one another'

Phinehas R. F D R. and Samuel W Richards. so you can see that some one looks to your Intrest when you are not here to look to it your self. I have permision to write all I know about the City. (you may judge how far my knowledge extends) but as the Twelve are about to Publish a burcler [brochure]. you will excuse me if I for bear to write any thing about it. and when you come I will tell you all I have heard. a word to the wise tis not nessasary that the world should know all our prospects

[*page 3*] I am very sorry that Br Littlefield has done as he has. (but should be more sorry if it had been my Samuel. but thank heaven I have no truoble on that score) I should not be soprised if he gets a reppremand from the 12 and called home into the bargin. me thinks if he had done as he was expected to do' I should have had my husband at home this Winter.[15] I have not bought a house' and the reason why I made mension of it in my letter was because that bros Willey (who you once took care off when sick) and Sheets had just sold their houses for six dollers each and they were very comportable ones and such as would just have suted me for this Place. and I thought how pleasent it would seem to go and keep house for you should you return this fall. and that to before you was abliged to build one for I dreded the thought of having to live in with another family. and I hoped 'twould be the desire. of my Samuel to live along [alone] also.I received your letters by Bro Scovil on the 3rd of Oct the next day I received [*hole*] 3 pounds you sent by him. which were very acceptable as I had [*hole*] one dollar remaining. plenty of calls for that. but the letters [*hole*] was what was the most wellcome that night we all feasted upon [*hole*] I assure you. the Money you sent by Candland. I have not received I beleve I wrote you an account of his trials when coming [*hole*] on a Scrap that I put in a letter that father wrote. on rather I beleve in one that Jane wrote. to F. Bro C I expect is in rather poor sircumstances' would I beleve be glad to pay me if he had the means. I rejoice to hear that the work of ~~God~~ God is still prospering among the Nations of the Earth and I feel to praise his holy name for all the blessings' werewith he has blessed you in that he has made you instrumental in his hand in bringing many Souls unto a knowledge of the truth. oh may you be blessed & prosperd in all your in all your [*sic*] endeavers to do good. and ever be enabled to live with an Eye single to the Glory of God. is the sincere prayer of your Mary. I was very glad to hear that my freinds in Eng were all well. have you seen sister Ann. I should much [like] to hear from her please remember me very kindly to them all. I should hope to see some of them with you when you come. May the Lord bless them all. I have received all your letters as far as I have had any knowledge of them the letter dated July 5th was I beleve the last letter [*washed out*] rote you. but I expect you will have learned by this time that it is [*washed out*] the last time that I have writon to you or that you have had the privelige of hearing from me. father wrote 2 letters to you & F in July on the 26th I wrote you a Scrap which he enclosed in one of them. in September I wrote a letter to my folks in Eng. on the 28th I wrote a half sheet to you which I sealed and enclosed in the former. on the 4th of Oct I wrot another letter to Brothers & Sisters in order that <u>you</u> might hear from me should you still be there. on the 17th I wrote another Scrap to you. which Sister Jane who started on that day for St Joseph Mo. took with her' and I expect enclosed in a letter to F. F. if you should happen to hear from me by the above wont you then give me the credit of writing to you once in 3 <u>Months</u> Oh Samuel my dear you need not upbraid me if I did say I would write again in 3 months for I think there is scribling enough in one of [*tear*] letters to last that long or at least to weary your patiance (as I should think it would.) so that you would be glad to have a intervall at least of 3 months. 'tis 10 Oclock here so I must bid you a good night. or rather wish you a good Morning for I sopose 'tis morning with you.

Friday morn 19th Good morn to you my love' and may you this morn enjoy <u>health</u>. Peace. and plenty. Mother has just returned from Uncle Levis were she has been watching all night with with Amelia who is very sick with the Measles' Heber John & Rhoda Ann have just recoverd from the Measles. little willard has now got them. Uncles Willard & Levi and the rest of the family are as well as usual for them. Aunt Rhoda is some what tried and worn out with taking care of Amelia.

evening since writing the above. I have had a Chill. after which I was very much afflicted with Pain for a short time. got father to lay hands on me and got immediate relefe. feel quite comfortable this eve. I broke them the last time with Quinine. and Uncle W. and my freinds put on the climax of faith and prayer. I shall try them again if my case requires it. but I pray my heavenly father that he will grant that the past may sofise

[*page 4*] if I was only permited to look into' the future and know of a certainty that I should be no worse' I would not write tonight. but lest it should be otherwise I will endeavour to write a few lines. last Tuesday eve I had a first rate visit with Bro H B Jacobs and his wife' he arrived here about a week ago. <u>his health</u> is quite pour. he wishes me to give his love to you' and tell you he is still trubled with bleeding at the lungs. he speeks very highly of the English Bre Sisters and often prays the lord to bless them. he says he said something to you about bringing him a Cap. he wishes you to bring him a <u>Plaid</u> also and he will pay you Bro Scovil seems very healthy. the other bre I beleve have not yet arrived. Mother wishes me to write her love to you and Franklin. says she is waiting very impatiantly to see you return' but will try & be as patiant and [as] posable. she has just reminded me that it is the <u>Annversary</u> of the <u>Night</u> that <u>Brother Joseph died</u> there was a couple of the Brethren who helped take care of him when Sick and bury him when dead. stayed with us one night ashort time ago. from whom we learned the perticulars of his <u>illness</u> and <u>death.</u> he was able to walk about more or less unto the day of his death. he talked much about and was very anxious to return

<u>home</u> we were all mutch pleased with the Poetry you wrote on his <u>death</u> think it is very appropriate and worthy a peace in print Henry sends his love (Mother says he is siting in the Corner Cracking Hazle nuts) he says he has only gethered one Bushel. but if you will come home this winter he will give <u>you</u> <u>some</u> to pay for that <u>Candy</u> that you are agoing to bring him I think he merits it pretty well' so you may venture to bring him some. he asks me every once and again if it can comfort my heart any—if he will do something or other for me. I have not heard from Maria of late. expect to hear frome her when Jane returns. who we are now expecting dayly. and my anxiaty to see her makes the time seem very long I asure you. Jane seems very dear to me' the more so I sopose because we have we have [*sic*] been together in hours of affliction and sorrow and because our situations are some what similar and we can sympathize with each other. Bro Fs letter accompanyed by the 17th and 18th Numbers of the Star. came in the same Mail with you[r]s. so we are Ignorant of what he has writon as yet. wish Jane was here to enjoy them.

Saturday 20th feel as well as usual. this morn' how are you my love. hope you are well. Maria was well when we last heard from her. Wolter had gone to St Louis to get a fit out. will I expect stay till Spring. Mother wants you to bring her a woolen lincy dress when you ~~to br~~ come she will need one very much by another winter. you will also remember that she needs Muslin for a Cap to wear at certain times. &C if you bring any dresses for me' I <u>need</u> <u>dark ones</u> for every day wear the worst. I would bring me a pair of Slippers No. 3 large or 3 & ½. Mother I expect would be glad of a pair also. the same size would fit her also. we shall need considerable Cotten Cloth before we go to the mountains' I have usued one of the waggon Covers to line a cupple of quilts with this Summer. you will remember my dear that there is a good deal to be done preparatory to our journey' should we go West next Spring. you will also have heard that we have no Waggons or Oxen. and only one ~~cow~~ Cow. and as the Companyes will start much earlier next Spring' it will be nessasary that you should start at least (and latest) by the first of January. as my sheet is full I must draw to a Close the Lord <u>bless</u> and <u>preserve you</u> <u>love.</u> from your wife Mary H Richards

[*left margin of page 2*] Aunt Rhoda Amelia Uncle Willard & Levi wish a rememberance to you and F. with many of our freinds please remember me very kindly to Brother Franklin tell him Jane was well with the exception of a cold when we last heard from her. which was about 2 weeks ago. I saw Brother Spencers family on Thursday eve. were all well except his 2nd Daughter who is just recovering from the Measles. and she is doing well are sweet girls

[*upside down on page 2*] I read him the verses you composed on Joseph's death. to the 3rd he claped his hands' and exclamed Oh Glory. when I had finished he requested me to write him a coppy which I agreed to do. good night love and the lord bless you

Oh! may the Bareque that bears you o'er
The ever restless <u>Sea,</u>
In safty reach' its destine'd Shore.
And you' your Native Country ~~greet or~~ see

O may no object ~~intervene~~ intervene
To stay you on your way.
But to your freinds and kindred dear
May you soon in safty make your way.

O could I gaze upon thy Brow
And Print there on a kiss
on it recline and hear thy vows
'Twould be a source of bliss–

   I composed the above lines a few minutes ago when recovering from a <u>Chill</u> you will be able to judge from thier appearance
   [*left margin of page 3*] I saw Bro G A Smith yesterday. he told me he heard good reports from you and F. said Bro Hyde said in Council' that he did not know the worth of them Boys till he had proved them &C (need not feel vain) I told him I hoped you would soon be permited to come home and report yourself. &C my dear I hope you will continue to write to me every oppertunity. I should like to know when you epect to sail. Oh that you may have a swift and prosperous voige. and that I may soon be permited to <u>imbrace you</u>. the Lord bless you forever is the prayer of your Mary
   [*left margin of page 1*] <u>Whisper</u>; I have heard by the bye' that there is quite a number of labourers going out soon to gether up the w[h]eat. and I should not <u>wonder</u> if Eng. & Cot [Scotland] gets a viset from [*wax seal*] if so they may be the bearers of a letter to you. you need not be soprised either' if you should see a [*wax seal*] from the Dozen among the rest. I have heard some hints on the subject. they say they have first rate meetings now [*wax seal*] Mary has not been able to attend them for 4 Sundays but she will [*wax seal*] must sacrifize in some degree. to retain a blessing so sweet to me as health.
   [*upside down on page 3*] 22nd Uncle Willard has just been here and made us a sweet little visit. he sends much love to you and says he will write by the next mail if he can get time
[*addressed to*]
Mr. Samuel W. Richards
Star Office 39 Torbock St.
Liverpool.
England.
Care of Mr. Franklin D. Richards
Received Jan 18th 1848

Camp of Israel Winter Quarters[16]
Febuary 25th 1848 Noon

My Dear Samuel. 'Tis a beautyfull day. and I have just returned after spending Six days abroad visiting among my friends. and have taken up my Pen to spend this afternoon writing to you Oh! how happy I should be' could I spend it in your presence. and have a real good tete' tete <u>with you</u> all <u>alone.</u> I am antisapating such a visit before long. and rejoice in the prospect. I have of soon <u>wellcomeing</u> you. to your <u>own.</u> my health I am happy to say. is prety good at present. have not had a <u>Chill</u> for near 4 weeks. nor the dumb Ague for about one week. hope we have declined partnership forever. which may the Lord grant and the glory shall be his own.

   I was indeed made glad. on the eve of the 17th by receiving your kind letter dated at the Close of the of the Old Year. it gave me much joy to hear that you was well. but am sorry to hear that you had been <u>sick.</u> I rejoice to hear that the Lord has prospered your labours. and that you have been as an Instrument in his hand in bringing many to the knowledge of the Truth. but <u>nothing</u> can give me greater joy. than it does to learn that it is still your unchanging desire to do that which is right and well pleasing in the sight of <u>God</u> and those whom he has appointed to be our leaders here on the Earth. as well as all his Saints. Oh! that you may ever be blessed with wisdom and strenth to fortify you against every temptation and enable you to bid deffiance to all the powers of the Evil <u>one</u> it gives me secret joy to hear my Brethren speak well of you. and learn that they have great confidance in you & F and my joy' shall ever increase' with the knowledge that you have not betrayed the Confidance that has or may be reposed in you. but have been faithfull in keeping all your sacred Covnants. and humble under all sircumstances' wither in prosperity or adversity. followed by praise' and flattery. or Evil spoken off. loved. or ~~despesed~~ despised or what ever may be your lot

   [*left margin of page 1*] I am told by many' that Samuel will bring lots of money with him when he comes. I tell them I am perfectly willing it should be so though I have no such epectations myself. if it only pleases the Lord to return you to me in safty' I care not if you have not a Cent left. if you are blest with your health and [*wax seal*] of Heaven we can live

   [*page 2*] last Saturday I went to Uncle Willards' and visited there and at Uncle Levi's until Wednesday. the former has been very sick mostly confined to his bed for the last 2 months. I think he is now recovering. I had some good visits with him. wish I could write you all the perticulars. but be patiant and I will tell you' when you come home. one <u>thing</u> I have got the promis off. and that is. that it will be many years err you will be permited to settle down with the saints. and if you are permited to remain one year with them now' twill be more than I expect. but this does not truble me much at present. I endeaver to bear as patiantly as possable my present sofferings.

without borrowing truble for the future. for I am aware that it will bring with it' all that I shall want to endure. and my prayer is' that we may have strenth according to our day to endure the trials of the same. and ever be found in the Path of our duty. and the Lord has promised if we <u>love</u> and put our <u>trust in him</u>. that all things shall work together for our good. and this is my desire I called on Francis Swan last Sunday and told her what you wished me to. she seems to take the death of her mother very hard. last wednesday I visited at Bro Benson's with Sisters O & P P Pratt. spent the night with Sister Jane. and yesterday visited with her at Sister Lennards. from whence I returned this AM Sister Jane is well She with all the rest of our connections sends much love to you and F. we have just heard that Brother Wolter has returned from St Louis' and taken Maria from St. Joseph to Westren' [Weston] were they are now living' and may remain there til you come. should be glad to see them come up with you. Uncle Levi and his Wife. Bro O Pratt and his Wife. and several others will start for England in the Spring. Aunt Rhoda is going to take little Levi into her charge expects to go West this Spring. her health is quite poor. tis now night most dark. and I must bid you a good night. so if now my dear your on the <u>Sea</u> may the winds and waves be fair for thee.

[*left margin of page 2*] I have contracted no debts as yet my dear for you to pay when you return. would I could say the same by or about another person who I could name. I should like to talk with you a while after you return. e'er you make all things publick in regard to what you possess. <u>Not because</u> I wish to influance your <u>mind</u> for or against any person. but that you may know what I think you had ought to know

[*page 3*] Sunday 27th 12 Oclock father and Mother are gone to meeting' Henry is up to Brother Brighams farm. were he is gone to husk Corn on shares. and Mary is at home alone. trying to Scribble a line to you with a miserable Pen.

My dear husband' me thinks by this time you are or ~~ot~~ aught to be' at or near' New Orleans. would I knew were you now are and wither it be will with you' or not. but why should I wish this' for it may be you are in danger. and did I know this' I should be miserable. but now that I do not know I will pray for your safty' and hope for the best.

Eve Mother sends her kind love to you and Franklin she has just returned from Uncle Willards. she says he thinks he is getting better' though he is confined to his bed most of the time. he has had a long siege of sickness' but I trust he will soon be well. I send you a few lines by Brother Scovil to New Orleans. were I expect you will meet him. if you should not get them. I made mention of your bringing me a foot stove if you thought best I have had to beg all the letter Paper I have usued' from father for a long time. but although he has plenty I do not like to beg. he told me when I asked him for this sheet. that I must write you to bring I dont know how much with you. I have bought some for journals. and if you intend ~~I should~~ me to continu keeping one. I shall Need to have you bring me some Paper. I have now' not more than 2 Teaspoons full of Ink. I fear 'twill not last me till you come you will please bring some with you. I ~~have been~~ bought me six Quills as many months ago. and have used them till there is no more use to them. I begin to think 'tis about time for my Husband to come so that I need not have to write so many letters. I am tired of this way of telling my thoughts and wishes with a <u>Pen</u> would much rather do it with my Tounge. I think you will see by this' that I need a new soply before I write many many more letters.

[*left margin of page 3*] please give as much of my love as you can spare to fathers folks. I sent a letter to them last week in which I coppyed one from Brother Roger. I have not had a line from them since the letter sent by Bro Phelps. my health I am happy to say is still improving hope I shall be healthy and ruged when you come home

[*page 4*] if you have not all ready got them' I shall need much a soply of thread. Needles. Pins. Pens. &C I should also like 2 or 3 Pounds of cotten Batten. and a Pound or so of Cotten Yarn for stoc the Clock has just struck 10 this eve I have been reading a Star which Jane has received to day Publiced Dec first. I must now bid you a good night. praying the blessings of the Heaven to rest upon you do hast home as soon as you can I am as ever your unchanged and affectionate Wife

     Mary H Richards

[*addressed to*]
Mr. Samuel W Richards
St. Louis Missouri
Care of Mr. John Parker
between Franklin Avenue and wash
recd April 31st 1848

Valentine sent by Samuel from Scotland to Mary. Courtesy of Alton F. Richards Family, in possession of Rama Richards Buchanan, great-granddaughter of Samuel and Mary. A poem on the back of the valentine reads,

> This Valentine sheet With love so replete
> In <u>constancy</u> to thee is sent
> The Offering receive, The giver believe
> Till him you receive as he went
> S.W.R. to M.H.R.

CHAPTER NINE
As "a steam Boat hove in sight"

Spring came, bringing with it a feeling of excitement, as the populace in Winter Quarters planned to leave the Missouri River. President Brigham Young and the first pioneers had settled the Great Salt Lake Valley, with many returning to gather their families. A letter from Samuel verified his departure from Liverpool in February. Mary continued sewing, quilting, and braiding. She watched for steamboat arrivals, and when one came in sight, she and Jane hastened to the landing, hoping Samuel and Franklin were on board. Mary's journal ends with an unfinished sentence four days before Samuel's arrival. After that, there was no reason to write more. Her beloved companion was in her arms again.[1]

Journal Six
Friday, March 31, 1848, to Tuesday, May 16, 1848
Winter Quarters, Nebraska[2]

A Journal and Memorandom of Mary H Richards. commencing ~~Mach~~ March 31ˢᵗ 1848

today the weather was pleasent. was Ironing and fixing my Cloths and packing them away. was not very well.

Saturday 2ⁿᵈ April first. weather windy AM' PM pleasent. today I Cleaned up my Husbands Cloth's and put them out to Air. and went in search of swifts to doble of some Cotten Yarn. but was unsucsessfull called to see Sister Rollings little sick Son and spent a short time there knitting Edging. then returned home and put away My husbands Cloths &C Eve was cutting out stars for Quilt and about 8 oclock Bros Robert and Charls Burton came in from Mo the former spent a short time with us then went to Br Barlows. and Charls spent the Night with us. was much pleased to see them and hear from frends in Mo. Robert told me he had a little Daughter one Week Old [Theresa Hannah Burton].

Sunday 2ⁿᵈ a very windy day this morning Robert and Charls Burton took breakfast with us. let R read one of my letters. and had a good visit with him. AM was writing in my Journal PM I visited at Br Isreal Barlows' Where I saw Br Trueman Barlow' who had latley arrive in the City on a visit.

he met with a cruel missfortune one Year ago' wile blasting a Well and is Now entirely blind.

he seemed much pleased to hear my voice once more' and expressed a fevent wish (to all appearance) to see me.

we had quite a chatt about our old freinds' and the times we spent in Nauvoo. &C &C

I spent the Evening at home. Charls Burton spent the night with us.

Monday 3ʳᵈ a windy day was sewing &C &C felt very lonely

Tuesday 4ᵗʰ the weather pleasent today ~~Ellen Wilding visited with us. and I had some ple~~ Mother and me' visited at Br Slaids' [George Washington Slade] and had an excellant visit. Sisters Hartwell & Fuller visited with us.

Eve Henry. & Robert Burton came there and desired me to go' and spend the Evening with them at Br Barlows. which I did. saw Ellen Rockwood there. We sung some, had some Music. and finely wound up our evening visit by a dance enjoyed my self tollerable well

Wednesday 5ᵗʰ a pleasent day to day Ellen Wilding made us a visit. with her babe. and I fitted the lining of a new dress to her. we had some plain talk together about some ~~the~~ things that she had told about my Husband and myself. in which she had betrayed Confydence but she seemed unwilling to acknowledge it however I told her just what I thought in regard to the matter and so satisfy'd my mind. (all done in good feelings) I went with her to see Br Barlows folks. and walked with her part way home. Eve the folks went to meeting and I was alone

Thursday 6ᵗʰ weather pleasent to day we washed and Ironed after which I started to go to Sister Janes' Met with Sister Lennard who prevailed with me to Join her in a walk to Sister Bensons after which I spent the Night with Jane very agreeabley' we lay awake and conversed till long past midnight

Friday 7ᵗʰ a pleasent day morn took breakfast with Jane then went to Br Woolleys to assist Ellen about making a dress. on my way there' I called to see Sisters Haven and Rockwood. and invited them for Sister Jane' to visit her the next day. I sowed for Ellen untill eve then called in to see Sister Noon and her family also Aunt Rhoda.

when I came to Janes house she was not there' so I went to her mothers where I found her and spent the eve. then went home with Jane and spent the Night

Saturday 8ᵗʰ weather pleasent to day Jane said I must stay and visit with her and her company. which I did. about 10 oclock PM Sister Jane had the misfortune to Badly Scold her foot. was lifting the Tea kettle' when the Bail broke and the lid fell off' and turned the then boiling water onto her foot' twas cruel to see her suffer with the pain this caused her. I then turned Cook' made some Pyes &C and got ready to receive the company. PM I enjoyed a sweet visit with Sisters Haven & Rockwood. and our Mother and Mother Snyder. got Supper &C eve Br Right came in and chatted a while with us. spent the Night with Jane

Sunday 9th   weather cold was with Jane all day. and did what ever needed to be done' PM Uncle Willard came on foot' was the fartherest or longest walk he had taken for more than 3 Months. he lay down a while' after which I combed his hair for him. Amelia was here also til eve spent this night with Jane also

Monday 10th   weather pleasent was with Jane until 4 PM then Lovisa came to stay with her' and I came home.

her foot appears to grow worse after I got home I wrotte off some Verses for Trueman Barlow' to gra[t]ify a wish he made. and answer his request. after which I wrote a letter to my Father in St Louis.

Tuesday 11th   weather pleasent to day Br Rowe was in our house on a visit

I was very busy all day' helping about the wort [work]. and repairing the lining to a comforter &C &C

Wednesday 12th   weather pleasent Morn Br Rowe made me a set of quilting Frames. AM I put a Comforter in the Frames to tie and finished tieing it by 4 oclock PM Br R helped me to put it in the fram's roal [roll] it' &C I had quite a high fever before & for some time after I finished it. to day Sister Orcer was here and made a visit. Evening I went to prayer meeting' with father & mother. was a good meeting

Thursday 13th   pleasent weather to day we quilted a Scirt quilt for Mother. Sister Orcer came and helped us. I quilted two thirds of it myself. and we finished by 4 oclock PM to day I learned some thing by talking to Sister O' that I had not learned before

this PM I had a high fever again and felt sick.

the room we quilted in' was one belonging to Br Woolley which is vacant. eve I bound my Comforter. Trueman Barlow spent eve with us

Friday 14th   the weather changeable this morn Sisters Benson and Lennard sent us word that they were coming in the PM to make us a visit. so we went to work and cleaned the house &C and I made a couple of pyes they came at the appointed time' and we enjoyed their company much

Eve I wrote a letter to Elizabeth Fory to send by Trueman Barlow

Saturday 15th   weather moderate. to day I doubled a pound of Cotten Yarn' then went to Br. Robinsons and twisted about ½ of it. took supper there eve I was sewing

Sunday 16th   weather pleasent AM was at Meeting. Bro Young preached on various subjects relative to our going West. He said' it had been said by many' that it was not [ne]sessary to take so much provision this year' as last but said he' I should not feel willing to start with one pound less provision this year then those who went last year for their Crops were destroyed last year through carelessness and altho they have got 2 thousand Achres plowed' they have got no Fences. and what know we but they will be destroyed. I tell you I have no confidance in them' that they will preserve their Crops. John Taylor himself would lay in bed and let his Cattle destroy his Crops.

and if they do watch' the Indians might ride through and destroy it. for we know not but there are thousands of them in the Neighborhood

he then said that a brother who had writon back from the Valley' said' they had not left all the Thives back in Winter Quarters. for some of them had found their way to the Valley. he then swore with up lifted hands. that a theif should not live in the Valley after he got there if he knew it' for he would cut off their heads or be the means of haveing it done as the Lord lived. for they had tormented this People long enough &C &C

he then called upon Br Mccord who had just returned from the Valley' to give some account of that place. which he did. said the Bre and Sisters were generaley well had not had more than 10 deaths since they had been there' and he thought they had Averiged 3 Births in a day. had gotten considerable wheat planted. and about 1500 Achres of land plowed &C after meeting I went I [to] sister Janes and spent the PM then called to see Sister Jenne. eve we had a pleasent shower of rain was writing in my journal

Monday 17th   a very Windy & cold day. AM I was sewing PM I visited at sister Obanks Eve Uncle Levi and Aunt Sarah visited with us. and I think I never saw them appear so interesting before

Tuesday 18th   weather moderate to day I put a bed quilt in the frames and commenced quilting it. eve was sewing' and felt very unwell

Wednesday 19th   weather pleasent was quilting PM Sister Orcer came on purpose she said to talk with me. she helped me quilt a little a little

eve I went to the prayer meeting

Thursday 20th   A pleasent day Morn I sent for Sister Lennard who came & helped me quilt all day eve I went home with her and spent the night. she read to me all the eve. I enjoyed myself well.

Friday 21st   weather pleasent came home this morn and quilted all day. just at eve sister Lennard s[t]oped in to see me. at the same moment Br Camball rode up to the door with a letter from Samuel and F dated feb 20th in Liverpool. they were then expecting to sail in about 3 hours thanks be unto the Lord for this prospect. and may he bless him with prosperous and speedy passage home. his lines were very short. but the[y] were truely sweet. eve I wrote a letter to Elizabeth Fory in Davenport Iowa

Saturday 22nd   weather pleasent til eve then windy. to day I finished quilting my quilt and felt very tired. eve was sewing.

Sunday 23rd   a very windy day' went to see Sister Jenne who was very sick having gotten a little son yesterday. stayed with her a while' then went to mother Snyders were I dictated part of a letter for Lovisa Jenne soon after I got there Jane' and Melinda Wood came in. and we all stayed and took supper. after which we all turned our Cups and got Melinda to tell our fortunes eve br Chester Snyder waited upon me home.

Monday 24th   weather somewhat windy. was helping about the work and sewing' PM Br Robins visited with us. and took supper and bro Chester Snyder came and invited me to his weding and told me Miss Melinda Wood was his intended bride this somewhat soprized me for altho I spent last eve with both of them' I never once thought this would ever take place. he wanted I should go and help his mother which I did as soon as I could get ready. Br Robins walk'd up St with me. when I got there I found them waiting for me to make the Cake Cake Cake so I went to work and made made it. also some Cookeys. after which I went up to Sister Janes' with her' Phenihas Young and Henry. here the Weding party assembled. and soon this worthy Couple were made husband and Wife by Elder Joseph Young O may they live a life of peace Of love' of truth' of Righteousness

after this Cake and sling were passed around. several toasts were drank to the new Marrid pair and jou [joy] seemed to beam upon every countinance. Br Jacobs now arrived with his Violin. and I with some others joined the Bride and Groom in the dance.

I enjoyed myself much this evening and after the party were dismissed I and Jane waited upon the Bride to her bed. and bid her sweet repose. I slept with Jane

Tuesday 25th   weather pleasent morn took Breakfast with the Groom & Bride at Sister Janes PM Jane made a visit with me at Br Davis. Sisters Woolley & Mellen visited there also. Sister D entertained us with reading hers and her Husbands blessings showing us her numerous presents and so forth. we had a good Supper' and a pleasent visit. on our way home we called to see Sister Haven and Uncle Willards folks. eve Br Grant and his Ladys were at Janes. they sung several songs. I spent the night with Jane

Wednesday 26th   a pleasent day took breakfast with Jane. then came home and made me a Garment. PM went into sister Mellens house and sat a while with her eve I was sewing.

Thursday 27th   weather Cloudy. had had some rain. AM I assisted about the work as usual and was sewing. PM I attended a sewing bee at Br Barlows. with Sisters Rockwood' Haven' Palmer. and Burnham. and enjoyed my visit. eve was sewing.

Friday 28th   weather windy AM was sewing. PM helped Mother Mother tie a Comforter. and Sister Davis visited with us. I got Supper &C was much pleased with her Company. eve was very tired

Saturday 29th   weather changeable helped clean the house. wrothe in my Journal. Sewed &C &C

Sunday 30th   weather pleasant AM was at the meeting. and heard an Interesting discourse delivered by Erastus Snow. who had Just returned in company with Br Benson and others' from the East' where they had been gethering donations for the Church. they brought a good account of the feelings of the Eastren people towards the people of this Church. Br Bullock then read an Epistle from the Saints in the Valley to the Saints in this place which brought some good news from the Saints in that quarter. said health prevailed. and they were putting in large Crops. After Meeting I walked up to Sister Janes were I saw Amelia. PM I attended Meetting with them and Melinda. Br Benson preached. after Meeting I went to see Uncle Willard who was very Sick (Sister Bullock went with with me.) found him blind with the sore Eyes.³ I sat on his bed side' and talked with him about an hour mostly about Samuel. he expressed a good deal of anxiaty for the well fare and prosperity of both Samuel and Franklin. and a hope that they would not do as some other had done. but come home as they had left. only better wiser and more experinced. &C &C

on my way home I called to see Sis Jenne. Eve I was writing in my journal

Monday May First.   weather pleasant AM Mother and I washed and Uncle Willard came to our door in a Carrige and brought Jane Hall to stay a few days with us she being sick and blind with the sore Eyes. I was very tired after my washing I did some sewing &C &C

Tuesday 2nd   weather pleasant tied some Yarn and sent it to Mother Snyders to be Coller'd [colored]. folded the Cloth's and commenced making me a new dress.

to day Uncle Willard came and took Mother Jane and myself out riding in the Carrige. we had a pleasant ride. but he was very sick.

Wednesday 3rd   weather pleasant Ironed my clothes. helped about the work &C &C just as we were eating dinner Uncle W and Br Benson came again in the Carrige and invited us all to take a ride so we left our dinner half eat and went. we had a very pleasant ride indeed. Uncle W being much better was able to converse' which made it far more agreeable. PM & eve I was sewing.

Thursday 4th   weather windy till eve. to day Jane was quite sick waited upon her' helped about the work sewed &C &C Eve Sister S Woolley and I went and spent the eve with Miss Walker. one of Br A A Liman's [Amasa Lyman] family. who for a pass time told us our fortunes. we enjoyed oursefs much. this night I slept with Sister Woolley in her Waggon

Friday 5th   weather pleasant helped about the work as usual. PM Jane being bette[r] we visited at Br Woolleys and had a pleasent visit and spent the Eve. I sleep'd with Sister W again

Saturday 6ᵗʰ   weather windy to day Jane went home. and I finished making my dress.

Sunday 7ᵗʰ   the weather pleasent AM I attended meeting Br O Pratt delivered a very interesting fare well address' he expressed great love and respect for this People and said it was with them he wished to live and die. he said his prayer should ever be in behalf' and for the wellfare and prosperity of this People. and he asked our prayers in his behalf and a promis was given him of the same. many tears were shed during his discourse

at the intermisson I went and took dinner with Br & Sister Wareham enjoyed my self much and attended meeting with them in the PM when we were addressed by Presedent Young on various subjects. he apointed a gard to protect the Cattle & City both day and night as long as we stay here. William Cuttler and James Comings were apointed Captins each to take their ten men every other day and place them on the most prominnant points of land to gard their Cattle from the Indians while feeding. &C &C he said he was thronged all the time with folks coming to be Sealed and he wished the Saints to understand that all these things would have to be done over again and that he could tend to sealing no more till he got to the Valley and after I am gone said he let no one else try to seal any one ~~when I am gone.~~ if they do the[y] will burn their fingers. try it if you want to &C &C &C

after Meeting I went to Sister Janes and found her sick with the teeth ache got supper for her and in the eve went down to Uncle Willards in her stead to plead the cause of Sister Jenne whose husband was trying to get her' to go down into MO against her will' her desires being to go west. from there I returned to Janes and spent the night with her

Monday 8ᵗʰ   weather pleasent to day Mother and I washed after which I walked up to Sister Janes. was very tired when I got there. I lay down and had a sweet Nap. Eve I walked down to Uncle Ws with Jane who wanted to see him about Sister Jennes case. but did not. we then called to see Br Young but he was not at home. we then went home. and a few minutes went down to see Br Bullock on the same buisness. after which I spent the night with Jane.

Tuesday 9ᵗʰ   weather pleasent this morn I helped Jane get breakfast' and did up the work then helped put a bed Quilt into the frams. Uncle Levi came in while we were doing this' and Nailed it for us. we had quite a pleasent chatt with him. I never saw him more socible

I then went to the store and bought some thread and we went to quilting. Mother came and helped us. PM Lovisa and Miss Allen came and quilted. about 4 oclock a steam Boat hove in sight. which caused hearts to rejoice for a faint hope lingerd in our bosoms that our husbands might posabley be there. our Work felt itself neglected for our Eyes were turned from it to the long desired Object. e'er Sundown we saw it land and as soon as it was down we all rode down to the Boat to get all the information we could. as soon as we got there a Br who came aboard invited us to go on which we did. he kindly conducted us to the midst of the pasengers. and were we wished to go and back to to our waggon. we saw a sister Roper just from England who gave us some information concerning our husbands &C &C after we returned home' went to Uncles Willards. were we saw Bro Hyde and conversed with him and had a long chatt with Amelia. we then returned home went to bed' and talked about two thirds of the night.

Wednesday 10th   morn had a pleasent shower of rain. after which the weather was pleasent. to day I helped Jane Quilt and do her work. PM I went down to Sisters Jennes in her stead' to converse with her on the subject of her husbands going down into MO' their going West[4] &C &C had a long chatt with her' and helped her make a Waggon Cover' and left her satisfyed in my own mind that she would do about right. I then went to Mother Snyders and got some Yarn she had been colloring for me. saw Jane' bid her good night and returned home. found Br Rowe in from MO' and learned that Br Parker and Mrs Willson' from New Orleans, were now boarding with us.

Thursday 11th   weather pleasent helped Mother about the work and repair'd a quilt for myself. eve I went with Henry and Jane to a party on the boat. found quite a number of Sisters there whom I was acquainted with' and enjoyed myself tollerable well. danced with Henry. G Spencer. N Daniels. and one or 2 others of the brethren got home about 2 oclock Morning

Friday 12th   weather Moderate helped mother about the work as usual. and wrote in my Journal.

Saturday 13th   weather pleasent helped clean the house. Scouer'd the tin ware, knives, Shelves, &C &C then took my sewing and went an[d] sat a while with Sister Willson then came home and Cut out a dress for Mother. which I had bought her' and part made it eve was sewing. and enjoyed a good wash

Sunday 14th   weather. windy AM I went to Meeting. Br Woodruff preached his fare well sermond is going on a mission to the East he instructed the Saints to be faithfull and do their duty and increase in all good works. desired an intrest in their prayers and said we should ever be rememberd by him &C &C bro Benson then made a few remarks. after which bro Brigham arose' and [made] some pointed and appropriate remarks. he called upon the Lord to bless this place for the good of the saints. and curse every Jentile who should attempt to settle here' with sickness, rotenness, and death also to course the Land of Missouri that it might sease to bring forth Grain or fruit of any kind to its inhabitance' and that they Might be cursed [with] Sickness, rotenness and death. that their flesh might consume away on their bones' and their blood be turned into Maggots. and that their torments never sease, but increase until they leave the Land' and it be blessed for the possessions of the Saints. he also cursed Mr. Miller the Indian Agent who came upon the Boat and said if there was any Lickur unloaded here he would spill it Br Young dared him to do it. and said if he had done it' he would have taped his vains for him. if he had died the next moment for doing so. for he had no right to come here and interfere with that which was none of his business. for his place was among the Indians.

he upbraided the Gard for neglecting their duty and exposing their Cattle to the Indians &C &C

after Meeting I went to see Uncles Willards and Levis folks. found uncle W sating up and being shaved. the rest about as usual. saw and [talked] with Brs G A Smith & Woodruff. I then called to see Sister Jane and Stayed till eve then called to see Sister Snyder and took [talk] with her' saw Mrs Cathrine Snyder just returned from the East. Philo and Lovisa then accompanyed me home. on our way we enquired of the Miss Spencers who had just [received] letters from England if they had heard any thing from our husbands or S & F. but. there was not a word concerning them. night it rained. and I was obliged to leave my bed

Monday 15ᵗʰ a rainey morn but a pleasent day. to day I finished making Mothers ~~bed~~ dress. dryed my bed and beding. and cleaned all arround it. &C &C.

eve I took a walk to see Mrs Willson after which I was writing in my Journal. to day Br Rowe left us for his home

Tuesday 16ᵗʰ the weather

BIOGRAPHICAL REGISTER

This biographical register lists each person Mary mentions in her memorandum, journals, and letters. Although Mary records most people with only their surnames, preceded by "brother" or "sister," most of the time their identity is known. These individuals are shown with their correct name and spelling. In the event that there are multiple possibilities, or a definite identification is not known, Mary's spelling of the name has been retained, and a description of the role of that person in her writings is included. All known individuals who might have played that role are then identified, and these names, with relevant information, are set off. Each entry lists birth, marriage, and death data, where known, and the person's association with Mary or the Richards family. The sources for each entry are cited fully in the bibliography; abbreviations are listed at the beginning of the bibliography.

AARON, Reverend. Church of England minister who visited Mary in late 1838 after her baptism into the Church of Jesus Christ of Latter-day Saints and tried to convince her she had made a mistake.

ABBOTT, Abigail. Born April 26, 1829/30, Wayland, Middlesex, Massachusetts, to Lewis Abbott and Ann Marsh. Married Albert Peck Tyler, December 26, 1850. Died December 12, 1854. Was one of Mary's best friends in Nauvoo and in Winter Quarters. Crossed Iowa with John Van Cott's company in 1846. [SEB 1:3]

ABBOTT, Lewis. Born December 18, 1795, Wayland, Middlesex, Massachusetts, to Amos Abbott and Lydia Moore. Married Ann Marsh, June 22, 1829, Wayland, Middlesex, Massachusetts. Died August 26, 1861, Salt Lake City, Salt Lake, Utah. His family, including daughter, Abigail, crossed the plains in John Van Cott's company, leaving Elkhorn camp on June 15, 1847. In first High Council of the Mormon church in Salt Lake City. [SEB 1:27-29; HTW 8:416]

ALLEN, Brother. Mary, Jane, and Henry went to a meeting at Brother Allen's house in January 1847, where they were addressed by Wilford Woodruff. Two Allen families are known to have been in Winter Quarters.

ALLEN, Daniel. Born December 9, 1804, Whitestown, Oneida, New York, to Daniel Allen and Agnes Stewart. Married, first, Mary Ann Morris, October 6, 1828/31. Married, second, Louisa/Eliza Jane Berry, June 22,

1847, Winter Quarters. Other wives in Utah. Died January 15, 1892, Escalante, Garfield, Utah. [ARCH]

ALLEN, Orville Morgan. Born June 9, 1805, St. Ferdinand Township, St. Louis, Missouri, to John Edmond Allen and Pamela Perry. Married Jane Wilson, August 4, 1825, in Missouri. She left him at Winter Quarters, and he married Susannah Ward. When she married another man, Orville married widow Elizabeth Ann Burkett Williams, August 4, 1850. Died November 12, 1893 in Pima, Graham, Arizona. Headed a relief team to bring the poor camp from Nauvoo to Winter Quarters. Listed in bishop's reports of Winter Quarters First Ward in December 1846 and January 1847. When Winter Quarters was evacuated, Orville moved his family into Iowa until 1852, when they left for Salt Lake Valley. [EH; MEMA: 21-35]

ALLEN, Brother. In April 1847 while returning from the Samuel Burton home near the Missouri/Iowa border, Mary camped near brother Allen in quite a settlement of Mormons.

ALLEN, Andrew Lee. Born November 27, 1794, Wakefield, Carroll, New Hampshire, to Elijah Allen and Mehitable Hall. Married Clarinda Knapp, December 11, 1826. Died August 14, 1870, Provo, Utah, Utah. Other wives. Was a counselor to Libbeus Coons in the Coonville Branch, now Glenwood, Iowa. Also a high priest in the Coonville Branch in January 1848. This settlement was one day's journey from the Burton home. On the way to Samuel Burton's, Mary stayed at Libbeus Coons's home the last night on the trail. [SEB 1:479-92; CBM: 1; MCCB; PHP: 7]

ALLEN, Miss. She and Lovisa Jenne quilted at Mary's in May 1848.

ALLEN, Elizabeth Catherine. Born June 4, 1834, Louisiana, Pike, Missouri, to Orville Morgan Allen and Jane Wilson. Married George W. Shepard/ Thorpe, Cornelius Lott, James Abbott, and Mr. Wing. Died December 11, 1911. [MEMA: 34]

ALLEN, Lucinda. Born June 2, 1824, Dresden Centre, Washington, New York, to Nehemiah Allen and Hannah Dunham. Second wife of Joseph Young. Married 1846, Nauvoo, Hancock, Illinois. Died July 16, 1881. She left Elkhorn for Salt Lake Valley in Brigham Young's Company June 1, 1848. [SEB 2:24-25]

ALLRED, Reuben Warren. Born November 18, 1815, Bedford County, Tennessee, to James Allred and Elizabeth Warren. Married, first, Lucy Ann Butler, December 4, 1836. Lived at Council Point, member of the Council Point Branch in May 1849. Transported Mary from her visit in Iowa to his home in April 1847. [CPBM: 1; SEB 2:232-35]

ALSTON, John. Talked at a Mormon church service at the home of John Parker Sr., in Chaigley, Lancashire, England, in 1838.

ANDERSON, Augustus Leander. Born June 27, 1832, to William Anderson and Emeline Tilton Stewart. One of three people killed by anti-Mormon mobs during the "Battle of Nauvoo" September 10-12, 1846. [WON: 175; SEB: CD-ROM]

ANDERSON, William. Born March 29, 1809, Lincoln, Penobscot, Maine, to William Anderson Sr. and Mary Joy Morrell. Married Emeline Tilton Stewart.

Moved to Nauvoo September 1844. Killed in the "Battle of Nauvoo" September 12, 1846. Mary identified him as Mr. Henderson. [WON: 175; SEB: CD-ROM]

BABBITT, Almon Whiting. Born October 9, 1812, Cheshire, Berkshire, Massachusetts, to Ira Babbitt and Nancy Crosier. Married Julia Ann Johnson, November 23, 1833/34, Kirtland, Geauga, Ohio. Died October 24, 1855/56, Nebraska. In September 1846, brought news to Winter Quarters of the mob action in Nauvoo and the temple destruction. [SEB 3:1-5]

BADLAM/BADHAM, Alexander. Born November 28, 1808, Norfolk, Norfolk, Massachusetts, to Ezra and Mary Badham. Married Mary Ann. Died 1894 in Davies County, Missouri. While in Boston, received a letter from Samuel Whitney Richards, which he forwarded to Mary. [SEB 3:110-12]

BAKER, Brother. Visited by Mary and Jane in Winter Quarters in December 1846.

BAKER, Simon. Born October 18, 1811, West Winfield, Herker, New York, to Benjamin Baker and Rebecca Thorn. Married, first, Mercy Young, December 21/31, 1829, Winfield, Herker, New York. She died and he married Charlotte Leavitt, April 8/18, 1845, Nauvoo, Hancock, Illinois. Other wives in Utah. Died October 22, 1863, Mendon, Cache, Utah. Simon and Charlotte were in the vicinity of Winter Quarters when their second child was born in July 1847. [SEB 3:316-21]

BALDING, Miss. Went with Mary to visit Mrs. Shimers in November 1847.

BARLOW, Elizabeth Haven. Born December 28, 1811, Holliston, Middlesex, Massachusetts, to John Haven and Elizabeth Howe. First wife of Israel Barlow, married February 23, 1840, Quincy, Adams, Illinois. Died December 25, 1892, Bountiful, Davis, Utah. She was a first cousin to Phinehas Richards and Brigham Young; their mothers were sisters. Elizabeth was a sister to Mary Ellen Palmer and Nancy Rockwood and a half-sister to Maria Haven Burton and Eliza Ann Burton, all of whom Mary mentions in her writings. [SEB 21:713-15; IB; NDM: 89]

BARLOW, Israel. Born September 13, 1806, Granville, Hampden, Massachusetts, to Jonathan Barlow and Annis Gillett. Married, first, Elizabeth Haven, February 23, 1840, Quincy, Adams, Illinois. Married, second, Elizabeth Barton, January 28, 1846, Nauvoo, Hancock, Illinois. Other wives in Utah. Died November 1, 1883, Bountiful, Davis, Utah. Sources conflict as to when Israel arrived in Winter Quarters. One source says his family spent the winter of 1846 in Iowa before going on to Winter Quarters the fall of 1847. This correlates with Mary's journal about Brother Barlow just arriving from Farmington with the corpse of Mother Barton, perhaps the mother of his second wife. However, that Brother Barlow may have been Truman Barlow. Israel may have been in Mt. Pisgah in 1846 when the Mormon Battalion volunteers were recruited and then in Winter Quarters to help build the first homes. [SEB 3:562-68; IB; HTW 9:471-72; NDM: 89]

BARLOW, Truman Root. Born August 9, 1818, Granville, Hampdon, Massachusetts, to Jonathan Barlow and Annis Gillett. Married Safrona Reed. Died February 1858, probably in Harlan, Shelby, Iowa, where Truman owned land and was living in September 1856. One of the first police of Nauvoo. Remained in Nauvoo after his brother Israel left so he could sell Israel's lands.

May have been the Brother Barlow just in from Farmington, Iowa, in October 1847. Traveled to Davenport, Iowa, April 1848. Lost the sight of both eyes by blasting a well while living in Iowa. [IB]

BARNES, Sister. Is mentioned visiting Mary in Winter Quarters during 1847 or helping her wash clothes. A sister Barnes is also found at Mt. Pisgah.

BARNES, Hulda. Born October 1, 1806, to Abijah Barnes and Abi Bradford. She lived in the house of the Prophet Joseph Smith in Kirtland. Married Heber C. Kimball, 1843, Nauvoo, Hancock, Illinois, his twenty-eighth or twenty-ninth wife. Died September 20, 1898, Holden, Millard, Utah. [SEB 3:640-41; 26:640; AF; HCKW]

BARNES, Lorenzo Dow. Born 22 March 1812, Tolland, Hampton, Massachusetts, to Phinehas Barnes. Married Isabella Pratt. Died on a mission to England on December 20, 1842. His wife may have been in Winter Quarters. [SEB 3:660-62]

BARROWS, Brother E./ BARROWS, Brother/ BARROWS, Sister/ BURROWS, Brother/ BURROWS, Sister. With the exception of meeting Brother E. Barrows at Mt. Pisgah, all of the other references to Brother or Sister Barrows/ Burrows indicate that they were living close enough to Mary so that she could visit or borrow coffee. Mary also mentioned Sister Barrows's three sick children.

BARRIES/BARRUS, Emery. Born April 8, 1809, Hanover, Chautauqua, New York, to Benjamin Barrus and Betsy Stebbins. Married, first, Huldah Abigail Nickerson, December 19, 1833. Other wives. Four children born before 1846. Died October 5/6, 1899, Grantsville, Tooele, Utah. Not known if he was in the Winter Quarters area. Was in Nauvoo. Emigrated to Salt Lake Valley October 1853 in Appleton Harmon Company. [SEB 4:20-24]

BARRIES/BARRUS, Huldah Abigail Nickerson. Born April 16, 1816, Springville, Susquehanna, Pennsylvania, to Freeman Nickerson and Hulda Chapman. Married Emery Barries/Barrus, December 19, 1833. Died August 22, 1872. [SEB 32:645-46]

BURROWS/BARROWS, Ethan Allen. Born January 12, 1817, Dalton, Coos, New Hampshire, to Jacob Barrows and Emily Waterman. Married, first, Lorena Covey, January 1, 1837, no known children. Married, second, Lucy Hardy, perhaps in Salt Lake City. Died 1904, Salt Lake City. Winter Quarters First Ward shows Ethan in the bishop's report and paying tithing in December 1846, also owning two head of cattle in June 1847. This is the ward Mary lived in. [SEB 4:13-14; EH]

BURROWS/BARROWS, Lorena Covey. Born August 4, 1820, Scipio, Cayuga, New York, to Benjamin Covey and Sally Vanderhoff. Married Ethan Barrows, January 1, 1837. [SEB 12:29]

BARTON, Mother. Brother Barlow came from Farmington with the corpse of Mother Barton in his wagon. She could have been Israel Barlow's second wife, Elizabeth Barton. A brief sketch of the life of Elizabeth Barton, however, indicates that after her mother's death, she cared for her father until his death; all of her brothers and sisters were then married. She then joined the church and moved to Nauvoo, where she married Israel. [IB: 240-41]

BATES, Ormus E. Born March 25, 1815, Henderson, Jefferson, New York, to Cyrus Bates and Lydia Harrington. Married, first, Phebe Marie Matteson, in 1835, Ellisburgh, Jefferson, New York. Married, second, Marilla Spink, in 1844, Nauvoo, Hancock, Illinois. Both wives had children in Winter Quarters during 1847 and 1848 and had children in Pottawattamie County, Iowa, in 1849. Other wives. Died August 4, 1873, Rush Valley, Tooele, Utah. [SEB 4:241-48]

BENSON, Ezra Taft. Born February 22, 1811, Mendon, Worcester, Massachusetts, to John Benson Jr. and Chloe Taft. Married, first, Pamelia Andrus, January 1, 1831, Uxbridge, Worcester, Massachusetts. Married, second, Adeline Brooks Andrus, April 27, 1841, Nauvoo, Hancock, Illinois. Married, third, Eliza Perry, March 4, 1847, Council Bluffs, Pottawattamie, Iowa. Other wives in Utah. Died September 3, 1869, Ogden, Weber, Utah. Member of the High Council at Nauvoo. Filled mission to the East and brought a large company of Saints from the Boston area. Ordained an apostle on July 16, 1846, to take the place of John E. Page, who was excommunicated. One of the original pioneers of 1847, returning to Winter Quarters in the fall of 1847 with Brigham Young. Mary attended meetings where Benson was the preacher. Appointed over the Saints in Pottawattamie County with Orson Hyde and George A. Smith in 1848. Member of the Blockhouse Branch, Iowa. [SEB 5:3-11; MPJ; HS: 50; PHP: 1]

BENSON, Pamelia Andrus. Born October 21, 1809, Windsor, Hartford, Connecticut, to Jonathan Harvey Andrus and Lucina Parsons. First wife of Ezra Taft Benson, married January 1, 1831, Uxbridge, Worcester, Massachusetts. Visited often at the home of Mary and Wealthy in company of other New England women and in turn was visited by Mary. [SEB 2:437-39]

BENT, Samuel. Born July 19, 1778, Barre, Worcester, Massachusetts, to Joel Bent and Mary Mason. Married Mary Kilburn, May 3, 1805, Barre, Worcester, Massachusetts. She died in Missouri. Other wives. Died August 16, 1846, Garden Grove, Decatur, Iowa, where he was the presiding elder. Was also in Kirtland, with Zion's Camp, and in the High Council in Nauvoo. Mary called him "Father Bent" in her letter to Samuel in September 1846. [SEB 5:55-59]

BENTLEY, Elizabeth Price. Born June/July 29, 1821, Gloucestershire, England, to William Price and Mary Ann. Married Richard Bentley, September 9, 1843, Nauvoo, Hancock, Illinois. Died December 6, 1882, St. George, Washington, Utah. [SEB 35:638-39; NDM: 106]

BENTLEY, Richard. Born October 1, 1820, Great Aycliff, Durham, England, to Thomas Bentley and Ann Wood. Married Elizabeth Price, September 9, 1843, Nauvoo, Hancock, Illinois. Other wife in Utah. Died March 24, 1906, St. George, Washington, Utah. Lived at Hyde Park, six miles east of Council Point and thirteen miles south of Kanesville with the families of Orson Hyde, who was his wife's brother-in-law, and his wife's family. The 1847 reorganization of the First Presidency was done at his home, where Orson Hyde lived. [SEB 5:82-85; RB; NDM: 106]

BIG ELK. Principal chief of the Omaha nation. [MAM: 71-72]

BIRD, Brother. Lived about sixteen miles from Keg Creek, Pottawattamie, Iowa. Mary stayed there the night of April 3, 1847, then attended church in the Bird home the following day.

BIRD, Benjamin Freeman. Born January 19, 1778, Rahway, Essex, New Jersey, to Jeremiah Bird and Elizabeth Marsh. Married Marabe Reeves, February 22, 1801, Morris, New Jersey. Died February 23, 1861, Springville, Utah, Utah. Became bishop on east of river July 24, 1846. Member of the Tabernacle/Blockhouse Branch, Iowa, January 1848, also Branch President of Lake Branch, Iowa, December 1848. [SEB 5:443-46; PHP: 2; MPJ; MAM: 218]

BIRD, Charles. Born September 19, 1803, Flanders, Morris, New Jersey, to Benjamin Freeman Bird and Marabe Reeves. Married Mary Ann/ Maryan Kennedy, March 22, 1826, Covington, Tioga, Pennsylvania. Died September 29, 1884, Mendon, Cache, Utah. Family were members of Council Point Branch, Iowa, organized May 23, 1847. [SEB 5:450-55; CPBM: 3]

BIRD, Richard. Born October 13, 1820, Portsmouth, Chenango, New York, to Benjamin Freeman Bird and Marabe Reeves. Married Emeline Crandall, March 27, 1845. Died February 27, 1895, Springville, Utah, Utah. Member of McOlney Branch, Iowa, in 1848. Two children born in Council Bluffs, September 1848 and December 1849. Moved to Salt Lake Valley in 1850. [IBI: 19; SEB 5:480-83; NDM: 99]

BLEASDALE, Jeanette. Born February 10, 1826, Thornley, Lancashire, England, to William Bleasdale and Margaret Moss. Married John Rawlston Poole, July 16, 1848, Farmington, Van Buren, Iowa. Died May 20, 1921, Menan, Jefferson, Idaho. Was Mary's friend in England. Temporarily remained in England when her parents emigrated to Nauvoo with Mary. Arrived in Winter Quarters and learned her parents were in Farmington, Iowa, so she left to live with them, where she met her husband. [JBP; AF]

BLEASDALE, Margaret Moss. Born May 17, 1798, Barton, Lancashire, England, to Robert Moss and Margaret Kelsall. Married William Bleasdale, September 27, 1820, Goosnargh, Lancashire, England. Died May 16, 1877, Centerville, Davis, Utah. Emigrated to America with Mary. [MMB; AF; ALL; MCCB]

BLEASDALE, William. Born December 4, 1796, Thornley, Lancashire, England, to Edward Bleasdale and Jeanette Clough. Married, first, Margaret Moss, September 27, 1820, Goosnargh, Lancashire, England. Other wives in Utah. Died August 1885, Centerville, Davis, Utah. LDS church meetings were often held in his home in England. Emigrated to America with Mary. Remained in the East to earn enough money to go to Illinois. Member of Camp Creek Branch, Illinois, in 1845, where Mary possibly stayed with him. [AF; WB; ALL; MCCB; CBR]

BOLEY, Barbara Harts. Born October 10, 1793, Berks County, Pennsylvania, to Conrad Hertz and Elizabeth Segner. Married Henry Boley. Died in 1869, American Fork, Utah, Utah. A neighbor of Mary's in Winter Quarters First Ward. She would not have been the woman who brought her children to visit, as they were grown, but Mary could have been writing about Barbara part of the time. [ARCH]

BOLEY, Betsy/Elizabeth Asenath Davis. Born September 12, 1822, Richester, Columbiana, Ohio, to Isaac Davis and Edith Richards. Married Henry Harts

Boley, June 19, 1846. Once brought her two children with her when visiting. Her sister, Edith Davis, also visited Mary with her. [SEB 13:398-99]

BOLEY, Henry. Born April 14, 1795, in Berks or Lancaster County, Pennsylvania, to Johan Peter Boley/Bolich and Catherine Ries. Married Barbara Harts. Other wife in Utah. Died January 2, 1881, American Fork, Utah, Utah. Is shown in the Winter Quarters First Ward bishop's report and tithing record for December 1846 and had three head of cattle in June 1847. [SEB 6:78-79; EH]

BOLEY, Henry Harts. Born October 11, 1823, Lancaster County, Pennsylvania, to Henry Boley and Barbara Harts. Married, first, Betsy Asenath Davis, June 19, 1846. Married, second, Hannah Jane Davis. Died June 19, 1876, American Fork, Utah, Utah. [SEB 6:81-83]

BOLEY, Mary Ann. Born April 21, 1833, Lancaster, Pennsylvania, to Henry Boley and Barbara Harts. Married Edward Sims, February 22, 1849. Died March 11, 1896. Identified in Mary's journal as Miss Boaley who was invited to a quilting party. [SEB 6:84]

BOSS, David. Born 1801, Davidson, Cabarrus, North Carolina, to Peter Boss and Mary. Married Martha. Left for Utah on June 15, 1847, in second group of ten, first fifty, under Hector Haight. Apparently didn't feel the need to plow fields for others in May 1847, as he was planning to leave, despite covenanting to plow, and was publically chastized. [SEB 6:226; HTW 8:421]

BRIKINNIGHT, Sister. Mary stayed eleven days at her home in Liverpool, England, while awaiting departure for America.

BRINTON, David. Born December 29, 1814, Thornbury, Chester, Pennsylvania, to John Brinton and Priscilla Branson. Married, first, Elizabeth Garrett Hoopes, February 22, 1844, Nauvoo, Hancock, Illinois. Married, second, Harriet Wollerton Dillworth, as her third husband, January 14, 1848, four days before holding a dance at his home. Died May 17, 1878, Big Cottonwood, Salt Lake, Utah. Emigrated to Salt Lake Valley in 1848. Married Harriet's sister, Ann, after her first husband, William Bringhurst, died. [HTW 9:474; SEB 6:756-61; NDM: 96]

BROWETT, Martha Rebecca. Born June 22, 1818/19, Tewksbury, Gloucestershire, England. Second wife of Orson Hyde, married in 1843. Later in life separated from him. Died October 30, 1904. Visited Mary with Sister Hyde. [SEB 7:4-5]

BULLOCK, Thomas. Born December 23, 1816, Leek, Staffordshire, England, to Thomas Bullock and Mary Hall. Married, first, Henrietta Rushton, June 25, 1838, in Leek, Staffordshire, England. Married, second, Lucy Caroline Clayton, January 23, 1846, Nauvoo, Hancock, Illinois. Other wife in Utah. Died February 10, 1885, Salt Lake City, Salt Lake, Utah. A clerk to Joseph Smith, then to the Twelve, finally to Brigham Young for more than ten years. Arrived in Winter Quarters with the Rushton families on December 6, 1846. [JTB: 5-14; FF]

BULLOCK, Henrietta Rushton. Born 1817 at Leek, Staffordshire, England, to Richard Rushton and Lettice Johnson. Married Thomas Bullock, June 25, 1838, Leek, Staffordshire, England. As his first wife, she would probably have been called "Sister Bullock" more than his second wife. Died October 19, 1897. [FF; JTB: 20]

BURNHAM, Mary Ann Huntley. born March 14, 1816, Waltsfield, Washington, Vermont, to Allen Huntley and Sally Hitchock. Married James Lewis Burnham, December 1, 1834. He may be the James who accompanied Levi Richards to England in 1840-43, so she would have been acquainted with the Richards family. When he died, she married Joseph Young as his fourth wife, February 6, 1846, Nauvoo, Hancock, Illinois. She then became a first-cousin by marriage to Phinehas Richards and Elizabeth Haven Barlow. Died November 10, 1903, Salt Lake City, Salt Lake, Utah. She attended a sewing bee at Elizabeth Haven Barlow's with Mary and Elizabeth's sisters and sister-in-law. [SEB 24:794-6]

BURNS, Mr. danced with Mary at a party at David Brinton's. Usually when Mary used the designation of Mr. it meant a non-member, while the word brother meant a fellow Latter-day Saint. There is one possible Mr. Burns who was a Mormon.

> BURNS, Enoch. Born November 12, 1807, Ascot, Sherbrooke, Quebec, Canada, to James Burnes and Hannah Tupper. Married Elizabeth Jane Pierce, January 11, 1842, Nauvoo, Hancock, Illinois. He was living in eastern Iowa in 1845 and was in Fremont County, Iowa, in August 1847 and January 1849. He may have been visiting Winter Quarters in January 1848. Died in Pima, Graham, Arizona, February 19, 1901. [SEB 7:647-50]

BURTON, Charles Edward. Born June 4, 1830, Adrian, Lenawee, Michigan, to Samuel Burton and Hannah Shipley. Married Harriet Maria Miner, March 20, 1860, Toledo, Lucas, Ohio. Died July 26, 1896, Mesa, Maricopa, Arizona. One of Mary's young friends. [RTB]

BURTON, Hannah Shipley. Born October 12, 1786, Gilberdyke, Yorkshire, England, to William Shipley and Jane Taylor. Married Samuel Burton, June 12, 1804, Luddington, Lincolnshire, England. Fourteen children, many of them friends to Mary and Samuel. Died July 26, 1846, Austin Township, Atchison, Missouri (now Fremont County, Iowa), and was buried in the bluffs. [RTB]

BURTON, Maria Susan Haven. Born April 10, 1826, Holliston, Middlesex, Massachusetts, to John Haven and Judith Woodby/Woodbury Temple. Married to Robert Taylor Burton, December 18, 1845, in her father's home in Nauvoo by Brigham Young. Died March 30, 1920, Salt Lake City, Salt Lake, Utah. First step-cousin to Phinehas Richards, and one of Mary's best friends. [SEB 21:724-25; IB: 15; RTB]

BURTON, Robert Taylor. Born October 25, 1821, Amherstburg, Essex, Ontario, Canada, to Samuel Burton and Hannah Shipley. Married, first, Maria Susan Haven, December 18, 1845, Nauvoo, Hancock, Illinois. Other wives in Salt Lake City. Died November 11, 1907, Salt Lake City, Salt Lake, Utah. Member of the Nauvoo brass band, William Pitt's band, and the Nauvoo Choir. In January 1845 went on a special mission with Samuel Whitney Richards to the central counties of Illinois to allay prejudice as a result of falsehoods against the church. He and Maria, along with both sets of parents and other family members, lived near the Nishnabotna River, near what was then called Austin Township, Atchison, Missouri, on the Missouri/Iowa border. Mary visited them there, also in Salt Lake City after both families had emigrated. [RTB; SEB 7:699-706; MPJ; HTW 9:476]

BURTON, Samuel. Born June 12, 1783, Garthorpe, Lincolnshire, England, to Samuel Burton and Mary Johnson. Married, first, Hannah Shipley, January 11, 1804, Luddington, Lincolnshire, England. When Hannah died, he married widow Louisa Chapin Smith, September 29, 1847, Winter Quarters. Died January 21, 1852, Suttersville, Sacramento, California. Friend and neighbor of Phinehas Richards's family in Nauvoo. [SEB 7:707-10; MPJ; HTW 9:476; RTB; N5HP]

BURTON, Theresa Hannah. Born March 26, 1848, Austin Township, Atchison, Missouri (near Hamburg, Fremont, Iowa) to Robert Taylor Burton and Maria Susan Haven. Married Lewis Samuel Hills, October 17, 1866. Died April 9, 1924. [RTB; SEB 7:700]

CAHOON, Andrew. Born August 4, 1824, Ashtabula County, Ohio, to Reynolds Cahoon and Thirza Stiles. Married, first, Mary Carruth, November 9, 1847. Married, second, Margaret Barr Carruth, July 17, 1848. Married, third, Jeanette Carruth, probably in Salt Lake City. Died December 13, 1900, Murray, Salt Lake, Utah. Was on a mission in Scotland from 1845 to 1848, returning on the ship *Carnatic* with Samuel Whitney Richards. Among the Scottish saints listed as accompanying him were Mrs. Mary Cahoon and Miss Margaret Carruth. [SEB 8:180-4: SWR]

CAHOON, Daniel Stiles. Born April 7, 1822, Harpersfield, Ashtabula, Ohio, to Reynolds Cahoon and Thirza Stiles. Married, first, Jane Amanda Spencer, July 17, 1843, Nauvoo, Illinois. Children born in Winter Quarters 1846 and in Council Bluffs area November 1848. Married, second, Jane's sister, Martha Ellen Spencer, 1847, in Pottawattamie County, Iowa. First child born May 1848 at Plum Hollow. Died November 13, 1903, Deseret, Millard, Utah. One of Mary's young friends, she often danced with him. At times, he was a fiddler at the dances. [SEB 8:185-89; NDM: 105]

CAHOON, William Farrington. Born November 7, 1813, Harpersfield, Ashtabula, Ohio, to Reynolds Cahoon and Thirza Stiles. Married, first, Nancy Maranda Gibbs, January 17, 1836, Kirtland, Geauga, Ohio. Married, second, Mary Wilson Dugdale, September 23, 1845, Nauvoo, Hancock, Illinois. Died April 4, 1893, Salt Lake City, Salt Lake, Utah. Worked on Kirtland Temple, member of Zion's Camp, early missionary, drummer in Nauvoo Legion band. Danced with Mary at the Council House. [SEB 8:225-30]

CAIN, Elizabeth Whitaker. Born August 4, 1828, Kidderminster, Worcestershire, England, to Thomas Whitaker and Sophia Turner. Married Joseph Cain, February 1, 1847, England. When he died, married his friend and business partner, Samuel Whitney Richards, January 27, 1859. Died March 26, 1880. Resident of Salt Lake City Fourteenth Ward. Known for her charitable disposition and pleasing personality. Sister to Sophia Whitaker who married John Taylor. [RFR; SEB 8:235; GW]

CAIN, Joseph. Born November 5, 1822, Douglas, Isle of Man, England, to James Cain and Ann Moore. Married Elizabeth Whitaker, February 1, 1847, England. Died April 20, 1857, Salt Lake City, Salt Lake, Utah. Emigrated to America in 1844. Printer in Nauvoo. Returned to England on mission in 1846.

To Salt Lake Valley in 1847 with John Taylor, who was his brother-in-law. Joseph and Samuel Richards were co-partners in a number of business ventures in Utah. When Joseph died, Samuel married his widow, Elizabeth, and took over Joseph's businesses. [SWR; SEB 8:237-40; HTW 8:424-25]

CAMPBELL, Robert Lang. Born January 21, 1825, Kilbarchan, Renfrenshire, Scotland, to Alexander Campbell and Agnes Lang. Married, first, Joan Scobie, November 20, 1845, Nauvoo, Hancock, Illinois. She and child died of exposure from leaving Nauvoo. Other wives. Died April 11, 1874, Salt Lake City, Salt Lake, Utah. Clerk for Patriarch John Smith and William Smith. Worked as clerk in the church historian's office under Willard Richards, where Mary had many opportunities to interact with him. [SEB 8:511-18; JTB: 35; HTW 9:477]

CANDLAND, David. Born October 15, 1819, Highgate, Middlesex, England, to Samuel Candland and Sarah Betts. Married March 27, 1844, Nauvoo, Illinois to Mary Ann Barton, younger sister of Israel Barlow's second wife, Elizabeth Barton. Other wives in Utah. Died March 8, 1902, Mt. Pleasant, Sanpete, Utah. Mission to England 1846-1847. Lived in Blockhouse Branch, Iowa, after vacating Winter Quarters. [SEB 8:535-40; IBI: 30; JTB: 39; IB: 322; NDM: 97; MBB]

CANDLAND, Mary Ann Barton. Born February 6, 1814, Shamokin, Northfield, Pennsylvania, to Noah Barton and Mary Cooley. Married David Candland, March 27, 1844, in Nauvoo. Died February 1859, Salt Lake City, Salt Lake, Utah. Younger sister of Elizabeth Barton Barlow. David described her as his "truest friend." [SEB 4:95-96; IBI: 30; IB: 322: NDM: 97; MBB]

CARMICHAEL, Mary Ann Wilson. Born October 29, 1808, Sussex County, New York, to Robert Wilson and Mary. First wife of William Carmichael. Visited Mary in July and August 1847. [SEB 46:904-5]

CARMICHAEL, William. Born August 15, 1804, New York County, New York, to William Carmichael and Agnes. Married, first, Mary Ann Wilson. Married, second, Emma Wright. Seventy in Nauvoo third ward. [SEB 8:669-70]

CARTER, Lydia Kenyon. Born December 11, 1801, Benson, Rutland, Vermont, to Daniel Kenyon and Mary Tanner. Married Simeon Carter, December 2, 1818, Benson, Rutland, Vermont. Died December 10, 1866, Salt Lake City, Salt Lake, Utah. Simeon was in England serving a mission while Samuel was in Scotland. Visited with Mary and the other wives of British missionaries. [SEB 26:482-83]

CARTER, Simeon. Born June 7, 1794, Killingsworth, Middlesex, Connecticut, to Gideon Carter and Johanah Sims. Married, first, Lydia Kenyon, December 2, 1818, Benson, Rutland, Vermont. Married, second, Hannah Dunham, January 19, 1846, Nauvoo, Hancock, Illinois. Other wives. Died February 3, 1869, Brigham City, Box Elder, Utah. Mission to England 1846-48. [SEB 9:61-65]

CARTER, Sister. Had a long talk with Mary after church meeting in Winter Quarters, May 30, 1847.

CARTER, Clarissa Amelia Foster. Married Daniel Carter, September 26, 1829, Benson, Rutland, Vermont. Family living in Winter Quarters when Daniel's second wife gave birth in December 1846. [SEB 16:872]

CARTER, Sarah. Born May 22, 1825, Herefordshire, England. Emigrated from Winter Quarters June 17, 1847. No other Carters were with her. [HTW 8:442; SEB 9:52]

CARTER, Sarah York. Married William Fourlsbury Carter November 11, 1834. He married his second wife in Winter Quarters, March 1846. Perhaps married his third wife in Winter Quarters, December 1846. [SEB 48:16; IBI]

CARTER, Lydia Smith. Married Dominicus Carter, May 21, 1828. Family living in Council Bluffs from August 1847 to June 1850. Dominicus a high priest in the Big Spring Branch January 1848 [PHP: 3; SEB 40:89-91]

CASSON, Mary. Born December 1, 1814, Forest of Ballond, Yorkshire, England. Endowed January 20, 1846, in the Nauvoo Temple. [SEB 9:138]

CHATMAN, Brother. Danced with Mary at the council house January 29, 1847. Only one Chatman/Chapman/Chitman family is known to have been in Winter Quarters. Other families were living on the east side of the river.

CHAPMAN, Welcome. Born July 24, 1805, Reedsboro, Bennington, Vermont, to Benjamin Chapman and Sibyl Amidon. Married Susan Amelia Risley in 1831. Ninth child born October 1846 in Winter Quarters. Other wives. Died December 9, 1893, Manti, Sanpete, Utah. [FF]

CHENEY, Elijah. Born September 14, 1785, Great Barrington, Berkshire, Massachusetts, to John Cheney and Elizabeth Granger. Married, first, Achsa Thompson, March 14, 1811. Died November 3, 1863, Centerville, Davis, Utah. High priest in Upper Keg Creek Branch, Iowa. Mary indicated he lived about two miles from the home of Samuel White at Keg Creek, Iowa. [PHP: 4; SEB 9:479-81]

CLAPP, Benjamin Lynn. Born August 19, 1814, Alabama, to Ludwick Clapp and Margaret Ann Loy. Married Mary Rachael Schults. Other wives in Utah. Died in California about 1860. On municipal high council in Winter Quarters and one of seven presidents of the Seventies Quorum. Was a frequent speaker at Sacrament meeting in Winter Quarters. Was excommunicated from the church April 7, 1859, for voicing opposition to officers of the church and for pride. [NJ51:26-28]

CLARK, Bishop. Offered to officiate at a dance at David Brinton's, but as it was not his ward, the party broke up.

CLARK, Isaac. Born May 7, 1806, in Bowling Green, Warren, Kentucky, to Robert Clark and Ruth Moore. Married Mary Timmons/Lemmons, January 16, 1850. Other marriages in Utah. Died January 24,1854, Ogden, Weber, Utah. Bishop Clark is shown in Bishop Edward Hunter's Winter Quarters First Ward record for relief to the poor, March 1847. Lived in Coonville, Iowa (now Glenwood, Mills County) and in Pottawattamie County, Iowa. [SEB 10:50-52]

CLARK, Hyrum. Born September 22, 1795, Wells, Rutland, Vermont, to Luman and Permelia Clark. Married Thankful Gill. Died December 28, 1853, San Bernardino, San Bernardino, California. Was a high priest in Kirtland. Served missions to England, Isle of Man, Ireland, and Scotland, returning to America in 1841, 1844, and 1846. [SEB 10:40-41]

CLARK, Sister William. Died about May 20, 1847.

CLARK, William. Plowing for Phinehas in June 1847.

CLAYTON, William. Born July 17, 1814, Charnock Moss, Penwortham, Lancashire, England, to Thomas Clayton and Ann Critchlow. Married, first, Ruth Moon,

October 9, 1836, Penwortham, Lancashire, England. Married, second, Margaret Moon, April 27, 1843, Nauvoo, Hancock, Illinois. Other wives in Utah. Died December 4, 1879, Salt Lake City, Salt Lake, Utah. In charge of emigration on the ship *North America* which carried John and Ellen Parker to America in 1840. One of the original pioneers to Utah in 1847. [SEB 10:300-309]

CLEVELAND, Henry Alonson. Born January 4, 1809, Schoharie, Schoharie, New York, to Sereign Cleveland and Martha Drake. Married Ann Slade. Died 1867, Centerville, Davis, Utah. Wounded in Far West. Shown in Winter Quarters First Ward report as owning four head of cattle in June 1847. Mary visited his home in July 1847. [SEB 10:379-81; EH]

COAL, Sister. visited with Mary in January and March 1848.

COLE, Charlotte Jenkins. Married John Cole, 1842, Nauvoo, Hancock, Illinois. Second child born October 1846 in Winter Quarters. Third child born July 1848 in Council Bluffs. [SEB 10:751-54]

COLE, Nancy Serepta Parrish. Married to William Riley Cole, March 19, 1840, Quincy, Adams, Illinois. Member of Nauvoo Fifth Ward with Phinehas when some of children blessed. Two children born in Iowa. [SEB 11:15-18, 33:914-16]

COLE, Phebe. Fourth wife of Benjamin Covey, who resided in Winter Quarters First Ward June 1847. [SEB 12:12]

COLFLESH, Harriet Wollerton Dillworth. Born February 24, 1824, Uwchland, Chester, Pennsylvania, to Caleb Dillworth and Eliza Wollerton. Married, first, William Henry Colflesh. Married, second, David D. Yearsley, February 7, 1846. Married him for time only the same day she was sealed to her deceased first husband. Was his plural wife. David Brinton's first wife died, afterwhich Harriet and David Yearsley were divorced. Harriet then married David Brinton, January 14, 1848, Winter Quarters. Died November 19, 1896. Often visited Mary with Sister Dillworth. [SEB 14:62-63]

COLTRIN, John. Born July 20/30, 1775, Tolland, Tolland, Connecticut, to John Coltrin Sr. and Rebecca Maxon. Married Sarah Graham. Died August 13/31, 1846, Pottawattamie County, Iowa, or Winter Quarters, Nebraska. In September 1846, Mary wrote that "Father Colton" died August 31, 1846. [SEB 11:193-96]

COLTRIN, Zebedee. Born September 7, 1804, Old Seneca, New York, to John Coltrin and Sarah Graham. Married, first, Julia Ann Jennings. Married, second, Mary Mott, February 5, 1841, Nauvoo, Hancock, Illinois. In first pioneer company to Salt Lake Valley, 1847. High priest in Blockhouse Branch January 1848. [SEB 11:210-15; JTB: 61]

COONS, Libbeus Thaddeus. Born May 13, 1811, Plymouth, Chenango, New York, to Thomas Coons and Elizabeth Crandall. Married Mary Ann Williamson. Other wife. Died July 7, 1872, Richfield, Sevier, Utah. President and bishop of the Coonville Branch (now Glenwood, Mills, Iowa). His home was one day's journey from the settlement where Samuel Burton lived. Mary and Samuel Burton spent the last night here on their way to the Burton residence. [SEB 11:498-501; CBM: 1; PHP: 4]

COONS, Mary Ann Williamson. Born August 11, 1812, Springfield, Otsego, New York, to John Williamson and Nancy Sickels. Married Libbeus Thaddeus Coons. Died November 27, 1867. [SEB 46:643-44; CBM: 1]

CORAY, Melissa Burton. Born March 2, 1828, Mersea, Essex, Ontario, Canada, to Samuel Burton and Hannah Shipley. Married, first, William Coray, June 22, 1846, Mt. Pisgah, Union, Iowa. At age eighteen and married one month, accompanied her husband on the Mormon Battalion, hiring on as a cook and washerwoman. Was one of only four women to complete the march. After Coray's death, she married, second, William Henry Kimball, December 24, 1851, Salt Lake City, Salt Lake, Utah. Died September 21, 1903, Salt Lake City, Salt Lake, Utah. [SEB 6:694-96; RTB]

CORAY, William. Born May 14, 1823, Alleghany County, New York, to Silas Corey and Mary Stevens/Stephens. Married Melissa Burton, June 22, 1846, Mt. Pisgah, Union, Iowa. Weakened from Mormon Battalion march, he died March 7, 1849, Salt Lake City, Salt Lake, Utah, one month after birth of his second child. Sealed to Melissa on his death bed by Brigham Young. [SEB 11:609-11; RTB]

CORBRIDGE, Alice Parker. Born April 16, 1820, Chaigley, Lancashire, England, to John Parker Sr. and Ellen Heskin. Married July 17, 1841/43 to Edward Corbridge. Died February 5, 1890. Mary's sister. [AG]

CORBRIDGE, Edward. Born January 10, 1806, Thornley, Lancashire, England, to William Corbridge and Ellen Bolton. Married Alice Parker, Mary's sister, July 17, 1841/43, Chipping, Lancashire, England. Died January 8, 1883, Bountiful, Davis, Utah. Emigrated to St. Louis, Missouri, about 1849. From there traveled to Utah with the company of his brother-in-law John Parker Jr. in 1852. [EC]

CORBRIDGE, Ellen. Married to Brother Walker, according to letter of June 8, 1847.

CORBRIDGE, Ellen Parker. Born July 7, 1817, Chaigley, Lancashire, England, to John Parker Sr. and Ellen Heskin. Married January 25, 1840, to William Corbridge. Died November 9/10,1906. Mary's sister. [AG]

CORBRIDGE, James. Born 1810/1811, Thornley, Lancashire, England, to William Corbridge and Ellen Bolton. Married Elizabeth Walmsley, February 16, 1835, Lancashire, England. Also married Mary Whitehead. Baptized March 24, 1840. Sunday morning church meetings were often held at his home three miles west of John Parker's home in Chaigley, Lancashire, England. A brother to Edward and William Corbridge and their sister, Ann Corbridge Slater, all of whom joined the LDS Church in 1839 and 1840. [EC; IGI]

CORBRIDGE, Mary. Mary's niece.

CORBRIDGE, William. Born March 9, 1808, Thornley, Lancashire, England, to William Corbridge and Ellen Bolton. Married Ellen Parker, Mary's sister, January 10, 1840, Clitheroe, Lancashire, England. Died October 30, 1888, Franklin, Franklin, Idaho. [AG; IGI; AF]

CORMACK, Brother. Hid in his cellar during the battle of Nauvoo, as he was sick, according to Mary's report from William Cutler and Daniel H. Wells.

CORNAY/CORNAYS, Mr. Lived in the Nishnabotna valley near the border of Missouri/Iowa by the Burton and Haven families, 1847.

COTTAM, Isabella Parker. Born April 12, 1799, Chaigley, Lancashire, England, to John Parker Sr. and Ellen Heskin. Married Thomas Cottam, January 16, 1826. Mary's oldest sister. [AG]

COVEY, Benjamin. Born March 7/9, 1792, Duchess County, New York, to Walter Covey and Sarah Hatch. Married, first, Sarah/Sally Vanderhoff, November

7, 1815. Married, second, Almira Mack, October 23, 1836, Kirtland, Geauga, Ohio, or Liberty, Clay, Missouri. Married, third, Diana Cole, who died in 1847. Married, fourth, Phebe Cole. Married, fifth, Elizabeth Shimer. Died March 13, 1868, Salt Lake City, Salt Lake, Utah. A member of Winter Quarters First Ward in June 1847. Was called in to administer to Mary in June 1847. [SEB 12:11-4; EH; N5HP; HTW 9:479]

CROOKSTON, Ann Welch. Born December 18, 1826, Brampton Moor, England, to Nicholas Welch and Elizabeth Briggs. Married Robert Crookston, June 20, 1847, Winter Quarters. Died February 3, 1904, Logan, Cache, Utah. Usually mentioned in connection with "Brother or Sister Welch." [ARCH]

CROOKSTON, Robert. Born September 21, 1821, Fife, Scotland, to James Crookston and Mary Young. Married Ann Welch, June 20, 1847, Winter Quarters. Died September 21, 1916, Logan, Cache, Utah. Was a member of Crooked Creek and Ramus Branches, Iowa. Usually mentioned in connection with "Brother or Sister Welch." [SEB 12:475-48; IBI: 45]

CROWEL, Rev. W., A.M. Editor of the *Christian*, Boston, Massachusetts. While Orson Spencer was serving a mission in Great Britain, he published a series of his letters to Rev. Crowel in the *Millennial Star*. Phinehas read two of these letters to Mary in January 1848. [MS 9:277]

CUMMINGS, James. Born January 26, 1780/90, Dunstable, Middlesex, Massachusetts, to James Cummings and Sarah Wright. Died March 28, 1847, Winter Quarters. His wife, Susanna Willard Cummings, also died there, February 28, 1847. Member of Winter Quarters First Ward in December 1846. Also a member of Crooked Creek and Ramus Branches, Iowa. One of the captains appointed to guard the cattle from Indians at Winter Quarters. [SEB 12:595-96; IBI: 46; EH]

CURTIS, Brother. A member of Jane's ward, January 1847. Many Curtis families are found in the Winter Quarters area.

> CURTIS, Enos. Born October 9, 1783, Kinderhood, Columbia, New York, to Edmond Curtis and Polly Avery. Married Ruth Franklin, December 15, 1805. Other wife in Utah. Died June 1, 1855, Springville, Utah, Utah. Emigrated to Utah in May 1848. His children living in Winter Quarters or Council Bluffs were David Avery Curtis, Ezra Houghton Curtis, Simmons P. Curtis. [SEB 12:683-87; ARCH]

> CURTIS, Moses Nahum. Born May 8, 1816, Connaught, Erie, Pennsylvania, to Nahum Curtis and Millicent Waite. Married, first, Amelia/Aurelia Ann Jackman, May 28, 1839, Nauvoo, Hancock, Illinois. Child born in Winter Quarters in 1850. Died May 5, 1907, Eden, Graham, Arizona. [FF; SEB 12:748-53]

CURTIS, Sister. Met Mary in Liverpool, the first American woman Mary had ever met.

CUTLER, Brother. Speaker at Sunday Meetings in Winter Quarters, 1847. Possibly Alpheus Cutler, president of the High Council, or William Cutler, who is specifically named in entry of May 7, 1848.

> CUTLER, Alpheus. Principal stonemason for Nauvoo Temple. Led advance party across Iowa. President of the High Council at Winter Quarters during 1846-47. Selected location for Cutler's Park. Branch president of

Silver Creek, Iowa Branch, 1849-52. Excommunicated in 1851 through series of conflicts with Orson Hyde and the High Council at Kanesville. Founded the Cutlerite Church in 1853, with headquarters in Manti (near present-day Shenandoah), Fremont, Iowa. Died 1860 at Manti. [HS: 32; NJ62: 45-64]

CUTLER, William Lathrop. Born February 6, 1821, East Bloomfield, Ontario, New York. Married Abigail E. Chase. Appointed captain to guard the cattle from Indians in Winter Quarters, according to Mary's journal, May 7, 1848. Served British Mission 1849-50. [SEB 13:30]

DALTON, Brother. Hosted party, where he danced with Mary in December 1847 and February 1848.

DALTON, Charles. Born August 22, 1810, Wysox, Bradford, Pennsylvania, to John Dalton and Elizabeth Cooker. Married Mary Elizabeth Warner, sixteen years his junior. Other wives in Utah. Died May 22, 1891, Ogden, Weber, Utah. Traveled to Utah with Willard Richards in 1848. [SEB 13:126-29; HTW 9:480]

DALTON, John. Born July 10, 1801, Wyoming, Luzerne, Pennsylvania, to John Dalton and Elizabeth Cooker. Married Rebecca Turner Cranmer, January 21/26, 1822, Towanda, Bradford, Pennsylvania. Other wives in Utah. Died January 5, 1885, Rockville, Washington, Utah. Traveled to Utah in 1848. [SEB 13:140-44; HTW 9:480; MPJ]

DALTON, Simon Cooker. Born January 1, 1806, Wilkes-Barre, Luzerne, Pennsylvania, to John Dalton and Elizabeth Cooker. Married, first, Annabell Anna Dalton/Anna Hannibal, August 5, 1825, Philadelphia, Philadelphia, Pennsylvania. Married, second, Elnora Lucretia Warner, February 4, 1846, Nauvoo, Hancock, Illinois. Died October 14, 1885, Springville, Utah, Utah. Most of his children born in Centerville, Davis, Utah. When Mary and Samuel lived in Salt Lake City, they often visited the Dalton family in Centerville. [SEB 13:156-59]

DANIELS, N. Danced with Mary at a party in May 1848.

DANIELS, Noble N. The only person in early records whom this might be. Was in the Nauvoo Fourth Ward, received his endowments in the Nauvoo Temple in February 1846, but it is unknown if he was in Winter Quarters or not. [SEB 13:236]

DAVENPORT, Almira Phelps. Born January 23, 1805, Canajoharie, Montgomery, New York, to John Phelps and Polly Rider. Married James Davenport, September 4, 1822, Olean, Cattaraugus, New York. Died December 28, 1881, Richmond, Cache, Utah. [SEB 34:731-72; FF]

DAVENPORT, James. Born May 1, 1802, Danville, Caledonia, Vermont, to Squire Davenport Jr. and Sarah Kittridge. Married Almira Phelps, September 4, 1822, Olean, Cattaraugus, New York. Died July 23, 1883, Richmond, Cache, Utah. Eleventh child born in Winter Quarters, March 1847. Was a blacksmith, one of the first pioneers to Salt Lake Valley with Brigham Young. Was chosen to ferry people over the Platte River. [SEB 13:283-77; HTW 8:403; HTW 9:481]

DAVIS, Edith. Born January 8, 1832, West Township, Columbus, Ohio, to Isaac Davis and Edith Richards. Married Joseph D. Riter, May 1, 1860. Died February 6, 1910. [SEB: 13:434-35; FF]

DAVIS, Edith Richards. Born March 16, 1784/94, to Abijah Richards and Esther Daniels. Married Isaac Davis, November 8, 1814. Died August 8, 1866, Iowa. Mother of ten children, including Betsy Arsena Davis, who was married to Henry Harts Boley. [SEB 36:605; FF]

DAVIS, Elisha Hildebrand. Born October 22, 1815, West Township, Columbia, Ohio, to Isaac Davis and Edith Richards. Married Mary Ann Mitchell, December 25, 1846, London, Middlesex, England. Died July 31, 1898, Lehi, Utah, Utah. After evacuation of Winter Quarters, moved into the Iowa settlements. [SEB 13:382-84]

DAVIS, Isaac. Born February 20, 1783, Pilesgrove, Salem, New Jersey, to Isaac Davis and Hannah Hildebrand. Married Edith Richards, November 8, 1814. Died May 20, 1847, Winter Quarters. Was shown in the records of Winter Quarters First Ward, shortly after his death, owning eleven head of cattle. [SEB 13:434-35; FF]

DAVIS, Mary Ann Mitchell. Identified in Mary's journal as Sister Elisha Davis. Born 1820, baptised February 4, 1842, in London, England. Married Elisha Hildebrand Davis, December 25, 1846, London, Middlesex, England, and emigrated the following day. [SEB 13:382-84]

DERBY, Herman Erastus. Born September 14, 1810, to Edward Derby and Ruth Hitchcock. Married Ruhamah B. Knowlton, August 10, 1834. Close friend of Joseph Smith during Nauvoo period and was given a special blessing by the Prophet. Member of Garden Grove Branch, 1848-52. Did not remain active in the church. [NJ41: 22-23; SEB 13:847-49]

DILLWORTH, Eliza Wollerton. Widow of Caleb Dillworth. Found in the bishop's report of the Winter Quarters First Ward in December 1846, as was her son John Taylor Dillworth. In June 1847, John is listed with ten head of cattle. Born October 14, 1793, West Chester, West Chester, Pennsylvania, to William Wollerton and Rebecca Harvey. Married Caleb Dillworth, January 14, 1813. Died December 21, 1876. Mother of Harriet Wollerton Dillworth Colflesh Yearsley Brinton. Miss Dillworth, mentioned by Mary, could be one of Eliza's two unmarried daughters. [SEB 47:601-2]

DILLWORTH, Maria Louisa. Born January 14, 1834, Uwchland, Chester, Pennsylvania, to Caleb Dillworth and Eliza Wollerton. Married John Leonard and George Nebeker. Died December 29, 1905. Perhaps she is the Miss Dillworth mentioned by Mary. [SEB 14:68-69]

DILLWORTH, Mary Jane. Born June 29, 1831, Uwchland, Chester, Pennsylvania, to Caleb Dillworth and Eliza Wollerton. Married Francis Asbury Hammond, November 17, 1848. Died June 6, 1877. First Relief Society president of Huntsville, Utah. Possibly she is the Miss Dillworth mentioned by Mary. [SEB 14:70-71]

DOUGLAS/DOUGLASS, Henrietta Wheeler. Married to Ralph Briggs Douglas, January 26, 1845, Nauvoo, Hancock, Illinois, by James Smithies. Ralph was stepson of John Parker Jr. In one entry, Henrietta is designated as the "daughter-in-law" of Mary's "sister-in-law." [SEB 45:540]

DOUGLAS/DOUGLASS, Ralph Briggs. Born December 28, 1824, Downham, Lancashire, England, to George Douglas and Ellen Briggs. Married Henrietta Wheeler, January 26, 1845, Nauvoo, Hancock, Illinois. Other wife. Died May 3, 1900, Ogden, Weber, Utah. His widowed mother was married to Mary's brother John Parker Jr. and was living in St. Louis, Missouri. Was a private in Company D of the Mormon Battalion. [SEB 14:271-73; DBMB: 64]

DUEL, Brother and Sister. Lived in the vicinity of the Havens and Burtons at Austin Township, near the Iowa/Missouri border. The Duel family took Mary back to Winter Quarters. Mary gave Sister Duel's two little girls ten cents.

DEUEL, Eliza Avery Whiting. Born October 14, 1819, Gilford, Windham, Vermont, to Nathaniel Whiting and Mercy Young. Married January 1, 1837, to William Henry Deuel. Died December 20, 1872. [SEB 45:845; HTW 8:448]

DEUEL, Mary Whiting. Born November 23, 1807, Whitehall, Washington, New York. Married Osmyn Merritt Deuel. [SEB 13:897; HTW 8:448]

DEUEL, Osmyn Merritt. Born January 1, 1802, Galway, Saratoga, New York, to Lewis Deuel and Mary Barton. Married Mary Whiting. Other wives in Utah. Died January 11, 1889. Emigrated to Utah June 17, 1847, with wife Mary, but no children shown. A brother Amos D., age fifty, also emigrated with them. [SEB 13:901-3; HTW 8:448]

DEUEL, William Henry. Born January 1, 1812, or December 31, 1811, in New York to Lewis Deuel and Mary Barton. Married Eliza Avery Whiting, January 1, 1837. Four of eleven children born before the Winter Quarters period. Emigrated to Utah with brothers Osmyn and Amos on June 17, 1847. Accompanying him was wife Eliza and two daughters ages four and one. Died April 30, 1891, Escalante, Garfield, Utah. [SEB 13:904-7; HTW 8:448]

DUNN, Crandall. Born August 11, 1817, Phelps/Ontario, Wayne, New York, to James Dunn and Sally/Sarah Barker. Married Mary Ann Cahoon, December 25, 1838. Died December 27, 1898. Mission to England in 1845. In September 1847, Mary discussed Crandall with his parents who lived near Keg Creek, Iowa. [SEB 14:689-91]

DUNN, James. Born September 26, 1788, Lancaster County, Pennsylvania, to Robert and Agnes Dunn. Married Sally/Sarah Barker. Member of Zion's Camp. Called "Father Dunn" by Mary. [SEB 14:700; ZC: xxiv, 41,44]

DUNN, Sally/Sarah Barker. Married James Dunn. Lived near the family of Samuel White at Keg Creek, Iowa. [SEB 14:689]

DUZETTE, Edward Peas. Born January 24, 1812, Boston, Middlesex, Massachusetts, to Philemon Duzette and Elizabeth/Betsy Jane King. Married Eliza Ann Cowan in Salt Lake City, Salt Lake, Utah. Died December 9, 1874, Rockville, Washington, Utah. Drummer in the Nauvoo Legion. Often danced with Mary in Winter Quarters. [SEB 14:868-72]

EGAN, Howard. Born June 15, 1815, Tuelemore, Kings, Ireland, to Howard Egan and Ann Meade. Went to Canada with his family at the age of eight. Married, first, Tamson Parshley, December 1, 1838, Salem, Essex, Massachusetts. Married, second, Nancy A. Redding, 1847. Other wife in Utah. Died March 18, 1878, Salt Lake City, Salt Lake, Utah. One of first pioneers to Salt Lake Valley in 1847. An agent for the Pony Express and Overland Mail. [SEB 15:168-72; HTW 9:483]

EGAN, Tamson Parshley. Born July 27, 1824, Barnstead, Belknap, New Hampshire, to Richard Parshley Jr. and Mary Coverly. Married Howard Egan, December

1, 1838, Salem, Essex, Massachusetts. Died March 31, 1905, Salt Lake City, Salt Lake, Utah. Fourth child born in Winter Quarters. Tamson is probably the person Mary calls Sister Egan, as she was the first wife of Howard. [SEB 33:953-55]

ELLSWORTH, Brother. Lived somewhere between Jane's home and Mary's home in Winter Quarters.

    ELLSWORTH, David. Born October 8, 1804, Pittsburgh, Rutland, Vermont, to Israel Ellsworth and Prudence Stevens. Married, first, Diana Livingston. Married, second, Catherine Lancaster. Other wife in Utah. Died October 1872, Kanab, Kane, Utah. Listed in the Winter Quarters First Ward records where he owned four head of cattle in June 1847. [SEB 15:420-22; EH]

    ELLSWORTH, Edmund Lovell. Born July 1, 1819, Paris, Oneida, New York, to Jonathan Ellsworth and Sarah Gailey/Gully. Married, first, Elizabeth Young, daughter of Brigham Young, July 10, 1842, Nauvoo, Hancock, Illinois. Other marriages. Was in Winter Quarters 1846-47. Assisted to build ferry at Platte River. Arrived in Salt Lake Valley October 12, 1847. [SEB 15:423-32; NDM: 101]

    ELLSWORTH, German. Born January 18, 1815, Bastard, Leeds, Ontario, Canada, to Israel Ellsworth and Prudence Stevens. Married Experience Almeda Brown, May 25, 1837, Leeds. Died November 9, 1849, Salt Lake City, Salt Lake, Utah. Known to have been in Council Bluffs, possibly Winter Quarters as well. [SEB 15:444-47]

ESS, Sister. visited with Sister Green at Mary's home. No woman by this name has been located in early records.

    HESS, Jacob. Born May 21, 1792. Died June 23, 1846. In the Mount Pisgah Branch. It is possible that Sister Ess is his wife. [IBI: 81]

    HESS, Mary. Wife of Peter M. Hess, whose daughter, Amanda A., died in Winter Quarters on August 26, 1847. Peter filled a mission to Lancaster County, Pennsylvania, April 1843. Lived in Nauvoo. [SEB 22:484, 507]

EVERETT, Brother and Sister. Had Mary to their home often for meals or to sleep. Mary indicated that they left for Salt Lake Valley with a Fuller Family, which suggests the family of John and Sarah Ann Everett. However, if Mary was talking about more than one Everett family in her visits, she may also be identifying Addison Everett, who was in Winter Quarters as well.

    EVERETT/EVARTS, John. Born June 10, 1803, or July 10, 1811, North Canaan, Columbia, New York, to Eli Evarts and Susan Merriman. Married Sarah Ann Evarts. [HTW 8:417; SEB 15:772]

    EVERETT/EVARTS, Sarah Ann. Born June 3, 1811, Richmond, Berkshire, Massachusetts. [HTW 8:417; SEB 15:773,785]

FAIRBANKS, Sister. Visited Mary while at Sister Grow's house.

    FAIRBANKS, Polly Brooks. Born February 16, 1780, Princeton, Worcester, Massachusetts, to David Brooks and Patience White. Married Joseph Fairbanks, October 3, 1803. Died January 24, 1860, Salt Lake City, Utah. Husband died in Winter Quarters February 25, 1847. Emigrated to Utah with son David's family June 17, 1847. [SEB 6:840-41; HTW 8:437]

FAIRBANKS, Sarah H. Van Wagoner. Born July 11, 1822, Pompton, Passaic, New Jersey, to Halmagh John Van Wagoner and Mary/Polly Van Houten. Married John Boylston Fairbanks, August 31, 1844, Pompton, Passaic, New Jersey. Died February 8, 1898. Second child born in Winter Quarters. [SEB 44:334-35; HTW 8:437]

FAIRBANKS, Susan Manderville. Born September 23, 1819, Pompton Plains, Passaic, New Jersey, to Cornelius Manderville and Jane Jones. Married David Fairbanks, November 26, 1838, Pompton Plains, Passaic, New Jersey. Died March 2, 1899, Payson, Utah, Utah. David was bishop of original Eighth Ward in Winter Quarters. He was also shown in records of Winter Quarters First Ward relief to the poor in March 1847. [SEB 29:207-8; HTW 8:437; EH]

FARNSWORTH, Julia Ann Clark. Married Stephen Martindale Farnsworth August 30, 1837. Jane Snyder Richards wrote that Mrs. Julia Farnsworth was among her women friends at Nauvoo. [JSR; SEB 10:107; CBM: 2]

FARNSWORTH, Philo. Born January 24, 1826, Hock Hacking, near Burlington, Lawrence, Ohio, to Reuben Farnsworth and Lucinda Kent. Married, first, Margaret Whipp Yates, October 29, 1848. Other wives. Died July 31, 1887, Beaver, Utah. Was teamster for Franklin D. and Jane Snyder Richards. [SEB 15:953-60; HTW 9:484]

FARNSWORTH, Stephen Martindale. Born October 8, 1809, Dorset, Bennington, Vermont, to Reuben Farnsworth and Lucinda Kent. Married, first, Julia Ann Clark, August 30, 1837. Other wives. Died September 19, 1885, Tuba, Coconino, Arizona. A member of the Coonville Branch, Iowa. Also shown in the Keg Creek Branch. Owned cattle in the Winter Quarters First Ward in June 1847. Mary suggests that he came to Winter Quarters in May 1847 from Loup Creek. [SEB 15:961-66: EH; CBM: 2; FF]

FELSHAW, Mary Harriet Gilbert. Born June 23, 1808, Otsego County, New York, to Josiah Gilbert and Susannah Hyde. Married William Felshaw, February 1, 1827, Washington County, New York. Died August 26, 1871, Fillmore, Millard, Utah. [ARCH; SEB 18:372-73]

FELSHAW, William. Born February 3, 1800, Granville, Washington, New York, to Lemuel Felshaw and Sarah Hicks/Hix. Married, first, Mary Harriet Gilbert, February 1, 1827, Washington County, New York. Mary mentions visiting them in August 1846 during the time she was living at Mosquito Creek. They may not have moved into Winter Quarters as three of their children were born at Galland's Grove, Shelby County, between 1848 and 1851. This is about fifty miles northeast of Winter Quarters. Also possible they lived in Winter Quarters and moved to Galland's Grove when Winter Quarters was evacuated in 1848. [SEB 16:117-21; JTB: 53; ARCH]

FIELDING, Amos. An Englishman who had arrived in Nauvoo on March 26, 1845. He stayed with Phinehas and family June 8, 1846, on his return to England. [TB: 69]

FIELDING, Hannah Greenwood. Born September 4, 1808, Bolton, Lancashire, England, to Thomas Greenwood and Ellen Haslam. Married Joseph Fielding, June 11, 1838, at Preston, Lancashire, England. Died September 9, 1877, Ogden, Weber, Utah. [SEB 19:198-99]

FIELDING, Hyrum Thomas. Born March 29, 1847, or April 4, 1847, Winter Quarters, Douglas, Nebraska, to Joseph Fielding and Hannah Greenwood. Died August 4, 1847, Winter Quarters. [SEB 16:226]

FIELDING, Joseph. Born March 26, 1796, Honidon, Bedfordshire, England, to John Fielding and Rachel Ibbotson. Married, first, Hannah Greenwood, June 11, 1838, at Preston, Lancashire, England. Married, second, Mary Ann Peake, 1845, Nauvoo, Hancock, Illinois. Other marriages. Died December 19, 1863, Mill Creek, Salt Lake, Utah. Was baptized May 21, 1836, by Parley P. Pratt in Canada. Mission to Preston, England, in June 1837. He and Willard Richards confirmed Mary after she had been baptized by William Kay. [SEB 16:228-34; HTW 9:484]

FONTENELLE, Logan. Interpreter for Omaha Chief Big Elk at the August 1846 meetings with the Mormons. Chief spokesman and first to sign sale of Omaha lands to U.S. Government in 1854. [MAM: 71-72]

FORY, Brother and Sister. Arrived in Winter Quarters from Nashville, Iowa (near the present-day Montrose), January 1847.

> FORY, Peter Joseph and Sophia. Parents of Elizabeth Fory, although her mother may have been dead by then. Elizabeth's brothers Gurdon, unmarried, and Augustine were in New Orleans, Louisiana, in June 1848. A married brother John was in Davenport, Iowa, in June 1848. [EF]

FORY, Elizabeth. Born August 27, 1825, probably to Peter Joseph and Sophia Fory. Close friend to Eliza Anne Haven and Mary. Moved to Davenport, Scott, Iowa, from Nauvoo to live with her brother. A June 1848 letter to Mary mentions sisters and brothers Augustine, Gurdon, John, Sophia, and Maria, as well as other friends Melissa Coray, Rebecca Jones, Ellen Wilding, and Maria Burton. Letter also tells of planned marriage to Levi Davis in September, a member of the Davenport Baptist Church. Elizabeth joined the Davenport Presbyterian Church because of her disbelief in plural marriage. [EF; N5HP; SEB 16:831; IGI]

FULLER, Catherine Walker. Born May 20, 1824, Peacham, Caldonia, Vermont, to John Walker and Lydia Holmes. Married Elijah Knapp Fuller, a widower with three children, January 18, 1846, in Nauvoo. Later divorced. Died August 31, 1885, Brigham City, Box Elder, Utah. Emigrated to Utah June 15, 1847, with the family of John and Sarah Ann Everett. Mary called to bid farewell to Catherine and Sarah Ann on June 3, 1847. Son of Catherine married a daughter of Sarah Ann Everett. [SEB 44:476-77; HTW 8:417]

FULLER, Sister. Visited Mary in April 1848 with Sister Hartwell. This would have to be a different woman than Catherine Walker Fuller, who emigrated to Utah in June 1847.

GASS, Mr. Lived near the Samuel Burton family at Austin Township, Atchison, Missouri (near present-day Hamburg, Fremont, Iowa). Danced with Mary at a party at Brother Swamlys. No person has been located by that name, but there was a Mr. G. B. Gaston living in the area, considered to be one of the old settlers around Austin. The town of Percival, an outgrowth of the Kansas City, St. Joseph and Council Bluffs Railroad, was originally named Gaston after G. B. Gaston. Later Gaston became prominent in Tabor, Iowa. [HFC: 372, 511, 542]

GATES, Elizabeth Caroline Hutchin/Hutchings. Born 1811. Married Jacob Gates, January 21, 1846. Died September 15, 1846, Cutler's Park, Douglas, Nebraska, leaving a baby girl, Mary E. Gates. Mary wrote to Samuel about this death. [IGI; SEB 17:1007; 18:23]

GLEASON, John Streeter. Born January 13, 1819, Livonia, Livingston, New York, to Ezekial Gleason and Polly Howard. Married, first, Desdamonia Chase, November 8, 1839, Nauvoo, Hancock, Illinois. Other marriages in Utah. Died December 21/22, 1904, Pleasant Grove, Utah. Major in the Nauvoo Legion. One of original pioneers to Utah, 1847. [SEB 18:489-96]

GLEASON, Desdemonia Chase. Born April 3, 1821, Sparta, Livingston, New York, to Isaac Chase and Phoebe Ogden. Married John Streeter Gleason, November 8, 1839, Nauvoo, Hancock, Illinois. Died February 18, 1884, Farmington, Davis, Utah. [SEB 9:366-67]

GODDARD, Alamantha. Born May 31, 1830, McDonough, Chenango, New York. First wife of Stephen Hezekiah Goddard. Mary called her a "very intelligent woman." [SEB 18:557]

GODDARD, Arquily. Probably a daughter of Stephen H. Goddard. While staying at his home, Mary sewed for her.

GODDARD, Emmy. Probably a daughter of Stephen H. Goddard. While staying at his home, Mary sewed for her.

GODDARD, Stephen Hezekiah. Born August 23, 1810, Champlain, Clinton, New York, to Stephen G. Goddard and Sylvia Smith. Married, first, Alamantha. Died September 10, 1898, San Bernardino, San Bernardino, California. Conducted singing school in Nauvoo and Winter Quarters and was director of Tabernacle Choir in Salt Lake City. One of original pioneers of 1847. Apparently lived east of the Missouri River close enough that he could cross to Winter Quarters and back easily. Mary remained at his home for two weeks in January 1848 while very ill. It was here that some sisters came to bless her and spoke in tongues. [SEB 18:569-72; HTW 9:487]

GOODALE, Isaac Newton. Born February 6, 1815, Berkshire, Tioga, New York, to Isaac Goodale and Electa Allen. Married two wives in Salt Lake City, Salt Lake, Utah. Died April 26, 1890, Ogden, Weber, Utah. [SEB 18:626-29; FF]

GOURDIAN, Sister. Called on Mary and Wealthy in May 1847 with Sisters Douglas and Greenalch.

GORDON, Mary Ballentyne. Married April 4, 1843, Nauvoo, Hancock, Illinois, to James P. Gordon, who was born April 18, 1820, Renfrew, Scotland. Third child supposedly born in Nauvoo 1848. Fourth child born in Utah 1850. Crossed plains to Utah in 1848. [SEB 3:420-21; HTW 9:487]

GORDON, Sophia. Wife of Gilman Gordon, who was born January 18, 1821, Brutus, Cayuga, New York, and who was in the Mormon Battalion. No date for marriage. If they were married prior to this time, it is possible she may have been in Winter Quarters. [SEB 18:710]

GRANT, Brother and ladies. A brother Grant had a school room where singing school was held. Brother Grant and his ladies visited at Jane's, where they sang several songs. George Davis Grant had only one wife at this time. David Grant had only one wife, Mary Ann Hyde Bullard, at this time. Jedediah M. Grant had only one wife, Carolyn Van Dyke, at this time.

GRANT, George Davis. Born September 10, 1812, Windsor, Broome, New York, to Joshua Grant and Athalia Howard. Married Elizabeth Wilson, January 22, 1834, Naples, Ontario, New York. Other wives in Utah. Died September 20, 1876, Bountiful, Davis, Utah. Danced with Mary or accompanied her to parties. In Nauvoo Legion. One of Joseph Smith's bodyguards. Officer in territorial militia in Utah during the Indian wars. Was in rescue party for handcart companies [SEB 18:874-79]

GRANT, George Roberts. Born July 14, 1820, Reading, Steuben, New York, to Lorin Grant and Betsy Keney/Keeney. Married, first, Mary Dorsey Barnery, September 28, 1840. Married, second, Mary Helen Van Orden, no date. Other wife in Utah. Died July 22, 1889, Placer County, California. Was in Winter Quarters, having been with first pioneers in 1847 and returned. [SEB 18:880-83]

GREEN, Sister. Is usually mentioned in connection with visits to or from Wealthy, indicating she was probably a mature woman, not one of Mary's young friends, or possibly a relative of Wealthy's. Mary may also have meant "Sister Gheen," instead of Green.

> GREENE, Susan Kent. Born April 3, 1816, Genoa, Cayuga, New York, to Daniel Kent and Nancy Young. Married August 29, 1835, to her cousin Evan Melbourne Greene. Second cousin of Samuel Richards. Evan was a high priest in the Big Spring Branch in January 1848; Susan a member of the Blockhouse Branch October 1848. Died April 17, 1888, Oakley, Cassia, Idaho. [FRN: 40; SEB 26:475-76; PHP: 3; MBB]

> GREEN, Susannah Phillips. Married John Hyrum Green in 1834, Acton, England, after his first wife died. Eighth child born in Winter Quarters, October 17, 1847. Husband was second counselor to William Kay in Kaysville, Davis, Utah. [SEB:19:102-3]

GREENE, Nancy Zerviah. Born September 17, 1827/29, Springwater, Livingston, New York, to John Portineus Greene and Rhoda Young. Sister of Evan Melbourne Green and second cousin to Samuel Richards. Member of Blockhouse Branch October 1848 [SEB 19:165; MBB]

GREENALCH, Sister and four children. Visited Mary during 1847.

> GREENALGH, Mary Clough. Born March 18, 1814, Breightmet, Lancashire, England. Married William Greenalgh, 1834, England. Husband and first four children born in Lancashire, England. Family is found in St. Louis, St. Louis, Missouri in 1851. William died 1882, Spring Lake, Utah, Utah. [SEB 10:468]

GROW, Henry, Jr. Born October 1, 1817, Morristown, Montgomery, Pennsylvania, to Henry Grow and Mary Riter. Married Mary Moyer, January 24, 1834, or August 1, 1837. Other wives, including widow Ann/Nancy Elliot Veach. Died November 4, 1891, Salt Lake City, Salt Lake, Utah. Was in Winter Quarters October 1846 and built the first log cabin, then went to Kimball's area six miles east and built a house. In the fall of 1847 he moved to near Weston, Platte, Missouri. Henry was found in the Winter Quarters First Ward records for March and December 1846. Bishop in Salt Lake City, architect and builder of social hall, tabernacle, Salt Lake City theater, first sugar factory in Utah, and saw mills for Brigham Young. [SEB 19:493-501; AF]

GROW, Mary Moyer. Born April 28, 1817, Germanton, Philadelphia, Pennsylvania, to Charles Moyer and Elizabeth Bird. Married Henry Grow Jr., January 24, 1834, or August 1, 1837. [SEB 31:931-32]

HALL, Brother. Met Mary in Chadburn, England, where she attended a church meeting.

HALL, Jane. See RICHARDS, Jane Hall.

HARDY, Miss. Quilted with Mary and washed clothes for Wealthy in exchange for having her bonnet cleaned in September 1847. Three unmarried daughters of Zachariah Hardy and Eliza Philbrook were probably in Winter Quarters and could have been the young woman mentioned.

> HARDY, Eliza Jane. Born April 3, 1827, Belfast, Waldo, Maine, to Zachariah Hardy and Eliza Philbrook. Married William Beal, January 25, 1852. Died January 3, 1881. [SEB 20:716]

> HARDY, Elmira. Born October 5, 1824, Belfast, Waldo, Maine, to Zachariah Hardy and Eliza Philbrook. Possibly unmarried. Died October 3, 1925. [SEB 20:719]

> HARDY, Lucy. born February 24, 1828, Belfast, Waldo, Maine, to Zachariah Hardy and Eliza Philbrook. Married Ezekial Wells Cheney, May 11, 1848. Died November 2/7, 1913. [SEB 20:756-57]

HARDY, Sister. Quilted at Mary's in September 1847 along with Sisters Leonard and Robbins. Three sons of Joseph Hardy and Elizabeth Thorndyke were members of the LDS church in Nauvoo, where Joseph and Elizabeth died. One of their wives may have been the Sister Hardy written about in Mary's journal.

> HARDY, Eliza Philbrook. Born July 25, 1807, Camden, Knox, Maine, or Isleboro, Waldo, Maine, to Elisha Philbrook and Doratha Witham. Married Zachariah Hardy in 1822 in Maine. He died February 13, 1846, in Nauvoo. She died January 5, 1881, Hooper, Weber, Utah. [SEB 34:794-96; FF]

> HARDY, Lucy Thorndyke Blanden/Blandon. Born February 9, 1812, Camden, Knox, Maine, to Jonas Blanden and Deborah Ogier. Married Joseph Hardy. Died May 4, 1891, Hooper, Weber, Utah. Sixth child born April 1848 in Council Bluffs. [SEB 5:738-39]

> HARDY, Phoebe French. Born June 2, 1810, Belfast, Waldo, Maine. Married Lewis Ogier Hardy, June 28, 1831, Belfast, Waldo, Maine. Fourth child born in Illinois, 1843. Fifth child born in Iowa, 1850. [SEB 17:270]

HARMON, Sophrona Melinda. See KIMBALL, Sophronia Harmon.

HARRIS, Emaline/Emmy. See WELLS, Emmeline Blanche/Belos Woodward Harris Whitney.

HARRIS, Martin. Born May 18, 1783, Easttown, Saratoga, New York, to Nathan Harris and Rhoda Lapham. Married Lucy Harris and Caroline Young. Died July 10, 1875, Clarkston, Cache, Utah. Assisted Joseph Smith in translating the Book of Mormon by acting as scribe and by financial help. Member of Zion's Camp. Excommunicated in 1837 and joined the Strangite Church. Mary heard that he was in England preaching for the Strangites. Later rejoined the Mormon church and moved to Utah. [SEB 21:84-89]

HART, Brother and Sister. Visited with Phinehas and Wealthy, December 1846, and with Mary, January 1847.

HART, Cornelia Staker. Born June 9, 1809, Ontario, Canada, to Conrad Staker and Cornelia Nooks. Married Elias Hart about 1830, Kingston, Ontario, Canada. Lived in Pike County, Illinois, 1841-45. Married Jared Porter, January 1, 1848, Kanesville, Pottawattamie, Iowa. Died July 6, 1850, of cholera while crossing the plains. [SEB 41:137-39]

HART, Elias. Born 1804, Canada. Married Cornelia Staker about 1830 in Kingston, Ontario, Canada. Family group sheet shows his death March 13, 1846, in Pike, Illinois, but his last child was born October 8, 1848 in Kanesville, Pottawattamie, Iowa. Sixth child died 1847 in Council Bluffs. [SEB 21:277-78; FF]

HARTWELL, Sister. Quilted and visited with Mary and Wealthy between September 1847 and April 1848. Once brought her baby.

HARTWELL, Lucinda Almeda Merritt. Married Reuben Parker Hartwell, who was born July 27, 1809, East Templeton, Worcester, Massachusetts. He was baptized in 1837. Resided near Council Bluffs, Pottawattamie, Iowa. Lucinda and Reuben joined the Reorganized Church of Jesus Christ of Latter Day Saints about 1860 while still in Pottawattamie County. [RLDS 3:343; SEB 30:808]

HATCH, Permelia Snyder. Born October 7, 1827, Quincy, St. Lawrence, New York, to Samuel Comstock Snyder and Henrietta Maria Stockwell. Married Meltiar Hatch, January 1, 1846, Job's Creek, Hancock, Illinois. Husband with Mormon Battalion. Died September 21, 1917, Hatch, Garfield, Utah. Visited Mary with Ellen and Jane on June 10, 1847. Jane's niece. [SEB 30:701-2; DBMB: 85]

HAVEN, Eliza Ann. Born May 15, 1829, Holliston, Middlesex, Massachusetts, to John Haven and second wife, Judith Woodby/Woodbury Temple. Married October 14, 1849, to Charles Westover. Died January 20, 1923, Washington, Washington, Utah. First step-cousin to Phinehas Richards and one of Mary's best friends. [SEB 21:711-12; RTB; IB: 15]

HAVEN, Jesse. Born March 28, 1814, Holliston, Middlesex, Massachusetts, to John Haven and first wife, Elizabeth Howe. Married Martha Spring Hall, November 24, 1842. Died December 13, 1905, Peterson, Morgan, Utah. First cousin to Phinehas Richards. [SEB 21:716-17; IB: 14]

HAVEN, John. Born March 9, 1774, Holliston, Middlesex, Massachusetts, to Jesse Haven and Catherine Marsh. Married, first, Elizabeth Howe, an aunt of Phinehas Richards, March 30, 1801. Their children included Mary Ellen Haven Palmer, Nancy Haven Rockwood, Elizabeth Haven Barlow, and Jesse Haven, all of whom are mentioned in Mary's journals. Married, second, Judith Woodby/Woodbury Temple, February 9, 1823. Their children were Maria Susan Haven Burton and Eliza Ann Haven, both close friends of Mary's. Died March 16, 1853, Salt Lake City, Salt Lake, Utah. [SEB 21:719-21; RTB; IB: 14-15]

HAVEN, Judith Woodby/Woodbury Temple. Born December 28, 1798, Holden, Worcester, Massachusetts, to Aaron Temple and Lydia Gleason. Married John Haven, February 9, 1823. Died August 25, 1891, Salt Lake City, Salt Lake, Utah. [IB: 15]

HAVEN, Martha Spring Hall. Born November 21, 1819, Sutton, Worcester, Massachusetts, to John Calvin Hall and Abigail Harback. Married Jesse Haven, November 24, 1842. When Jesse visited with Mary's family in May 1847, she remained in Mt. Pisgah. [SEB 21:716-17]

HEDLOCK, Reuben. Elders Quorum president of Kirtland, Ohio. President of the British Mission 1843-45. In January 1846, he was appointed president again of the British Mission. Because of mishandling the money received in the "Joint Stock Company," which was to be used to help the British Saints emigrate, he was released as president of the mission and disfellowshipped in July 1846. [SEB 22:188]

HENDRIX, Brother and Sister. Mary called on them, January 1847, after a party at the council house. Mary wrote on July 13, 1846, that Sister Hendrix expected to be confined any day. On September 30 Mary wrote that she had died on July 25, leaving a little two-week old daughter, who also died ten days later. It is unknown who Mary was referring to here.

HENDRICKS, Drusilla Dorris. Born February 8, 1810, Sumner County, Tennessee, to William Dorris and Catherine Frost. Married James Hendricks May 31, 1827. Died May 20, 1881, Richmond, Cache, Utah. [SEB 49:801-2; ITOW: 161-68]

HENDRICKS, James. Born June 23, 1808, Franklin, Simpson, Kentucky, to Abraham Hendricks and Charlotte Hinton. Married, first, Drusilla Dorris, May 31, 1827. Died July 8, 1870, Richmond, Cache, Utah. Badly wounded in Battle of Crooked River. A member of Nauvoo Fifth Ward High Priests Quorum, as was Phinehas. Emigrated to Utah 1847. [SEB 22:296-300; HTW 8:432; EH; N5HP]

HENDRIX, Daniel. Born August 6, 1801, Berkshire, Massachusetts, to Daniel Hendrix and Lydia Phelps. Married, first, Patsy Page, in 1831. Married, second, Louisa Marie Lester, December 3, 1835. She was born February 2, 1810, Berkshire, Massachusetts, to Silas Lester and Lucrecia. Daniel married, third, Caroline Lovina Orcott, 1846. She was born January 19, 1825. Other wife. Bishop of one of the branches of the church in Pottawattamie County, July 24, 1847. [SEB 22:346-48]

HINMAN, Aurelia Lewis. Born April 1819, Massachusetts. Married to Lyman Hinman. They were part of the Vermillion group with George Emmett and George Miller. Friends of the Richards family from Massachusetts. Introduced to Mary in July 1847. [RFH 3:263; LH]

HINMAN, Edna Sarah. Born February 28, 1828, West Stockbridge, Berkshire, Massachusetts, to Lyman Hinman and Aurelia Lewis. Married, November 9, 1845, Josiah Mosso. Died February 25, 1896. Friend of the Richards family from Massachusetts. She and her sister Evaline Potter visited Mary and Wealthy on April 21, 1847. [RFH 3:263; LH]

HERINGTON, Brother and Sister. Visited by Wealthy and Mary in April 1847.

HARRINGTON, Leonard Ellsworth. Born January 7/27, 1816, New Lisbon, Otsego, New York, to Spencer/James Harrington and Polly Evans. Married Louise/Lois Russell, February 3, 1840, Nauvoo, Hancock, Illinois. Other wives in Utah. Died June 12, 1883, American Fork, Utah,

Utah. Crossed plains to Utah with Edward Hunter company, October 1, 1847. [SEB 20:953-59]

HARRINGTON, Louise/Lois Russell. Born March 25, 1822/1824, Sparta, Livingston, New York, to Daniel Russell and Sarah/Sally Chase. Married Leonard Ellsworth Harrington, February 3, 1840, Nauvoo, Hancock, Illinois. Died June 19, 1902, American Fork, Utah, Utah. [SEB 38:29-30]

HILL, Sarah. Was living with Sister Haven. Jane and Mary helped her quilt, also took her to dancing school in March 1848.

HILL, Sarah/Sally Forbush. Was the wife of Leonard Hill, born 1800. He died in Council Bluffs, September 10, 1846. She died there March 17, 1847, so she wouldn't be the Sarah mentioned, unless this date is incorrect. Three conflicting records exist for their daughter, Sarah Jane Hill. One says she was born September 1, 1806, in Little York, Pennsylvania, and was married to Jacob Strong, June 8, 1850. Another indicates she was born November 21, 1830, Petersboro, Hillsborough, New Hampshire. Jacob's record says they were married February 28, 1822, and had children between 1829 and 1845. A George W. Hill was in the Winter Quarters First Ward in June 1847, but did not have a wife or daughter named Sarah. [SEB 22:950-1007; EH]

HORNE, Joseph. Born January 17, 1811, London, Middlesex, England, to Joseph Horne and Maria Maidens. Married, first, Mary Isabella Hale, May 9, 1836. Other wife in Utah. Died April 27/30, 1897, Salt Lake City, Salt Lake, Utah. Mary tried to visit them while she was living at Mosquito Creek. [SEB 23:883-89]

HORNE, Mary Isabella Hale. Married May 9, 1836, Joseph Horne. Living at Mosquito Creek in July 1846. Emigrated to Salt Lake Valley June 15, 1847, with Edward Hunter's group. [HTW 8:425; SEB 23:883-89]

HUNTER, Ann Stanley/Standley. Born February 16, 1808, Haverford, Delaware, Pennsylvania, to Jacob Stanley/Standley and Martha Vaughan. Married Edward Hunter as his first wife, September 30, 1830, Delaware County, Pennsylvania. Died November 9, 1855, Salt Lake City, Salt Lake, Utah. [SEB 41:191, 208-9]

HUNTER, Edward. Born June 22, 1793, Newton, Delaware, Pennsylvania, to Edward Hunter and Hannah Marsis. Married, first, Ann Stanley, September 30, 1830, Delaware County, Pennsylvania. Married, second, Laura Lovina Shimer, June 29, 1846, Nauvoo, Hancock, Illinois. Their first child born at Winter Quarters. Married, third, Susanna Wann, fall of 1845, Nauvoo, Hancock, Illinois. Other wife in Utah. Died October 16, 1883, Salt Lake City, Salt Lake, Utah. Bishop of the Winter Quarters First Ward where Mary resided the last year. Kept a notebook with some ward business. Member of Nauvoo Fifth Ward and high priest, as was Phinehas. [EH; SEB 24:691-96; N5HP; HTW 8:249]

HUNTER, Susanna Wann. Born February 18, 1825, Earl, Lancaster, Pennsylvania, to Daniel Wann and Catherine Jameson. Married Edward Hunter in the fall of 1845. Died December 17, 1885, Salt Lake City, Salt Lake, Utah. Visited with Mary in June 1847. [SEB 44:736-37]

HUNTINGTON, John. Visited by Mary in Preston, England. She called him her cousin.

HUNTINGTON, John Dickenson. Born February 11, 1827, Watertown, Jefferson, New York, to William Huntington and Zina Baker. Married Adelaide L. Danks, March 8, 1851. Carried a letter from Mary on the Iowa trail to Samuel in Nauvoo. [SEB 24:765-66]

HUNTINGTON, Magdelene. Mary's cousin. Unknown if she is related to Robert and John Huntington or if her last name is actually Huntington, but she is mentioned in connection to them. Mary calls her "cousin Magdelene" in her letters to England.

HUNTINGTON, Robert. Visited by Mary in Preston, England. She called him her cousin.

HUNTINGTON, William. Born March 28, 1784, Cheshire County, New Hampshire, to William Huntington and Prescinda Lathrop. Married, first, Zina Baker, December 28, 1806. Married, second, Lydia Clisbee Partridge, widow of Edward Partridge, September 29, 1840. Married, third, Doras Baker. Died August/September 29, 1846, Mt. Pisgah, Harrison, Iowa, where he was the presiding authority. [SEB 24:783-86; FF]

HUNSUCKER/HUNTSUCKER, Mr. In March 1847 met Mary at a party at Mr. Wells's house in Austin, Atchison, Missouri (near present-day Hamburg, Fremont, Iowa). Visited with her again at the home of Samuel Burton later the same month.

HUNSAKER, Daniel and Isaac. Came to the Pleasant Grove area near Austin about 1843. By 1844 they built and operated Hunsaker's ferry across the Nishnabotna. This was the first ferry in Fremont County and was situated in Austin. Later sold ferry to Archibald H. Argyle, along with the trading store nearby. [HFC: 373, 409, 447, 511, 557]

HYDE, Mary Ann Price. Born June 5, 1816, Gloucester, England, to William and Mary Ann Price. Married Orson Hyde, April 1843, as his third wife. Remained in Kanesville with him until 1850. After his death in 1878, lived with other wives in Spring City, Utah. She and her sister, Elizabeth Price Bentley, lived near each other at Hyde Park, near Keg Creek, Iowa. Mary visited them there. [SEB 24:979-87]

HYDE, Nancy Marinda Johnson. Born June 28, 1815, Pomfret, Windsor, Vermont, to John Johnson and Elsa Jacobs. Married Orson Hyde, September 4, 1834, Geauga County, Ohio. Died March 24, 1886. In August 1847 visited Mary with Orson's second wife, Martha Rebecca Browett. [SEB 25:677-79]

HYDE, Orson. Born January 8, 1805, Oxford, New Haven, Connecticut, to Nathan Hyde and Sarah/Sally Thorpe. Married, first, Nancy Marinda Johnson, September 4, 1834, Geauga County, Ohio. Married, second, Martha Rebecca Browett, 1843. Married, third, Mary Ann Price, April 1843. Other wives. Died November 28, 1878, Spring City, Sanpete, Utah. Apostle in 1835. Mission to England where he met Samuel and Franklin. In 1848 was left in charge of affairs at Kanesville, Iowa, with George A. Smith and Ezra T. Benson as his counselors. Published the *Frontier Guardian* until 1852. [SEB 24:957-64; HS: 30; IBI: 88]

HYDE, William. Born September 11, 1818, Livingston, York, New York, to Heman Hyde and Polly W. Tilton. Married, first, Elizabeth Howe Bullard, second cousin of Phinehas Richards, February 23, 1842, Nauvoo. Other wives in Utah. Died March 2, 1874, Hyde Park, Cache, Utah, which was named after him. Lived near Phinehas in Nauvoo. [SEB 24:979-87; NAU5; HTW 9:493]

JACOBS, Mother, Brother, Sister. Several references to Brother Jacobs in Winter Quarters playing his violin or dancing with Mary after November 16, 1847. He had recently returned from mission to England, where he had seen Mary's sister Ellen Corbridge. Sister Jacobs was in Mt. Pisgah. Mother Jacobs visited at the Jenne home in January 1847. Father Jacobs lived near Jane and the Snyder families in Winter Quarters, September 1846. Some of those mentioned in Mary's journal are known, others are possible.

JACOBS, Henry. Born July 14, 1788, Guilford, Windham, Vermont, to Stephen Jacobs and Hannah Rebecca Bailey. Married Maryette/Polly Youdell/Udall about 1811. Died June 9, 1834. Perhaps his wife is Mother Jacobs. [SEB 25:227-29]

JACOBS, Henry Bailey. Born May 5, 1814, Niagara, New York, to Henry Jacobs and Maryette/Polly Youdell/Udall. Married, first, Zina Diantha Huntington, March 7, 1841, Nauvoo, Hancock, Illinois. They separated after they had two children and Zina married Joseph Smith; after his death she married Brigham Young. Henry married, second, Sarah Taylor. Died August 1, 1886. Filled several missions to various states and Europe. Was in Great Britain the same time as Samuel and Franklin. Emigrated to Utah in 1848. [SEB 25:230-32]

JACOB/JACOBS, Norton. Born August 11, 1804, Sheffield, Berkshire, England, to Udney Hay Jacob and Elizabeth Hubbard. Married, first, Emily Horton Heaton, November 20, 1830, Bush, Chautaqua, New York. She was born November 28, 1801/1811, Burlington, Chittenden, Vermont, to Elias Heaton and Mary, and died December 6, 1859. Other wives. Died January 30, 1879, Glenwood, Sevier, Utah. Pioneer in first company to Salt Lake Valley then returned to Winter Quarters for the winter before emigrating again. [SEB 25:250-56]

JACOBS, Sister H. B. Visited with Mary, June 1847. Her husband was on a mission to England. Henry Bailey Jacobs's first wife, Zina Diantha Huntington, had left him and subsequently married Joseph Smith on October 27, 1841, and Brigham Young on February 9, 1846. Mary probably refers to his wife Sarah Taylor here. Jacobs may have married her in England while on his first mission, as there was a Sarah Taylor from the Manchester, England, Conference who was baptised on August 26, 1845. [SEB 22:846; 25:230-32]

JENNE, Benjamin Prince. Born May 16, 1806, Plymouth, Windsor, Vermont, to Prince Elisha Jenne and Olive Lincoln. Married Sarah Comstock Snyder, sister of Jane Snyder Richards, January 20, 1830, Port of Ferry, St. Lawrence, New York. Later divorced Sarah, who married Franklin Dewey Richards as a plural wife. Died February 1896, Idaho Falls, Bonneville, Idaho. [SEB 25:434-36; RFR]

JENNE, Brigham. Born January 25, 1846, Comos, Cook, Iowa, to Benjamin Prince Jenne and Sarah Comstock Snyder. Died December 1, 1847, Winter Quarters. Mary helped Jane make burial clothes for Brigham. [SEB 25:437]

JENNE, Lovica/Lovisa. Born June 15, 1832, Ernestown, Ontario, Canada, to Benjamin Prince Jenne and Sarah Comstock Snyder. Married Jared Roundy, February 26, 1851. Died October 5, 1917. Friend of Mary's and niece of Jane's; there are many references to her in Mary's journals. [SEB 25:434-36; FDR; ARCH]

JENNE, Olive. Born October 1/9, 1835, Canada, to Benjamin Prince Jenne and Sarah Comstock Snyder. Married, October 14, 1853, William Peck. Died April 29, 1921. Jane's niece. Mary has several references to her in the journals. [ARCH; SEB 25:434-36]

JENNE, Sarah Comstock Snyder. Born April 11, 1813, Ernestown, Ontario, Canada, to Isaac Snyder and Lovisa Comstock. Married Benjamin Prince Jenne, January 20, 1830, Port of Ferry, St. Lawrence, New York. After divorce from Benjamin, married Franklin Dewey Richards, October 13, 1849. Died October 4, 1894, Plain City, Weber, Utah. Sister of Jane Snyder Richards. [ARCH]

JENNE, William Henry. Born April 22, 1848, Winter Quarters, Douglas, Nebraska, to Benjamin Prince Jenne and Sarah Comstock Snyder. Married, October 17, 1873, Laura Minetta Johnston. Died October 9, 1927. [ARCH]

JOHNSON, Brother. Took a letter from Mary at Mt. Pisgah to Elizabeth Fory in July 1846.

JOHNSON men known to have been in Mt. Pisgah, Garden Grove, Council Bluffs or Winter Quarters are Aaron Johnson, bishop of Garden Grove; Artemus Johnson, one of first pioneers to Utah in 1847; Benjamin Franklin Johnson, with a child born in Winter Quarters, January 1847; Joseph Ellis Johnson; Joseph Watkins Johnson, with a child born in Mt. Pisgah, August 1846; and Lewis Robert Johnson, with a child born in Council Bluffs, September 1847. [SEB 25:512-631]

JONES, Clara Lucinda. Born March 17, 1846, Nauvoo, Hancock, Illinois, to Nathaniel Very Jones and Rebecca Burton. Married John Willard Young, February 4, 1868, Salt Lake City, Salt Lake, Utah. [JBS; SEB 25:986]

JONES, Mrs. Visited by Mary at Winter Quarters in November 1847. She was not Rebecca Burton Jones, or Mary would have referred to her as Rebecca.

JONES, Sarah Ann Malarnee/Mallonee. Born August 30, 1809, Baltimore, Baltimore, Maryland, to Isaac Mallonee and Amy Perrigo. Married October 17, 1829, Steubenville, Jefferson, Ohio, to James Naylor Jones. Died February 14, 1886, Fairview, Sanpete, Utah. Sixth child born February in Kanesville, Pottawattamie, Iowa. [FF]

JONES, Nathaniel Very/Vary. Born October 13, 1822, Brighton, Monroe, New York, to Samuel Jones and Lucinda Kingsley. Married, first, Rebecca Maria Burton, who was one of Mary's best friends, March 14, 1845, Nauvoo, Hancock, Illinois. Other wives. Died February 15, 1863, Salt Lake City, Salt Lake, Utah. Mormon Battalion. Nathaniel and Rebecca lived in the Nishnabotna area around Austin Township, Missouri/Iowa, during 1848-49, as did Samuel and Mary. Both couples had their first child there. Emigrated to Utah, May 1849. [SEB 25:985-92; ARCH; RTB; DBMB: 107]

JONES, Rebecca Maria Burton. Born February 16, 1826, Mersea, Essex, Ontario, Canada, to Samuel Burton and Hannah Shipley. Married Nathaniel Very/

Vary Jones, March 14, 1845, Nauvoo, Hancock, Illinois. Died November 19, 1888. One of Mary's dearest friends, whom Mary visited at Austin township, on the Missouri/Iowa border. Rebecca wrote letters from there to Mary at Winter Quarters. [SEB 25:993; RTB; RBJ]

KAY, William. Born April 11, 1811/1812, Chaigley, Lancashire, England, to William Kay and Elizabeth Mercer. Married Mary Twimberrow Wattis Bennett, February 7, 1844, Nauvoo, Hancock, Illinois. Died 1875. Baptized Mary on August 6, 1838. Emigrated to America in 1844. [JTB: 50; NDM: 13; SEB 26:134-38]

KENNEDY, Catherine. Took care of Samuel when he had smallpox in Scotland, 1846.

KERR, Sister. Took care of Samuel when he had smallpox in Scotland, 1846. Samuel also roomed at her home much of the time he was on his mission.

KIMBALL, Ellen Sanders. Born 1824, Thelemarken, Norway, to Ysten Sondrasen and Aagoata Ystendatter. Twentieth wife of Heber Chase Kimball, married January 7, 1846, Nauvoo, Hancock, Illinois. Was living at Cold Springs camp when she visited Mary and Wealthy on their arrival at the Bluffs. One of three women in the first pioneer company in 1847. Died November 22, 1871, Salt Lake City, Salt Lake, Utah. [SEB 26:637; HCKW: 21-23]

KIMBALL, Frances Jessie Swan. Born June 20, 1822, Edinburgh, Midlothian, Scotland, to Douglas Swan and Margaret Craig. Twenty-first wife of Heber Chase Kimball. One child. Samuel wrote to Mary about death of Frances's mother. Emigrated to Utah with Kimball's family in 1848. [SEB 26:638; 42:313; IGI, HTW 9:495; HCKW: 32-33]

KIMBALL, Heber Chase. Born June 14, 1801, at Sheldon, Franklin, Vermont, to Solomon Farnham Kimball and Anna Spaulding. Married, first, Vilate Murray, November 22, 1822, Mendon, Monroe, New York. Other wives. Died June 22, 1868, Salt Lake City, Salt Lake, Utah. Missionary to Great Britain, where he spent time in the home of Old John Parker, Mary's father. Baptized hundreds in England. First counselor to Brigham Young. One of original pioneers to Utah 1847. [SEB 26:623-54; HCKW]

KIMBALL, Mary Mariah/Marion Davenport. Born February 27, 1824, Covington, Genessee, to James Davenport and Almira Phelps. Married William Henry Kimball, February 11, 1845, Nauvoo, Hancock, Illinois. With other women from Cold Springs Camp, she visited Mary when she arrived at Mosquito Creek. [ARCH; NDM: 113]

KIMBALL, Sarah Peak Noon. Born 1811. Second wife of Heber Chase Kimball. Came to Nauvoo from England with first husband, William S. Noon. He deserted her and she married Heber sometime in 1842. Referred to in Heber's journals as Sarah Peak. Died 1873. Often helped Mary quilt or had Mary sew for her. [SEB; HTW 9:495; HCK]

KIMBALL, Solomon Farnham. Born February 2, 1847, Winter Quarters, Douglas, Nebraska, to Heber Chase Kimball and Vilate Murray. Married Mary Ursala Pomeroy, February 10, 1881. Died February 7, 1920. His mother wrote a poem for him when he was born. [SEB 26:626, 671-72]

KIMBALL, Sophronia Harmon. Born April 5, 1824, Conneaut, Erie, Pennsylvania, to Jesse Pierce Harmon and Anna Barns. One of Heber Chase Kimball's wives, married February 3, 1846, Nauvoo, Hancock, Illinois. Niece of another of Heber's wives, Hulda Barnes Kimball. Died January 26, 1847, Winter Quarters, Douglas, Nebraska. On January 29, 1847, Mary wrote to Samuel that Sofrone Harmon had died the previous Tuesday. [AF; HCKW: 34-35]

KIMBALL, Vilate Murray. Born June 1, 1806, Florida, Montgomery, New York, to Roswell Murray and Susannah Fitch. First wife of Heber Chase Kimball, married November 22, 1822, Mendon, Monroe, New York. Died October 22, 1867, Salt Lake City, Salt Lake, Utah. [SEB 32:114-16; ITOW: 137-39; HCKW: 8-12]

KIMBALL, William Henry. Born April 10, 1826, Mendon, Monroe, New York, to Heber Chase Kimball and Vilate Murray. Married, first, Mary Mariah/Marion Davenport, February 11, 1845, Nauvoo, Hancock, Illinois. Second wife was Melissa Burton Coray, one of Mary's best friends and widow of William Coray, who died from effects of Mormon Battalion. Died December 30, 1907, Coalville, Summit, Utah. Danced with Mary and accompanied her to parties and socials in Winter Quarters. Assisted in bringing emigrants to Utah, including the Martin Handcart Company. [SEB 26:626, 677-81; FF; HTW 9:494-95; NDM: 113]

KING, Brother. Mentioned as having a sick child in August 1846 while Mary lived at Mosquito Creek, Iowa. Several King families eventually lived around the Missouri River during the following two years, but it isn't known which one lived near Mary at that time.

KING families: Levi P. King owned cattle in Winter Quarters First Ward in June 1847. Eleazer King Jr. and his wife, Mary Caroline Fowler, had a child in Pottawattamie County in October 1847. His brother, John Morris King, and the latter's wife, Sally Ann Jewell, were in the Tabernacle/Blockhouse Branch, Iowa, in January 1848, as was Eleazer King Jr. or Sr. John Morris King was also in the Mormon Battalion. Thomas Rice King and Matilda Robison were living in Winter Quarters in March when their seventh child was born. [SEB 26:723-829; PHP; EH]

KNIGHT, Bishop, Brother. Invited Mary to a dance at the council house to benefit the poor. As a bishop, he also was called to supervise a dance in one of the Winter Quarters wards, not his own.

KNIGHT, Joseph. Born June 21, 1808, Halifax, Windham, Vermont, to Joseph Knight and Polly Peck. Married Betsey Covert, March 22, 1832, Kirtland, Geauga, Ohio. Other wives. Died November 3, 1866, Salt Lake City, Salt Lake, Utah. He was acting bishop of Winter Quarters and Council Bluffs. In March 1847, he donated to the poor of the Winter Quarters First Ward. He was in the Tabernacle/Blockhouse Branch, Iowa, in January 1848. [SEB 27:4-8; EH; PHP: 1]

LAMB, Abel. Born March 9, 1801, Rowe, Franklin, Massachusetts, to Enos Lamb and Anna Blackman. Married, first, Almira Merrill in 1826. Died April 14, 1874, Cedar City, Iron, Utah. Mary purchased a washboard from him. After living in Winter Quarters, he moved into the Tabernacle/Blockhouse Branch, where he was a counselor to the branch president in 1849. He was still in Kanesville, Iowa, in January 1850, when he performed two marriages. [SEB 27:201-5; IBI: 99; JTB: 52; FF; PHP: 1]

LAMB, Almira Merrill. Born June 5, 1807, Hartford, Hartford, Connecticut, to Daniel Merrill and Phoebe Shepherd. Married Abel Lamb in 1826 and by 1843 had born him eleven children. Died January 8, 1865, Salt Lake City, Salt Lake, Utah. Visited once with Mary. [FF; SEB 30:726-28; JTB: 62]

LAMBSON, Alfred Boaz. Born August 27, 1819/1820/1824, Royalton, Niagara, New York, to Boaz Lambson and Polly Walworth. Married Melissa Jane Bigler, March/November 25, 1845, Nauvoo, Hancock, Illinois. Died February 26, 1905. Brother-in-law of George A. Smith. Was visited by Mary in January 1847. Emigrated to Utah June 15, 1847. [SEB 27:285-88; HTW 9:496]

LAMBSON, Melissa Jane Bigler. Born March 24, 1825, Harrison, West Virginia, to Mark Bigler and Suzanna Ogden. Married Alfred Lambson, March/November 25, 1845, Nauvoo, Hancock, Illinois. Died October 25, 1899, Salt Lake City, Salt Lake, Utah. Visited by Mary in January 1847. First child born November 1846 in Winter Quarters. [SEB 5:284-85]

LAMOREAUX, Andrew. Danced with Mary at the council house in April 1847. There are two references in early church records to an Andrew Lamoreaux, which may indicate two different individuals. Neither show any record of being in Winter Quarters.

   LAMOREAUX, Andrew L. Born October 19, 1812, Pickering, York, Ontario, Canada, to John McCord Lamoreaux and Abigail Ann Losee. Married, first, Isabell Wilson, on October 12, 1833, Markham, York, Ontario, Canada. Died June 13, 1855, St. Louis, St. Louis, Missouri. His sixth child was born August 1845 in Nauvoo and the seventh child born 1848 in Utah. [SEB 27:293-98]

   LAMOREAUX, Andrew Losee. Born March 19, 1817, Scarborough, Ontario, Canada, to Joshua Lamoreaux and Ann Cross. Married Eleta Colton, October 11, 1841. [SEB 27:293-98]

LANG, Bishop Thomas. Bishop in one of the Winter Quarters wards. While in Mt. Pisgah, he loaned two yoke of oxen to William Hyde to return to Nauvoo for the poor camp. [MPJ; WQ: 66]

LEVETT, Sister. Visited in May 1847 by Wealthy, later in the day by Mary. Jane Snyder Richards later wrote that one of her women friends in Nauvoo was a Mrs. Leavitt, kind and motherly. She may have been referring to one of these women, who were sisters-in-law and who later lived in Winter Quarters.

   LEAVITT, Phoebe Cole. Born July 6, 1795, New Hampshire. Married to Weir Leavitt. Their son, George, age nineteen, is shown in the Winter Quarters First Ward records in June 1847 owning five head of cattle. He, his mother, and two sisters emigrated to Utah in 1847. Phoebe was apparently a widow at this time. [SEB 28:1; HTW 8:434]

   LEAVITT, Sarah Sturdevant. Born September 5, 1798, Lyme, Grafton, New Hampshire, to Lemuel Sturdevant and Priscilla Thompson. Married Jeremiah Leavitt, March 6, 1817. Died April 5, 1878. Her husband died August 20, 1856, in Bonaparte, Iowa, where he had gone for food while she and the family were in Mt. Pisgah. She moved the family to Winter Quarters, where they made a camp of hay until her older boys could build a house. After the Saints left Winter Quarters, she remained with her family, moving into one of the nicer houses, and took in boarders, leaving for Utah in 1851. [DL: 20-28; SEB 42:246-47]

LEONARD, Brother and Sister. Were good friends of Mary and Wealthy. Sister Leonard helped them quilt. Mary and Wealthy were often in the Leonard home, sometimes staying all night, sewing, visiting, or reading. Wealthy made Brother Leonard a hat.

LEONARD, Abigail Calkins. Born April 11, 1795, Burlington, Bradford, Pennsylvania, to Moses Calkins and Thankful Stevens. Married Lyman Leonard of Springfield, Hampden, Massachusetts. [SEB 8:306]

LEONARD, Lyman. Born June 3, 1793, Springfield, Hampden, Massachusetts, to Ezekial Leonard and Rhoda Saxton. Married, first, Abigail Calkins. Died March 1877. [SEB 27:974-76; HTW 8:436]

LEONARD, Ortentia White. Born November 30, 1825, Rushford, Alleghany, New York, to Ephraim Davis White and Sally Crane. Married Truman Leonard of Pottertown, Ontario, New York, January 1, 1846, Nauvoo, Hancock, Illinois. Died August 14, 1898, Farmington, Davis, Utah. [FF; SEB 45:726]

LEONARD, Truman, Jr. Born 1820, Pottertown, Ontario, New York, to Truman Leonard and Roxanna Allis. Married, first, Ortentia White, January 1, 1846, Nauvoo, Hancock, Illinois. First child born November 1846 in Winter Quarters. Died December 20, 1897, Farmington, Davis, Utah. [SEB 27:983-87; FF]

LITTLE, Edwin Sobieski. Born January 22, 1817, Aurelius, Cayuga, New York, to James Little and Susannah Young. Married Harriet Amelia Decker Hanks, March 22, 1842, Nauvoo, Hancock, Illinois. Died March 18, 1846, Richardsons Point, Lee, Iowa. Mary went to see his grave on the way through Iowa. [SEB 28:253-55; NDM: 100]

LITTLE, Jesse Carter. Born September 26, 1815, Belmont, Waldo, Maine. Married three times. Died December 25, 1893, in Salt Lake City, Salt Lake, Utah. Bishop in Pottawattamie County July 24, 1846. In first pioneer company in 1847. [SEB 28:276-81; HTW 8:405; IBI: 103]

LITTLEFIELD, Lyman Omer/Omen. Born November 21, 1819, Verona, Oneida, New York, to Waldo Littlefield and Sarah Mary Thompson/Mary Higgins. Married Adaline Hamblin. Died September 1, 1893. In April 1847 he started for a mission to England, stopping at the Richards home to see if he could carry letters to Samuel and Franklin. Returned to Winter Quarters in 1848. [SEB 28:285-87]

LOTT, Cornelius Peter. Born September 27, 1798, New York County, New York, to Peter Lott and Mary Jane Smiley. Married, first, Permelia Darow, April 27, 1823. Married, second, Rebecca Narcissus Fausett, January 22, 1846, Nauvoo, Hancock, Illinois. In Winter Quarters he married Phoebe Peck Knight, widow of Joseph Knight Sr., who died February 3, 1847. She was the mother of Newel K. and Joseph Knight. Died July 6, 1850, Salt Lake City, Salt Lake, Utah. Managed Joseph Smith's farm in Nauvoo and the church farm in Salt Lake City. Is mentioned in the Winter Quarters First Ward bishop's report, December 1846, and is shown owning cattle there in June 1847. [EH; HS: 65-66; FF]

LOUIS, Sister. Lived on the east side of the river. While Mary was staying with the Goddard family in February 1848, she fit and sewed a dress for sister Louis.

LEWIS, Duritha Trail. Born January 5, 1803, North Franklin, Simpson, Kentucky, to Soloman Trail and Nancy Durant. Married David Lewis, November 23, 1834/1836, Kentucky. Twins born to her while living at Mosquito Creek, Pottawattamie County in August 1848. [SEB 43:808; MPJ]

LEWIS, Malinda Gimlin/Gimblin. Born March 27, 1811, Cumberland County, Kentucky, to Samuel Gimlin and Elizabeth More. Married Tarleton Lewis, March 27, 1828. Died June 5, 1894. Sixth child born December 1846 in Winter Quarters. [SEB 18:439-40]

LEWIS, Rebecca Henricks. Married to Neriah Lewis Jr., who was born April 29, 1816, Simpson County, Kentucky. Fourth child born in September 1846, Council Point, Iowa. Husband died in Richmond, Cache, Utah. [SEB 28:86-88; MPJ]

LUTS, Sister. visited with Mary at the Mellon home in November 1847.

LITZ, Fanny Fairchild. Born November 22, 1796, Russell, Virginia, to Hezekiah and Jemima Fairchild. Married Stephen Litz, January 15, 1818. He was baptized by Joseph Wood near Brown County, Illinois, in 1840, moving to Nauvoo where he was a high priest in the Nauvoo Fifth Ward High Priests Quorum, as was Phinehas. He was shown in the Winter Quarters First Ward, donating to the poor in March 1846. [SEB 15:901; EH; N5HP]

LUTZ, Susannah Dubois. Born January 22, 1816, Penns Neck, Salem, New Jersey, to Robert Dubois and Jane Johnson. Married Albert Lutz. Died November 6, 1885, Randolph, Rich, Utah. Children born in Kanesville, Pottawattamie, Iowa, 1849 and 1850. Shown in Blockhouse/Tabernacle Branch, Iowa, in January 1848 and Lake Branch, Iowa, in 1849. Possible the family was in Winter Quarters earlier. [FF; PHP: 8; FG]

LYMAN, Amasa Mason. Born March 30, 1813, Lyman, Grafton, New Hampshire, to Roswell Lyman and Martha Mason. Married, first, Louisa Maria Tanner, June 10, 1835, Kirtland, Lake, Ohio. Other wives in Nauvoo, including Dionitia Walker, whom Mary mentions in her journal. Was in first pioneer company. Emigrated to Utah with his families in 1848. [SEB 28:780-95; HTW 8:405; HTW 9:497]

LYMAN, Dionitia Walker. Born March 10, 1816, Dayton, Montgomery, Ohio, to Oliver Walker and Crisse/Cressy Nancy. Fifth wife of Amasa Mason Lyman, married July 1843, Nauvoo, Hancock, Illinois. Died September 1896 or July 11, 1894. No children. Was a pioneer to Utah in 1848. Was a nurse. [SEB 44:480-91; DUP: 36]

MACE, Brother and Sister. Invited Mary to their home for dinner and visiting in July 1847 and in March 1848. In October 1847 Mary visited brother Mace, the first time she had seen him since leaving Nauvoo. His home was across the street from Brother Miller in Winter Quarters.

MACE, Elizabeth Armstrong. Born April 2, 1819, Seneca Castle, Ontario, New York, to Alexander Armstrong and Griswold Chapman. Married Hiram Mace, April 4, 1837. Died August 12, 1902. The Hiram Mace family was in Ponca with the Emmett and Miller group when their child was born in February 1847. Next child was born March 1849 in Harris Grove, Iowa. [SEB 2:522-23]

MACE, Hiram. Born May 5, 1811, Eurelious Station, Cayuga, New York, to Henry Mace and Clarilla DeWater. Married, first, Elizabeth Armstrong, April 4, 1831. Children born at Ponca, Dixon, Nebraska, and at Harris Grove, Iowa. Died August 28, 1896, Fillmore, Millard, Utah. [SEB 28: 969-73]

MACE, Margaret Merkle. Born October 22, 1810, New York County, New York, to Conrad and Margaret Merkle. Married Wandall Mace, November 9, 1828, New York County, New York. Died June 13, 1854, Keokuk County, Iowa. Unknown if she was in Winter Quarters. [SEB 30:695-97]

MACE, Wandall. Born February 19, 1809, Johnstown, Montgomery, New York, to John Henry Parcels Mace and Dinah Campbell. Married Margaret Merkle, November 9, 1828, New York. Died August 10, 1889/ 1890, Kanab, Kane, Utah. Skilled wheelwright. Designed all of the wooden framing used in the construction of the Nauvoo Temple and Nauvoo House. Member of Nauvoo Legion. May have been in Winter Quarters. Emigrated to Utah 1849. [SEB 28:987-93; JTB: 53]

MAJOR, William W. Born January 27, 1804, Bristol, Sommerset, England, to Richard and Constantia Major. Married Sarah Coles, April 2, 1832, in England. Died October 2, 1854, in England while on a mission. Joined the Mormon church in 1852. Emigrated to Nauvoo in 1844. Painted scenery of the murder of Joseph and Hyrum at Carthage and sketches of the scenery along the route to Utah. Preached in several of the Winter Quarters wards. [ARCH; HS: 25; EH]

MARTIN, Julia Priscilla Smith. Born March 5, 1815, Stockholm, St. Lawrence, New York, to Asahel Smith and Elizabeth Schellenger. Married Moses Martin, 1846. Died March 15, 1916. Mary wrote in June 1847 that she was expected in Winter Quarters soon. [SEB 40:56-57]

MARTIN, Moses. Born June 1, 1812, New Lisbon, Grafton, New Hampshire, to Moses Martin. Married Julia Priscilla Smith, 1846. Died May 5, 1900. With Zion's Camp. First Quorum of Seventy. Accompanied Samuel and Franklin on their missions. [SEB 29:547-48]

MATTESON/MATSON, Sister. Mentioned as one of Mary's new neighbors in July 1847. Mary often visited with her at the homes of either Edward Hunter or Sister Wilder, another neighbor.

MATTESON women: There are two Sister Mattesons who were in early church records, but both were the first wife and would have been called by their married name. Phebe Maria Matteson was married to Ormus E. Bates and gave birth to a child, January 1848, in Winter Quarters. A Phebe Matteson was married to Henry Pearmain, November 1843, in Nauvoo and may have been in Winter Quarters. Another possibility is Ann Pierson, born 1797 in Chester County, Pennsylvania, married to George B. Mattson. She was endowed in the Nauvoo Temple, and her son, George Brinton Matson, was a pioneer to Utah. [SEB 4:241; 29:653; NDM: 96]

McCORD, Brother. Spoke at church meeting after returning from Salt Lake Valley, April 1848.

    McCORD, Alexander. Born January 15, 1811, in New York City, New York, New York. Was 4th Sergeant in Company A of the Mormon Battalion. Married Sybil Bradenburg, Scarborough, Upper Canada. Died July 15, 1888, Harlan, Shelby, Iowa, or September 8, 1847, San Diego, San Diego, California. [SEB 30:56; DBMB: 118]

McGRAY, Brother. One of three fiddlers at Phinehas's home on October 19, 1847. Other two were William P. McIntire and Daniel Cahoon.

    McGRARY, John. Listed in one of the Pottawattamie branches. [IBI: 108]

    McRAE, Alexander. Born September 7, 1807, Anson County, North Carolina, to John B. and Mary Jane McRae. Married October 2, 1834, New Castle, Henry, Kentucky, to Eunice Fitzgerald. Other wife in Utah. Died June 20, 1891, Salt Lake City, Salt Lake, Utah. In Liberty Jail with Joseph Smith, winter 1838-39. Child born in Kanesville, September 1848. [SEB 30:447-52]

McINTIRE, Anna/Ann Patterson. Born December 19, 1811, Wheatfield, Perry, Pennsylvania, to William Patterson and Margaret Lynn. Married William Patterson McIntire, December 19, 1834, Indiana County, Pennsylvania. Died June 29, 1880. Accompanied husband as he played violin. [SEB 34:117-18; MBB: 9]

McINTIRE, William Patterson. Born May 29, 1813, Wheatfield, Indiana, Pennsylvania, to George McIntire and Sarah Davis. Married Anna Patterson, December 19, 1834, Indiana County, Pennsylvania. Died January 7, 1881/82, St. George, Washington, Utah. Phinehas twice brought William "Macantire" to his home to accompany dances and play tunes on his violin. Is shown as a member of Blockhouse Branch, organized December 27, 1846. [SEB 30:262-66; MBB: 9]

McLELLEN, Brother. Mary and Samuel Burton spent the night of February 16, 1847, at his home at the Pony Creek Indian Village.

    McLELLIN, James. A bishop in Pottawattamie County, Iowa, July 24, 1846. [IBI: 112]

MEEKS, Priddy. Born August 29, 1795, Greenville, Greenville, South Carolina, to Athe Meeks and Margaret Sneed. Married, first, Mary Bartlett, March 1815. After she died, he married, second, widow Sarah Mahurin Smith, December 24, 1826. Died 1886. Lived near the border of Iowa and Missouri close to William Slusher and Mr. Wilkinson, both mentioned in Mary's journal. It was at his home that Mary and John Haven read the letter about Joseph's death in the Mormon Battalion. Priddy was a Thomsonian doctor who continued to practice upon arriving in the Salt Lake Valley. [SEB 30:595-99; PM]

MELLEN/MELLON, Brother and Sister. Visited with Mary, fed her, shared patriarchal blessings, and hosted a dance at their home between July 1847 and March 1848.

    MELLEN, Grace Jane Ramsden. Born September 26, 1816, to James Ramsden and Catherine Horricks. Married John Mellen in 1836, Bolton, Lancashire, England. Died 1894, Woods Cross, Davis, Utah. Fifth child born in Winter Quarters, April 1848. [HTW 9:499; FF; SEB]

MELLEN, John. Born August 18, 1813, Little Bolton, Lancashire, England, to John Mellen and Ann Lever/Horrock. Married Grace Jane Ramsden, 1836, Bolton, Lancashire, England. Died February 16, 1896, Woods Cross, Davis, Utah. Emigrated to Utah, September 1848. [HTW 9:499; FF; SEB 30:628-30]

MILLER, Emeline Potter. Born May 18,1829, Plymouth, Litchfield, Connecticut, to Ransom Robert Potter and Rhoda Emeline Ferrell. Third wife of William Miller, married February 7, 1846, Nauvoo, Hancock, Illinois. [SEB 35:366]

MILLER, Marilla Lucretia Johnson. Born October 12, 1830, Haddam, Middlesex, Connecticut, to Aaron Johnson and Polly Zuriah Kelsey. Second wife of William Miller, married December 27, 1845, Nauvoo, Hancock, Illinois. [SEB 25:647]

MILLER, Phoebe Scott. Born August 19, 1816, Avon, Livingston, New York. First wife of William Miller, married May 4, 1834, Avon, Livingston, New York. [SEB 38:541]

MILLER, William. Born February 8, 1814, Avon, Livingston, New York, to Seth Miller and Martha Fielding. Married, first, Phoebe Scott, May 4, 1834, Avon, Livingston, New York. Married, second, Marilla Lucretia Johnson, December 27, 1845, Nauvoo, Hancock, Illinois. Married, third, Emeline Potter, February 7, 1846. Married fourth wife in Utah, although Mary mentions him with three and sometimes four ladies. Died August 7, 1875, Provo, Utah, Utah. With William Kay helped Phinehas move into his new house. Mary often visited at his home, where she rested or ate. [SEB 31:98-102]

MOON, F. Was a frequent visitor to the home of Old John Parker in Chaigley, Lancashire, England, along with Willard Richards, Joseph Fielding, and others. There are Matthias Moon, married to Alice Plumb, and Thomas Moon, married to Lydia Plumb, both of Lancashire. Perhaps Mary meant Father Moon, as no F. Moon is known. [SEB 31:430-38]

MORLEY, Isaac. Born March 11, 1786, Montague, Franklin, Massachusetts, to Thomas Morley and Edith Marsh. Married, first, Lucy Gunn, June 20, 1812. Married, second, Hannah Finch Blakeslee, 1844, Nauvoo, Hancock, Illinois. Married, third, Abigail Leonora Snow, 1844, Nauvoo, Hancock, Illinois. Died June/July 21, 1864, Fairview, Sanpete, Utah. First counselor to Bishop Edward Partridge, the first bishop in the church from 1831 to 1840. Ordained patriarch in 1838. Frequent preacher in Winter Quarters. Emigrated to Utah in 1848, bringing records of the church and some precious items from the Nauvoo Temple. [SEB 31:621-29; HS: 30]

MORSE, Mary Vail. Born December 8, 1809, Dublin, Cheshire, New Hampshire. Second wife of Phinehas Richards, married February 8, 1846, Nauvoo, Hancock, Illinois. Although Wealthy was opposed to the marriage, Heber C. Kimball told Phinehas not to let a woman steal his crown, that it was his duty to enter into plural marriage. Phinehas left Mary Vail Morse at Mt. Pisgah with one load of their supplies. When he went back for her and the supplies, she wouldn't accompany him. On December 5, 1846, Phinehas divorced her on the advice of Brigham Young. She married Levi Jackman, 1851, Salt Lake City, Salt Lake, Utah. [PR; SEB 31:754]

MOSES, Brother and Sister. Visited with Mary and Wealthy in May 1847. In May 1848, Mary was at their home. Two Moses brothers were living at the Bluffs. One or both families may have been mentioned by Mary.

MOSES, Barbara Matilda Neff. Born October 28, 1822, Lancaster County, Pennsylvania, to John Neff and Mary Barr. Married Julian Moses, March 25, 1845. Died May 29, 1890. [SEB 32:360-61]

MOSES, James. Born February 28, 1806, Norfolk, Litchfield, Connecticut, to Jesse Moses and Esther Brown. Married, first, Roxy Mariah Terry, April 9, 1833. Married, second, Eliza Spencer, October 7, 1839, Nauvoo. Two children born in Council Bluffs, August 1846 and May 1848. Was in Pleasant Valley Branch or McOlney Branch, Iowa, in 1848. Died March 30, 1891, Holliday, Salt Lake, Utah. [SEB 31:786-89; IBI: 122]

MOSES, Julian. Born April 11, 1810, Norfolk, Litchfield, Connecticut, to Jesse Moses and Esther Brown. Married Barbara Matilda Neff, March 25, 1845. Died February 12, 1892, Salt Lake City, Salt Lake, Utah. Emigrated to Utah June 17, 1847. [SEB 31:793-95; HTW 8:434]

MOSES, Roxy Mariah Terry. Married James Moses, April 9, 1833. [SEB 31:786-87]

MOSS, Elizabeth Cottam. Married to William Moss, May 17, 1828. Mary visited with Brother and Sister Moss while visiting with the Goddard family on the east side of the Missouri River. Member of Council Point Branch. [SEB 31:836-37]

MOSS, William. Born September 27, 1796, Barton, Lancashire, England, to Robert Moss and Margaret Kelsell. Married Elizabeth Cottam, May 17, 1828. Died 1872, Salt Lake City, Salt Lake, Utah. In Council Point Branch, 1847. [SEB 31:836-37; IBI: 122]

MURDOCK, John. Born July 15, 1792, Kortright, Delaware, New York, to John Murdock and Eleanor Riggs. Married, first, Julia Clapp, December 14, 1823. She died 1831. Her six-hour twins were given to Emma Smith to care for. Married, second, Amoranda Turner, February 4, 1836, New York. She died August 1837 in Missouri. Married, third, Electa Allen, May 3, 1838, Caldwell County, Missouri. She died 1838. Married, fourth, Sarah Zufelt, 1846, Nauvoo, Hancock, Illinois. Bishop in Nauvoo and Salt Lake City. Patriarch in Ohio. Several missions in early period of church. Member of Zion's Camp. Preached sermon in church meeting Mary attended at brother Bird's home on east side of river. Emigrated to Utah June 17, 1847. [SEB 32:20-29; HTW 8:441; IBI: 123]

MURRAY, Fanny Young. Born November 8, 1787, Hopkinton, Middlesex, Massachusetts, to John Young and Abigail/Nabby Howe. Married, first, Robert Carr, 1803. Married, second, Roswell Murray. Died June 11, 1859. First cousin to Phinehas Richards and stepmother of Vilate Murray Kimball. [SEB 48:109-10]

NEPHI, Brother. Called to see Mary in August 1847 with the family of Isaac Davis.

NOON, Betsy [Elizabeth Ann]. Daughter of Sarah Peak Noon Kimball and her first husband, William S. Noon. Came to America with her mother and sister in 1841. Mary altered a dress for her. Married James Lawson, May 6, 1856, Salt Lake City, Salt Lake, Utah. [HCKW: 13; SEB 27:570]

NOON, Sarah. See KIMBALL, Sarah Peak Noon.

NORRIS, David. Born August 10, 1800, Orange, Essex, New York, to David Norris Sr. Married Sarah Louise Ambler/Aser and received his endowments in the Nauvoo Temple. Killed during "Battle of Nauvoo," September 10-12, 1846. [SEB:CDROM; WON: 175]

OAKLEY, Brother and folks. Visited by Mary while camped at Mosquito Creek, July 30, 1846.

> OAKLEY, Ezra. Born April 10, 1788, Hemstead, Naussau, Long Island, New York, to Ezra Oakley and Elizabeth Stringham. Married Elizabeth DeGroot. Died January 29, 1879, Salt Lake City, Salt Lake, Utah. Their family at the bluffs included John DeGroot Oakley, who joined the Mormon Battalion, and his wife, Mary McCormall Patterson, married February 16, 1845, Nauvoo, and whose first child was born in Winter Quarters, February 1847; Mary Ann DeGroot Oakley, who married John Taylor in 1845; and a daughter, Margaret Oakley. Most of this family emigrated to Utah together in June 1847. [HTW 8:425; SEB 32:991-99; 33:1-10; NDM: 98]

OBANKS, Margaret Phillips. Born May 26, 1800, Kent, Putnum, New York, to Joseph Phillips and Sarah Farrington. Married Moses Banks/OBanks/ Osterbanks. He died 1845. Married, second, David Fullmer, as his second wife. He was president of Garden Grove Branch. His third wife was Sarah Sophronia Banks, Margaret's daughter. Possibly divorced Margaret, as she is known as sister OBanks in Phinehas's and Mary's journals, not as sister Fullmer. Margaret married Phinehas Richards, February 29, 1847, by Brigham Young in Winter Quarters. Because of Wealthy's opposition, they were divorced, February 17, 1852, in the President's Office, Salt Lake City, Salt Lake, Utah. She was sealed the same day to Brother Chamberlin of Parowan, Utah. [SEB 34:822-23; PR]

ONE, Miss Susan. See HUNTER, Susanna Wann.

ORCER/ORSER, Sister. Visited often by Mary, Wealthy, and Jane. She lived near Joseph Fielding's family.

> ORSER, Maria. Born March 15, 1803, Pompey, Onondago, New York. Married Zechariah Butterfield, August 4, 1844, Nauvoo, Hancock, Illinois. If she were his first wife, she wouldn't have been known as Sister Orser, but Sister Butterfield. No other Orser woman is known. [SEB 33:205; NDM: 112]

PACK, John. Born May 20, 1809, St. John, New Brunswick, Canada, to George Pack and Phylotte Greene. Married, first, Julia Ives, October 10, 1832, Watertown, Jefferson, New York. Married Nancy Aurelia Booth, Ruth Mosher, and Eliza Jane Graham, January 21, 1846, Nauvoo, Hancock, Illinois. Divorced Eliza Jane about 1846. Other wives in Utah. Died April 4, 1885, Salt Lake City, Salt Lake, Utah. Experienced trials in Missouri. Council of Fifty and Nauvoo Legion in Nauvoo. One of first pioneers to Utah in 1847. Emigrated with family, including widowed mother, in Heber C. Kimball's company, 1848. [RJP; FF; HTW 9:502]

PACK, Julia Ives. Born March 8, 1817, Watertown, Jefferson, New York, to Erastus Ives and Lucy Paine. Married John Pack, October 10, 1832, Waterton,

Jefferson, New York. Died June 23, 1903, Kamas, Summit, Utah. Remained in Winter Quarters while husband traveled with first pioneers to Utah in 1847. [SEB 25:20-22]

PAGE, John Edward. Born February 25, 1799, Trenton, Oneida, New York, to Ebenezer and Rachel Page. Married Lorain Stevens, December 26, 1833; she died in Missouri. Married Mary Judd, January 1839. Died October 14, 1867, Sycamore, DeKalb, Illinois. Early missionary to Canada. Involved in early church history in Kirtland and Far West. Apostle. Supported James Strang as successor to Joseph Smith. Excommunicated June 1846. Helped Hedrickites gain possession of the Independence Temple lot. He was replaced in the Quorum of the Twelve by Ezra Taft Benson. [SEB 33:555-60]

PAINE, Brother. Lived in Nauvoo. Received a letter from Samuel W. Richards dated August 31, 1846.

> PAINE, Samuel Langdon, Jr. Born September 1, 1808, Brookfield, Madison, New York. Married Mary. Endowed in the Nauvoo Temple, January 23, 1846. [SEB 34:163]

> PAYNE, Richard B. Married to Lurena. Endowed in Nauvoo Temple, February 7, 1846. Member Council Point Branch, May 1847. [SEB 34:162; CPBM: 3]

> PAYNE, Samuel. Born July 24, 1814, Melbourne, Cambridge, England, to Samuel Payne. Married Sarah Hills and Mary Barnes in England. Died Prairieville, Iowa, 1848. Child born Nauvoo 1844. [SEB 34:163]

> PAYNE, William. Born January 4, 1816, Houghton, Stropshire, England. Married Catherine Nichols, June 7, 1843, Nauvoo. [SEB 34:168]

PALMER, Joseph Farel/Ferron. Born October 7, 1802, Vermont, to Abner Palmer and Mary Harvey. Married Mary Ellen Haven, January 9, 1833. Died October 1885. Wife was first cousin to Phinehas Richards. [SEB 33:618-19]

PALMER, Mary Ellen Haven. Born June 26, 1803, Holliston, Middlesex, Massachusetts, to John Haven and first wife, Elizabeth Howe. Married Joseph Farel/Ferron Palmer, January 9, 1833. Died February 15, 1863. First cousin to Phinehas. [IB: 14; SEB 21:726-27]

PARKER, Alice. See CORBRIDGE, Alice.

PARKER, Ann. See WATSON, Ann/Nancy.

PARKER, Brother. Boarded with Phinehas and his family on May 10, 1848. From New Orleans.

PARKER, Ellen. See CORBRIDGE, Ellen.

PARKER, Ellen Briggs Douglas/Douglass. Born November 4, 1806, Downham, Lancashire, England, to Mr. Briggs and Isabell. Married, first, George Douglas, who died in Nauvoo. Married, second, John Parker Jr., March 29, 1846, Nauvoo, Hancock, Illinois. Sister-in-law to Mary. [SEB 6:687; SWR; NDM: 113]

PARKER, Ellen Hesken. Born January 23, 1778/1779, Ribchester, Lancashire, England, to Robert Hesken and Margaret Watson. Married John Parker Sr., January 14, 1799, Mitton Parish, Yorkshire, England. Died of malaria, September 22, 1845, Nauvoo, Hancock, Illinois. Mary's mother. [AG]

PARKER, Isabella. See COTTAM, Isabella.

PARKER, John, Jr. Born February 14, 1812, Chaigley, Lancashire, England, to John Parker Sr. and Ellen Heskin. Married, first, Alice Woodacre, October 5, 1835, in England. She died leaving him with small children. He emigrated to Nauvoo, where he married Ellen Briggs Douglas/Douglass, March 29, 1846. Other wife in Utah. Died March 24, 1886. Bishop of Virgin, Washington, Utah. Brother of Mary and father of Samuel Whitney Richards's second wife. [AG; NDM: 113]

PARKER, John, Sr. Born August 17, 1775, Chaigley, Lancashire, England, to Richard Parker and Alice Kenyon. Married Ellen Heskin, January 14, 1799, Mitton Parish, Yorkshire, England. Died January 8, 1857, Salt Lake City, Salt Lake, Utah. Emigrated to America on ship *North America*, first church-sponsored ship. Wife Ellen died in Nauvoo of malaria. Mary's father. [AG]

PARKER, Rodger/Roger. Born March 6, 1807, Chaigley, Lancashire, England, to John Parker Sr. and Ellen Heskin. Married Alice Bleasdale. Baptized in England. Came to America but apparently didn't remain in the church. Mary's brother. [AG]

PARKER, Robert. Born December 5, 1801, Chaigley, Lancashire, England, to John Parker Sr. and Ellen Heskin. Married Mary Hoyle, November 17, 1823. Remained in England. Mary's brother. [AG]

PARRY/PERRY, Brother and Sister. Mary talked to Sisters Parry and West in Winter Quarters, May 1847. In February 1848 she rode home from the Goddard home on the east of the river with Brother Perry. This could be the same family or two different ones. Several Perry families are located in Iowa or Council Bluffs. The most logical individuals are here listed.

> PERRY, Eliza B. Born October 5, 1810. Plural wife of Ezra Taft Benson, married March 4, 1847, Council Bluffs. [SEB 34:523-24]

> PERRY, Eunice Wing. Born July 8, 1794, Hinsdale, Berkshire, Massachusetts, to Elisha Wing and Anna Boardman. Married Gustavus Adolphus Perry. Member of Lake Branch, Iowa, 1848-50. [SEB 47:62; LBM: 1; IBI: 135]

> PERRY, Gustavus Adolphus. Born January 4, 1797, Wilton, Hillsboro, New Hampshire, to Abijah Perry and Elizabeth Tippets. Married Eunice Wing and others. Died May 28, 1868, Perry, Box Elder, Utah. Member of Lake Branch, Iowa, 1848-50. [SEB 34:531-33; LBM: 1; IBI: 135; PHP: 2]

> PERRY, Isaac. Born May 4, 1807, Madison, Madison, New York, to Asahel Perry and Polly Chadwick. Married Lucinda Cooley, October 17, 1832. Shown in the Winter Quarters First Ward donating to the poor, March 12, 1847. [EH; SEB 31:534-35]

> PERRY, Orrin Alonzo. Born September 11, 1817, Lewis, Essex, New York, to Gustavus Adolphus Perry and Eunice Wing. Married Mary Hoops, 1841. Child born June 1847 in Council Bluffs. Died June 1901, Perry, Box Elder, Utah, which was named for him. [SEB 34:548-50]

PARSONS, Brother and Sister. Called to see Mary and Wealthy, July 1847.

> PARSONS, Mary Jenkins. Born September 28, 1813, Worcestershire, England. Baptized 1839 by Wilford Woodruff. In Lake Branch, Iowa, 1848-50. [IBI: 131; SEB 25:391; LBM: 3]

PARSONS, William, Sr. Born March 27, 1807/8, Bosbury Lane, Herfordshire, England, to Richard Parsons and Mary Gouldrick. Married, first, Mary Jenkins. Child born in Farmington, Iowa, March 1847, and another born in Council Bluffs, December 1849. In Lake Branch, Iowa, 1848-50. Died September 20, 1882, Willard, Box Elder, Utah. [SEB 34:1-5; IBI: 131; LBM: 3]

PARTINGTON, Ellen Marie. Born September 14, 1834, Preston, Lancashire, England, to Ralph Partington and Ann Taylor. Married John Moburn Kay, June 19, 1851, Salt Lake City, Salt Lake, Utah. Died 1903, Salt Lake City, Salt Lake, Utah. Partington family emigrated to Nauvoo, where the parents could not find work, and lived next to Willard Richards. Willard had Ellen and her sister Catherine sealed to him in the Nauvoo Temple as adopted daughters. Richards family records indicate that Ellen left Nauvoo with Willard's family to live in Winter Quarters. The rest of the Partington family moved to St. Louis from Nauvoo. In 1850 she was in St. Louis with her parents. [WR; ID: 483, 567, 619; SS]

PATTON, William. Sold his house to Phinehas in April 1847. Phinehas paid for it with one dollar and his son Joseph's coat. The house was situated on the south line of Winter Quarters.

PATTEN, William Cornwell. Born March 16/24, 1799, Chester, Pennsylvania, to John Patten and Ann Cornwell. Married Harriet Cooper and Julianah Bench. Married, third, Jane Crouse, January 14, 1844/45, Nauvoo, Hancock, Illinois. Other wives. Died March 9, 1883. Emigrated to Utah in 1850. [SEB 34:108-12]

PATTEN, William W. Born October 14, 1816, Herkimer, Herkimer, New York, to John Patten and Abigail Stiles. Married Betsey Dorrow. Died 1851. Was in Nauvoo February 1846. Emigrated to Utah in 1850. [SEB 34:113-14]

PEART, Jacob. Born June 3, 1801, St. Johns, Carrigill, Cumberland, England, to George and Nancy/Ann Peart. Married, first, Elizabeth Haldon, December 30, 1824. Married, second, Phoebe Thompson, May 6, 1842, Nauvoo, Hancock, Illinois. Married, third, Philanda Angela Loss, November 21, 1847. Died April 20, 1874, Salt Lake City, Salt Lake, Utah. Adopted into the family of Willard Richards. While living in Winter Quarters, they provided a home for Phoebe's daughter, Mary Thompson, one of Willard's wives. Emigrated to Utah in 1848. [SEB 34:255-61; HTW 9:503; ID: 480; NDM: 100]

PEIRCE, Mary. Born November 27, 1821, to Robert Peirce and Hannah Harvey. Sealed to Brigham Young on January 22, 1846, Nauvoo, Hancock, Illinois. Died March 16, 1847, Winter Quarters, Douglas, Nebraska. Mary's letter to Samuel dated April 15, 1847, mentioned the death of Mary in about April. [ERS: 246 SEB 34:379-82]

PEIRSON, Edwin Dwight. Born December 10, 1819, Richmond, Berkshire, Massachusetts, to William Peirson and Nancy Richards. Married Clamenza Eunice Wells, April 7, 1847. Died December 16, 1885. Samuel's first cousin and brother to Eliza Ann and Amelia Elizabeth Peirson. [AF; RFH 1:276, 269, 283]

PEIRSON, Eliza Ann. Born April 14, 1822, Richmond, Berkshire, Massachusetts, to William Peirson and Nancy Richards, who was a sister of Phinehas, Willard, and Levi Richards. Joined the LDS church along with her sisters Amelia Elizabeth and Susan Sanford, although their father was very much opposed. Eliza and Amelia left the family to be with the main body of the Saints. Eliza Ann died in Winter Quarters, October 12, 1846. First cousin of Samuel Whitney Richards. [RFH 1:10-11, 108, 169, 268-83]

PEIRSON, Nancy Richards. Born November 22, 1792, Hopkinton, Middlesex, Massachusetts, to Joseph and Rhoda Howe Richards. Married William Peirson, March 4, 1819. A sister of Phinehas, Levi, Rhoda, and Willard Richards and mother of Amelia Peirson Richards. Baptized June 2, 1838, but her husband wouldn't accept the religion. She finally left him to travel to Utah, where she could be with her family and the church. Died July 14/15, 1852, Platte River, Nebraska. [RFH1:268-82]

PHELPS, Brother. At Levi Richards's in February 1848. When Levi and Sarah cited their Greek lessons to Mary, Brother Phelps translated the words.

    PHELPS, Morris Charles. Born December 20, 1805, Northampton, Hampshire, Massachusetts, to Spencer Phelps and Mary Kenneipe. Married, first, Laura Clark, who died about 1840. Married, second, Sarah Thompson, March 27, 1842. Child born October 1848 in Winter Quarters. Died May 22, 1876, Montpelier, Bear Lake, Idaho. [SEB 34:763-69]

    PHELPS, William Wines. Born February 17, 1792, Hanover, Morris, New Jersey, to Enon Phelps and Mehitable Goldsmith. Married three wives, Stella Waterman, Laura Stowell, and Elizabeth Dunn. Died March 6, 1878, Salt Lake City, Salt Lake, Utah. Emigrated to Utah in 1848 with Brigham Young. [SEB 34:787-93]

PITT, William. Born August 16, 1813, Dymock, Gloucestershire, England, to Robert Pitt and Hannah Hill. Married, first, Caroline Smith, April 28, 1841, West Bromwich, Warwickshire, England. Married Cornelia Melvina Divine and Mary Jane Collins Dyer. Died February 21, 1873, Salt Lake City, Salt Lake, Utah. He and his band were all converted at the same time as a result of the missionary work of Wilford Woodruff and Heber C. Kimball in England. They emigrated to Nauvoo as a group. Gave concerts in the settlements in Iowa to earn money during the exodus. [FF; HS: 55]

PLUMB, Elizabeth Cleopatra Bellows. Born September 8, 1829, Jefferson County, Illinois. Married Merlin Plumb, 1843. Lived near Keg Creek, Pottawattamie, Iowa, within one mile from Samuel Dennis White, whom Mary visited. [SEB 35:112-16]

PLUMB, Merlin. Born August 14, 1826, Mulberry, Clermont, Ohio, to Merlin Plumb and Sarah Roberts. Married Elizabeth Cleopatra Bellows, 1843. Second child born November 1847, Keg Creek, Pottawattamie, Iowa. Died September 21, 1901, Eden, Graham, Arizona. [SEB 35:112-16].

POTTER, Eveline Hinman. Born August 8, 1829, West Stockbridge, Berkshire, Massachusetts, to Lyman Hinman and Aurelia Lewis. Married Gardner Godfrey Potter, December 1844, Iowa River, Johnson, Iowa. Married Thomas Sasson Smith. Died March 11, 1903, Farmington, Davis, Utah. Eveline and Gardner with her parents accompanied the Emmett/Miller group to Ft. Vermillion, winter 1846-47. Arrived in Winter Quarters spring 1847. Eveline and her sister Edna called to see Wealthy and Mary in April 1847. [SEB; FF; LH]

POTTER, Sister. Took a letter from Mary to her relatives in St. Louis, August 1847. Possibly Eveline Hinman Potter or Emeline Potter, wife of William Miller.

POTTER, W. Suitor of Mary's in England

PRATT, Martha Monks. Born April 28, 1825, Raynor, England. Ninth wife of Parley Parker Pratt, married April 28, 1847, Winter Quarters. Emigrated to America with other Saints the same time that Parley returned from England. Said she loved Mary because they were both from the same country. [SEB 35:568-82; APPP: 463]

PRATT, Orson. Born September 19, 1811, Hartford, Washington, New York, to Jared Pratt and Charity Dickenson. Married one of his converts, Sarah Marinda Bates, July 4, 1836. Other wives: Charlotte Bishop, 1844; Adelia Ann Bishop, December 13, 1844; Mary Ann Merrill, January 13, 1846; Louisa Chandler, January 17, 1846. Other wives in Utah. Died October 3, 1881, Salt Lake City, Salt Lake, Utah, the last of the original Council of Twelve Apostles of the church. Published many books of religious doctrine, astrology, and mathematics, as well as missionary tracts. One of the most intellectual and influential leaders of the LDS church. Frequent speaker in Winter Quarters. Spoke at Mary's funeral in Salt Lake City Fourteenth Ward, June 4, 1860. [HS: 53; NJ51: 39-41; SEB 35:550-66]

PRATT, Parley Parker. Born April 12, 1807, Burlington, Otsego, New York, to Jared Pratt and Charity Dickenson. Married, first, Thankful Halsey, September 9, 1827, who died in Kirtland in 1837. Nine other wives. Killed May 13, 1857, near Van Buren, Arkansas, by Hector McLean. One of the most effective proselyters of the early LDS church after his baptism in 1830. Apostle in 1835. Emigrated to Utah in 1847. Visited with Samuel in Great Britain then reported to Mary that he was well. [APPP; SEB 35:568-82]

PRATT, Sarah Marinda Bates. Born February 5, 1817, Henderson, Jefferson, New York, to Cyrus Bates and Lydia Harrington. First wife of Orson Pratt, married July 4, 1836, Henderson, Jefferson, New York. Died December 25, 1888, Utah. As first wife, was probably the woman mentioned in Mary's journal who visited at Sister Benson's with Sister Parley P. Pratt and Mary in February 1848. [SEB 4:255-57]

PRATT, Sister Parley P. Mentioned by Mary in December 1846, June 1847, and February 1848. Parley married several wives after his first wife died: Mary Ann Frost, 1837; Elizabeth Brotherton, July 24, 1843; Mary Wood, September 9, 1844; Hannahette Snively, November 2, 1844; Belinda Marden, November 20, 1844; Sarah Huston, October 15, 1845; Phoebe Sopher, February 8,1846; Martha Monks, April 28, 1847; Ann Agatha Walker, April 28, 1847; other wives in Utah. [APPP: 462-64; SEB 35:568-82]

PRICE, William, Jr. Born December 4, 1815, Lea, Gloucestershire, England, to Wiliam Price and Mary Ann. Died September 18, 1906. Baptized 1841 in England. Member of the Seventies Quorum. [SEB 35:683-84]

PROCTOR, Richard. Because he was leaving for St. Louis, Mary sent her letter of January 29, 1847, with him to forward to Samuel.

PULSIPHER, Brother. Phinehas requested Mary to read a letter of Samuel's to him and Brother Campbell in February 1848.

PULSIPHER, Elias. Born November 12, 1805, Newberry, Orange, Vermont, to David Pulsipher and Terza Newton. Married Polly Ann Chubbuck, January 31, 1828. Died August 30, 1850, Winter Quarters or Iowa. Child born March 1848, Iowa. His widow and children were in the Little Pigeon Branch, 1851-52. [SEB 35:858-60; FF]

REDFIELD, Brother. Mary and her friends called here to collect things she had left behind at Samuel Burton's home.

REDFIELD, David. Born August 31, 1807, Herkimer, Herkimer, New York. Married Fanny M. McAtherton. Member of Nauvoo Fifth Ward high priests, as was Phinehas. Also a high priest in the Farmersville Branch in January 1848. Not known if he was in Winter Quarters. [SEB 36:236-37; N5HP; PHP: 3]

REDFIELD, Levi/Eli Harlow. Born September 25, 1801, Connecticut, to Levi Redfield and Wealthy Stevens. Married Caroline Foster, December 23, 1834. Married Alpha Foster, October 11, 1835. Married Francis A. Worsley, 1839. Died August 3, 1866. High priest in Tabernacle/Blockhouse Branch, January 1848. [SEB 36:238-39, 244-46; MBB; PHP: 1]

RHODES, George. Sailed with Mary and William and Margaret Beasdale. Shown on the passenger list of the ship *Alliance*, age twenty-six. Also shown on the same passenger list is the name of William Rhodes, age one year three months. Much conflicting information is found in LDS Ancestral File and other records about George and his family. Most logical information follows: Born October 5, 1815, Thornley, Lancashire, England, to William Rhodes and Ann Adder. On March 20, 1835, married Margaret Corbridge, sister of William and Edward Corbridge, who married Mary's sisters. A daughter, Ellen, and his wife died prior to his leaving England with young son William Henry. [AF; SEB 36:542-55; ALL]

RICE, Sister. Lived on the west line when Mary visited her June 1847.

RICH, Charles Coulson. Born August 21, 1809, Campbell County, Kentucky, to Joseph Rich and Nancy O'Neal. Married, first, Sarah DeArmon Pea, February 11, 1838, Far West, Caldwell, Missouri. Married the next four wives at Nauvoo, Hancock, Illinois: Eliza Ann Graves, January 2, 1845; Mary Ann Phelps, January 6, 1845; Sarah Jane Peck, January 9, 1845; Emeline Grover, February 2, 1846. Other wives. Died November 17, 1883, Paris, Bear Lake, Idaho. Presided over Mt. Pisgah Branch the winter of 1846-47. Involved in Battle of Crooked River and with Zion's Camp. High Council and Stake Presidency in Nauvoo. Helped colonize California and Cache County, Utah. [SEB 36:542-55; N5HP]

RICH, Sarah DeArmon Pea. Born September 23, 1814, St. Clair County, Illinois, to John Peay and Elizabeth Knighton. Married Charles Coulson Rich, February 11, 1838, Far West, Caldwell, Missouri. They had been recommended to each other by mutual friends, then corresponded. Charles proposed through a letter and Sarah accepted before they ever met. Died September 12, 1893, Paris, Bear Lake, Idaho. Was one of Mary's choice friends, having known her before her marriage to Samuel. In Salt Lake City, Sarah helped Mary sew for Samuel before his subsequent missions to Great Britain. [SEB 34:176-81; SDPR]

RICHARDS, Amelia Elizabeth Peirson. Born April 16, 1825, Richmond, Berkshire, Massachusetts, to William Peirson and Nancy Richards. Joined the LDS church with sisters Susan and Eliza Ann against father's wishes. Was taught church doctrine by uncle Willard and baptized by uncle Phinehas Richards. With Eliza Ann moved to Nauvoo. Married Willard Richards, January 22, 1846. She and Sarah Longstroth were the two wives he took with him to Winter Quarters. Cared for children of Willard and Jennetta Richards after Jennetta's death. Died February 23, 1851, Salt Lake City, Salt Lake, Utah, three days after giving birth to a son who died at birth. Mary and Samuel named first daughter, Mary Amelia, after her mother, Mary, and Amelia Peirson Richards. [RFH 1:269, 283; RFH 3:255-78; SEB 34:954; RFR]

RICHARDS, Elizabeth McFate. Born October 28, 1829, Mahoning, Armstrong/Mercer, Pennsylvania, to James McFate and Elizabeth Williams. Second wife of Franklin Dewey Richards, married January 31, 1846, Nauvoo, Hancock, Illinois. Died March 29, 1847, Winter Quarters, Douglas, Nebraska. [SEB 30:201; 36:607; RFR]

RICHARDS, Franklin Dewey. Born April 2, 1821, Richmond, Berkshire, Massachusetts, to Phinehas Richards and Wealthy Dewey. Married, first, Jane Snyder, December 18, 1842, Nauvoo, Hancock, Illinois. Married, second, Elizabeth McFate, January 31, 1846, Nauvoo. Thirteen more wives, some of whom were Willard's widows. Died December 9, 1899, Ogden, Weber, Utah. Mission president to England several times. Church historian 1889-89. Mary's brother-in-law. [SEB 36:609-19; RFR]

RICHARDS, George Spencer. Born January 8, 1823, Richmond, Berkshire, Massachusetts, to Phinehas Richards and Wealthy Dewey. Killed October 30, 1838, at Haun's Mill, Missouri. Mary's brother-in-law. [SEB 36:620-21; RFR]

RICHARDS, Heber John. Born October 11, 1840, to Willard Richards and Jennetta Richards. Married Mary Julia Johnson, April 9, 1862, Salt Lake City. Died May 12, 1919, Provo, Utah, Utah. Mary wrote about him getting over the measles. [SEB 36:622-24; RFH 3:139, 214, 254]

RICHARDS, Henry Phinehas. Born November 30, 1831, Richmond, Berkshire, Massachusetts, to Phinehas Richards and Wealthy Dewey. Married Margaret Minerva Empey, December 30, 1852, Salt Lake City, Salt Lake, Utah. Died October 29, 1912, Salt Lake City, Salt Lake, Utah. Mary's brother-in-law. [SEB 36:625-31; RFR]

RICHARDS, Isaac Phinehas. Born July 23, 1846, in Iowa, 72 miles west of Nauvoo, to Franklin Dewey Richards and Jane Snyder. Died the same day. Buried in Mt. Pisgah Cemetery, Iowa. Mary's nephew. [SEB 36:611; RFR]

RICHARDS, Jane Hall. Born February 18, 1826, Chatburn, Lancashire, England, to William Hall and Alice Veevers. Sixth wife of Willard Richards. Married January 31, 1846, in Nauvoo, Hancock, Illinois. Died December 10, 1849, Salt Lake City, Salt Lake, Utah. [RFH 3:306; RFR]

RICHARDS, Jane Snyder. Born January 31, 1823, Palmelia, now Watertown, Jefferson, New York, to Isaac Snyder and Lovisa Comstock. Married Franklin Dewey Richards, December 18, 1842, at the home of Jane's father who was living on Job Creek, near La Harpe, Hancock, Illinois. Died November 17, 1912, Ogden, Weber, Utah. Shared in Mary's experiences of Winter Quarters while their husbands served missions together in Great Britain. [SEB 40:687-89; RFR; FDR; ITOW: 169-77]

RICHARDS, Jennetta Richards. Born August 21, 1817, Walkerfold, Lancashire, England, to Reverend John Richards and Ellin Charnock. Married Willard Richards, who was a missionary in England, September 24, 1838. Died July 9, 1845, Nauvoo, Hancock, Illinois. Jennetta was a friend of Mary's older sisters. Taught school at her father's chapel in Walkerfold, where Mary attended for a time. [SEB 36:633-34; RFR; RFH 3:203-54]

RICHARDS, Joseph William. Born May 25, 1829, Richmond, Berkshire, Massachusetts, to Phinehas Richards and Wealthy Dewey. Died November 21, 1846, Ft. Pueblo, Colorado, where he had been sent with the sick detachment from the Mormon Battalion. Was a musician in Company A of the Battalion. [SEB 36:644-45; RFR]

RICHARDS, Levi. Born April 14, 1799, Hopkinton, Middlesex, Massachusetts, to Joseph Richards and Rhoda Howe. Married Sarah Griffith, December 25, 1843, Nauvoo, Hancock, Illinois. Married, second, Persis Goodall. Died June 13, 1876, Salt Lake City, Salt Lake, Utah. Played many musical instruments, taught school at age nineteen, and was a Thomsonian doctor. Mission to England in 1840, where he met Sarah Griffith. In Winter Quarters, he and Sarah were called on a five-year mission to England and advised to leave their small son, who was sickly, with Levi's sister, Rhoda. Samuel's uncle. [SEB 36:647-51; RFH 2:1-135; RFR]

RICHARDS, Levi Willard. Born June 12, 1845, Nauvoo, Hancock, Illinois, to Levi Richards and Sarah Griffith. Married Louisa Lula Greene, June 16, 1873, Salt Lake City, Salt Lake, Utah. Other wife. Died March 30, 1914, Salt Lake City, Salt Lake, Utah. Samuel's cousin. [SEB 36:652-54; RFR]

RICHARDS, Phinehas. Born November 15, 1788, Framingham, Middlesex, Massachusetts, to Joseph Richards and Rhoda Howe. Married Wealthy Dewey, February 24, 1818, Richmond, Berkshire, Massachusetts. Five other wives. Died November 25, 1874, Salt Lake City, Salt Lake, Utah. Thomsonian doctor. Member of High Council at Kirtland, Nauvoo, and Council Bluffs, and of the first High Council in Salt Lake City. First cousin of Brigham Young and John Haven's children. Mary's father-in-law. [SEB 36:667-72; HS; RFH 1:110-266; RFR]

RICHARDS, Rhoda. Born August 8, 1784, Framingham, Middlesex, Massachusetts, to Joseph Richards and Rhoda Howe. Married to Joseph Smith, June 12, 1843, Nauvoo, Hancock, Illinois. Died January 17, 1879, Salt Lake City, Salt Lake, Utah. Was in Winter Quarters with Willard's and Levi's families. When Levi and Sarah were called on mission to England in May 1848, their three-year-old son was left in Rhoda's care for five years. Samuel's aunt. [RFH 1:34-109; RFR]

RICHARDS, Rhoda Ann Jennetta. Born September 15, 1843, Nauvoo, Hancock, Illinois, to Willard Richards and Jennetta Richards. Married Benjamin Franklin Knowlton, October 31, 1863. Died May 3, 1882, Farmington, Davis, Utah. [RFH 3:142, 237-54; RFR]

RICHARDS, Samuel Whitney. Born August 9, 1824, Richmond, Berkshire, Massachusetts, to Phinehas Richards and Wealthy Dewey. Married Mary Haskin Parker, January 29, 1846, Nauvoo, Hancock, Illinois. Five other wives in Salt Lake City. Died November 26, 1909, Salt Lake City, Salt Lake, Utah. Was instrumental in building up the Scottish Mission, 1846 to 1848. British Mission president twice, also president of Eastern States Mission. Entrepreneur in Salt Lake City; owned mill in Farmington, Utah, and ranch in Wyoming. Was a carpenter and finisher. Worked on the Salt Lake City Temple. [SEB 36:680-88; RFR]

RICHARDS, Sarah Griffith. Born December 26, 1802, Monmouth, Monmouthshire, England, to David Griffith and Mary Stead. Married Levi Richards, December 25, 1843, Nauvoo, Hancock, Illinois. Died June 7, 1892, Salt Lake City, Salt Lake, Utah. Was tutored in London, then acquired position as private governess/tutor and lived in France for six years. Baptized in July 1842, then emigrated to Nauvoo, where she married Levi. She was forty-one and he was forty-four. Samuel's aunt. [RFH 2:136-205; RFR]

RICHARDS, Sarah Langstroth. Born February 25, 1826, Anncliffe, Yorkshire, England, to Stephen Langstroth and Ann Gill. Third wife of Willard Richards, married 1843, Nauvoo, Hancock, Illinois. Died 1858, Salt Lake City, Salt Lake, Utah. [RFH 3:279-83]

RICHARDS, Wealthy Dewey. Born September 6, 1786, Pittsfield, Berkshire, Massachusetts, to Samuel Dewey III and Mille McKee. Married Phinehas Richards, February 24, 1818, Richmond, Berkshire, Massachusetts. Died October 13, 1853, Salt Lake City, Salt Lake, Utah. Investigated the church for over five years after Phinehas joined. All her children were baptized before her. Struggled with her husband's plural marriages. Took great comfort in having Mary live with her in Winter Quarters. [RFR; RFH 1:110-266]

RICHARDS, Wealthy Lovisa. Born November 2, 1843, Nauvoo, Illinois to Franklin Dewey Richards and Jane Snyder. Died September 14, 1846, Cutler's Park, Douglas, Nebraska. Mary's niece. [SEB 36:611; RFR]

RICHARDS, Willard. Born June 24, 1804, Hopkinton, Middlesex, Massachusetts, to Joseph Richards and Rhoda Howe. Married, first, Jennetta Richards, September 24, 1838, Preston, Lancashire, England. Married seven more wives in Nauvoo, Hancock, Illinois: his niece, Amelia Elizabeth Peirson, December 22, 1845; Sarah Langstroth, January 22, 1846; Nanny Langstroth, January 25, 1846; Mary Thompson, January 27, 1846; Jane Hall, January 31, 1846; Susanna Lee Liptrot Walker, February 6, 1846; Ann Read Braddock, February 6, 1846. Married Susanna Bayliss, December 22, 1847, Winter Quarters, Douglas, Nebraska. May have also married Ann King Fox in January 1846, Nauvoo, Hancock, Illinois. Died March 11, 1854, Salt Lake City, Salt Lake, Utah. Jennetta died in Nauvoo. Amelia and Sarah Longstroth accompanied Willard to the Bluffs. Nanny, Jane, and Ann Braddock went first to St. Louis with the Longstroth family. Mary Thompson went to St. Louis first with her mother and stepfather, Jacob Peart, as did Ann Fox, then moved to Winter Quarters. British missionary. Apostle April 14, 1840. In Carthage Jail with Joseph Smith. Second Counselor to Brigham Young. Spiritual leader of the Richards family. Younger brother of Phinehas. [SEB 36:695-702; RFR; RFH 3:1-201; ID]

RICHARDS, Willard Brigham. Born January 25, 1847, Winter Quarters, Douglas, Nebraska, to Willard Richards and Sarah Langstroth. Mary's letter of January

29, 1847, informed Samuel of his new cousin, who was a "fine little gent." [RFH 3:145]

RICHARDSON, Brother T. Mary stayed with his family in Preston when her parents left for America.

RICHMOND, Brother. Mary called him one of Uncle Willard's "boys," and wrote that he was a fickle-minded youth. He visited at the home of Phinehas during November and December 1847 and told them about the army.

> RICHMOND, Benjamin Boyce. Born October 20, 1825, Upper Providence, Canada, to Thomas and Margaret Richmond. Married Sarah Elizabeth Garlick. Died 1854, Fillmore, Millard, Utah. Was a private in Company C of the Mormon Battalion. [SEB 36:789-90; DBMB: 144]

> RICHMOND, William. Born in England. Was in Nauvoo. Private in Company D of the Mormon Battalion. Died in Gold Hill, Storey, Nevada. [SEB 36:799; DBMB: 144]

RIGDON, Sidney. Born February 19, 1793, St. Clair, Alleghany, Pennsylvania, to William Rigdon and Nancy Galliger. Married Phebe Brook, June 12, 1820. Died July 14, 1876. Founded the Campbellites with Alexander Campbell. Converted to Mormonism in 1830 by reading the Book of Mormon. Was in Liberty Jail the winter of 1838-39. Acted as first counselor to Joseph Smith 1833-44, then tried to take control of the church at Joseph's death. Excommunicated. Mary wrote that he had returned to the Campbellite Church about 1847. [SEB 36:894-99]

RIPELY, Brother. Visited by Mary and Miss Boly in July 1847.

> RIPLEY, Alanson. Born January 8, 1798. Member of Zion's Camp. Lived in Nauvoo and Winter Quarters. [SEB 36:957-58]

RISTON, John. Young man who had taken care of Joseph when sick in Pueblo and helped bury him, visited with Phinehas and family.

> CLIFFORD, John Price [John Price Wriston]. Born April 13, 1823, Hopkinsville, Christian, Kentucky, to John Clifford and Elizabeth Price. His grandfather, Elias Clifford, had taken his stepfather's name, Wriston. In Utah, Brigham Young advised family members to use the original surname of Clifford. Married Mary Lois Van Leuven, December 15, 1852. Died March 4, 1899. Member of Company A of the Mormon Battalion. Wintered in Pueblo, Colorado, with the sick detachment. Arrived in Salt Lake Valley July 29, 1847, then returned to Winter Quarters. Spoke Shoshone and Bannock dialects and acted as interpreter. President of Indian Mission in 1859. [SEB 10:401-2; DUPMB: 79; DBMB: 51-52]

ROBINS, Brother and Sister. Arrived from Nauvoo in January 1847. Mary spent many days visiting, quilting, and reading Samuel's letters with sister Robins.

> ROBINS, Ann Johnson. Born about 1820. Married Thomas Fullwell Robins. Member Council Point Branch, 1851. Child born December 1851 in Council Bluffs. [SEB 37:186-88]

> ROBINS, Elizabeth Lambert. born March 19, 1818, Ledbury, Herefordshire, England. Married James Robins, 1840, Nauvoo, Hancock, Illinois. Child born in Winter Quarters December 1847. [SEB 27:24]

ROBINS, James. Born January 18, 1818, Little Comberton, Cambridgeshire, England, to Richard Robins and Ann Fullwell. Married Elizabeth Lambert, 1840, Nauvoo, Hancock, Illinois. Died August 8, 1907, Kaysville, Davis, Utah. [SEB 37:177-79]

ROBINS, Thomas Fullwell. Born August 13, 1824, Deerhurst, Gloucestershire, England, to Richard Robins and Ann Fullwell. Married Ann Johnson. Died June 6, 1895, Scipio, Millard, Utah. Member of Council Point Branch 1851. [SEB 37:186-88; IBI]

ROBINSON, Brother. Mary went to his home in April 1848 and twisted about half a pound of cotton yarn.

ROBINSON, Joseph L. Born February 18, 1811, Shaftsbury, Bennington, Vermont, to Nathan Robinson and Mary Brown. Married, first, Maria Wood, July 23, 1832, Booneville, Oneida, New York. Married, second, Susan McCord, sealed January 31, 1846, Nauvoo, Hancock, Illinois. Married, third, Laurinda Maria Atwood, March 20, 1847. Died January 1, 1893, Uintah, Weber, Utah. Member of Winter Quarters First Ward. Was in bishop's report December 1846, donated to the poor in March 1847, and owned nine head of cattle in June 1847. [FF; EH]

ROCKWOOD, Albert Perry. Born June 9, 1805, at Holliston, Middlesex, Massachusetts, to Luther Rockwood and Ruth Perry. Married, first, Nancy Haven, February 4, 1827, or April 3, 1827, Holliston, Middlesex, Massachusetts. Married, second, Alvira Teeples Wheeler, 1846. Other wives. Died November 25, 1879, Sugar House, Salt Lake, Utah. One of presidents of the First Quorum of Seventy from 1845 until his death. Drill officer and a general in the Nauvoo Legion. With first pioneers to Utah in 1847. First adopted son of Brigham Young, which allowed him many privileges and responsibilities. Warden of the territorial prison in Utah for fifteen years. Director of the Deseret Agricultural and Manufacturing Society. Married to Phinehas's cousin. [SEB 37:420-31; HS: 58-59; HTW 9:508; IB: 14]

ROCKWOOD, Ellen Acklund. Born March 23, 1829, Holliston, Middlesex, Massachusetts, to Albert Perry Rockwood and Nancy Haven. Married, first, Brigham Young, January 21, 1846. Died January 6, 1866. Second cousin to Samuel Richards. [SEB 37:432-33]

ROCKWOOD, Nancy Haven. Born June 13, 1805, Holliston, Middlesex, Massachusetts, to John Haven and first wife, Elizabeth Howe. Married Albert Perry Rockwood, February 4, 1827, or April 3, 1827. Died January 1876. Sister to Elizabeth Haven Barlow and Mary Ellen Haven Palmer. Half-sister to Eliza Ann Haven and Maria Haven Burton. First cousin to Phinehas Richards. [IB: 14; SEB 21:728-29]

RODYBACK, Brother and Sister and daughter. Between November 1847 and May 1848, Mary had many associations with a Rodeback family, visiting, sewing, and reading letters. Once when Mary was very ill, she stayed home from Sunday meeting and was watched by a young Rodeback daughter. Two Rodeback/Rhodeback families were in Winter Quarters during this time.

RODEBACK, Charles. Born June 8, 1811, Newlin, Chester, Pennsylvania, to Charles Rodeback and Sarah Quaintance. Married Jane Morgan, October 18, 1838, Newlin, Chester, Pennsylvania. Died June 1, 1907,

Hoytsville, Summit, Utah. After moving from Winter Quarters, the family settled in Council Bluffs until leaving for Utah after 1852. [FF; CR]

RODEBACK, James. Born May 22, 1807, Newlin, Chester, Pennsylvania, to Charles Rodeback and Sarah Quaintance. Married Phebe Beagle, 1832. Buried May 25, 1875, Cedar Valley, Utah, Utah. Lived in Nauvoo Fifth Ward, as did Phinehas. Member of North Pigeon Branch 1849-52. [FF; NAU5; IBI: 147]

RODEBACK, Jane Morgan. Born March 28, 1811, Uchland, Chester, Pennsylvania, to James/Benjamin Morgan and Mary Fisher. Married Charles Rodeback. Died September 14, 1890, Hoytsville, Summit, Utah. Child born July 1847 in Montrose, Iowa, who died October 1847 in Winter Quarters. Next child born in Council Bluffs, October 1848. [FF; SEB 31:594]

RODEBACK, Mary Ann. Born June 30, 1839, Uchland, Chester, Pennsylvania, to Charles Rodeback and Jane Morgan. Would have been age eight if she were the little Rodeback girl tending Mary. [FF]

RODEBACK, Phebe Ann. Born November 2, 1835, West Chester, Chester, Pennsylvania, to James Rodeback and Phebe Beagle. Died May 4, 1910. Would have been age twelve if she tended Mary. [FF; IBI: 147]

RODEBACK, Phebe Beagle. Born June 25, 1811, Uchland, Chester, Pennsylvania, to Henry Beagle and Margaret Evens. Married James Rodeback. Died September 17, 1898, Cedar Valley, Utah, Utah. Sixth child born November 1849, Council Bluffs. [FF; SEB 49:312]

ROLLINS, Brother and Sister. Visited by Mary in the spring of 1848. Sister Rollins helped Mary and Wealthy with washing. Several possibilities.

ROLLINS, Enoch Perham. Born January 14, 1805, Jefferson, Lincoln, Maine, to Ichabod Rollins and Mary Perham. Married Sophia Wing Fillbrook. Died November 9, 1877. Council Point Branch, 1847 and 1851. [SEB 37:619-22; IBI: 147]

ROLLINS, Eveline Walker. Born May 26, 1823, Randolph County, Indiana. Married James Henry Rollins. Child died in Winter Quarters, August 1847. [SEB 44:491]

ROLLINS, Henry. Born August 1790, Lincolnshire, England, to Austin Rollins and Betsy Wells. Married, first, Sophia Bray/Brag. Married, second, Ann Weathershogg. Died June 9, 1865, Centerville, Davis, Utah. All children born in Lancashire, England, and Steuben County, New York. Baptized in 1844. Not known if family was in Winter Quarters. Emigrated to Utah in 1848. [SEB 37:624-26]

ROLLINS, James Henry. Bishop in Pottawattamie County, July 24, 1846. Donated supplies for wagon to return to Nauvoo for poor camp while at Mt. Pisgah. High priest in Honey Creek Branch. Married Evaline Walker. Child died August 1847 in Winter Quarters. [PHP; MPJ; SEB 631-37]

ROLLINS, Sophia Wing Fillbrook. Born December 12, 1805, Hamdon, Penobscot, Maine. Married Enoch Perham Rollins. Last child born in Nauvoo. [SEB 26:283; IBI: 149]

ROPER, Sister. Arrived at Winter Quarters from England in May 1848; gave Mary's family information on Samuel and Franklin.

ROWE, Brother. Visited Phinehas and family. Told them how he had held Joseph in his arms when he died in Pueblo, Colorado.

> ROWE, Caratat Conderset. Born May 11, 1823, Perry, Delaware, Indiana, to William Noble Rowe and Candace Blanchard. Married Mary Napier. Died February 12, 1904, Mountainville, Sanpete, Utah. According to Claire Noall in *Intimate Disciple*, Caratat and his wife, who had enlisted as a laundress, were with Joseph in Pueblo and cared for him. No woman by the name of Mary Rowe is shown in Mormon Battalion records. [IB: 514; NJ21: 34; ARCH; DBMB: 147]

> ROWE, William. Born February 20, 1826, West Burlington, Delaware, Indiana, to David Rowe and Hannah Manning. Married March 1853 to Elizabeth Murdock. Died July 24, 1905; buried Thayne, Uinta, Wyoming. Company D of Mormon Battalion. [DUPMB: 127; NJ21: 34; DBMB: 147]

RUSHTON, Isabella Hannah. Born September 15, 1845, Nauvoo, Hancock, Illinois, to John Rushton and Margaret Hall. Died December 3, 1846, near Winter Quarters, Douglas, Nebraska. [FF]

RUSHTON, John. Born May 20, 1821, Newton Township, Yorkshire, England, to James Rushton and Isabella Hoyle. Married Margaret Hall, June 25, 1843, Nauvoo. Died in St. Louis, Missouri. Families of John Rushton and Thomas Bullock arrived in Winter Quarters together on December 6, 1846. John was a brother of Henrietta Bullock. [NDM: 105; JTB: 66; FF]

RUSHTON, Margaret Hall. Born July 28, 1822, Chatburn, Lancashire, England, to William Hall and Alice Veevers. Married John Rushton, June 25, 1843, Nauvoo. When he died, married Joseph Alston, August 12, 1851. Died April 29, 1872, American Fork, Utah, Utah. Sister of Jane Hall Richards. First child died the day before reaching Winter Quarters. Second child born in Winter Quarters, March 1847. [FF; NDM: 105]

RUSSELL, Daniel. Born March 8, 1811, China, New York. Bishop in Pottawattamie County, July 24, 1846. A Brother Russell held Sunday meeting at his home January 1847. He, Bishop Lang, and Phinehas spoke. Five Russell families were known to have lived either in Winter Quarters or on the east of the Missouri River between 1846 and 1850; however, Phinehas recorded the name as D. Russell in his journal. Phinehas also often attended prayer meetings at the home of D. Russell or Samuel Russell [IBI; PR]

SANDERS, Helen. See KIMBALL, Ellen Sanders.

SCOFIELD, Sister. Visited by Mary in May 1847.

> SCOFIELD, Clarissa Aurilla Terry. Born November 9, 1820, Perry, Ontario, New York, to Henry Terry and Sarah Williams. Married Joseph Smith Scofield, June/July 11, 1838. He was one of original pioneers to Utah. [SEB 42:955]

SCOTT, John. Born May 6, 1811, Armagh, Armagh, Ireland, to Jacob Scott and Sarah Warnock. Married, first, Elizabeth Menerey, April 15, 1836, Tranfalger, Ontario, Canada. Married, second, Mary Pew/Pugh, 1844, Nauvoo, Hancock, Illinois. Married, third, Sarah Ann Willis, 1846. Died December 16, 1876, Mill

Creek, Salt Lake, Utah. A Danite at Far West. Colonel in the Nauvoo Legion in charge of the artillery. Transported the Nauvoo Legion cannon to Utah. Early member of the Council of Fifty. [SEB 38:516-22]

SCOVIL, Alice Graves Hurst Wallwork. Born February 18, 1819, Shaw/Crompton, Lancashire, England, to William Hurst and Ann Graves. Married, first, William Wallwork, October 8, 1838. Married Lucius Scovil after his first wife died. Second child born August 1848 in Winter Quarters and died October 1849 near Pigeon Creek, Iowa. Alice died April 5, 1885. Was sick with quincy when Mary visited her. [FF; FG: 19]

SCOVIL, Emma Whaley. Born April 12, 1823, Sheffield, Yorkshire, England, to William Whaley and Emma Johnson. Married first to Mr. Curtis. Fourth wife of Lucius Nelson Scovill. Accompanied him home from his mission in England. In October 1847, she visited with Mary many times, often with Sister Turner and the Crookston family. In February 1848, Mary called to see Emma at the Scovil home, as she was sick. [SEB 45:516]

SCOVIL, Lucius Nelson. Born March 18, 1806, Waterbury, New Haven, Connecticut, to Joel Scovil and Lydia Manville. Married, first, Lucy Snow, June 1824/1828. She died in Nauvoo. Married, second, Alice Graves Hurst Wallwork. Fourth wife was Emma Whaley from England, who came to America with Lucius when he returned from his mission. Other wives. Died February/March 14, 1889, Springville, Utah, Utah. Was on a mission to England the same time as Samuel and Franklin. Arrived at Winter Quarters October 1847, bringing letters and parcels for Mary and Jane. High priest in Ferry Branch, Iowa, 1848. [PHP: 4; FF; FG: 19; IBI: 152; HS: 17-18; SEB 38:565-68]

SCRODSHAM, Brother. Neighbor of Jane's in Winter Quarters.

SEEDS, Mr. Mary's employer in England who tried to discourage her from joining the Latter-day Saint church.

SESSIONS, Brother. With other men in Winter Quarters had agreed to share in plowing the fields for planting crops, regardless of whether they were staying another season or leaving for Utah. Brothers Sessions and Boss refused to allow their cattle to plow and were publically chastized in a Sunday meeting, May 23, 1847. David Sessions and his son, Perrigrine, with their families, were in the companies which left June 17, 1847.

    SESSIONS, David. Born April 4, 1790, Orange County, Vermont, to David Sessions and Rachel Stevens. Married, first, Patty Bartlett, January 28, 1812, Newry, Oxford, Maine. Married, second, Harriet Worthing, Nauvoo, Hancock, Illinois. Died August 11, 1850, Salt Lake City, Salt Lake, Utah. [SEB 38:712-20]

    SESSIONS, Perrigrine. Born June 15, 1814, Newry, Oxford, Maine, to David Sessions and Patty Bartlett. Married, first, Julia Ann Killgore, September 21, 1834, Newry, Oxford, Maine. She died January 25, 1845. Married sisters Lucina and Mary Call, June 28, 1845, Nauvoo, Hancock, Illinois. In Nauvoo police force. First settler in Bountiful, Davis, Utah, and built first home there. [SEB 38;738-49; PS]

SEVERAGE, Mr. Lived near the Burton and Haven families on the Missouri/Iowa border. Took Mary on a sleigh ride when she was visiting the area.

SHEETS, Brother. Was selling his home in Winter Quarters for $6.00 in November 1847. Mary thought of buying it.

    SHEETS, Elijah Funk. Born March 22, 1821, Charlestown, Chester, Pennsylvania, to Frederick Sheets and Hannah Page. Married Margaret Hutchinson, England, January 16, 1846. She died February 1, 1847, Winter Quarters. Married Susanna Musser, April 6, 1847, Winter Quarters, Douglas, Nebraska. Other wives in Utah. Died July 3, 1904, Rexburg, Madison, Idaho. Worked on Nauvoo Temple. Mission to England 1844. Mission to Illinois, Indiana, Pennsylvania. Assistant trustee in trust of LDS church, 1873. [SEB 38:927-38]

SHERWOOD, Henry G. Born April 20, 1785, Kingsbury, Washington, New York, to Newcomb Sherwood. Married, first, Jane J. McManagal. Married, second, Marcia Abbott. Died November 24, 1862, San Bernardino, San Bernardino, California. Marshall of Nauvoo and Kirtland. High Council in Nauvoo, Kirtland, Salt Lake City. One of original pioneers in 1847. Surveyed the property purchased at San Bernardino. Agent for the Pony Express in Salt Lake City. Returned to San Bernardino where he died. [SEB 39:82-85]

SHIMERS, Mrs. or Sister. Visited by Mary in November 1847 and in February 1848.

    SHIMER, Elizabeth. Born January 1, 1805, Charleston, Cheshire, Pennsylvania. Fifth wife of Benjamin Covey. [SEB 12:11-14; 39:113]

    SHIMER, Laura Lovina. Born March 23, 1825, Charlestown, Chester, Pennsylvania, to David and Elizabeth Shimer. Second wife of Bishop Edward Hunter, married December 15, 1845, or June 29, 1846, Nauvoo, Hancock, Illinois. First child born October 1847 in Winter Quarters. Married two more times in Utah. Died July 16, 1894. [SEB 39:114-16]

SINGLETON, A. J. Lived near the Haven and Burton families on the Missouri/Iowa border in Pleasant Grove. One of the old-time settlers. Constable of Franklin precinct in the Austin area, which included Austin, the first county seat of Fremont County, Iowa. His son, born October 1840, was the second child born within the limits of Fremont County. Probably he is the Mr. Singleton Mary met at a party given by Mr. Wells. [HFC: 450, 509-11, 536, 614]

SLADE, George Washington. Born December 15, 1816, Bainbridge, Chenango, New York, to Aaron Slade Jr. and Mary/Polly Knight. Married, first, Jane Miller. Married, second, Eliza Jane Atwood, daughter of Elisha Atwood and Anna Hartshorn, born February 20, 1825, Mansfield, Tolland, Connecticut, and who died November 1893. Member of Winter Quarters First Ward, in bishop's report December 1846, owned cattle in June 1847. [SEB 39:546-47; EH]

SLATER, Ann Corbridge. Born November 16, 1812, Thornley, Lancashire, England, to William Corbridge and Ellen Bolton. Married Richard Slater, September 29, 1834, Chipping, Lancashire, England. Died August 17, 1902, Ogden, Weber, Utah. Sister of Mary's brothers-in-law, Edward and William Corbridge. [NJ42:29]

SLATER, Richard. Born September 26, 1811, Little Bowland, Lancashire, England, to Thomas Slater and Margaret Cutler. Married Ann Corbridge, sister of Mary's brothers-in-law, Edward and William Corbridge, September 29, 1834, Chipping, Lancashire, England. Died November 26, 1893, Slaterville, Weber,

Utah. Private in Company B of the Mormon Battalion. [SEB 39:573-56; NJ42:28-29; DBMB: 156]

SLUSHER, William. Lived near the Burton and Haven families at the Missouri/Iowa border. His home was at the foot of the bluffs, just south of Mr. George Wilkinson's on the Missouri bottoms in the Austin area. Invited Priddy Meeks and Samuel Clark to move onto his land, build their homes, and herd their stock the winter of 1846-47, also offered them unpicked corn and cucumbers from his fields. The Slusher home was always open for gambling, drinking, card playing, and visiting, which created a good market for the elderberry wine Meeks and Clark made, giving them money for an outfit to go west. [HFC: 384, 511; PM]

SMITH, Bathsheba Wilson Bigler. Born May 3, 1822, Shinnston, Harrison, West Virginia, to Mark Bigler and Susannah Ogden. Married George A. Smith, July 25, 1841, Nauvoo, Hancock, Illinois. Died September 20, 1910. Fourth general president of the Women's Relief Society. [SEB 5:261-64]

SMITH, DAVID. Born July 20, 1820, Newry, Oxford, Maine, to Josiah Smith and Lucy Meserve Bean. Married Phoebe Bowley, May 7, 1843, Nauvoo, Hancock, Illinois. A David B. Smith married Lucinda W. Morgan, May 9, 1840, Nauvoo, Hancock, Illinois. This may be the same person. Mary visited at his home. [SEB 39:750]

SMITH, George A. Born June 26, 1817, Potsdam, St. Lawrence, New York, to John Smith and Clarissa Loomis Lyman. Married the following women in Nauvoo, Hancock, Illinois: Bathsheba Wilson Bigler, July 25, 1841; Lucy Meserve Smith; Nancy Clement, February 1, 1845; Zilpha Stark, March 8, 1845; Sarah Ann Libby, November 20, 1845; Hannah Maria Libby, November 20, 1845. Other marriages in Utah. Died September 1, 1875, Salt Lake City, Salt Lake, Utah. Cousin to Joseph Smith. Apostle at age twenty-two. Council of Fifty. One of original pioneers in 1847. First counselor to Brigham Young from 1868 to 1875. Involved in church leadership in Winter Quarters. [SEB 39:838-50; HS: 9; FF; PHP: 1]

SMITH, Lucy Mack. Born July 8, 1776, Gilsum, Cheshire, New Hampshire, to Solomon Mack and Lydia Gates. Married Joseph Smith Sr., January 24, 1796, Tunbridge, Orange, Vermont. Died May 5, 1855, Nauvoo, Hancock, Illinois. Mother of the Prophet Joseph Smith Jr. [SEB 29:8-12]

SMITH, Mrs. or Sister. Visited Mary with Ellen Wilding Woolley at the Woolley home in December 1846. Called on Mary when she was sick, January 1847, again with Ellen and others. Records show many Smith families living in Council Bluffs, who may or may not have been in Winter Quarters: Elias Smith and Lucy Brown; Jackson Smith and Mary Marie Owens; John Smith and Elizabeth Martha Koons; John A. Smith and Ann Anderson; John Calvin Lazelle Smith and Sarah Fish; John Lyman Smith and Augusta Bowen Cleveland; John Sivel Smith and Jane Wadley, of Worcestershire, England; Thomas Sasson Smith and Polly Clark; Thomas Washington Smith and wives; William P. Smith and Mary Grimshaw, of Lancashire, England. Other possibilities of families in Winter Quarters include John Smith and Clarissa Loomis Lyman, parents of George A. Smith; and George Albert Smith and Bathsheba Wilson Bigler. [SEB 39:771-952; 40:316-95]

SMITH, Mrs. Visited with Mary while she was at the home of John White at Keg Creek, September 1847.

SMITH, Olive. Visited with Mary in February 1848. The only Olive Smith known is Olive Amanda Smith, born September 18, 1825, Livermore, Androscoggin, Maine, to Hawley Decker Smith and Martha Allen. Married Milton Cook about 1842. Child born in Nauvoo or Carthage. Married John Solomon Fullmer as his second wife. Child born October 1846 in Winter Quarters. Possibly went by her maiden name Smith instead of first married name Cook. Died March 17, 1885, Orangeville, Emery, Utah. [SEB 40:142-44]

SMITH, Phoebe Bowley. Born February 28, 1820, Weld, Franklin, Maine. Married David B. Smith, May 7, 1843, Nauvoo, Hancock, Illinois. Visited by Mary. [SEB 6:353]

SMITH, Widow. Lived about sixteen miles from Keg Creek. Brother Deuel and Mary spent the night here on their way back from the Burton home on the Missouri/Iowa border.

> SMITH, Louisa Chapin. Born about 1818, Onondaga County, New York, to Adolphus and Cynthia Chapin. Married, first, a Mr. Smith. Married Samuel Burton, September 29, 1847, in Winter Quarters after his first wife died. [JBS]

SMITHIES, Ann/Nancy Knowles. Born August 2, 1809, Chaigley, Lancashire, England, to Robert Knowles and Ann Parker. Married James Smithies, September 1847, Lancashire, England. Died March 3, 1883, Salt Lake City, Salt Lake, Utah. First cousin of Mary's. Ann's mother and Mary's father were brother and sister. [ARCH; SEB 27:88-89]

SMITHIES, James. Born October 29, 1807, Downham, Yorkshire, England, to Richard Smithies and Mary Robison/Robinson. Married, first, Ann/Nancy Knowles, September 1847, Lancashire, England. Other wife in Salt Lake City. Died June 26, 1881, Salt Lake City, Salt Lake, Utah. Their children with them in Winter Quarters were Mary, Robert, Joseph, Richard, James Alma, Sarah Ellen. Emigrated to Utah in June 1847. Organized first choir in Salt Lake City. Wife was cousin to Mary. [SEB 40:408-12; ARCH; HTW 8:439]

SMITHIES, Mary. Born October 7, 1837, Bashall Eaves, Yorkshire, England, to James Smithies and Ann/Nancy Knowles. Married January 25, 1856 to Heber Chase Kimball, Salt Lake City, Salt Lake, Utah, his twenty-second wife. Died June 8, 1880, Salt Lake City, Salt Lake, Utah. [SEB 26:638; 40:415-17; ARCH; HCKW: 48-49]

SNOW, Erastus Fairbanks. Born November 9, 1818, St. Johnsbury, Caledonia, Vermont, to Levi Snow and Lucina Streeter. Married, first, Artemesia Beamon, December 3, 1838. Married, second, Minerva White, April 2, 1844, Nauvoo. Married, third, Inger Nielsen. Married, fourth, Elizabeth Rebecca Ashby, December 19, 1847. Other wives. Died May 27, 1888, Salt Lake City, Salt Lake, Utah. To Utah with first pioneers in 1847. Went with Ezra T. Benson and others to the East in 1848 to gather donations for the church. Apostle February 12, 1849. [SEB 40:532-43]

SNYDER, Chester. Born June 10, 1815, Camden East, Midland, Ontario, Canada, to Isaac Snyder and Lovisa Comstock. Married, first, Catherine Montgomery, June 12, 1838, Canada. Married, second, Malinda Wilcox Wood, April 24,

1848, Winter Quarters, Douglas, Nebraska. Died March 22, 1888, Snyderville, Summit, Utah. Brother of Jane Snyder Richards. He, his brother Jesse, and their mother were at Montrose when Franklin D. Richards moved Jane from Nauvoo across the river. They started their trek across Iowa together, but the wagons became separated. Mary helped prepare for the wedding of Chester and Malinda. [SEB 40:661-65; FDR: 66]

SNYDER, Elsie Pamela Jacob/Jacobs. Born May 13, 1831, Busti, Chantaugua, New York, to Norton Jacob and Emily Horton Heaton. First or second wife of Jesse Snyder, married May 17, 1846, Nauvoo, Hancock, Illinois. Other wife was Catherine Duff. When Jesse died in 1853, Elsie married his brother, George Gideon Snyder, December 3, 1854, Salt Lake City, Salt Lake, Utah. Died March 2, 1891. Sister-in-law of Jane Snyder Richards. [SEB 25:188-89; IGI; AF]

SNYDER, George Gideon. Born June 12, 1819, Palmyra, Wayne, New York, to Isaac Snyder and Lovisa Comstock. Married, first, Sarah Wilder Hatch, April 17, 1840, Hancock County, Illinois. Other wives, including Jesse Snyder's widow, Elsie Pamela Jacobs. Emigrated to Utah in 1849. Brother of Jane Snyder Richards. [SEB 40:674-83; IGI; AF]

SNYDER, Jesse. Born April 12, 1825, Pamelia, Jefferson, New York, to Isaac Snyder and Lovisa Comstock. Two marriages in Nauvoo, Hancock, Illinois, to Catharine Duff and Elsie Pamela Jacob/Jacobs. Died May 20, 1853. [ARCH; SEB 40:690; AF; IGI; FDR: 66]

SNYDER, Lovisa Comstock. Born May 22, 1789, Great Barrington, Berkshire, Massachusetts, to Samuel Comstock and Sarah Grippen. Married Isaac Snyder, March 13, 1807, Fort Ann, Washington, New York. He died February 24, 1844 in Nauvoo, Hancock, Illinois. She died March 20, 1856, Salt Lake City, Salt Lake, Utah. Mother of Jane Snyder Richards. [ARCH]

SNYDER, Sally. See JENNE, Sarah Comstock Snyder.

SNYDER, Sally's baby. See JENNE, Brigham or JENNE, William Henry.

SNYDER, Samuel Comstock. Born February 14, 1808, Fort Ann, Washington, New York. to Isaac Snyder and Lovisa Comstock. Married Henrietta Maria Stockwell, March 1826, New York. Died April 8, 1886. Established the first saw mill in Utah at Parley's Park, later named Park City, Summit, Utah, purchased from Parley P. Pratt. Built first road through Parley's Canyon to Park City. Brother of Jane Snyder Richards. [SEB 40:709-11; ARCH]

SPENCER, Aurelia Reed. Born October 4, 1834, Deep River, Middlesex, Connecticut, to Orson Spencer and Catherine Curtis. Married Thomas Rogers, March 21, 1851. Died August 19, 1922. Her mother died and her father went on mission to England, leaving six children under age of thirteen in a log cabin at Winter Quarters, in the care of Thomas Bullock. She and her sister Ellen were friends of Mary's and helped her quilt. She crossed the plains in Brigham Young's company in 1848. Founder of the first Primary meeting in the church, Farmington, Davis, Utah. [SEB 40:837-39]

SPENCER, Claudius. Born April 2, 1824, West Stockbridge, Berkshire, Massachusetts, to Daniel Spencer and Sophronia Eliza Pomeroy. Married his cousin, Marie Antoinette Spencer, January 25, 1847, in Winter Quarters, Douglas, Nebraska. Mary wrote to Samuel of this marriage. Died January/March 5, 1910. [SEB 40:847-52]

SPENCER, Daniel, Jr. Born July 20, 1794, West Stockbridge, Berkshire, Massachusetts, to Daniel Spencer and Chloe Wilson. Married, first, Sophronia Eliza Pomeroy, January 16, 1823/24. Married, second, Sarah Lester Van Schoonoven, June 30, 1834. Married, third, Mary Woolerton, 1846. Married, fourth, Mary Spencer, 1845, Nauvoo, Hancock, Illinois. Married, fifth, Emily Shafter Thompson, widow of his brother Hiram, January 25, 1847, Winter Quarters, Douglas, Nebraska. Died December 8, 1868, Salt Lake City, Salt Lake, Utah. Presided over a small branch called Richmond and West Stockbridge Union Branch in Berkshire County, Massachusetts. Served out Joseph Smith's term as mayor of Nauvoo. Bishop in Winter Quarters. [SEB 40:853-62; HS: 9; AF]

SPENCER, Ellen Curtis. Born November 21, 1832, Middlefield, Hampshire, Massachusetts, to Orson Spencer and Catherine Curtis. Married Hiram Bradley Clawson, March 18, 1850. Died August 24, 1896, Salt Lake City, Salt Lake, Utah. She and her sister Aurelia were friends of Mary's and helped her quilt. [SEB 40:867-68]

SPENCER, G. Danced with Mary aboard a boat on the Missouri River, May 1848.

SPENCER, Hiram. Born November 30, 1798, West Stockbridge, Berkshire, Massachusetts, to Daniel Spencer and Chloe Wilson. Married, first, Mary Spencer, December 20, 1820. Married, second, Emily Shafter Thompson, January 1, 1843, Nauvoo, Hancock, Illinois. Died August 12, 1846, near Mt. Pisgah, Harrison, Iowa. [SEB 40:878-81; NDM: 102]

SPENCER, Marie Antoinette. Born January 22, 1826, West Stockbridge, Berkshire, Massachusetts, to Hiram Spencer and Mary Spencer. Married her cousin, Claudius Spencer, January 25, 1847, Winter Quarters, Douglas, Nebraska. Died March 11, 1850. Mary wrote to Samuel of her marriage. [SEB 40:910-11]

SPENCER, Mary. Born April 12, 1824, West Stockbridge, Berkshire, Massachusetts, to Hiram Spencer and Mary Spencer. Fourth wife of Daniel Spencer Jr., married 1845, Nauvoo, Hancock, Illinois. Died August 12, 1846, Council Bluffs, Iowa, or Winter Quarters, Nebraska. Her unnamed baby also died the same time. Mary wrote to Samuel of these deaths in September 1846. [AF]

SPENCER, Orson. Born March 14, 1802, West Stockbridge, Berkshire, Massachusetts, to Daniel Spencer and Chloe Wilson. Married Catherine Curtis, April 13, 1830. When she died, he left their six children in Winter Quarters while he filled a mission for the church in England. Married, second, Martha Knight. Died October 15, 1855, St. Louis, St. Louis, Missouri. President of St. Louis Stake. Emigrated to Utah in 1849 as captain of his own company. [HS: 14; SEB 40:919-24]

STANDING ELK. Son of Big Elk, chief of the Omaha nation. Involved in the negotions between the Omahas and the Mormons. [MAM: 71-72]

STANLEY, Sister. Visited Mary in July 1847 with sisters Barns and Douglas.

> STANLEY/STANDLEY, Ann. First wife of Edward Hunter. As first wife, she would have been called Sister Hunter, not Sister Stanley. See HUNTER, Ann Stanley/Standley.

> STANLEY/STANDLEY, Philinda Upson. Born August 1, 1815, Randolph, Portage, Ohio, to Freeman Upson and Sarah Culver. Married Alexander Scoby Stanley/Standley, March 19, 1829. Died January 27,

1892. Child born May 1847, Pottawattamie County, Iowa. [SEB 44:153]

STEVENS, Brother. Traveled alongside Phinehas's family from Mt. Pisgah to the Bluffs.

    STEVENS, Roswell, Jr. Born October 17, 1807/1808, Mt. Pleasant, Brant, Canada, to Roswell Stevens and Sybell Spencer. Married Polly Maria Doyle. Other wives. Died May 14, 1880, Bluff, San Juan, Utah. Converted to Mormonism in 1834. Helped manage the evacuation of Missouri. In 1846, enlisted in the Mormon Battalion as a private in Company E. At Santa Fe, Roswell, John D. Lee, and Howard Egan returned to Winter Quarters with the Battalion money. Wife gave birth to a baby in September 1846 in Pottawattamie County, Iowa. [SEB 41:477-82; HS: 111-12; DBMB: 165]

    STEVENS, Roswell, Sr. Born February 27, 1772, Litchfield, Litchfield, Connecticut, to Nehemiah Stevens and Hepsibah Kellum. Married Sarah Spencer, Dolly Williams, and Sybell Spencer. Member of the Council Point Branch in May 1847. Died July 3, 1847, in Council Bluffs, Pottawattamie, Iowa. [SEB 41:474-76; CPBM: 2]

STRATTON, Joseph Albert. Born September 11, 1821, Bedford, Bedfordshire, England, to Calvin Stratton and Gabrilla Johnson. Married Mary Ann Covington. Died October 1850. Mission to England 1844-46. Branch president in St. Louis, Missouri. Carried letters between Mary and her family in St. Louis. Emigrated to Utah 1847. [SEB 42:73-74]

STRATTON, Mary Ann Covington. Born March 31, 1815, Bedford, Bedfordshire, England, to Berrill Covington and Elizabeth Hodges. Married, first, William Smith. Married, second, Joseph Albert Stratton. Married, third, Chauncey Walker West. Died October 5, 1907. Accompanied husband from St. Louis to Winter Quarters where she met Mary in April 1847. [SEB 12:57-58; 42:75]

SWAMLYS, Brother. Mary attended a party at his home while she was visiting with the Samuel Burton family on the Missouri/Iowa border.

SWAN, Francis or sister. See KIMBALL, Frances Jessie Swan.

TAFFINGDER, William. Mary spent the last night in Liverpool with his family.

TAYLOR, John. Born November 1, 1808, Milnthorpe, Westmoreland, England, to James Taylor and Agnes Taylor. Married, first, Leonora Cannon, January 28, 1833, Toronto, Ontario, Canada. Married the following wives in Nauvoo, Hancock, Illinois: Elizabeth Kaighin, December 12, 1843; Jane Ballentyne, February 25, 1844; Mary Ann Oakley, January 14, 1846. Married Sophia Whitaker, April 23, 1847, Winter Quarters, Douglas, Nebraska. Other wives in Utah. Died July 25, 1887, Kaysville, Davis, Utah. Converted to the LDS faith in Canada. Apostle, December 19, 1838, Far West, Missouri. After the departure of Brigham Young and the first pioneers in April 1847, he and Parley P. Pratt supervised the affairs of the church in Winter Quarters. Third president of the church. Author of many LDS publications. [SEB 42:729-45; HS: 7]

TAYLOR, Leonora Cannon. Born October 6, 1796, Peel, Isle of Man, England, to George Cannon and Leonora Callister. Married John Taylor, January 28, 1833. Left Winter Quarters for Utah June 21, 1847. Mary called to tell her goodbye before she left. [SEB 8:598-99; ITOW: 101-7]

TAYLOR, Mother. Possibly John Taylor's mother, brought a letter to Mary at the Bluffs from Samuel in Nauvoo about July 1846. Agnes Taylor was born August 22, 1787 in Westmoreland, England, to John Taylor and Agnes Whittington. Married James Taylor, December 23, 1805. Died November 14, 1868. Emigrated to Utah with the John Taylor company in 1847. [SEB 42:617-68]

TAYLOR, Sophia Whitaker. Born April 21, 1825, Blakedown, Worcestershire, England, to Thomas Whitaker and Sophia Turner. Married John Taylor, April 23, 1847, Winter Quarters, Douglas, Nebraska, having arrived with him from his visit in England. Died February 27, 1887. Her sister Harriet also married John Taylor, December 7, 1847. A brother, Moses, married to Alice Longstroth, and sister, Mary Ann, married to Richard Harrison, had emigrated to Nauvoo in 1842. Another brother, George, was a teamster for Parley P. Pratt. A sister, Elizabeth, was married to Joseph Cain and later, Samuel Whitney Richards. [SEB 46:17-18; FF; HTW 8:424]

THOMPSON, Charles Blanchard. Born January 27, 1814, Niskayuna, Schenectady, New York, to David Thompson and Sarah Blanchard. Married Elizabeth Yincks/Jencks, December 4, 1836. Married Catherine Ann Houck, December 24, 1845. Died February 25, 1895, Philadelphia, Philadelphia, Pennsylvania. Opposed Joseph Smith's teachings on Daniel's prophecies. Mary wrote to Samuel that Charles Thomson, who had joined Strang, had written to the church asking permission for rebaptism. [SEB 43:243-46]

TOOTLE, Thomas E. Postmaster and merchant at Austin, Missouri, post office. Hired the store built near the site of the ferry for one hundred and five dollars, March 8, 1848. The store later was sold to A. H. Argyle along with Hunsaker's ferry. Became quite interested in Mary when she visited the home of Samuel Burton on the Missouri/Iowa border in March 1847. He frequently asked Eliza Ann Haven and Rebecca Burton Jones about her. In December 1847 he brought her a letter from Samuel to Winter Quarters. Mary referred to him as Mr. Tuttle or Thomas Tuttle. [MHPR April 15, 1847; RBJ; EAH; HFC: 337]

TURNER, Sister. Visited with Mary at the Crookston home, October 1847, also spent time with Mary when she was ill.

VAN COTT, John. Born September 7, 1814, Canaan, Columbia, New York, to Losee Van Cott and Lavinia Jemima Pratt. Married, first, Lucy Lavina Sackett, September 15, 1835, Canaan, Columbia, New York. Other wives. Died February 18, 1883, Salt Lake City, Salt Lake, Utah. Left New York for Nauvoo in 1846 with wife and mother. Continued on to Winter Quarters. Made it possible for Phinehas and Levi Richards to leave Nauvoo by lending them outfits and oxen. Emigrated to Salt Lake Valley, June 15, 1847. President of Scandinavian Mission twice. [SEB 44:213-20; ARCH; HTW 8:417]

VAN COTT, Lovina Jemima Pratt. Born August 6, 1787, Canaan, Columbia, New York, to Obadiah Pratt and Jemima Tolls. Married Losee Van Cott, September 5, 1812. He died June 29, 1824, in Canaan. She died May 18, 1878, Salt Lake City, Salt Lake, Utah. [ARCH; HTW 8:417; SEB 35:540]

VAN COTT, Lucy Lavinia Sackett. Born July 17, 1915, Stephentown, Rensselaer, New York, to Calvin Pardee Sackett and Hannah Douglas. Married John Van Cott, September 15, 1835, Caanan, Columbia, New York. Died January 31,

1902, Salt Lake City, Salt Lake, Utah. Van Cott family members were good friends of the Richards family. [ARCH; HTW 8:417; SEB 38:93]

VEACH, Nancy Ann/Ann Elliott. Married William Veatch/Veach January 14, 1830, Trumbull, Ohio. William died November 2, 1845, probably in Montrose, Lee, Iowa. Winter Quarters First Ward records, December 1846, show Nancy Veach as one of three widows in the ward. Married Henry Grow Jr. as his second wife. [SEB; EH; SJVL]

WALKER, Miss. See LYMAN, Diontia Walker.

WAREHAM, Brother and Sister. Invited Mary to dinner in May 1848.

> WAREHAM, Harriet Adams. Born May 22, 1818, Dayton, Montgomery, Ohio, to Edmond Adams. Married James Wareham, August 13, 1835, West Milton, Montgomery, Ohio. [SEB 1:159]

> WAREHAM, James. Born July 2, 1813, Bedford County, Pennsylvania, to Philip and Elizabeth Wareham. Married Harriet Adams, August 13, 1835, West Milton, Montgomery, Ohio. Was a seventy in Nauvoo. Emigrated to Utah in 1852 with William Wood Company. [SEB 44:861-63]

WATSON, Ann/Nancy Parker. Born March 11, 1809, Chaigley, Lancashire, England, to John Parker Sr. and Ellen Heskin. Married Thomas Watson, February 16, 1835. Mary's sister who remained in England. [AG]

WAYLEY, Hmma. See SCOVIL, Emma Whaley.

WEBB, Elizabeth Lydia Taft. Born December 6, 1827, St. Clair, St. Clair, Michigan, to Seth Taft and Harriet Ogden. Second wife of Chauncy Griswold Webb, married January 21, 1846, Nauvoo, Hancock, Illinois. His first wife gave birth to her third and last child in Nauvoo in 1842/44. Unless she had died, Elizabeth would normally have been known as Elizabeth Taft; but no other Elizabeth Webb is known who could have visited with Mary in Winter Quarters. [SEB 42:424]

WELCH, Eliza Billington. Born December 16, 1825, Oolom, Chesterfield, Derbyshire, England, to Joseph Billington and Martha Brown. Married John Welch, May 18, 1845, Nauvoo, Hancock, Illinois. Died August 16, 1907, Brigham City, Box Elder, Utah. Eliza, her mother-in-law, Elizabeth Briggs Welch, and her sister-in-law, Ann Welch, often visited with Mary during 1847. [ARCH]

WELCH, Elizabeth Briggs. Born England. Married to Nicholas Welch II. Mother of John Welch. Endowed in the Nauvoo Temple. Died January 7, 1867. [SEB 45:294]

WELCH, John. Born January 6, 1823, Brampton, Derbyshire, England, to Nicholas Welch II and Elizabeth Briggs. Married, first, Eliza Billington, May 18, 1845, Nauvoo, Hancock, Illinois. Other wife in Utah. Died November 8, 1910, Paradise, Cache, Utah. His sister, Ann, was the wife of Robert Crookston. John and Robert gave Mary priesthood blessings when she was very ill. [SEB 299-303]

WELLS, Clamenza Eunice. Born 1819, Tyler, Virginia, to Duckett Wells. Married Edwin Dwight Peirson, Samuel's first cousin from Massachusetts, April 7, 1847. [AF; RFH 1:276]

WELLS, Daniel Hanmer. Born October 27, 1814, Trenton, Oneida, New York, to Daniel Wells and Catherine Chapin. Married Eliza Rebecca Robison/

Robinson, Commerce, Hancock, Illinois, March 12, 1837. Died March 24, 1891, Salt Lake City, Salt Lake, Utah. Non-Mormon who lived in Commerce before the Latter-day Saints arrived and changed its name to Nauvoo. Was baptized in 1846. Second counselor to Brigham Young in the First Presidency, 1857-77. Mary described him as "Squire Wells," who arrived from Nauvoo bearing news of the battle in Nauvoo and the destruction of the temple. [SEB 45:325-34]

WELLS, Emmeline Blanche/Belos Woodward Harris Whitney. Born February 29, 1828, Petersham, Worcester, Massachusetts, to David Woodward and Diadama Hare. Married James Harvey Harris at age fifteen, July 29, 1843. Married Newel Kimball Whitney as his second wife, February 24, 1845. After he died, married Daniel H. Wells, 1852, Salt Lake City, Salt Lake, Utah. Died April 25, 1921, in Salt Lake City, Salt Lake, Utah. Mary called her Emaline or Emmy Harris as they shared poems and writings. Known as Emmeline B. Wells, she helped Eliza R. Snow organize the Relief Societies in various ward in the church in 1866. Editor and publisher of *The Woman's Exponent*. President of the Relief Society from 1910 to 1921. [SEB 47:523-26; ITOW: 43-49]

WELLS, Mr. and Mrs. Neighbors of Samuel Burton on the Nishnabotna River near the Missouri/Iowa border. Mary attended a party at their home in March 1847.

WEST, Joseph. Born June 23, 1822, Homer, Cortland, New York, to Alva West and Sally Benedict. Married Lucinda Burton. Sealed in Nauvoo Temple, February 7, 1846. Died about 1846. Mary indicated in April 1847 that Lucinda had chosen Ezra T. Benson as her next guardian. [AF; SEB 45:448-49]

WEST, Lucinda Burton. Born October 22, 1825, Seneca County, New York. Married Joseph West. He died about 1846. She married Ezra Taft Benson, March 4, 1847, Council Bluffs or Winter Quarters. Mary wrote to Samuel of the marriage. [SEB 7:692]

WEST, Sister. Talked with Mary in May 1847. She could have been referring to Lucinda Burton West or one of the following women.

> WEST, Margaret Cooper. Married January 29, 1829, to Samuel Walker West, who was born March 30, 1804, Dixon County, Tennessee. Last child was born April 1847 in Kanesville, Pottawattamie, Iowa. Samuel died in Washington County, Utah, February 22, 1870. Susan and Samuel had unmarried teenage daughters, but they would have been known as Miss West. [SEB 45:463-64]

> WEST, Mary Hoagland. Born February 11, 1829, Royal Oak, Oakland, Michigan, to Abraham Hoagland and Margaret Quick. Married Chauncey Walker West, May 1846. Died January 2, 1873, Ogden, Weber, Utah. [SEB 49:961]

WHEELOCK, Sister Cyrus. Mary wrote on January 29, 1847, that Sister Wheelock had died three weeks previous. Cyrus was then serving a mission in England. His family records show three wives. There are no records for his first wife, Desdamonia Jemima Rose. His second wife, Olive Parrish, gave birth to her last child in 1843, but apparently died in 1902 in Cokeville, Wyoming. He married his last wife in Utah. [SEB 45:579-84, AF]

WHITAKER, Widow. Lived near the home of Samuel White at Keg Creek, Iowa. Visited by Mary in September 1847.

WHITE, Joel William. Born March 10, 1831, Erie, Erie, Pennsylvania, to John Griggs White and Lucy Maranda Bailey. Younger brother of Mary's friend Samuel Dennis White. Lived with his parents near Keg Creek, Iowa. [SEB 45:695]

WHITE, John Griggs. Born October 25, 1776, Massachusetts, to John White and Jemima Griggs. Married, first, Lucy Maranda/Amanda Bailey, February 17, 1808, Roxbury, Suffolk, Massachusetts. Died February 1851, Lehi, Utah, Utah. Called "father White" by Mary, his farm was near Keg Creek, Iowa, about twenty miles from Winter Quarters. [SEB 45:694-96]

WHITE, Lucy Maranda/Amanda Bailey. Born February 6, 1790, Connecticut, to Samuel Bailey and Mary Carter. Married John Griggs White, February 17, 1808, Roxbury, Suffolk, Massachusetts. Died February 17, 1874, Salt Lake City, Salt Lake, Utah. Lived at Keg Creek, Iowa. [SEB 3:200]

WHITE, Mary Elizabeth. Born November 7, 1846, Garden Grove, Decatur, Iowa, to Samuel Dennis White and Mary Hannah Burton. Mary said that this child was her namesake. [SEB 45:732; JBS]

WHITE, Mary Hannah Burton. Born August 31, 1818, Pultneyville, Ontario, New York, to Samuel Burton and Hannah Shipley. Married Samuel Dennis White, October 24, 1841, Walnut Grove, Knox, Illinois. Died December 2, 1894, Beaver, Beaver, Utah. Lived near Mary in the outskirts of Nauvoo. Sister of Rebecca Burton Jones and Robert Taylor Burton. [RTB]

WHITE, Samuel Dennis. Born March 9, 1818, Parishville, St. Lawrence, New York, to John Griggs White and Lucy Maranda Bailey. Married, first, Mary Hannah Burton, October 24, 1841, Walnut Grove, Knox, Illinois. Died October 17, 1868, Salt Lake City, Salt Lake, Utah. Became friends with Mary when they both lived in the farming area of Nauvoo, before Mary and Samuel were married. [RTB; SEB 45:731-35]

WHITECAR, Sophia. See TAYLOR, Sophia Whitaker.

WHITNEY, Helen Mar Kimball. Born August 25, 1828, Mendon, Monroe, New York, to Heber Chase Kimball and Vilate Murray. Married Horace Kimball Whitney, February 4, 1846. Died November 15, 1896. First child was delivered stillborn in Winter Quarters while her husband was with the original pioneers to Utah. Was one of the first women to greet Mary and Wealthy when they arrived at the Bluffs. [SEB 26:626, 657-58]

WHITNEY, Newel Kimball. Born February 5, 1795, Marlborough, Windham, Vermont, to Samuel Whitney and Susannah Kimball. Married, first, Elizabeth Ann Smith, October 20, 1822, Kirtland, Geauga, Ohio. Married, second, Emmeline Blanche/Belos Woodward Harris, February 24, 1845. Married, third, Anna Houston, February 8, 1846. Married next four wives on January 7, 1846: Olive Maria Bishop, Elizabeth Mahala Moore, Elizabeth Almira Pond, and Abigail Augusta Pond. Married, eighth, Henrietta Keys, January 26, 1846. Many of the wives had children in Winter Quarters. Died September 23, 1850. Bishop of Kirtland and Adam-ondi-Ahman. Member of the Council of Fifty. Second presiding bishop of the church. [SEB 45:963-71; HS: 14]

WHITNEY, Orson Kimball. Born January 20, 1830, Kirtland, Geauga, Ohio, to Newel Kimball Whitney and Elizabeth Ann Smith. Married, first, Johannah Hickey Robertson. Died July 31, 1884, Salt Lake City, Salt Lake, Utah. One of the original pioneers of 1847. [SEB 45:973-75]

WILCOX, Cynthia Maria. Born July 26, 1846, Council Bluffs, Pottawattamie, Iowa, to Walter Eli Wilcox and Maria Wealthy Richards. Mary helped deliver her during a severe thunderstorm shortly after arriving at Mosquito Creek from Mt. Pisgah. Samuel's niece. [SEB 46:172-74]

WILCOX, Huldah Lucas. Born January 22, 1781, Westfield Parish, Middleton, Hartford, Connecticut, to Richard Lucas and Hannah Royce Penfield. Married September 16, 1802, Missleton, Middlesex, Connecticut, to William Wilcox. Died August 26, 1846, Council Bluffs. Mother of Samuel's brother-in-law, Walter Eli Wilcox. Mary called her "Mother Wilcox" when she wrote to Samuel of her death on September 30, 1846. [AF]

WILCOX, Maria Wealthy Richards. Born June 17, 1827, Richmond, Berkshire, Massachusetts, to Phinehas Richards and Wealthy Dewey. Married to Walter Eli Wilcox, December 10, 1844, Nauvoo, Hancock, Illinois. Died January 13, 1909, Salt Lake City, Salt Lake, Utah. Sister of Samuel Whitney Richards. [SEB 36:657-68; RFR; NDM: 113]

WILCOX, Walter Eli. Born April 11, 1821, Dorchester, Suffolk, Massachusetts, to William Wilcox and Huldah Lucas. Married, first, Maria Wealthy Richards, December 10, 1844, Nauvoo, Hancock, Illinois. Other marriages in Utah. Died May 8, 1919, Salt Lake City, Salt Lake, Utah. Phinehas's son-in-law. Moved from the Bluffs to Weston and St. Louis, Missouri, to work and earn money. [SEB 46:229-37; NDM: 113]

WILDER, Sister. With Sister Matson/Matteson was visited by Mary in May 1847. Mary says they were new neighbors. It isn't known who this refers to. The Wilder name shows up often in the Hatch family. Sarah Wilder Hatch was the first wife of Gideon Snyder; they gave one of their children Wilder as a middle name, as did Meltiar Hatch and Permelia Snyder. Orin Hatch and Elizabeth Melissa Perry named a child with Wilder as his first name. The Levi and Joseph Wilder families were in Nauvoo, but remained with the RLDS Church. [SEB 3:674-81, 30:701-2, 46:262-63]

WILDING, Ellen. See WOOLLEY, Ellen Wilding.

WILKEY, Brother. With Mormon Battalion, sent letter to Brother Meeks telling them that Joseph Richards was dead. Mary read the letter at the Meeks home February 22, 1847.

WILKIN, David. Born August 1, 1819, Ennikillen, Ireland, to David J. Wilkin and Isabella Hunter. Married Isabella McNair. Other wives. Died January 21, 1891, Orangeville, Emery, Utah. Shown as David Wilkey, Wilkie, or Willkey in the muster-in records of the Battalion. [DBMB: 185]

WILLEY, Jeremiah. Born November 6, 1804, Northfield Depot, Merrimack, New Hampshire, to Isaiah Willey and Sarah Ann Daniels. Married, first, Bashabe Stevens, November 29, 1827. No death date is known for her, but only one wife is mentioned in Winter Quarters. Married, second, Samantha Call, April 28, 1839, Warsaw, Hancock, Illinois. Her children born in Winter Quarters 1847 and in Pottawattamie County, Iowa, in 1849. Other wives. Died May 21, 1868, Bountiful, Davis, Utah. Private in Company A of the Mormon Battalion. Escorted General Kearney from California to Fort Leavenworth, Kansas, in 1847, then rejoined his wife in Winter Quarters. Mary wrote to Samuel in

November 1847 that Brother Willey, whom he once took care of, was selling his house in Winter Quarters for six dollars and that she had thought of buying it from him. [SEB 46:409-14; DBMB: 186]

WILLEY, Samantha Call. Born November 15, 1814, Fairfax, Fairfax, Vermont, to Cyril Call and Sally Tiffany. Married Jeremiah Willey, April 28, 1839, Warsaw, Hancock, Illinois. Died November 13, 1905, Bountiful, Davis, Utah. Mary called to see Sister Willey at Mt. Pisgah in June 1846 and at the Bluffs in July 1846. [SEB 8:390-91]

WILLIAMS, Sister. It is probable that Mary wrote of more than one Williams family, one who lived near the home of Samuel Burton near the Missouri/Iowa border in March 1847; Sister G. Williams, who helped Mary quilt in September and October 1847; and Mother Williams, who helped Mary and Wealthy raise their tent at Mosquito Creek in July 1846.

WILLIAMS, Abigail Celecity Lewis. Born July 26, 1823, Addison, Montgomery, New York. Married to Andrew Boakman Williams in 1839. Third child born January 1849 at Plum Hollow, Fremont, Iowa. Andrew was appointed bishop of Plum Hollow Branch, June 1851. He died in McCammon, Bingham, Idaho. [SEB 46:444-45; 50:25; IBI: 187]

WILLIAMS, Clarissa Harding/Harden. Born September 26, 1820, Parisburgh, Cattaraugus, New York, to Miller Harding and Elizabeth Taber. Married, first, John Benjamin Williams, 1838, Venice, Cayuga, New York. Child born August 1848, Mosquito Creek, Pottawattamie, Iowa. Other husbands. Died February 17, 1901. [SEB 20:637-38]

WILLIAMS, Hannah Maria Andrus. Married Gustavus Williams, January 21, 1833. She is the only Williams woman who could be Mrs. G. Williams. Gustavus was born 1807 in Berkshire County, Massachusetts, and died in Teasdale, Wayne, Utah. [SEB 46:524-25]

WILLIAMS, Harriet Baldwin. Born September 13, 1808, Bradford, Orange, Vermont, to Theophilus Baldwin and Hannah Mann. Married Charles Hamilton Williams. Died February 10, 1860. Child born November 1847, Pottawattamie County, Iowa. [SEB 3:358]

WILLIAMS, Harriet Sobrina. Married to Daniel S. Williams. Lived in Nauvoo Fifth Ward with Phinehas. Members of Blockhouse Branch, Iowa, in January 1848. [PHP: 8; NAU5]

WILLIAMS, Rebecca Swain. Born August 8, 1798, Loyalsock, Lycoming, Pennsylvania, to Isaac Swain and Elizabeth Hall. Married Frederick Granger Williams, December 25, 1815, Wyandotte, Wayne, Michigan. He died October 25, 1842. Married, second, Heber Chase Kimball, February 7, 1846, Nauvoo, Hancock, Illinois. Died September 25, 1861, Smithfield, Cache, Utah. [SEB 42:303-4; HCKW: 35-37]

WILLIAMS, Zilpha Baker Cilley. Married January 15, 1833, Erie, Erie, Pennsylvania, to Almond Mack Williams. Three of her children were born in Mills County, Iowa. Almond is listed in the Pottawattamie Branch Index. He was one of the original pioneers of 1847, but returned to Mills County where he died December 13, 1874. [IBI: 188; SEB 49:619]

WILSON, Sister. Lived with Phinehas and his family for awhile in May 1848 when she moved to Winter Quarters from New Orleans.

WILSON, Mrs. A woman Mary knew in England.

WILLSON, William. Mary's suitor in England.

WOOD, Malinda Wilcox. Born November 18, 1823, Dorchester, Suffolk, Massachusetts, to Moses Wood and Malinda Wilcox. Married, first, Chester Snyder, April 24, 1848, Winter Quarters, as his second wife; divorced. Other husbands. One of Mary's close friends. Probably lived with the Joseph Young family in Winter Quarters. Niece of Mary's brother-in-law, Walter Eli Wilcox. Mary baked the cake and cookies for her wedding to Chester Snyder. [SEB 47:319]

WOODRUFF, Wilford. Born March 1, 1807, Farmington, Hartford, Connecticut, to Aphek Woodruff and Beulah Thompson. Married, first, Phoebe Whittemore Carter, April 13, 1837, Scarsborough, Cumberland, Maine. Married, second, Mary Ann Jackson, April 15, 1846. Both wives gave birth to children in Winter Quarters. Died September 2, 1898, San Francisco, San Francisco, California. Apostle, April 26, 1839, at Far West, Missouri. One of original pioneers in 1847. Frequent preacher at Sunday meetings in Winter Quarters. Fourth president of the LDS church. [SEB 47:469-81]

WOOLLEY, Catherine Elizabeth Mehring. Born November 19, 1826, Hull, Lancaster, Pennsylvania. Married Samuel Woolley, May 11, 1846. Was Mary's next-door neighbor in Winter Quarters. [SEB 30:694; NJ42: 55]

WOOLLEY, Edwin Dilworth. Born June 28, 1807, East Bradford, Chester, Pennsylvania, to John Woolley Jr. and Rachel Dilworth. Married, first, Mary Wickersham, March 24, 1831. Married, second, Louisa Chapin Gordan. She remained in Montrose, Iowa, then went to Illinois, where she died. Married, third, Ellen Wilding, February 6, 1846, Nauvoo, Hancock, Illinois. Died October 14, 1881, Salt Lake City, Salt Lake, Utah. [SEB 47:603-10; N5HP; NJ42: 49-50]

WOOLLEY, Ellen Wilding. Born April 8, 1819/1820/1822, Lancashire, England, to Thomas Wilding and Ellen Porter. Third wife of Edwin Dilworth Woolley, married February 6, 1846, Nauvoo, Hancock, Illinois. Died 1910/1911, Paris, Bear Lake, Idaho. One of Mary's closest friends; they met for the first time in Preston, England. Samuel and Mary discussed the possibility of him marrying Ellen as a plural wife. Mary helped care for Ellen when she gave birth to her first baby. [FF; SEB 46:275; HTW 9:520]

WOOLLEY, Samuel. Born September 11, 1825, Newlin, Chester, Pennsylvania, to John Woolley Jr. and Rachel Dilworth. Married Catherine Elizabeth Mehring, May 11, 1846. Other wives in Utah. Died March 23, 1900, Salt Lake City, Salt Lake, Utah. When his parents died, he lived with his brother Edwin, where he heard the gospel and was baptized. Lived in the Winter Quarters First Ward and is shown paying tithing in December 1846 and owning cattle in June 1847. Was a next-door neighbor of Phinehas in Winter Quarters. At one time Mary used his empty room to quilt in. [EH; NJ42: 54-55; SEB 47:647-56]

WOOLLEY, Sarah. Born December 27, 1847, Winter Quarters, Douglas, Nebraska, to Edwin D. Woolley and Ellen Wilding. Mary helped care for Sarah after her birth. [SEB 47:605]

WRIGHT, Jonathan Calkins. Born November 29, 1808, Rome, Oneida, New York, to Peter Bice Wright and Elizabeth Shead/Shed/Shad. Married, first, Rebecca

Wheeler, March 1, 1838, Waynesville, DeWitt, Illinois. Children born November 1846 in Winter Quarters and May 1848, Harris Grove, Pottawattamie, Iowa. Married, second, Sarah C. Boyce, May 1847. Died November 8, 1880, Brigham City, Box Elder, Utah. Marshall of Nauvoo and Winter Quarters. Sent on short-term missions to Nauvoo and other areas to encourage the Saints to gather to Utah. High priest in Blockhouse Branch. Possibly lived in Jane S. Richards's ward in Winter Quarters, where he held meetings in his home. Danced with Mary at the council house. Emigrated to Utah in 1850. [SEB 47:863-72; PHP: 1; MBB]

YOUNG, Brigham. Born June 1, 1801, Whittingham, Windham, Vermont, to John Young and Abigail/Nabby Howe. Married the following wives before and during the Winter Quarters period: Miriam Works, who died September 8, 1832; Mary Ann Angell, 1834, Kirtland; Lucy Ann Decker, 1842; Harriet Elizabeth Cook Campbell, 1843; Augusta Adams, 1843; Clara Decker, 1844; Olive Grey Frost, 1845; Louisa Beaman, 1846; Clarissa Ross, 1844; Emily Dow Partridge, 1844; Emmeline Free, 1845; Margaret M. Alley, 1846; Susan Snively and Margeret Pierce, 1845; Ellen Acklund Rockwood, 1846; Maria Lawrence, 1846; Martha Bowker, 1846; Zina Diantha Huntington Jacobs, 1846; and Naamah Kendel Jenkins Carter, 1846, all married in Nauvoo. Others were Mary Jane Bigelow, 1847, and Lucy Bigelow, 1847, married in Winter Quarters. Died August 29, 1877, Salt Lake City, Salt Lake, Utah. Second president of the church. Led exodus from Nauvoo to Winter Quarters and from there to the Salt Lake Valley. First cousin to Phinehas Richards. [SEB 48:3867]

YOUNG, Little Brigham. Danced with Mary in January 1847 at the council house. Brigham Young Jr., the son of Brigham and Mary Ann Angell was born December 18, 1836. This would make him only nine years old and probably too young to attend the dance.

    YOUNG, Brigham Hamilton. Son of Phinehas Howe Young and Clarissa Hamilton, born January 3, 1824, Hector Hills, Tompkins, New York. Died June 5, 1898, Alameda, Alameda, California. Second cousin of Samuel Richards, he is the most probable choice for the person Mary writes about. [SEB 48:68-81]

YOUNG, Mary Ann Angell. Born June 8, 1803, Seneca, Ontario, New York, to James William Angell and Phoebe Ann Morton. Married Brigham Young, February 18, 1834, Kirtland, Geauga, Ohio, after the death in 1832 of his first wife, Miriam Works. Died June 27, 1882, Salt Lake City, Salt Lake, Utah. Was known as "Mother Young" by Brigham's other wives and children. Spent an evening with Mary when she was ill. [SEB 2:452-54; ITOW: 140-42]

YOUNG, John. Born May 22, 1791, Hopkinton, Middlesex, Massachusetts, to John Young and Abigail/Nabby Howe. Married Theodocia Kimball, 1813. Other wives in Utah. Died April 27, 1870, Salt Lake City, Salt Lake, Utah. President of Kirtland Stake. Missionary in Pennsylvania and New York. First cousin of Phinehas Richards. [SEB 48:136-39; HS: 230]

YOUNG, Joseph. Born April 7, 1797, Hopkinton, Middlesex, Massachusetts, to John Young and Abigail Howe. Married, first, Jane Adeline Bickness, February 18, 1834, Kirtland, Geauga, Ohio. Married the next three wives in Nauvoo,

Hancock, Illinois: Lucinda Allen, 1846; Lydia Flemming, 1846; Mary Ann Huntley, widow of James L. Burnham, February 6, 1846. Other marriages in Utah. Died July 16, 1881, Salt Lake City, Salt Lake, Utah. One of first seven presidents of the Seventies from 1835 to 1881. Member of Zion's Camp. Survivor of the Haun's Mill massacre in Missouri. First cousin to Phinehas Richards. Frequent speaker at Sunday meetings in Winter Quarters. [SEB 48:169-78]

YOUNG, Phinehas. Born February 16, 1799, Hopkinton, Middlesex, Massachusetts, to John Young and Abigail/Nabby Howe. Married, first, Clarissa Hamilton, January 18 or September 28, 1818, Auburn, Cayuga, New York. Married, second, Lucy Pearce Cowdery, 1836. Other wives in Utah. Died October 10, 1879, Salt Lake City, Salt Lake, Utah. Member of the first pioneer company to Utah in 1847. First cousin to Phinehas Richards. [SEB 48:233-41]

YOUNG, Vilate. Born January 1, 1830, Monroe, Mendon, New York, to Brigham Young and Miriam Works. Married Charles Franklin Decker, February 4, 1847, Winter Quarters, Douglas, Nebraska. Died November 18/19, 1902, Lewisville, Jefferson, Idaho. One of the group of women who visited Mary and Wealthy upon their arrival at the Bluffs. [SEB 48:267-69; HTW 9:521]

YOUNG, Brother W. Ferried Mary, Maria Wilcox, and Eliza Ann Peirson across the Missouri River in June 1847.

YOUNG, William Goodall. Born February 21, 1827, Canadaigua, Ontario, New York, to Lorenzo Dow Young and Persis Goodall. Married Adelia Clark, June 1, 1845. Died April 15, 1894, Salt Lake City, Salt Lake, Utah. Second cousin to Samuel Whitney Richards. [SEB 48:277-78]

NOTES

Chapter 1

1. "The Memorandum of Mary H. Parker," in editor's possession, copy in Church of Jesus Christ of Latter-day Saints Archives Division, Salt Lake City; hereinafter cited as LDS Archives.
2. The Bishop's Transcripts of Great Mitton, Yorkshire, England show that Mary was baptized on October 5, 1823. This date agrees with her age of seventeen found on the passenger list of the ship *Alliance*, dated January 1841, and with the Family Record of Samuel Whitney Richards found in the LDS Archives, which lists her birth as September 8, 1823. However Mary's "Memorandum," Nauvoo Temple endowment, and sealing records show her birth as September 8, 1825. Her obituary and crossing the plains information in the supplement to the 1849 Journal History of the Church, LDS Archives, also point to the year of 1825 for her birth. Yet the Salt Lake City Fourteenth Ward records show her birth in 1824.
3. The surname of Mary's mother, Ellen, is found spelled as Heskin or Hesking. Mary and Samuel both wrote Mary's middle name as "Haskin," however.
4. The name "Old John Parker" was used by his friends to differentiate him from his son, John.
5. "Memorandum of Mary H. Parker."
6. Richard L. Jensen, "Transplanted to Zion," *BYU Studies* 31 (Winter 1991): 78.
7. Information received by the author from descendants of William and Margaret Bleasdale.
8. Kate B. Carter, comp., "Historic Letters of the Past," *Our Pioneer Heritage*, vol. 3 (Salt Lake City: Daughters of the Utah Pioneers, 1960), 156.
9. Joseph Grant Stevenson, ed., *Richards Family History*, vol. 3 (Provo, Utah: J. Grant Stevenson, 1991), 237.
10. Ague was one of the most common diseases in the frontier period.

> The symptoms were unmistakable: yawnings and stretching, a feeling of lassitude, blueness of the fingernails, then little cold sensations which increased until the victim's teeth chattered in his jaws and he "felt like a harp with a thousand strings." As the chills increased, the victim shivered and shook "like a miniature earthquake." After an hour or so warmth returned, then gradually merged into raging heat with racking head pains and aching back. The spell ended with copious sweating and a return to normal.

Various types of ague were known as the dumb ague, shaking ague, chill fever, and other variations. Some individuals had chills and fever on the same day.

Other people had them on alternating days or every two or three days. Each person seemed to have a specific pattern, whatever the variety. Even the fever was identified as intermittent, remittent, erratic, etc., depending upon the frequency and pattern of occurrence. Madge E. Pickard and R. Carlyle Buley, *The Midwest Pioneer: His Ills, Cures, & Doctors,* (New York: Henry Schuman, 1946), 16-20.

11. Records showing varying degrees of muscular dystrophy in the descendants of Mary Haskin Parker Richards and John Parker Jr. are found in the Muscular Dystrophy Clinic, University of Utah Medical Center, Salt Lake City, Utah, and in the personal files of Rose Adele Gwynn, Centerville, Utah. Their father, John Parker Sr. is often mentioned in written accounts as being "frail" or quite "feeble," so he is probably the one who passed the gene down to Mary and John Jr. The medical records of his other children's family lines are unknown or unavailable.

12. August 7, 1846, letter to her father and brother John's family while they were in St. Louis. This letter later had one side cut off and was attached as a cover to Mary's sixth journal, which is located in the LDS Archives.

14. All information on the life of Samuel Whitney Richards is found in his diaries, which span more than half a century; his family records; articles written about him and by him in LDS church periodicals and newspapers; and *A Biographical Sketch of Samuel Whitney Richards* by Ramona W. Cannon, a grandniece.

15. Samuel's account of this experience is published in the *Young Woman's Journal* 18 (December 1907); the *Elders' Journal,* dated December 1, 1905; and other sources. For Joseph Smith's call for the expedition and a list of volunteers, including Samuel Richards, see Joseph Smith, *History of the Church of Jesus Christ of Latter-day Saints,* edited by B. H. Roberts, 7 vols., 2d ed. (Salt Lake City: Deseret Book, 1957; reprint, 1973), 6:224.

16. The Quorum, or Council, of the Twelve Apostles consists of twelve men who have been ordained to the Melchizedek Priesthood with the office of apostles. They are chosen through inspiration by the president of the church and ordained by the First Presidency and the Quorum of the Twelve by the laying on of hands. As a priesthood quorum, the Quorum of the Twelve Apostles is next in authority to the Quorum of the First Presidency. At the death of Joseph Smith, the Quorum of the First Presidency was dissolved and Brigham Young, as head of the Quorum of the Twelve, asserted authority over the church. Daniel H. Ludlow, ed., *LDS Encyclopedia* (New York: Macmillan Reference, 1992), 1185-89.

17. The temple endowment is one of the ordinances performed in the Latter-day Saint temples, along with baptisms for the dead, washings and annointings, and marriages or sealings for eternity. In the endowment, worthy members are taught about the plan of salvation and commit to a Christlike life. Ludlow, 2:455-56.

18. Joseph Young, president of the Seventies Quorum in which Samuel was a member. The Seventies were called originally to travel to all areas of the church and to preach the gospel. The seven presidents of the First Quorum of Seventies were sustained as General Authorities of the church, and were to act under the direction of the Quorum of the Twelve Apostles. Ludlow, 3:1300-1305.

19. Many theories of medicine abounded in the early nineteenth century. A particularly prominent group of practitioners were the Thomsonians, named

after their founder, Samuel Thomson. He believed that all illness was caused by a lack of heat in the body. He returned the heat through the use of steaming and herbs. The second component of his remedy was cleansing the stomach, usually through the use of an emetic such as lobelia, known as the "Puke Weed." Steaming was accomplished by immersing red-hot stones into pans of hot water and making a tent over the patient to prevent the steam from escaping. Thomson denounced the practice of bleeding and the then new use of poisonous drugs as medicines.

By 1820, Thomson was publishing pamphlets that promoted his medical sect, giving lectures, and providing his concoctions wholesale. Licensed practitioners were required to purchase his book for $20 and pass a brief examination before being granted their certificate. Pickard and Buley, 167-79.

Willard Richards obtained his patent after studying six weeks with Thomson at his infirmatory in Boston in July 1834. He spent a short time on the medical circuit before being taught about the Latter-day Saints church by his cousin Brigham Young, thereafter devoting his time to the church. However he was known as Dr. Richards by many, including himself. Claire Noall, *Intimate Disciple: A Portrait of Willard Richards* (Salt Lake City: University of Utah Press, 1957), 600-602.

Levi Richards also received his training in Boston with Thomson at the same time as Willard. He was known throughout his life as Dr. Levi Richards. Joseph Smith called Levi and Willard his personal physicians. Stevenson, vol. 2 (1981), 9, 35, 144.

Phinehas Richards may or may not have received his license from Thomson; however, he is shown as a Botanical Doctor in the 1850 Utah Census. His journal indicates that he practiced medicine his first six years in the Salt Lake Valley, administering medicines and setting broken bones. There, also, he assisted in creating the Council of Health, which was used to teach the settlers good health habits.

20. Although the Word of Wisdom was received by Joseph Smith in February 1833 in Kirtland, Ohio, it first was taken as a guide to health, not a commandment. This "principle with a promise" is found in the Doctrine and Covenants section 89. Abstinence from tea, coffee, tobacco, and alcohol are urged, as well as eating meat sparingly. Whole grains, especially wheat, are advised as good for man. Those who follow these admonitions are promised spiritual and temporal blessings. Church presidents beginning with Brigham Young emphasized the importance of keeping the Word of Wisdom; however, interpretations of it varied. Coffee, tea, and alcoholic beverages were used on occasion by leaders of the church as well as by lay members. It was Mormon President Joseph F. Smith in the early 1900s who began to standardize the interpretation of the Word of Wisdom and to tie adherance to it to the standard of worthiness required for temple attendance and leadership positions in the church. Thomas G. Alexander, *Mormonism in Transition: A History of the Latter-day Saints, 1890-1930* (Urbana: University of Illinois Press, 1986), 258-61.

21. The Saints leaving Nauvoo used a variety of wagons, but most were ordinary reinforced farm wagons which had been covered by cloth or waterproof canvas that could be closed at each end. The bottoms were usually caulked or covered with canvas so that they would float if necessary. Even though these wagons were slow, awkward, and miserable to ride in, they were the best way

of carrying goods and provisions. They also provided shelter during and after the trip. Travelers perferred oxen for pulling the wagons, due to their strength. Women and children also found them easier to handle than the horses and mules they sometimes used.

22. Phinehas wrote in his journal on Saturday, February 8, 1846, that he and Mary Vail Morse were sealed by Brigham Young in a private room in the Nauvoo Temple in the presence of H. C. Kimball and Sarah Ann Sanders, then added, "Although Wealthy being opposed, yet says Br Kimball don't let a woman take your crown Br. Richards." The "Journal of Phinehas Richards" substantiates and clarifies events surrounding Mary's life. It is located in the Richards Family Collection, LDS Archives.

23. John Mack Faragher, *Women and Men on the Overland Trail* (New Haven: Yale University Press, 1979), 11.

24. Jane Snyder Richards described Elizabeth McFate as young, about seventeen, and pretty and also as very considerate, amiable, and kind: she claimed that the two women never had an unkind word pass between them "Reminiscences of Jane Snyder Richards" (1880), original at Bancroft Library, University of California, Berkeley, California; copy at the Utah State Historical Society, Salt Lake City, Utah. Franklin married Elizabeth on January 29, 1846, the same day as Samuel and Mary were married. Franklin and Jane Snyder had married on December 18, 1842.

25. This is the poem as Samuel wrote it in his letter to Mary:

> What do I Love?
> I love the day in which I chose
> The partner of my early life
> But sweeter still I love the girl
> Which I obtained by faith and strife.
>
> O yes dear Mary true it is
> That earth ne'er had a prize for me
> Of half the value that I gained
> When I the covenant made with thee.
>
> Now with that treasure in my heart
> And there forever shall remain
> Although my body absent is
> It shall return to thee again.
>
> Then shall I have a kind return
> Of love, reciprocate, my Dear.
> My love, and all that I possess
> Is thine, Is whispered in my ear.
>
> Then, Mary, shun the discontent
> that flows from life's most rugged stream.
> The happiness that's yet for thee
> will make it but a pleasant dream.
>
> We meet, we part, and part again,
> As is the common lot of man.
> Tis greater glories to obtain,
> According to the heavenly plan.

Then happy be, and seek to spread
Its influence on all around.
A messenger of peace and love
Be to thy kindred ever found.

Although thro. foreign climes I range
I know your heart will never change
That bosom burns with honors glow
My kind and faithful, Mary O,

You have my heart you have my hand
By sacred truth and honors band
Nought from this bond shall make us free
For thou art mine and I'm for thee.

The copy he entered into his journal of poetry has some words changed and is missing the last two verses.

26. Stevenson, 3:262.

27. The Mormon Battalion was a volunteer unit in the 1846 United States campaign against Mexico. There were 497 men, plus 80 women and children, who made up five companies that marched to California, clearing roads which helped secure California as a United States territory. Brigham Young initiated the proposed enlistment, hoping that the military pay would help purchase supplies for the Saints in Iowa and at the Missouri River settlements. He also hoped the enlistment would allay fears about Latter-day Saints loyalty to the United States, help transport hundreds of Mormons to the Western frontier, and give him some bargaining power with the government in obtaining the privilege of settling his people on Indian lands for a few years. Ludlow, 2:933-36.

28. Wealthy wrote to Samuel and Franklin on the back page of one of Mary's letters dated July 13, 1846, in which she states: "Joseph is about to take his departure for Santafee Willard says he must go, you know when the word goes forth there is no revoking it, so you see one trial after another comes, but I have got so used to trials that this don't try me as much as some things, Joseph is willing to go." In the same letter, Mary confided to Samuel: "Uncle Willard . . . said if you had not gon to Eng he would now have sent you & Franklin into the army." Samuel Whitney Richards Collection, LDS Archives.

29. "Reminiscences of Jane Snyder Richards." Franklin D. Richards identified this baby with the name Franklin in a letter written to Samuel telling him of Jane's situation. Mary's letter to Samuel, dated September 30, 1846, identifies him as Franklin Snyder. His memorial monument, located at the former Mt. Pisgah, Iowa, cemetery, shows his name as Isaac Phineas.

30. By August 1846, ten to fifteen hundred individuals were still in Nauvoo; 750 called on the Nauvoo trustees daily for food, clothing, and aid to leave the city. Harrassment from anti-Mormon mobs escalated into a five-day fight called the Battle of Nauvoo. Several people were killed on both sides before the Saints surrendered on September 17. At this time hundreds of refugees fled Nauvoo across the river to Iowa, where they camped without food or shelter. Many were ill or crippled. None had money to enable them to join the main company of pioneers. Orville M. Allen was assigned to head a relief company to bring the poor camp to the Bluffs, where they were advised to stay in the Iowa settlements.

31. Other than the journals written by Mary during this particular time and the memorandum, no other of her diaries or journals are known. On June 3, 1846, Mary reported to Samuel that she had kept a journal since the time she left Nauvoo. In a February 25, 1848, letter to Samuel, Mary informs him that if he intends her to continue keeping a journal he would have to bring her some more paper, ink, and quills.

32. Kenneth W. Godfrey, "Winter Quarters: Glimmering Glimpses into Mormon Religious and Social Life," in *A Sesquicentennial Look at Church History*, proceedings of the Sidney B. Sperry Symposium (Provo, Utah: Brigham Young University Press, January 26, 1980), 149-61.

33. Heber C. Kimball and Willard Richards were members of the Quorum of the Twelve Apostles under the leadership of quorum president Brigham Young. When Young was sustained by the membership as the second president of the Church of Jesus Christ of Latter-day Saints on December 27, 1847, Kimball was sustained as his first counselor and Richards as the second.

34. Straw for braiding was traditionally made from the dried stems of wheat, oats, or barley. They were cut in the "milk stage," before the heads were ripe. The heads, outer layer, and hard joints were then removed. This left straight stems eight to ten inches long, which were usually sorted by size. Sometimes they were also softened and split with scissors or sharp knives and then flattened for a uniform piece. Bleaching the hats could be accomplished in two ways. Initially, the straw was scalded in hot water and dried in the sun for many days. Afterwards, if a lighter shade was desired, the bundles of straw could be bleached in sulfur fumes. The hats were created with a variety of braiding styles. The finishing step in making a hat was blocking it with starch, steam, and a flatiron. Veronica Patterson, "The Elusive Braided Straw Hat," *Piecework* 2 (July-August 1994): 61-64.

    Rhoda Richards's life story indicates that as a young child, she learned the household tasks of knitting, carding, spinning, braiding, and sewing straw hats and bonnets from her mother and "did everything that girls and women of a self-sustaining community would need to do." Stevenson, vol. 1 (1977), 34.

35. Phinehas Richards, "Journal," entries dated May 1847 through May 1848, Richards Family Collection, LDS Archives; also a letter to Willard Richards, dated June 13, 1847, Stevenson, 1:189.

36. Journal History of the Church, February 5, 1847, LDS Archives.

37. Maureen Ursenbach Beecher, "Women in Winter Quarters," *Sunstone* 8 (July-August 1984): 12.

38. The letter, dated November 17, 1847, from St. Louis, Missouri, is located in the Samuel Whitney Richards Collection, LDS Archives.

39. Maureen Ursenbach Beecher, *Eliza and Her Sisters* (Salt Lake City: Aspen Books, 1991), 80.

40. These letters are found in the Samuel Whitney Richards Collection, LDS Archives.

41. Letter of Samuel Whitney Richards dated June 26, 1846, Samuel Whitney Richards Collection, LDS Archives.

42. The main diseases mentioned in pioneer journals, including Mary's, were "black leg" or "black canker," meaning scurvy; "chills and fever" and "ague," usually meaning malaria; and "consumption," meaning tuberculosis. Other

discomforts included toothache and boils. Children often died of "inflamation."

Richard E. Bennett, *Mormons at the Missouri, 1846-1852: "And Should We Die. . ."* (Norman: University of Oklahoma Press, 1987), 132, 134, has estimated that between 1846 and 1848, 550 deaths occurred in Winter Quarters, Cutler's Park, and Cold Springs; 220 deaths in Council Bluffs; about 115 deaths at Mt. Pisgah; 95 at Garden Grove; and 23 at Ponca, situated above the head of the Niobrara River on the Nebraska border. This is a total of 1,003 estimated deaths. Heber C. Kimball stated that he had never before seen so much sickness as he did in August 1846 at the Missouri.

43. Fourteen-year-old Lovisa Jenne, a niece of Jane Snyder Richards, tells of her experience with black canker:

> We had a very poor living, mostly corn meal for bread, no vegetables. It was very hard on the people; caused much sickness. We had what they called scurvy, black leg, and canker; with it I had all three. My mouth was so bad with canker that I never tasted food for six weeks; only as sometimes the folkes would toast some bread, browned it, and made coffee with it and I would drink it. I could only drink, my mouth was so badly eaten with canker, and my legs were all drawn up. I could not straighten them no more than if I was sitting down. They were that way for a long time, but at last they grew some better. Until they were straightened out a little, one of my legs was two inches shorter. I walked with a cane for a long time, but it lengthened to be as long as the other was. (Conrey Bryson, *Winter Quarters* [Salt Lake City: Deseret Book, 1986], 73)

44. In a letter to Samuel on June 3, 1846, shortly after parting, Mary indicated that besides writing a journal since the time she left Nauvoo, she had also "written some in my other & intend to complete it as soon as time & sircumstances will admit." By comparing writing and color of ink with the memorandum and the first few journals, one may conclude that she was writing the memorandum at the same time as her journals.

45. Samuel Whitney Richards Journals, 1839-1909, and Journals and Family Record, 1846-1876, LDS Archives.

46. The boundary line between the territory of Iowa and the state of Missouri was at first disputed, almost causing a civil war. The Iowa authorities had fixed a line that has since been established as the permanent boundary line. The Missouri constitution defined the northern border from the rapids of the Des Moines River, just below Keosauqua, thus taking from Iowa a strip of about eight miles.

Missouri officials attempted to collect taxes in the contested territory, sending sheriffs to get the taxes or confiscate property. The Iowa leaders retaliated by putting the Missouri sheriffs in jail. Governor Boggs, of Missouri, called out his militia to enforce the decision. Iowa's Governor Lucas then called out his militia and soon had about twelve hundred men enlisted with five hundred armed and ready to fight. The United States Congress finally settled the confrontation in favor of Iowa. *History of Fremont County, Iowa* (Des Moines: Iowa Historical, 1881), 177-78.

47. Oliver Cowdery had grown dissatisfied with the leadership of the church and had left it eleven years before his arrival in Winter Quarters. However, in Kanesville, at a church conference in October 1848, Oliver shared his

testimony of the restored church and expressed his desire to renew his baptism and his hope to join the main body of the church in Salt Lake. The account of Oliver's written and verbal testimonies to Samuel are found in the *Deseret Evening News*, December 21, 1901, p. 11; the *Improvement Era* 2 (December 1898): 90-96; Smith, *History of the Church*, 1:42; statement of Samuel Whitney Richards, May 21, 1907, in LDS Archives; and other places.

48. Journal History of the Church supplement, 1849.

49. Sanpete Valley was originally called San Pitch Valley after the Ute Indian leader San Pitch. The name has been retained today in the mountain range running between Levan and Freedom, Utah.

50. Mary's ill health was evident to all of her friends throughout her life. On May 28, 1856, Wilford Woodruff wrote to Orson Pratt: "There are a few sick here; among whom are sisters Mary Ann Young and Mary Richards, who are a little easier to day." Journal History of the Church.

51. Edward W. Tullidge's account of the British Mission states,

    And so also the historian can tell of tens of thousands of souls sent over to this country from Great Britain under the administration of Franklin D. Richards and his brother Samuel. The Richardses were among the founders of the British Mission: under them it reached the zenith of its glory.

    Franklin replaced Samuel as president of the British Mission in 1854. The two brothers served a combined nineteen years in the capacity of president; Samuel served nine. Together they emigrated 14,364 British and Scottish Saints.

52. The Big Field ran from 200 West to 1300 East and 900 South to 2100 South in Salt Lake City and was used as farm land for the early pioneers. Samuel's property, lots 18 and 19 in block 15, was between 800 and 900 East, approximately between Bryan Avenue on the north and Logan Avenue on the south. (Salt Lake Recorder's Office Land Records, copy, LDS Archives; also Map of the Big Field, copy, LDS Historical Department Library.)

53. Mary Ann Parker was the youngest of Samuel's wives. He often wrote of "attending Mary Ann to her grammar school" in his diaries. After Mary's death, Mary Ann raised her three children, ages 2, 9, and 13. Perhaps this explains the confusion found in the many records in which Mary Haskin Parker is not mentioned and her children are shown as the children of Mary Ann Parker. Mary Ann also outlived all of Samuel's wives. She accompanied Samuel when he served as mission president of the Eastern States Mission in 1895. She was the mother of ten children.

54. Richard Ballentyne surveyed 148 acres of pasture land, with the section for the Fourteenth Ward running from 900 West to the Jordan River and from 1300 South to 1700 South. On February 23, 1855, Samuel recorded in his journal that he attended a meeting at Jacob Peart's of persons claiming land in the Ballentyne Survey east of Jordan and drew lot number 10, a five acre lot lying at the southeast corner. Twenty-four lots were drawn. Pioneer plat records confirm Samuel's lot, situated on the corner of 900 West and 1700 South. Pioneer Plat Records, 1852-1888, Salt Lake County, copy, LDS Archives.

55. Samuel owned a forty-five acre farm and home near 1600 South and 2100 East in Sugar House. He often called it his Bench farm. Ann Cash Richards was

living there, in the Sugar House Ward, when she died. Mary Ann's family also lived there periodically. Cannon, *Biographical Sketch of Samuel Whitney Richards*, 19, 20.

56. According to Samuel's journal, on April 16, 1855, he "bargained a yoke of cattle" to John Oldfield for lot 3, block 11 in the Fifth Ward. The cattle were worth $90; the remaining $60 on the property was to be paid in shingles from Cedar Valley. The transaction in the Salt Lake Deed Records simply records that Samuel paid $60 for the land. This land was situated on 500 West between 750 and 775 South.

   On September 17, 1855, Samuel purchased from J. William Farrer lot 3, block 30 in the Sixth Ward for $100. This property is located on the corner of 300 West and 600 South.

   On May 7, 1856, Samuel purchased lot 7, block 19 in plat B from Edward Hunter for $160 This acre and one quarter was on 600 East between 850 and 875 South in the Second Ward. Samuel's journals do not mention the purchase of Edward Hunter's property, but they record a transaction not found in the deed records. On March 14, 1856, Samuel wrote that he bought a house and lot from Samuel Bennett in the Second Ward for $150. Six days later he rented a house and lot in the Second Ward to Brother Bryant for $45 for a year. Salt Lake Deed Records, Book A, 1850-1859, copy, LDS Archives, 31, 51, 190.

57. Ann Jones was married first to John Valleley, by whom she had two children, Margaret and John. When Valleley died, she married James Cash, a widower with a small daughter, Mary Ellen. Cash was a member of the Church of Jesus Christ of Latter-day Saints in the Liverpool Branch; Ann was not. However, she joined the church two months after he died. She subsequently worked as a housekeeper in the mission office in Liverpool before emigrating to America.

58. Samuel's letters dated December 22 and 29, 1855, and Mary's responding letters, in the Samuel Whitney Richards Collection, LDS Archives.

59. Helena Lydia Robinson came from the Isle of Man. Not only was she accomplished on the melodian, but she sang on the stage of the Salt Lake Theater. During the United States government's later campaign against polygamy, Samuel divided his families and sent them to different locations. Helena and her children lived on his Spring Ranch near Cokeville, Wyoming. The isolation there away from the fine things she loved was very difficult for her, although she and the children attended parties in the neighboring settlements and she taught music lessons at Smith's Fork. She died at the age of forty-eight and was the mother of twelve children. According to her descendants, she was so embittered about her life that she made her children promise never to marry a Mormon, although some did.

60. Jane Elizabeth Mayer and Samuel only had one son, Henry Phinehas. When she took him with her to visit in Arkansas and Louisiana, it was to be for a short time only. However, her family members kept pressuring her to stay longer, knowing they might never see her again. In her letters to Samuel she repeatedly asked him for permission to remain longer in the East; consequently, her stay lengthened into almost three years. Her letters are full of praise for their little son. She finally made plans to return to Salt Lake City, but because of the Civil War she could not leave. Young Phinehas died in Arkansas. Jane later returned and died in Salt Lake at the age of thirty-six. In

a tribute written in May 1867 in her memory, Eliza R. Snow talked of Jane's cheerful spirit, her truthful nature, and her devotion to her church. Carter, *Our Pioneer Heritage*, vol. 12 (1969), 397-98.

61. Samuel's incomplete journals rarely mention where his families are living. Except for the reference to the Sugar House Ward where Ann Cash Richards died, all of the records on his wives and children are found in the Salt Lake Fourteenth Ward where he and Mary first settled. The boundaries for the Fourteenth Ward were Main Street on the east, 500 West on the west, North Temple Street on the north, and 300 South on the south. Samuel may have preferred keeping everyone as members in the same ward, regardless of where they actually lived. In the early 1870s, Samuel mentions that Helena is living in the Twelfth Ward. Carter, *Our Pioneer Heritage*, vol. 16 (1973), 532, indicates that Helena lived in a log cabin on the southwest corner of South Temple and Second or Third East. This was close to the northwest boundary of the Twelfth Ward.

62. Apostle Lorenzo Snow began the Polysophical Society in 1854 as a means of gathering together an elite group of intelligent men and women. They first met at his large home every other week where they shared original poetry, performed music, held discussions, and gave extemporaneous speeches. A master of ceremonies conducted the meeting. Samuel wrote of handling that responsibility more than once.

     Two years later, the intellectual community was looked on with suspicion by some. Jedediah Grant, Salt Lake City mayor and Mormon leader, remarked that the Polysophical Society was a stink in his nostrils, and Heber C. Kimball declared that there was an adulterous spirit in it. See Beecher, *Eliza and her Sisters*, 115. It was soon replaced by the Deseret Theological Class, under the direction of President Brigham Young.

63. Elizabeth Whitaker and Joseph Cain were the parents of two children. After Joseph's death, Samuel administered his estate. Samuel's journals indicate that he showed concern and love for not only his natural children but the children of Elizabeth Cain and Ann Cash.

64. Ten letters from Jane to Samuel and thirteen letters from Samuel to Jane, written during the time she was in Arkansas, are in the Samuel Whitney Richards Collection, LDS Archives. Additional letters between the two are in the private possession of Frederick S. and Rama Richards Buchanan, Salt Lake City, Utah.

65. "Journal of Phinehas Richards," Richards Family Collection, LDS Archives. Also "Historian's Office Journal," 1860-1861, LDS Archives, pp. 56-57.

66. "Autobiography of Sarah DeArmon Pea Rich," typescript, LDS Archives.

67. *Deseret Semi-Weekly News*, Wednesday, June 6, 1860.

Chapter 3

1. Mary's memorandum is in the possession of Maurine Carr Ward, Hyrum, Utah, with a copy in the LDS Archives. It is comprised of yellowed pages, 4 inches wide by 6½ inches long. The pages are sewn on the left side where the sheets are folded. The ink varies between brown and blue. Very faint lines

appear on some of the pages, however on many pages it appears that Mary wrote two lines in each space, instead of one line. Eight pages at the end of the booklet are bare.

2. George Rhodes would sail from England with his fifteen-month-old son, William Rhodes. It is likely that this is the George Rhodes who was married to Margaret Corbridge, a sister-in-law to two of John Parker's daughters, who married into the Corbridge family.

3. William and Margaret Moss Bleasdale were neighbors of John and Ellen Parker and joined the Latter-day Saints church about the same time. According to a history furnished by descendants of the Bleasdales, William had a neighbor couple who wanted to emigrate to America, but they could not afford to take their daughter. William Bleasdale promised this neighbor that he and Margaret would take the girl with their family. When the time came for William to leave, he did not have enough money for both his daughter, Jennette, and the neighbor's daughter, who was probably Mary Haskin Parker, so he left Jennette home with an uncle who planned to emigrate later. When the uncle chose to remain in England, Jennette sailed by herself.

Family records of Samuel Whitney Richards show that John and Ellen Parker's son Roger/Rodger married William and Margaret Bleasdale's other daughter Alice.

Chapter 4

1. Journal Number One covers the trek across Iowa and is located in the LDS Archives. It is six inches long and four inches wide. It is made of cream-colored paper and is written in brown ink. The sheets are sewn with heavy white thread on the fold at the top of the page. A letter from Mary to her brothers and sisters in England, dated July 13, 1845, has been cut down one side and sewn as a cover on the journal at a later date.

2. Hiram Kimball's landing, also called the upper landing, has not been definitely located. According to James Kimball, from the LDS Historical Department, the steamboat landing area covered two or three acres fronting the old village of Commerce, Illinois. Hiram Kimball had a pier that jutted out from the shore. Based on Commerce tax records and histories, this pier could have been located anywhere alongside the old town, from present-day Cutler Street on the south to Brattle Street on the north.

3. This refers to the temple undergarments that Mary, and other Saints, would have worn after being endowed in the Nauvoo Temple (see Mary's letter dated June 3, 1846). A few other times when Mary talks about sewing a garment she refers to the temple garment, but sometimes she is referring to another article of clothing.

4. On the ninth of March, Edwin Little had taken sick at Sugar Creek. Suffering from fever and lung problems, he was counseled to leave the camp and stay with some of the brethren in the vicinity. He died on the eighteenth and was buried at dusk between the Fox and Chequst Rivers. The Journal History of the Church, March 18, 1846, LDS Archives, gives detailed directions to his burial spot.

5. According to Phinehas Richards's journal, his family only traveled until they found a dry camping place each day. When the sun came out, they were able to dry their wet clothing and bedding.

6. This day was the third day in six days of traveling that one of the wagon tongues broke and had to be fixed or repaired. Unfortunately, this was not the last time repairs had to be made. Phinehas records the breakdowns with the wagons where Mary does not.

7. Mary's brother, John Parker Jr., and his wife, Ellen, had gone to St. Louis, Missouri, to see about investing in a soft-drink business, hoping to earn money to go west later. It appeared to be a good venture for them, so Ellen returned to Nauvoo to collect their children. On June 5, Samuel, who was still in Nauvoo, put Ellen and the children, plus his father-in-law, John Sr., on the steamer, *The Prairie Bird,* and gave them a letter of recommendation to Joseph Stratton, the presiding elder in St. Louis.

8. The church's presidency at Mt. Pisgah consisted of Charles C. Rich, Ezra T. Benson, and William Huntington.

9. Phinehas recorded that the journey this time was better than it had been on the way to Mt. Pisgah. Records from other travelers also indicate that this part of the trip was more pleasant. Some mention seeing wild strawberries amidst the prairie grass. However, the wind on the evening of July 4 was so strong it "prostrated" tents, according to Phinehas.

10. On this day, Samuel and Franklin finally left Nauvoo for their mission to Great Britain.

11. The women were from Cold Springs Camp.

12. Samuel Whitney Richards Collection, LDS Archives. The letter is 11 by 17 inches, folded to 8½ by 11, then folded again, with the address on the back page. Other attributes include brown ink, 6⅜ inch holes on fold lines, and two larger ½ by 3 inch and ½ by 1½ inch holes. Missing words due to holes have been assumed and inserted in brackets.

13. Phinehas recorded that he "passed through Farmington crossed the Desmoin River and camped 5 miles west for the Night." Stanley B. Kimball states that the pioneer trail went north from Croton, following the Des Moines River, through Farmington to Bonaparte, where the Mormons forded the river. The old crossing place is near the modern bridge over the River. Kimball, *Historic Sites and Markers Along the Mormon and Other Great Western Trails* (Urbana: University of Illinois Press, 1988), 24.

14. Samuel Whitney Richards Collection. The letter is 15½ by 9¼ inches folded to 7¾ by 9¾ inches and is in brown ink.

15. Commenting on the temple garment which Mary refers to here, Samuel wrote on June 4, 1846: "I commend you to the protection of him, who has power to rule your destiny for good. believing that you will use every precaution. and in faith the garment of the Priesthood which will prove a shield. both to your body and soul." Later in the same letter Samuel added: "Was glad to hear that you had got your garment made and wearing them. The Lord bless you with them, also that you was writing a journal. I am satisfied that you will do every thing I enjoined upon you. Therefore I go my way in peace." Samuel Whitney Richards Collection.

16. In answer to Mary's letter, Samuel wrote on June 4, 1846: "You say you would rather see the Boy that weares the curl, than his likeness. I did not mean myself, but that which might come ~~of~~ us. No doubt you would be glad to see him, and he would make you happy, and so would I when I return to your kind bosom." In the same letter Samuel wrote:

> Did I know, my love! what your condition ~~was~~ is, in relation to that, of which we often used to speak, and to which <u>you consented</u> for my sake (<u>which strengthened my love for you</u>,) I should perhaps be more free in writing to you, in relation to that matter, However, your circumstances, (be what they may.) will no doubt subject you to many feelings, and perhaps of a trying nature. But, <u>Mary</u> never submit to feelings, or be governed by them. (Samuel Whitney Richards Collection)

Samuel was, of course, expecting to hear whether Mary was pregnant.

17. Mary's menstrual period. On June 26, 1846, Samuel's letter again shows his concern for her "condition": ". . . has the <u>visitor</u> been faithful with you or not." Samuel Whitney Richards Collection.

18. Samuel Whitney Richards Collection. The letter is a single sheet, 7½ by 9 inches, in brown ink.

19. Samuel Whitney Richards Collection. The letter is 15½ by 9¾ inches, folded to 7¾ by 9¾ inches, in brown ink. It was written right side up, then turned and written upside down in the spaces.

20. On June 26, 1846, Samuel wrote:

> You ask about Ellen what her prospect is for going west &C. . . . She told me that she was going with Bro. Hunters folks to <u>help them</u> had no expectation of going to be one of the family or staying with them as such, neither of going back to Wooleys. we talked over her circumstances and what had passed between us 3 before she was sealed, she thought, had she taken a different course she might have been happier than she had been, upon which I told her that I should say nothing to induce her to leave him to whom she belonged, but in case she was liberated, she might know that the offer was still for her, she replyed, that probably she would accept it after my return. . . . Now Mary I want you should use your influence, in wisdom, to secure her for me when I return, if she leaves Bro. Wooley. Be wise in all you say and do, but if she is once made free, and acts independent you can secure her, and you know that our happiness depends upon that society which is congenial to it, and she is constant, and a tried friend. . . . and if you expect another to share in my affections with you, pray that may be one who can make <u>you</u> happy as well as <u>me</u>. (Samuel Whitney Richards Collection)

21. A term used to designate when a woman was ready to give birth.

22. Mary is giving Samuel her version of a statement Samuel wrote on June 26, 1846: "I understand that one Derby has left the camp being guilty of adultery with one of Haws daughters, who by the laws of the land was Whitmarsh wife, but sealed to Brigham, as a penalty for which he had either to loose his head, or his manhood (testicles) the only means of salvation for him. I have not heard what is to be done with the woman, should like to know, if death as used to be." Samuel Whitney Richards Collection.

According to Hosea Stout, Erastus Derby was found in bed with Emiline Haws when a group of boys overturned the wagon they were in. The next morning Emiline threw a cup of hot coffee in the face of Benjamin Denton, nearly blinding him, as she believed him to be the cause of her embarrassment. Juanita Brooks, ed., *On the Mormon Frontier: The Diary of Hosea Stout, 1844-1861* (Salt Lake City: University of Utah Press and Utah State Historical Society, 1964), 1:160.

Consequently, Erastus left the camp, but wrote to Brigham Young asking forgiveness and requesting permission to return to the Saints. Brigham told him to return to his family and be a good husband. However, he and his family eventually left the church. Journal History of the Church, June 1, 1846, LDS Archives.

Chapter 5

1. Journals Two through Six are located together in the LDS Archives. Journal Two is five inches long and four inches wide. It is made of cream-colored paper. The sheets are sewn with heavy white thread where they fold at the tops of pages. The beginning entries are written in dark brown ink, which changes to light brown, then to blue, and ends with light brown ink again.

   The first four pages are missing or contain partial texts that are not completely legible. An incomplete entry on page five is apparently Wednesday, July 22, 1846; however, the date is on the previous page. There are six and one-half blank pages after the last entry in this journal. The partial texts on the first four pages include the following:

   [*page 2*]
   Church in
   leave their
   their comfort
   w they enj
   had tried
   [*page 3*]
   sentation to put
   sed God to
   [?]
   by Bro J
   where about
   for 200 dolars.
   for the former
   had and good
   a [?]
   was waiting
   with
   [*page 4*]
   ever had
   stayed here
   be as forward
   went onto
   22th
   Smithes hair
   yet with me
   Heber Kimba
   more than

Father & Mother
pet

2. Either Heber C. Kimball or Willard Richards.

3. The law of adoption was one of the doctrines that the Prophet Joseph Smith introduced to the Twelve Apostles in the fall and winter of 1841-42. This principle allowed many of the leaders of the LDS church to adopt members and their families as their own children, with the idea of sharing exaltation in the hereafter. Brigham Young had adopted at least forty men, who helped run his farm in Winter Quarters. Heber C. Kimball, likewise, had a farm run by many of his adopted sons. After the Mormons reached the Salt Lake Valley, the practice became so confusing that it was discontinued.

4. Wilford Woodruff described the storm of July 28, 1846, thusly:

   It immediately presented the Appearance of a severe storm, thunder, lightening strong wind And a heavy body of Water Almost instantly rushed upon [us]. The water beat through our waggon Covers And nearly evry thing in our waggon. The wind drove our family carriag down a steep hill & turned it bottom side upwards And smashed the top to peaces but providentually there was no one of the family in the Carriag. And evrything was saved that was in it bottols &C. Vary heavy storms of thunder & rain continued through the night. Much rain fell. The beds bedding & family was drenched with water. Several tents were torn down in camp. It was A vary disagreeable night. (Scott G. Kenney, ed., *Wilford Woodruff's Journal*, [Midvale, Utah: Signature Books, 1979], 64)

5. It is not known what Mary meant by the "soft side of a bord" to sleep on, but the tent must have been extremely crowded that night. According to Brigham Young's writings as found in the Journal History of the Church, LDS Archives, Willard Richards had gone to John Taylor's camp, where he found Orson Hyde, Parley P. Pratt, and John Taylor ready to start for England, accompanied by Jesse C. Little as far as New York:

   After supper a tremendous storm of wind, thunder and rain commenced. Elder John Taylor lowered two of his tents, and the third prepared to lodge Elders Richards and Little, blew down and covered them while the water fell in torrents. They soon repaired to Brother [Walter] Wilcox's tent which had blown down and left his wife, Wealthy Maria, exposed to the storm, who, although delivered of a daughter the Sunday previous, fled to her Father's (Phinehas Richard's) tent, where Elders Richards and Little stayed and watched with the family the remainder of the night.

6. According to Parley P. Pratt, when he reached New York he joined with Samuel, Franklin, and Moses Martin as they sailed to Great Britain on September 22, 1846. Parley P. Pratt, *Autobiography of Parley P. Pratt* (1938; reprint, Salt Lake City: Deseret Book, 1975), 346.

7. At this time, Samuel and Franklin were still pursuing their way eastward. Upon leaving St. Louis, they traveled to Pittsburgh. Franklin was ill with chills and fever. At one landing place after leaving Pittsburgh, the two brothers went into the woods, offered up a prayer and read the Bible. One day Samuel discovered his gold ring from Mary was missing. He recalled: "I deeply regretted this misfortune more than any thing that had happened since I left the west. I suppose that I wiped it off my finger (being very loose) when I washed in the

morning being in a great haste." They arrived in Columbia, near Philadelphia, on August 5, 1846, and spent the night with Brother John P. Smith. Here they were able to undress for the first time since leaving St. Louis some twenty days previous. Samuel Whitney Richards Journals, LDS Archives.

8. Ursalia Hascall, another woman who lived around Council Bluffs, wrote a letter to her family in the East in which she described "black walnuts in abundance and hundreds of bushels of grapes, orchards of mild plumbs. Fifty bushels in a place. You never saw anything better [to] make pies and preserves." Letter of Ursalia B. Hastings Hascall to Col. Wilson Andrews, September 19, 1846, Utah State Historical Society.

The Biography of Margaret Jane McIntire Burgess, written by her daughter Margaret V. Burgess McMurtie from her mother's records (Harold B. Lee Library Special Collections, Brigham Young University), tells that she lived with her parents and four other families on the east side of the Missouri River in a wooded ravine. Below their cabins was the Potawatomi Indian village. Wild grapes grew in abundance on the sides of the hills, also elderberries and hazel nuts.

9. The bluffs on the Missouri River are among the finest examples of loess (meaning "loose particles") hills in the world. Only a region in China has a similar land formation. Wind carried the silt, comprised of fine mineral particles, across the central and northwestern states. In Iowa, the loess hills follow a narrow band from north of Sioux City to the Missouri border along the course of the nearby Missouri River. The top soil of yellow loess is finer than sand but coarser than dust or clay and is approximately fifteen feet deep on these bluffs. When undisturbed, the hills are stable, but any crack in the ground allows water to seep in, turning the soil to slippery mush. Mike Whyte, "Voices of the Loess Hills," *The Iowan* 41 (Spring 1993): 39-47, 69.

10. Samuel Whitney Richards Collection, LDS Archives. This letter is 9¾ by 15½ inches, folded to 9¾ by 7¾ inches, on blue paper with blue ink. It is written first right side up and then upside down between the lines. At the end is a scrap of cream paper, 4¾ by 2½ inches, written in brown ink on both sides of the paper.

11. Richard Neitzel Holzapfel and Jeni Broberg Holzapfel, *Women of Nauvoo* (Salt Lake City: Bookcraft, 1992), 175.

12. On May 29, 1846, ten days after Phinehas left Nauvoo, he wrote in his journal: "I lost my Dog Watch." From Nauvoo, Samuel wrote to Mary on June 27, 1846: "Most all of our acquaintants have left the city. Joseph Youngs folks and John's folks, are on the Bluff. Bro Godales family are with them. Our dog watch is with them. They will take him to you."

Chapter 6

1. Journals Two through Six are located together in the LDS Archives. Journal Three is 7½ inches tall by 5 inches wide. It has been written with brown ink. The sheets are cream-colored paper and are sewn with heavy thread where the pages fold on the left side of the journal. There is a period of three months between the end of Journal Two and the beginning of Journal Three, indicating that a journal has been lost or that Mary did not write during this time.

Consequently, little is known of her stay with Jane at Cutler's Park and of her move to Winter Quarters.

2. James Smithies was married to Ann Knowles, Mary's first cousin. Mary writes this name as either Smithis or Smithes.

3. Although Mary does not mention it, Phinehas was still having difficulties in his plural marriage to Mary Vail Morse. Earlier she had refused to accompany him from Mt. Pisgah to the bluffs, finding her own way there. Finally, on December 5, on the advice of Brigham Young, Phinehas went to Mary's wagon and gave her a verbal discharge. She told him that she did not have any hard feelings toward him, but agreed to the "divorce." Phinehas still showed an interest in her and recorded in his journal her subsequent marriage to Levi Jackman on July 22, 1851, in Salt Lake City.

4. The two chiefs were Big Elk, chief of the Omaha Nation, and his son, Standing Elk. Logan Fontenelle was the interpreter.

5. Hosea Stout recorded in his journal,
> Towards day the howling North wind, which had not yet ceased to blow, began to howl with renewed strength and filled our little Shanty full of its cold and piercing breath. The weather had increased in coldness & when morning light came I found one of those intolerable cold clear days that bids the most industerous to cease his labours & keep within. There was no stiring only by those who were either out of wood or hay or compelled by some means to meet the "chilling blast."

The day before, Stout had written that it was the coldest day of the year and that in spite of the best fires, his family was uncomfortable all day. Brooks, ed., *On the Mormon Frontier*, 1:223.

6. Hosea Stout wrote, "This was one of the most cold & disagreeable day[s] ever met with The wind in the North beating a driving snow which entirely obstructed the sight." Ibid., 1:229.

7. Joseph Hovey also wrote about this dance:
> The brethren built a Council House, and they called a meeting to dedicate it, Brother Brigham [was] there and and a number of the Twelve. They talked about having a dance for those who had built it or assisted. Brother Brigham said he was going to have the first dance and his brethren with him so they would set a pattern for the rest. They called for the band, and on they came forthwith. Brother Brigham organized a number of couples and set the band to playing a tune, after which we knelt down and prayed to the God of Heaven. I can truly say that the prayer that was offered up and the music and the dance were controlled with the Spirit of God which caused me to shed a flow of tears for joy. . . . Truly I was led to say this was the way the ancient fathers praised the Lord in a dance. ("Autobiography of Joseph Hovey," Harold B. Lee Library, Brigham Young University)

8. Approved dances of the time consisted of square dances, cotillions, Virginia and Scotch reels, polkas, varsouvienne, quadrille, schottische, and money musk. Annie C. Carr, ed., *East of Antelope Island* (Bountiful, Utah: Carr Printing Company and Daughters of the Utah Pioneers, Davis County Company, 1961), 433.

9. Helen Mar Kimball Whitney gave added insight into her mother's feelings on plural marriage: "I had, in hours of temptation, when seeing the trials of my

mother, felt to rebel. I hated polygamy in my heart." Augusta Joyce Crocheron, ed., *Representative Women of Deseret* (Salt Lake City: J. C. Graham, 1884), 112.

10. Robert Burton's journal describes their home:

> We thought it would be better for our family—that we could obtain the outfit for our journey quicker by moving down into the state of Missouri.
>
> Accordingly leaving the Bluffs and traveling down the Missouri River arriving at Atchinson Co., about the middle of August [1846].
>
> In our little company were my father and family and my father-in-law (John Haven) and family. I purchased a claim near the mouth of the Nishbotna River. Here we erected cabins, cultivated land and I obtained labor, part of [the] time in Missouri. (Janet Burton Seegmiller, *"Be Kind to the poor": The Life Story of Robert Taylor Burton* [Robert Taylor Burton Family Organization, 1988], 70)

11. This is Libbeus Coons, who, with his wife, Mary Ann Williamson, had settled a place which they called Coonville, near present-day Glenwood, Iowa.

12. While Mary was visiting at the Nishnabotna, Phinehas was working on his house in Winter Quarters. He wrote that he finished covering the house and put up one-half of each end with turf. However, a few days later, he was attacked with a sharp pain in his left shoulder which lasted a week and left him feeble for a long time. Shortly after that, Wealthy had complications from her rheumatism. They must have felt the hardship with Mary not there to help them.

13. When Franklin heard of the death of his brother Joseph, he exclaimed, "May the Spirit of the Lord be upon mother and father and enable them to bear these afflictions, conflicting dispensations and feel willing, if necessary to give up all their sons to the Lord." Franklin Dewey Richards, Journals, Richards Family Collection, LDS Archives. Samuel expressed his feelings in a poem entitled "Joseph, Our Brother, is Dead." It was printed in the *Millennial Star* 9 (June 1, 1847): 175–76.

14. According to Caratat C. Rowe,

> The Battalion left Point Pool, on the Missouri River on the 24th day of July, 1846, and marched to Fort Levenworth on foot, without tents or shelter of any kind, sleeping on the ground, which was sometimes saturated with rain and heavy dews. Some rain storms fell upon us while thus sleeping under the open canopy of the heavens. At Fort Levenworth Joseph William Richards took sick, doubtless from exposure on the road. When the command left the garrison he remained in the hospital, unable to be moved... he was soon able to be forwarded and overtook us at Council Grove. When the Battalion was divided . . . and the stronger portion put on a forced march to be in Santa Fe in time to cross the mountains to California the same fall, he being stronger than usual, was selected as one of them. When I arrived, I found Joseph again prostrated.... On the sad night of his departure, he gradually sank down and . . . quietly passed away.

Franklin L. West and Clair Noall (p. 514) indicate that Rowe and his wife, who had enlisted as a laundress, took care of Joseph at Pueblo. To the last of his life, Joseph offered no complaint, and he died in Rowe's arms. Other tributes to Joseph by his associates in the battalion are found in West's book, *Life of Franklin Dewey Richards* (Salt Lake City: Deseret News Press, 1924); and Claire Noall, *Intimate Disciple.*

15. One of the inconveniences for the Saints while on the trail and also in the little cabins in Winter Quarters or in Iowa was the lack of privacy, not only for personal hygiene and marital relations, but also for individual prayer and contemplation. Mary often found unique ways to be alone.

16. In 1839 and 1840, the A. J. (or J. J.) Singleton family was one of the first four families to settle in Pleasant Grove, four miles southeast of Sidney. Daniel and Isaac Hunsaker came to Pleasant Grove in 1843. They built the first ferry over the Nishnabotna River the following year. Eli Slusher moved to the Pleasant Grove area, not far from Singleton's, in 1844. Archibald H. Argyle arrived in 1845 and purchased the ferry, which apparently retained the name of Hunsaker's ferry. Argyle also bought a small trading store at that point.

    By 1846, the area around the ferry was known as Austin and was still thought to be in Atchison County, Missouri. This was about seven and one-half miles south of the town of Sidney.The only other village in the county at that time was a small one named McKissick's Grove. On March 8, 1848, Thomas E. Tootle, postmaster, entered into a contract with Thomas R. King, builder, for the construction of a store, which Argyle then purchased. It was also later used as a courthouse. Argyle's store, along with his home, was situated on the hill above the ferry.

    Fremont County, Iowa, was organized in the spring of 1849 at Argyle's store in Austin. The names of Singleton, Hunsaker, and Slusher are found often in the early records of the townships and the county. *History of Fremont County, Iowa* (Des Moines: Iowa Historical Company, 1881).

17. On this day, John Smith wrote in his journal, as recorded in the Journal History of the Church: "The cold weather has continued until yesterday; it has been very severe ever since it commenced in December. At this time the weather is more moderate. . . . We have had the coldest winter I ever experienced, or at least it seems to me."

18. At the age of fifteen, George had been murdered at Haun's Mill, Missouri, on October 30, 1838.

19. One week later, Brigham Young wrote to Orson Spencer in England asking if he could permit some of the American elders to return home that summer, then added: "If either Franklin or Samuel Richards could be spared, consistently, it would be right, also Lucius N. Scovill and others the same, but if not in accordance with the spirit of the time, let them wait in patience, and they shall have their rewards." Journal History of the Church, April 12, 1847, LDS Archives.

    Orson Hyde also wrote a letter on May 30, 1847 to Orson Spencer:
    I have seen and conversed with brother Franklin's and Samuel's wives to-day, and also with their parents. They are all well at this time and cheerful. I saw brother Scovill's wife at the meeting to-day, and she was well. Brother Wheelock's wife is dead: she died of the chills, canker, and other complaints at her friends in the Potowatamie nation. As brother Wheelock now has nothing urgent to call him home, he had better remain in England until I counsel him to return. The wives of all the Elders in England, that went from this country, are *particularly* anxious for their return as you may all well judge; yet inasmuch as they still remain in England, their families can be sustained if they will send them what they consistently can for their help. (*Millennial Star* 9 [August 15, 1847]: 243)

20. Phinehas replaced Samuel Russell who was put into the presidency of the Seventies Quorum.
21. Brigham Young, many of the Council of the Twelve, and others left for the Salt Lake Valley on April 7, 1847. More of them, including Willard, left on April 8.
22. Parley P. Pratt had recently arrived in Winter Quarters from Great Britain.
23. John Taylor arrived in Winter Quarters from England, bringing with him $2000 in gold for the church. Brigham Young and the Twelve returned from starting west to meet with him.
24. On January 18, 1847, Franklin and Samuel spent most of the day in the mission office packing things to send to their wives with Joseph Cain on his return to Winter Quarters. Both men had been given straw bonnets for their wives, trimmed and ready to wear, by a Brother and Sister Carmichael. Margaret Kerr and Margaret Dyer had previously led an enterprise of gathering clothing and other goods to send to the destitute families of Samuel and Franklin. These items were included in the chest being prepared. Franklin D. Richards, Journals, Richards Family Collection, LDS Archives.
25. Phinehas was in the Winter Quarters First Ward, with Bishop Edward Hunter. Records of this ward are found in the LDS Archives and include the bishop's report, December 16, 1846; tithing, December 1846; relief for the poor, March 1847; and a list of cattle in the ward, June 22, 1847. These records help to identify many of Mary's neighbors.
26. Additional information on the Mormons' problems with the Indians around Winter Quarters can be found in the journal of Hosea Stout, the police chief of Winter Quarters. Brooks, ed., *On the Mormon Frontier.*
27. Samuel Whitney Richards Collection, LDS Archives. The letter is 15½ by 9¾ inches folded to 7¾ by 9¾, then folded again with the address on the back; it is written in blue ink.
28. In Samuel's letters (Samuel Whitney Richards Collection), he often counseled Mary in regard to her feelings of unhappiness and of the importance of a positive attitude, as in the following examples:

> Mary never submit to feelings, or be governed by them. but act upon Principle and you will act upon inteligence, be governed by it and you will be governed by inteligence and all will be well. . . Yes my dear make up a face, to go through any thing that comes before you. . . you have a mind that ought to tread upon the trifling trials of this life as one would upon the serpents head, and welcome to your bosom, naught, but that which makes for peace, happiness, and virtue. (June 4, 1846)
>
> You say it is very pleasant to see so many of the brethren returning. though the unbidden tear steals down the cheek when you see so many of your sisters enjoying the society of their husbands. but when you have looked at them 'till your feelings can scarcely enduce then turn and look at those whose husbands have just left them and you will no doubt find a contrast, and then think 'perhaps my husband will be with me before theirs' and let the tear be dry. (October 27, 1852, during Samuel's second mission)

29. Samuel Whitney Richards Collection. The letter is 15 by 9¾ inches, folded to 7¾ by 9¾ and written in brown ink. It is quite worn. Pages one and two have

been taped, making the paper dark and hard to read. Pages three and four have a large tear and hole.

30. Samuel Whitney Richards Collection. This letter has no heading or date but appears to be an addition to the previous letter. It is a single sheet of paper, 7¾ by 5 inches, written in brown ink. It has a large hole in it approximately 1½ inches in diameter.

Chapter 7

1. Journals Two through Six are located together in the LDS Archives. Journal Four is 7½ inches tall and 5 inches wide. It is sewn with heavy thread where the sheets fold on the left margin. The journal is written on cream-colored paper with brown ink at the beginning, later changing to blue ink.

2. While Parley P. Pratt was in England, he wrote a letter in blank verse to his family on the Missouri River, beginning with the words, "My Dearest Wife." According to his autobiography, "It was published in England . . . on a beautiful sheet with a handsome border, and designed to be put in a frame as a household ornament. . . . May it be handed down to posterity as a monument of suffering and self-denial of women and children for the gospel's sake." Pratt, *Autobiography*, 347-53.

3. Because Phinehas, Levi, and Willard Richards were Thomsonian doctors, they were active in their use of herbs and plants. Mary received many of the standard herbal treatments during her illnesses. Boneset was considered a cure-all at that time. It was thought to be an excellent remedy for "Intermittent and Bilious Fevers, in Fever and Ague, as well as in Affections of the Liver, Lungs, and in Dyspepsia." When the leaves were boiled down into a tea, it was claimed to induce perspiration and vomiting. Comfrey was another name for boneset. John Charles Gunn, *Gunn's Newest Family Physician* (New York: Baird and Dillon, 1885), 815.

   Lobelia was used for treating cough, asthma, and epilepsy. Samuel Thomson claimed he discovered the medicine when he coaxed a friend to chew a leaf of the plant. The friend immediately fell deadly ill. When he drank some water, he vomited and recovered from its effects and felt better than he had before eating the plant. In reality, lobelia is a poisonous plant which causes vomiting and affects the central nervous system. See Claire Kowalchik and William H. Hylton, eds., *Rodale's Illustrated Encyclopedia of Herbs* (Emmaus, Pennsylvania: Rodale Press, 1987), 364. Tincture of lobelia was prepared by filling a jar with green leaves, well bruised and pressed, then adding three or four pods of common red pepper for each quart of herbs. Enough whiskey was poured in the jar to cover the lobelia, and the concoction was allowed to stand until used. Pickard and Buley, 187.

   Composition powder was a combination of one pound bayberry, one-half pound ginger, and one ounce each of cayenne and cloves. It was pulverized, and then a tea was made of a large tablespoon of powder in a pint of boiling water. Like boneset, composition was used to produce perspiration. *Gunn's Newest Family Physician*, 1138. When Mary's illness became extremely critical, she was given quinine. This was a fever suppressant derived from the bark of the South American quinchona tree. It was a new medicine that was gaining popularity in the 1840s and was highly mistrusted, very expensive, and scarce.

4. Anciently, horseradish was considered valuable as a plaster, especially for swelling of joints, gout, and spleen and liver ailments. It was also used as a stimulant, laxative, diuretic, and antiseptic. Perhaps it was used by Mary to sooth her inflamed stomach and bowels from outside her body. Kowalchik and Hylton, 470-72.

5. On September 2, 1847, Phinehas complained to Hosea Stout, chief of the police, that Henry Boley's ox had done damages in his garden and he wanted to have it arrested and put in the stray pen. Henry and his son followed the officers who took the ox and violently tried to get it back, requiring the officers to draw their pistols on Henry. Henry's son then threatened to shoot the officers and had to be taken to a bishop's court, where he was fined five dollars. Perhaps the bad feelings between Henry and Phinehas this day kept Henry's daughter from attending the quilting bee at Mary's home. Miss Davis, who also did not attend, may have been Betsy Asenath Davis, who was Henry Boley Jr.'s first wife, or, more probably, Hannah Jane Davis, his second wife. Brooks, 1:271.

6. Animadverting is an archaic term meaning to notice or observe, to remark by way of criticism, or to censure. *The Oxford English Dictionary*, 2d Edition.

7. When Mary copied this poem in a later letter to Samuel, she wrote this word as "hard."

8. Samuel Whitney Richards Collection, LDS Archives. The letter is 15½ by 9¾ inches, folded to 7¾ by 9¾ and written in blue ink.

9. Records of the Winter Quarters First Ward, dated December 1846 (bishop's report and tithing), March 1847 (relief of the poor), and June 1847 (list of cattle) are found in a notebook of Bishop Edward Hunter, along with small records of the Nauvoo Fifth Ward and Salt Lake City Thirteenth Ward, at the LDS Archives. Phinehas is included in the June 1847 listing of cattle but not in the other two records because he had not moved into his house by then. According to Conrey Bryson (*Winter Quarters*, 66,67), when the first thirteen wards were organized in Winter Quarters, Edward Hunter was the bishop of the Seventh Ward. As the city grew, the number of bishops increased to twenty-two, and the boundaries changed. Bishop Hunter was then called to preside over the First Ward, which included all the inhabitants of the south side of Joseph Street. This was the geographically largest ward in the city, as most wards were comprised of only one block.

10. Samuel Whitney Richards Collection. This letter appears to be an addition to the previous letter. There is no date, salutation, or ending. It is 7½ by 7½ inches and written in blue ink.

11. This refers to sisters Harriet, Sophia, and Elizabeth Whitaker. They had emigrated from England in a group with John Taylor, Parley P. Pratt, and others. While still in Liverpool, Elizabeth married Joseph Cain. Sophia married John Taylor in Winter Quarters in April 1847. Harriet also married John Taylor on December 7, 1847.

12. Bedspread.

13. Samuel Whitney Richards Collection. The letter is a single sheet measuring 7¾ by 9¾ inches and is written in blue ink. There is a small hole in the center and a wax seal on one side.

14. Abigail Abbott to Mary Haskin Parker Richards, July 25, 1847, Samuel Whitney Richards Collection.

Chapter 8

1. Journals Two through Six are located together in the LDS Archives. Journal Five is 6¼ inches tall and 4 inches wide and is sewn with heavy white thread on the left fold. The journal is made of blue-lined paper; however, Mary writes smaller and does not follow the lines. A cream-colored paper has been sewn on later for a cover. It is covered with poetry, written in Mary's handwriting. Each line of writing is separated with a line of identical marks, designs, or capital letters. The text on the cover is as follows:

> Miss Mary H Parker RWS we Parted in Silance
>
> we parted in Silance. we parted at Night.
> On the Banks of that lonely River. where
> the fragrant lymes there Baughs. unite.
> We met & we parted for ever. The night
> Birds Song & the Stars above. tould many
> a tutching Storey.
> Of Scenes long gone in the kingdomes of love.
> where the Soule wears its mantle of Glory.
> ~~We parted in silence.~~ we parted at night.
> ~~On the banks of that lonely River.~~ we parted in Silance
> Our Cheeks Where wet with the tears that where past controlling.
> We vowed we never no never forget. & those vowes at that time.
> where consoling.
> Remember well and keep in mind a trusty
> but the lips that echoed this vow of mine are as could as that
> lonely River. And that Sparkling eye The Spirits shrine,
> Has enshrouded its fire forever. and now on the midnight Sky
> I look my Heart grows full to weeping. each Star to me is a Sealed Book.
> Some tale of that loved one wending.

> We parted in Sileance we parted ~~at Night~~ in tears On the Banks of that lonely River. But the flours an Bloom of those Bygone years. Shall hang O're its Waters forever. friend is hard to find MHP

2. Mormon Battalion.
3. It is unclear what Aunt Sarah meant by "tipping her hair" as it was "old of the moon." Possibly it indicated getting the ends of her hair trimmed as it had been a long time since her last hair cut.
4. On November 27, 1847, Phinehas was married to Martha Allen by Brigham Young, with Willard and Levi as witnesses. This marriage was soon dissolved. Mary does not mention the marriage, and no records note that Martha ever lived with the family.
5. A felon is a small abscess, inflamed sore, or boil.
6. This conference was held on Monday, December 28, 1847, in the newly constructed Log Tabernacle in Council Bluffs across the river. This was later called the Kanesville Tabernacle. It was at this conference that Brigham Young, president of the Council of the Twelve Apostles, was formally

sustained by the Iowa members of the church as the president of the Church of Jesus Christ of Latter-day Saints. Heber C. Kimball and Willard Richards were chosen as his counselors in the First Presidency of the church.

7. Several letters from Orson Spencer to Rev. W. Crowel, A.M., editor of *The Christian*, Boston, Mass., were printed in the *Millenial Star* at various times during the period Spencer was in the British Mission. *Millenial Star* 9 (September 15, 1847): 277.

8. Bishop of the Twenty-third Ward.

9. Isaac Clark was bishop of the Fifteenth Ward, consisting of Block 35. See Bryson, 67. Hosea Stout wrote of that evening: "Several of the police & myself went to the South Line of the City to Break up a dancing party but finding Bp Clark there we said nothing." Brooks, *On the Mormon Frontier*, 298.

10. Warm sling here refers to a drink popular in America at the time. It was a concoction of brandy, rum, or other alcohol sweetened, flavored, and mixed with water. *Oxford English Dictionary*, 2d Edition.

11. The gift of healing and the practice of speaking in tongues and the subsequent interpretation of tongues were found among the Latter-day Saints early in the history of the church. These gifts were given to any worthy member, male or female. After the female Relief Society was organized by Joseph Smith and the temple endowment ceremony was introduced, prayer and laying on of hands were often used for healing by the officers of the Relief Society and other endowed women. After the Mormons' expulsion from Nauvoo, Brigham Young disbanded the Relief Society but could not take away the faith in their spiritual gifts of the sisters at Winter Quarters. Small informal meetings, called blessing meetings, were held where women as well as men spoke in tongues and had experiences of the spirit. Since many men were away in the Mormon Battalion or working, it became necessary for women to handle spiritual as well as temporal crises, and many healings were brought about because of their administrations. Linda King Newell, "Gifts of the Spirit: Women's Share," in Maureen Ursenbach Beecher and Lavina Fielding Anderson, eds., *Sisters in Spirit* (Urbana: University of Illinois Press, 1992), 111-19.

An undated letter from Amelia Peirson Richards to her mother and sister in Massachusetts also mentions the blessing meetings:

Every Thursday is held a day of Prayer and Fasting, both in this camp and the last one. Prayer meetings are held at every convenient place and many are blessed. They have poured out on them the spirit of Prophesy, talking, singing, and blessing each other in tongues. Aunt Rhoda had a glorious blessing poured out upon her head last Thursday by Sister Kimball and Sister Pitcan. (She lived by Aunt Hepsy in Missouri) It was given in tongues, and after interpreted and it was truly glorious. Their meeting commence at 10 O'clock and we fast until after meeting. (Typescript of letter in possession of Patricia Jorgenson, Payson, Utah)

12. Phinehas married the widow Margaret Phillips Obanks Fuller on February 29, 1848. The marriage was performed by President Brigham Young with Joseph Knight and Thomas Bullock as witnesses. Margaret Phillips had previously been married to Moses Obanks and David Fullmer, both of whom died. She was Phinehas's third plural wife; the other two marriages had dissolved. Mary

made no mention of this marriage in her journal, although Mary wrote of Sister Banks coming to the home prior to that time to help.

13. LDS Archives. The letter is 15½ by 9¾ inches folded to 7¾ by 9¾, then folded again to create an envelope with Samuel's address on the back.

14. Possibly Uncle Willard Richards.

15. Lyman O. Littlefield left Winter Quarters in April 1847 on his way to Great Britain. With him were letters from Mary dated April 15, 22, and 27 and three letters from Phinehas, Wealthy, and Henry dated April 20. Mary's April 15 letter to Samuel indicated that Willard had received permission from the Council of the Twelve for Samuel and Franklin to come home that fall and that he was going to write a letter to his two nephews apprising them of that fact. Willard's instructions were no doubt carried by Littlefield as well. Samuel's mission journal, dated September 28, 1847, shows that Littlefield arrived in Liverpool two days earlier, where he turned over his packet of correspondence to Franklin. Had Littlefield gone directly to England when he left the Camp of Israel, as he had been instructed, Samuel and Franklin could possibly have returned home that fall instead of the following spring.

16. Samuel Whitney Richards Collection, LDS Archives. The letter is 7¾ by 9¾ inches, written in blue ink.

Chapter 9

1. An account of Franklin's reunion with Jane is found in the Richards Family Collection, LDS Archives. Samuel's and Mary's reunion would have been very similar:

> We made fast at a place lower part of Town all was soon stirring lively Father, Uncles Willard, & Levi br Henry & friends, brethren came to see us and hail us welcome. Many hearts were made glad today of the Camp & this Company. . . .
>
> As W Q is to be evacuated soon, Jane had moved her things over the River & was living in her wagon by her sisters. on the approach of the Boat she made ready & came over but I had by this time got the business so arranged as to go up in to the town & met her in the street, did not know her till I came directly up to her. took her into my arms & kissed her. . . . We went to Fathers nearby & saw my mother, Sister (S's wife) and arranged things at the boat then spent the night at Fathers with my wife again in my bosom.

2. Journals Two through Six are located in the LDS Archives. Journal Six is on blue-lined paper, written in blue ink. The journal is 6⅛ inches tall and 4 inches wide and is sewn together on the left margin. A letter dated August 9, 1846, which was written by Mary to her father in St. Louis, has been cut to fit the journal and sewn on for a cover.

3. Willard possibly had chronic inflammation of his eyes, which was caused by poor nutrition, a run-down condition, exposure to irritants (especially wind, dust, and smoke), insufficient sleep, and overuse of the eyes. It also was found in persons needing glasses. The margins of the eyelids became red and swollen and whitish scales formed around the eyelashes. In severe cases, a yellow crust glued the eyes shut and small ulcers formed beneath the crust. Itching,

soreness, runny eyes, sensitivity to light, and eyes that tired easily all combined to create sickness, aches, and pains.

    Conjunctivitis had all the above symptoms, but also affected the membrane covering the white portion of the eye. Newton Evans, ed., *Home Physician and Guide to Health* (Mountain View, Nebraska: Pacific Press Publication Association, 1923), 563-65.

4. Benjamin Prince Jenne agreed to go to Salt Lake Valley with his wife, Sarah, traveling in company with his brother-in-law, George Snyder, in 1848. However, there still must have been disharmony between Benjamin and Sarah, as she divorced him. She became a wife of Franklin D. Richards on October 13, 1849.

BIBLIOGRAPHY

Abbreviations used in the Biographical Register and Bibliography

AF	Ancestral File, FHL.
AG	Parker Family Records of Rose Adele Gwynn.
AJ	Jenson, *LDS Biographical Encyclopedia.*
ALL	*Alliance* passenger list.
APPP	*Autobiography of Parley P. Pratt.*
ARCH	Temple Archive Sheets, JSMB.
BYU	Harold B. Lee Library Special Collections, Brigham Young University.
CBM	Coonville or Union, Iowa, Branch Record.
CBR	Chaigley, Lancashire, Branch Record.
CPBM	Council Point, Iowa, Branch Record.
CR	Olsen, "Sketch of Charles and Jane Morgan Rhodeback."
DBMB	Larson, *A Data Base of the Mormon Battalion.*
DL	Brooks, *On the Ragged Edge: The Life and Times of Dudley Leavitt.*
DUP	Jakeman, *Daughters of the Utah Pioneers and their Mothers.*
DUPMB	Carter, *The Mormon Battalion.*
EAH	Eliza Ann Haven to Mary Haskin Parker Richards.
EC	Eddins, "Life History of Edward and Alice Corbridge."
EF	Elizabeth Fory to Mary Haskin Parker Richards.
EH	Hunter, "Bishop's Record Winter Quarters 1st Ward."
ERS	Beecher, *The Personal Writings of Eliza Roxcy Snow.*
FDR	West, *Life of Franklin Dewey Richards.*
FF	Four-Generation Family Group Sheets, JSMB.
FG	Cook, *Death and Marriage Notices from the "Frontier Guardian" 1849–1852.*
FHL	Family History Library, The Church of Jesus Christ of Latter-day Saints.
FRN	Barlow, *Family Recordings of Nauvoo: Descendants of Phinehas Howe and Susannah Goddard.*
GW	"Autobiography of George Whitaker."
HCK	Kimball, *On the Potter's Wheel: The Diaries of Heber C. Kimball.*
HCKW	Carter, *Heber C. Kimball and his Wives.*
HFC	*History of Fremont County, Iowa.*
HS	Brooks, *On the Mormon Frontier, The Diary of Hosea Stout 1844–1861.*

HTW	Carter, *Heart Throbs of the West.*
IB	Barlow, *The Israel Barlow Story and Mormon Mores.*
IBI	Watt, *Iowa Branch Index 1839–1859.*
ID	Noall, *Intimate Disciple: A Portrait of Willard Richards.*
TOW	Madsen, *In Their Own Words: Women and the Story of Nauvoo.*
JBP	"Biography of Jeanette Bleasdale Poole."
JBS	Janet Burton Seegmiller to Maurine Ward.
JSMB	Joseph Smith Memorial Building.
JSR	"Reminiscences of Jane Snyder Richards."
JTB	Knight, "Journal of Thomas Bullock."
LDS Archives	LDS Archives Division, Church Historical Department, Church of Jesus Christ of Latter-day Saints.
LBM	Lake, Iowa, Branch Record.
LH	Lyman Hinman to Brother and Sister Taylor.
MAM	Bennett, *Mormons at the Missouri, 1846–1852.*
MBB	Blockhouse, Iowa, Branch Record.
MCCB	Camp Creek, Illinois, Branch Record.
MEMA	McIntire, *My Early Mormon Ancestors.*
MHPR	Mary Haskin Parker Richards to Samuel Whitney Richards.
MMB	"Biography of Margaret Moss Bleasdale."
MPJ	Mt. Pisgah, Iowa, Branch Journal.
MS	*Millenial Star* 9 (September 15, 1847).
NAU5	Hunter, "Bishop's Record Nauvoo 5th Ward."
NAU5HP	Nauvoo 5th Ward High Priest Minutes.
NDM	Cook, *Nauvoo Deaths and Marriages 1839–1845.*
NJ21	Ward, "The Mormon Battalion."
NJ41	Ward, "1842 Census of Nauvoo" (Spring 1992)
NJ42	Ward, "1842 Census of Nauvoo" (Fall 1992).
NJ51	Ward, "1842 Census of Nauvoo" (1993).
NJ62	Gunzenhauser, "The Settlement at Garden Grove, Iowa."
PHP	Pottawattamie County High Priests Minutes.
PM	"Autobiography of Priddy Meeks."
PS	Sessions, *The Diaries of Perrigrine Sessions.*
PR	Phinehas Richards Journals.
RB	Carter, "Autobiography of Richard Bentley."
RBJ	Rebecca Burton Jones to Mary Haskin Parker Richards.
RFH1	Stevenson, *Richards Family History,* vol. 1 (1977).
RFH2	Stevenson, *Richards Family History,* vol. 2 (1981).
RFH3	Stevenson, *Richards Family History,* vol. 3 (1991).
RFR	Richards Family Records.
RJP	Bitton, *The Redoubtable John Pack.*
RLDS	Black, *Early Members of the Reorganized Church of Jesus Christ of Latter Day Saints.*
RTB	Seegmiller, *Be Kind to the Poor: The Life Story of Robert Taylor Burton.*
SEB	Black, *Membership of the Church of Jesus Christ of Latter-day Saints, 1830–1848.*
SJVL	Bishop, "History of Sarah Jane Veach Lewis."

SS   Partington Family Records of Sheri Eardley Slaughter.
SWR   Samuel Whitney Richards Journals and Family Record.
USHS   Utah State Historical Society.
WB   "Biography of William Bleasdale."
WQ   Bryson, *Winter Quarters.*
WON   Holzapfel and Holzapfel, *Women of Nauvoo.*
WR   Willard Richards Journals.
ZC   Bradley, *Zion's Camp 1834.*

Unpublished Sources

Abbott, Abigail, to Mary Haskin Parker Richards, July 25, 1847. Samuel Whitney Richards Collection. LDS Archives Division, Church Historical Department, Church of Jesus Christ of Latter-day Saints, Salt Lake City, Utah (LDS Archives).
Alliance Passenger List, New York, January 26, 1841. Family History Library, Church of Jesus Christ of Latter-day Saints, Salt Lake City, Utah (FHL).
Ancestral File. FHL.
"Autobiography of George Whitaker." Typescript. Utah State Historical Society, Salt Lake City, Utah (USHS).
"Autobiography of Joseph Hovey." Typescript. Harold B. Lee Library Special Collections, Brigham Young University, Provo, Utah (BYU).
"Autobiography of Priddy Meeks." Typescript. USHS.
"Autobiography of Sarah DeArmon Pea Rich." Typescript. LDS Archives.
"Biography of Jeanette Bleasdale Poole." In editor's possession.
"Biography of Margaret Moss Bleasdale." In editor's possession.
"Biography of William Bleasdale." In editor's possession.
"Biography of Margaret Jane McIntire Burgess." BYU.
Bishop, George E. "History of Sarah Jane Veach Lewis." Manuscript. Daughters of Utah Pioneers Cache Pioneer Museum, Logan, Utah.
Bleasdale Family History. In editor's possession.
Blockhouse [Iowa] Branch Record of Members. LDS Archives.
Camp Creek [Illinois] Branch Record of Members. LDS Archives.
Chaigley, Lancashire, England Branch Record. LDS Archives.
Coonville [Iowa] Branch Record of Members. LDS Archives.
Council Point [Iowa] Branch Record of Members. LDS Archives.
Eddins, Ada Sessions. "Life History of Edward and Alice Corbridge." In editor's possession.
Fory, Elizabeth, to Mary Haskin Parker Richards, June 2, 1848. Samuel Whitney Richards Collection. LDS Archives.
Four-Generation Family Group Sheets. Family File Section, Joseph Smith Memorial Building, Salt Lake City, Utah (JSMB).
Hascall, Ursalia, to Col. Wilson Andrews, September 19, 1846. USHS.
Haven, Eliza Ann, to Mary Haskin Parker Richards, May 11, 1847, and December 1, 1847. Samuel Whitney Richards Collection. LDS Archives.
Hinman, Lyman, to Brother and Sister Taylor, June 27, 1847. Typescript. USHS.
Historian's Office Journal. LDS Archives.

Hunter, Edward. "Bishop's Record, 1844–1848, Nauvoo 5th Ward and Winter Quarters 1st Ward." LDS Archives.

Journal History of the Church. LDS Archives.

"Journal of Phinehas Richards." Richards Family Collection. LDS Archives.

Jones, Rebecca Burton, to Mary Haskin Parker Richards, May 8, 1847, and May 11, 1847. Samuel Whitney Richards Collection. LDS Archives.

Lake [Iowa] Branch Record of Members. LDS Archives.

"Memorandum of Mary H. Parker." In editor's possession, and copy in LDS Archives.

Morgan, Nicholas Groesbeck, comp. "Pioneer map . . . Five-acre Plat A portion of the Big Field Survey, Great Salt Lake City." Library, Historical Department, Church of Jesus Christ of Latter-day Saints, Salt Lake City, Utah.

Mt. Pisgah [Iowa] Branch Journal, 1846. LDS Archives.

Nauvoo 5th Ward High Priest Minutes. LDS Archives.

Olsen, Luella Wells. "Sketch of Charles and Jane Morgan Rhodeback." USHS.

Parker Family Records. Private possession of Rose Adele Gwynn, Centerville, Utah.

Partington Family Records. Private possession of Sheri Eardley Slaughter, Salt Lake City, Utah.

Pioneer Plat Records 1852–1888, Salt Lake County. Copy. LDS Archives.

Pottawattamie County High Priests Minutes. LDS Archives.

"Reminiscences of Jane Snyder Richards." Original in Bancroft Library, University of California, Berkeley. Copy in USHS.

Richards, Amelia Peirson, to Nancy Richards Peirson. Typescript. Private possession of Patricia Jorgenson, Payson, Utah.

Richards Family Records. Private possession of Joseph Grant Stevenson, Provo, Utah. Copy in editor's possession.

Richards, Franklin Dewey. Journals. Richards Family Collection. LDS Archives.

Richards, Jane Mayer, to Samuel Whitney Richards. Samuel Whitney Richards Collection. LDS Archives. Copy in private possession of Frederick S. and Rama Richards Buchanan, Salt Lake City, Utah.

Richards, Mary Haskin Parker, to Samuel Whitney Richards, May 1846 to May 1848, 1854, 1855. Samuel Whitney Richards Collection. LDS Archives.

Richards, Mary Haskin Parker, to Samuel Whitney Richards, November 17, 1847. LDS Archives

Richards, Mary Haskin Parker, to John Parker, August 7, 1846. Attached as a cover to Mary Haskin Parker Richards, Iowa Journal. LDS Archives.

Richards, Mary Haskin Parker. Iowa Journal. LDS Archives.

Richards, Mary Haskin Parker. Winter Quarters, Nebraska Journals. LDS Archives.

Richards, Phinehas. Papers. Richards Family Collection. LDS Archives.

Richards, Samuel Whitney. Journals, 1839–1909. LDS Archives.

Richards, Samuel Whitney. Journals and Family Record, 1846–1876. LDS Archives.

Richards, Samuel Whitney, to Mary Haskin Parker. Samuel Whitney Richards Collection. LDS Archives.

Richards, Samuel Whitney. Statement about Oliver Cowdery, May 29, 1907. LDS Archives.

Richards, Wealthy Dewey, to Samuel Richards. Attached to a letter of Mary Haskin Parker Richards. Samuel Whitney Richards Collection. LDS Archives.

Richards, Willard. Journals. LDS Archives.
Salt Lake Deed Records. Book A, 1850–1859. Copy, LDS Archives.
Salt Lake Recorder's Office Land Records. Copy, LDS Archives.
Seegmiller, Janet Burton, to Maurine Ward, July 13, 1993. In editor's possession.
Temple Archive Sheets, JSMB.
Wilcox, Walter, to Samuel Whitney Richards, November 17, 1847. Samuel Whitney
    Richards Collection. LDS Archives.

Published Sources

Alexander, Thomas G. *Mormonism in Transition: A History of the Latter-day Saints,
    1890–1930.* Urbana and Chicago: University of Illinois Press, 1986.
Barlow, Ora Haven, comp. *Family Recordings of Nauvoo: Descendants of Phinehas Howe
    and Susannah Goddard.* Salt Lake City: Stanway Printing, 1965.
Barlow, Ora H. *The Israel Barlow Story and Mormon Mores.* Salt Lake City: Ora H.
    Barlow. 1968.
Beecher, Maureen Ursenbach. *Eliza and Her Sisters.* Salt Lake City: Aspen Books,
    1991.
———. *The Personal Writings of Eliza Roxcy Snow.* Salt Lake City: University of Utah
    Press, 1995.
———. "Women in Winter Quarters," *Sunstone* 8 (July–August 1984): 11–12.
Bennett, Richard E. *Mormons at the Missouri, 1846–1852: "And Should We Die. . . ."*
    Norman: University of Oklahoma Press, 1987.
Bitton, Davis. *The Redoubtable John Pack: Pioneer Proselyter Patriarch.* USA: Eden Hill,
    for the John Pack Family Association, 1982.
Black, Susan Easton, comp. *Early Members of the Reorganized Church of Jesus Christ of
    Latter Day Saints,* 6 vols. Provo, Utah: Religious Studies Center, Brigham
    Young University, 1993. Also available on CD-ROM.
———, comp. *Membership of the Church of Jesus Christ of Latter-day Saints, 1830–1848,* 50
    vols. Provo, Utah: Religious Studies Center, Brigham Young University, 1989.
Bradley, James L. *Zion's Camp 1834: Prelude to the Civil War.* Salt Lake City: Publishers
    Press, 1990.
Brooks, Juanita, ed. *On the Mormon Frontier: The Diary of Hosea Stout 1844–1861.* 2
    vols. Salt Lake City: University of Utah Press, Utah State Historical Society,
    1964.
———. *On the Ragged Edge: The Life and Times of Dudley Leavitt.* Salt Lake City: Utah
    State Historical Society, 1973.
Brown, S. Kent, Donald Q. Cannon, and Richard H. Jackson, eds. *Historical Atlas of
    Mormonism.* New York: Simon & Schuster, 1994.
Bryson, Conrey. *Winter Quarters.* Salt Lake City: Deseret Book, 1986.
Cannon, Ramona W. *A Biographical Sketch of Samuel Whitney Richards.* n.d.
Carr, Annie C., ed. *East of Antelope Island.* Bountiful, Utah: Carr Printing, Daughters
    of Utah Pioneers, Davis County Company, 1961.
Carter, Kate B., comp. "Autobiography of Richard Bentley." In *Heart Throbs of the
    West,* 370–74. Salt Lake City: Daughters of Utah Pioneers, 1946.
———, comp. *Heart Throbs of the West,* 12 vols. Salt Lake City: Daughters of Utah
    Pioneers, 1939–1951.

———, comp. "Historic Letters of the Past." In *Our Pioneer Heritage*, vol. 3. Salt Lake City: Daughters of Utah Pioneers, 1960.

———, comp. *Our Pioneer Heritage*, 20 vols. Salt Lake City: Daughters of Utah Pioneers, 1958–1977.

———. *The Mormon Battalion*. Salt Lake City: Utah Printing, Daughters of Utah Pioneers, 1956.

———, comp. and ed. *Heber C. Kimball and His Wives*. Salt Lake City: Utah Printing, Daughters of Utah Pioneers, 1967.

Cook, Lyndon W, comp. *Death and Marriage Notices from the "Frontier Guardian" 1849–1852*. Orem: Center for Research of Mormon Origins, 1990.

———, comp. *Nauvoo Deaths and Marriages 1839–1845*. Orem: Grandin Book, 1994.

Crocheron, Augusta Joyce, ed. *Representative Women of Deseret*. Salt Lake City: J. C. Graham, 1884.

Deseret Evening News. December 21, 1901.

Deseret Semi-Weekly News. June 6, 1860.

Elders' Journal. December 1, 1905.

Evans, Newton, ed. *Home Physician & Guide to Health*. Mountain View, Nebraska: Pacific Press Publication Association, 1923.

Faragher, John Mack. *Women and Men on the Overland Trail*. New Haven: Yale University Press, 1979.

Givens, George W. *In Old Nauvoo: Everyday Life in the City of Joseph*. Salt Lake City: Deseret Book, 1990.

Godfrey, Kenneth W. "Winter Quarters: Glimmering Glimpses into Mormon Religious and Social Life." In *A Sesquicentennial Look at Church History*, proceedings of the Sidney B. Sperry Symposium, 149–61. Provo, Utah: Brigham Young University Press, 1980.

Gunn, John Charles. *Gunn's Newest Family Physician*. New York: Baird and Dillon, 1885.

Gunzenhauser, Karla. "The Settlement at Garden Grove, Iowa." *The Nauvoo Journal* 6 (Fall 1994): 14–44.

History of Fremont County, Iowa. Des Moines: Iowa Historical, 1881.

Holmes, Gail George. *Winter Quarters Revisited*. Omaha: the Author, 1979.

Holzapfel, Richard Neitzel, and Jeni Broberg Holzapfel. *Women of Nauvoo*. Salt Lake City: Bookcraft, 1992.

Hylton, William H., ed. *The Rodale Herb Book*. Emmaus, Pennsylvania: Rodale Press, 1974.

Improvement Era 2 (December 1898): 90–96.

Kowalchik, Claire and William H. Hylton, ed. *Rodale's Illustrated Encyclopedia of Herbs*. Emmaus, Pennsylvania: Rodale Press, 1987.

Jakeman, Jas. T. *Daughters of the Utah Pioneers and their Mothers*. The Western Album Publishing Company, n.d.

Jensen, Richard L. "Transplanted to Zion." *BYU Studies* 31 (Winter 1991): 77–87.

Jenson, Andrew. *LDS Biographical Encyclopedia*. 4 vols. Salt Lake City: Western Epics, 1971.

Kenney, Scott G., ed. *Wilford Woodruff's Journal*, 8 vols. Midvale Utah: Signature Books, 1983.

Kimball, Stanley B. *Historic Sites and Markers along the Mormon and Other Great Western Trails.* Urbana: University of Illinois Press, 1988.

———, ed. *On the Potter's Wheel: The Diaries of Heber C. Kimball.* Salt Lake City: Signature Books in association with Smith Research Associates, 1987.

Knight, Gregory R., ed. "Journal of Thomas Bullock." *BYU Studies* 31 (Winter 1991) 5–75.

Larson, Carl V., comp. and ed. *A Data Base of the Mormon Battalion: An Identification of the Original Members of the Mormon Battalion.* Providence, Utah: Keith W. Watkins and Sons, 1987.

Ludlow, Daniel H. ed. *Encyclopedia of Mormonism.* 4 vols. New York: Macmillan Reference, 1992.

Madsen, Carol Cornwall. *In Their Own Words: Women and the Story of Nauvoo.* Salt Lake City: Deseret Book, 1994.

McIntire, Ronald Bruce. *My Early Mormon Ancestors.* Bountiful: Family History Publishers, 1991.

Millennial Star 9 (June 1, 1847): 175–76; (August 15, 1847): 243; (September 15, 1847): 277.

Newell, Linda King, "Gifts of the Spirit: Women's Share." In *Sisters in Spirit*, edited by Maureen Ursenbach Beecher and Lavina Fielding Anderson, 111–20. Urbana: University of Illinois Press, 1992.

Noall, Claire. *Intimate Disciple: A Portrait of Willard Richards.* Salt Lake City: University of Utah Press, 1957.

The Oxford English Dictionary, 2d edition, 20 vols. Oxford: Clarendon Press, 1989.

Patterson, Veronica. "The Elusive Braided Straw Hat." *Piecework* 2 (July–August 1994): 61–64.

Pickard, Madge E. and R. Carlyle Buley. *The Midwest Pioneer: His Ills, Cures, & Doctors.* New York: Henry Schuman, 1946.

Pratt, Parley P. *Autobiography of Parley P. Pratt.* 1938. Reprint, Salt Lake City: Deseret Book, 1975.

Seegmiller, Janet Burton. *Be Kind to the Poor: The Life Story of Robert Taylor Burton.* USA: Robert Taylor Burton Family Organization, 1988.

Sessions, T. Earl, ed. *The Diaries of Perrigrine Sessions.* Bountiful: Carr Printing, 1967.

Smith, Joseph, *History of the Church of Jesus Christ of Latter-day Saints*, edited by B. H. Roberts, 2d ed., 7 vols. 1957. Reprint, Salt Lake City: Deseret Book, 1973.

Stevenson, Joseph Grant, ed. *Richards Family History*, 3 vols. Provo, Utah: Stevenson's Genealogical Center, 1977–1991.

Ward, Maurine Carr, ed. "1842 Census of Nauvoo." *The Nauvoo Journal* 4 (Spring and Fall 1992): 22–23.

———, ed. "1842 Census of Nauvoo." *The Nauvoo Journal* 5 (Spring 1993): 26–27.

———, ed. "The Mormon Battalion." *The Nauvoo Journal* 2 (1990): 13–27.

Watt, Ronald G. *Iowa Branch Index 1839–1859.* Salt Lake City: Historical Department of the Church of Jesus Christ of Latter-day Saints, 1991.

West, Franklin L. *Life of Franklin Dewey Richards.* Salt Lake City: Deseret News Press, 1924.

Whyte, Mike. "Voices of the Loess Hills." *The Iowan* 41 (Spring 1993): 39–47, 69.

Young Women's Journal 18 (December 1907): 524–84.

Index

A

Aaron, Reverend, 57, 219
Abbott, Abigail, 16, 19, 30, 65, 66, 84, 103, 107, 142, 177, 219
Abbott, Lewis, 119, 142, 219
Adoption, law of, 83, 301n3
Ague. *See under* Sickness
Allen, Andrew Lee, 220
Allen, Brother, 105, 115, 219–20
Allen, Daniel, 219–20
Allen, Elizabeth Catherine, 220
Allen, Lucinda, 220
Allen, Miss, 215, 220
Allen, Orville Morgan, 220, 291n30
Alliance (ship), 6, 60
Allred, James, 24, 116
Allred, Reuben Warren, 115, 220
Alston, John, 55, 220
Anderson, Augustus Leander, 93, 220
Anderson, William, 220–21

B

Babbitt, Almon Whiting, 96, 221
Badlam, Alexander, 120, 136, 221
Baker, Brother, 104, 221
Balding, Miss, 180, 221
Ballentyne, Richard, 294n54
Banks, Brother, 136
Barlow, Elizabeth Haven, 143, 180, 187, 188, 196, 221
Barlow, Israel, 93, 188, 190, 191, 192, 195, 209, 210, 213, 221
Barlow, Truman Root, 164, 210, 211, 221–22
Barnes, Hulda, 144, 222

Barnes, Lorenzo Dow, 222
Barnes, Sister, 125, 152, 183, 222
Barries, Emery, 222
Barries, Huldah Abigail Nickerson, 222
Barrows, Brother, 124, 125, 152, 161, 163, 180, 222
Barrows, E., 66, 222
Barrows, Ethan. *See* Burrows, Ethan Allen
Barrows, Lorena. *See* Burrows, Lorena Covey
Barrows, Sister, 67, 222
Barrus, Emery. *See* Barries, Emery
Barrus, Huldah. *See* Barries, Huldah Abigail Nickerson
Barton, Mother, 164, 222
Bates, Ormus E., 195, 223
Beecher, Maureen: on female friendships, 29; on women's documents, 29
Benson, Ezra Taft: appointed captain, 127; appointed to Twelve, 76; biographical sketch, 223; delivers gifts, 126; delivers money, 173; marries Lucinda West, 133; Mary visits, 101, 206; in presidency, 298n8; speaks at meeting, 67, 100, 103, 183, 214, 216; speaks of Mt. Pisgah, 17; visits Mary, 87, 117, 132
Benson, Pamelia Andrus, 66, 99, 108, 110, 191, 197, 210, 211, 223
Bent, Samuel, 93, 223
Bentley, Elizabeth Price, 89, 153, 223
Bentley, Richard, 89, 153, 223
Big Elk (Indian chief), 101, 223, 303n4
Big Field, 38, 294n52